The Moral Psychology of Hope

Moral Psychology of the Emotions

Series Editor: Mark Alfano, Associate Professor, Department of Philosophy, Delft University of Technology

How do our emotions influence our other mental states (perceptions, beliefs, motivations, intentions) and our behavior? How are they influenced by our other mental states, our environments, and our cultures? What is the moral value of a particular emotion in a particular context? This series explores the causes, consequences, and value of the emotions from an interdisciplinary perspective. Emotions are diverse, with components at various levels (biological, neural, psychological, social), so each book in this series is devoted to a distinct emotion. This focus allows the author and reader to delve into a specific mental state, rather than trying to sum up emotions en masse. Authors approach a particular emotion from their own disciplinary angle (e.g., conceptual analysis, feminist philosophy, critical race theory, phenomenology, social psychology, personality psychology, neuroscience) while connecting with other fields. In so doing, they build a mosaic for each emotion, evaluating both its nature and its moral properties.

Titles in the Series

The Moral Psychology of Hope

Edited by Claudia Blöser and Titus Stahl

ROWMAN & LITTLEFIELD
INTERNATIONAL

London • New York

Published by Rowman & Littlefield International, Ltd.
6 Tinworth Street, London SE11 5AL
www.rowmaninternational.com

Rowman & Littlefield International, Ltd. is an affiliate of
Rowman & Littlefield
4501 Forbes Boulevard, Suite 200, Lanham, Maryland 20706, USA
With additional offices in Boulder, New York, Toronto (Canada), and London (UK)
www.rowman.com

British Library Cataloguing in Publication Information
A catalogue record for this book is available from the British Library

ISBN: HB 978-1-78660-972-4

Library of Congress Cataloging-in-Publication Data

Library of Congress Control Number: 2019952147

ISBN: 978-1-78660-972-4 (cloth : alk. paper)
ISBN: 978-1-5381-6548-5 (pbk : alk. paper)
ISBN: 978-1-78660-973-1 (electronic)

Contents

Chapter One

The Moral Psychology of Hope

An Introduction

Claudia Blöser and Titus Stahl

Drawing on the recent surge of interest in hope in philosophy and moral psychology, this volume collects contributions outlining the most influential historical and contemporary philosophical and psychological thinking on the role of hope in human life. In particular, it focuses on three areas: Part I assembles current research on accounts of hope from the history of philosophy; part II contains systematic discussions of the nature and moral psychology of hope; and part III focuses on applications of the analysis of hope in social and political philosophy.

Hope has always been of interest to philosophers in the Western tradition, from the ancients, who treated it as an emotion that can support or undermine virtuous behavior, to medieval Christian philosophers and theologians, according to whom hope is one of the three fundamental theological virtues, to early modern philosophers, who tried to integrate analyses of hope into their comprehensive treatments of human psychology (for an overview of the historical significance of this topic, see Blöser and Stahl 2017). However, modern analytic philosophy's focus on belief, justification, and knowledge has long pushed hope to the sidelines of that tradition. Only recently, prompted by new publications—first and foremost Adrienne Martin's *How We Hope*—and a well-funded research initiative at Cornell University and the University of Notre Dame, hope has received more systematic attention. This has also coincided with a resurgence of references to hope in public discourse. From Barack Obama to the post-crisis movements in Europe, many political forces base their legitimacy on a claimed capacity to revive hope in the public sphere. These developments have generated great interest in hope among researchers and in terms of the topic's increased visibility in philosophy courses, and it thus seems timely to assemble some of the most prominent scholars in the debate in a volume that both provides an entry point for interested non-experts and highlights new contributions to these debates.

This volume provides an overview of the present state of research on hope and aims to highlight some of the main questions animating the debate today. One set of questions concerns the nature of hope: How ought we to describe hope? Most accounts of the nature of hope are based on what has been called the "standard account" (Meirav 2009, 217) or the "orthodox definition" (Martin 2013, 211), according to which "hope that x" is constituted by a desire for x and the belief that x is possible (Downie 1963). It is commonly accepted, however, that the standard definition fails to give sufficient conditions for hope. Many authors have come up with examples of two people who equally desire an outcome and who both believe in its possibility but who nonetheless differ with regard to their affective outlook or behavior—thus differing with regard to whether or not they are hopeful. In an example originally introduced by Bovens (1999) and based on Frank Darabont's film *The Shawshank Redemption*, two prisoners, Andy and Red, both desire to be free and believe that there is a (very small) chance that they will escape prison. Andy hopes for freedom, while Red despairs over his situation (Meirav 2009, 222). Adrienne Martin's *cancer research* example has a similar structure: Alan and Bess, two terminally ill cancer patients, have equally strong desires for a "miracle cure," and both know that there is a less than 1 percent chance that an experimental drug will be successful. They both enroll in the drug trial, but whereas Bess really "hopes to be in the 1 percent," Alan focuses on how slim his chances are, and thus his hope is weaker (Martin 2013, 15). The failure of the standard definition shows either that it must be revised or that hope is entirely different from belief and desire, and hence irreducible to them. There are an increasing number of accounts that take the first route and build on the standard definition (e.g., Calhoun 2018, Milona 2018, and Kwong 2019). However, alternative approaches that argue for the irreducibility of hope have also been proposed (Segal and Textor 2015, Blöser 2019), such that it remains an open debate whether hope should be seen as—ontologically or conceptually—reducible to belief and desire.

Even if one does not subscribe to a reductive analysis of hope in terms of belief and desire, however, one can acknowledge that hope has a theoretical and a practical aspect: On the one hand, there are epistemic constraints on what one is able to hope for because one cannot hope for what one takes to be impossible (or certain). On the other hand, a hoping person takes a pro-attitude toward the hoped-for object: When the object can be promoted through one's actions, hope plausibly involves a disposition to do so. Where hope is directed toward objects that are fully beyond the power of the hoping subject, this disposition seems to be absent (but see McGeer 2004), but what remains is a positive evaluation of the object as good or desirable in some respect.

Other questions that animate the debate on the nature of hope are whether hope can be understood as an emotion or a virtue. In the history of philosophy, Thomas Aquinas has prominently suggested these two views of hope. The thesis that hope is an emotion was common in ancient Greece and in the philosophy of the seventeenth and eighteenth centuries but has long been neglected in contemporary debate, which—based on the standard definition—has focused on hope as a cognitive and conative state and its relation to action. Recently, however, and inspired by new developments in the philosophy of emotion, seeing hope as an emotion—or at least as having important emotional aspects—has enjoyed renewed interest (Döring 2014, Milona and Stockdale 2018). Similarly, the question of whether hope can be a virtue has been dissociated from the distinctively religious context in which Aquinas envisages it. There are authors who believe that hope is a civic or democratic virtue (Lamb 2016, Moellendorf 2006, Snow 2018) or an intellectual virtue (Snow 2013).

Further questions relate to the normative standards governing hope. Whereas many classic authors who see hope as an affect (like Hume) deny that it is subject to rational norms at all, hope has come to be regarded as a reason-responsive attitude. As hope involves a theoretical and a practical aspect, it is plausible to assume that both theoretical and practical norms are relevant to assessing hope's rationality. Adrienne Martin argues that theoretical norms govern a probability assignment to the outcome, but whether it is rational to hope depends more crucially on practical norms: on whether it promotes the agent's rational ends to perform hopeful activities (Martin 2013). Miriam Schleifer McCormick largely follows Martin but argues that the theoretical dimension of rationality is more important than Martin thinks. More evidence in favor of the realization of a certain outcome makes it more rational to hope for it (McCormick 2017). In general, the question of exactly which theoretical and practical norms are relevant to hope is subject to debate. Do we need positive evidence to be justified in hoping, or does "Kantian minimalism" suffice, according to which the object of hope merely must not be proven impossible? Are the practical norms that govern hope simply instrumental norms of rational end promotion, as Martin claims, or can we have noninstrumental reasons to hope (see Blöser and Stahl 2017)?

Finally, public discourse on hope as a feature of interpersonal relationships and even political practice (which has an affinity with pragmatist and early modern treatments of hope) raises the question of what we can hope for together and what hopes we should place in one another. While some of these questions are applications of arguments from the standard case to intersubjective contexts—for example, whether political or intersubjective hope is instrumentally or intrinsically valuable—focusing on the intersubjective context also raises new questions for the definition and the standards of rationality for hope. Intersubjective hope is hope for outcomes that depend on the agency of other people and is thus dependent on rational expectations toward the actions of other agents who are themselves driven by rational hopes; intersubjective hope incorporates expectations and desires not only into the agency of the hoping individual, but potentially into the collective agency of groups, or even entire societies. This raises not only the question of whether intersubjective hope (hope by which one agent becomes invested in the agency of another) and collective hope (hope by which an entire group incorporates shared beliefs and desires in their collective agency in a hopeful way) are possible and rational, but also the question of whether there are specific grounds on which such hopes ought to be judged desirable. This is most obvious in the political case, where hope has traditionally either been viewed with suspicion or exalted as an alternative to an overly rationalistic picture of politics.

The contributions to this volume relate to one or several of these questions, from historical, systematic, applied, and political perspectives. The first part, "Hope in the History of Philosophy," presents central historical positions on hope, ranging from the ancient Greeks, to Christian theology, to the philosophy of Immanuel Kant, to post-Kantian positions such as those held by Søren Kierkegaard and the American pragmatists.

In "Hope in Archaic and Classical Greek," Douglas Cairns investigates the congruence between the Greek *elpis* and "hope" as we use it today, in terms of their semantics and their evaluation. Important differences between this term and modern "hope" include the fact that *elpis* can focus on bad outcomes as well as good ones and does not always exhibit hope's motivational aspect. Tracing *elpis* in Plato and Aristotle, Cairns shows that the term has a wide semantic range, which raises difficulties in the search for ancient approaches to the moral psychology of hope. Still, Plato's discussion in the *Laws* reveals the positive and sustaining role of *elpis* in an ethical life by favoring cooperation, community, and deference to greater power. In Aristotle, *elpis* may also refer to negative events in the future; when its orientation is positive, Aristotle also uses terms such as *euelpis* or "good *elpis*." The latter is not always positive, however: the courage that rests on *elpis* is no more than irrational optimism. Cairns points out that the kernel of ancient Greek attitudes is to be found not in philosophical texts but in poetry, where hope is often depicted as valuable for providing motivation and sustenance in Greek poetry. Overall, however, the Greek attitude toward *elpis* is not as positive as it has been in modern times. Cairns surmises that this is because Greek thinking reflects a greater awareness that important aspects of human existence depend upon factors beyond the control of the individual and a corresponding skepticism about the power of positive thinking in itself when it comes to ameliorating one's lot.

Whereas the role of hope in ancient philosophy is disputed, Christian thinkers put hope on the agenda in theology and moral philosophy. In her contribution "Hope in Christianity," Anne Jeffrey highlights central elements of a Christian account of hope and shows how this account resonates in contemporary, secular thinking about hope. In particular, Jeffrey discusses the questions of the proper object of hope, the psychological conditions necessary for hope and what makes hope rational and valuable in human life. Jeffrey distinguishes between objectual hope, which concerns future events, and interpersonal hope, which is hope in persons, mainly in god. Whereas some contemporary accounts take up this distinction (see Martin's contribution on interpersonal hope), Jeffrey argues that Christian thinking has a distinctive view on the relationship between the two kinds. Other differences between contemporary, secular accounts and the Christian position include the feeling of certainty that is bound up with Christian hope and the Christian assumption that there is an objective standard of moral goodness which must be fulfilled in all hope that assumes a central place in a good human life.

In seventeenth- and eighteenth-century philosophy, hope is primarily discussed in the context of psychology and often viewed as a "passion." As such, it is a noncognitive attitude that is not subject to rational evaluation. By way of exception, Immanuel Kant treats the question "What may I hope?" as one of the fundamental questions of reason and, in answering this question, gives an account of hope's rationality. However, it is not easy to pin down his answer, which can be found across many of his writings and in different contexts. Claudia Blöser's contribution, "Hope in Kant," aims to provide an overview of the relevant contexts in which Kant discusses hope. Highlighting the central elements of Kant's conception of hope, Blöser shows how this general framework is at work in different contexts. In particular, she aims to clarify the relationship between hope and faith: According to Kant, we may hope for moral objects (such as the highest good) if we may reasonably assume—have faith in—its grounds (such as god), even in the absence of knowledge.

In post-Kantian philosophy, the value of hope is disputed. While thinkers such as Arthur Schopenhauer and Friedrich Nietzsche criticize and reject hope, others such as Søren Kierkegaard not only defend its value but view it as essential to a coherent practical identity. In "Kierkegaard on Hope as Essential to Selfhood," Roe Fremstedal unfolds Kierkegaard's thinking about hope and briefly situates it with regard to Schopenhauer and Nietzsche. Following Kierkegaard's *via negativa* methodology, Fremstedal approaches hope (as well as selfhood and practical identity) indirectly, by focusing on despair. Starting from the observation that Kierkegaard characterizes despair both as hopelessness and as double-mindedness, Fremstedal argues that on Kierkegaard's view, "hope against hope" (i.e., hope in a hopeless situation) is necessary for human agency and selfhood. The double-minded characteristic of despair involves a tension between ideals and reality. To overcome this tension, the subject needs a wholehearted commitment in the form of an orientation toward the good. Since hope is the expectation of the possibility of the good, according to Kierkegaard, an agent must have hope in order to retain his commitment to his ideals and values.

In her contribution "Pragmatist Hope," Sarah Stitzlein shows that hope is intimately connected to central elements of pragmatism, including its accounts of truth, inquiry, meliorism, growth, and habits. Stitzlein emphasizes that while many contemporary philosophers describe hope in individualist terms, pragmatists envisage the larger social process of hoping. Whereas Charles Sanders Peirce largely constrains the role of hope to its role in scientific inquiry, William James and John Dewey focus on human struggles and our ability to improve the world. Hope, on their picture, is essentially tied to action, and it is an attitude that can and should be supported by education. Stitzlein points out that a distinctive feature of a pragmatist notion of hope concerns hope's proper objects: rather than ultimate hopes that we may hold, pragmatists—notably Dewey—focus more on what one can feasibly do in the present. Turning to contemporary pragmatists Richard Rorty, Judith Green, Cornel West, Patrick Shade, and Colin Koopman, Stitzlein develops a pragmatist conception of hope as a set of habits: As a flexible set of habits, hope allows us to act in moments of struggle without succumbing to despair or apathy, thereby improving one's life and the lives of others.

Katie Stockdale's contribution "Emotional Hope" opens the section on the nature of hope. Although her chapter does not aim to offer a theory or analysis of hope, it contributes to our understanding of the nature of hope by focusing on its affective dimension: how hope makes us feel. The traditional assumption is that hope is positively valenced and therefore pleasant to experience. Stockdale challenges this picture by drawing attention to "fearful hopes": hopes we form in response to nonideal conditions, hopes that are tainted by the negatively valenced emotion of fear. Many authors, such as Descartes, Spinoza, and Hume, acknowledge that hope and fear often occur alongside each other because both are responses to a situation of uncertainty. Stockdale goes further, however, and argues that in some cases fear actually *constitutes* hope: when we hope that *p* and the content of *p* is perceived as threatening, we experience fearful hope. When a woman hopes that a man who is aggressively catcalling her on the street will not assault her, for example, she experiences fearful hope. By way of various examples, Stockdale vividly portrays how forms of oppression (based on race, gender, etc.) shape the character of people's hopes and make fearful hope part of everyday experience. Following this line of thought, she explores how sustained experiences of oppression and violence not only shape episodes of hope but affect a more basal form of hope (see Ratcliffe 2013, Calhoun 2018) that constitutes a sense of being in the world. Stockdale closes by pointing out that paying attention to hope as an emotion with an affective dimension may advance our understanding of its role in motivation.

Matthew A. Benton investigates "Epistemological Aspects of Hope," starting from the linguistic and conceptual finding that hope that *p* is incompatible with knowledge whether *p*. He suggests a "Chances License Hope" principle, according to which one may hope that *p* if there is an epistemic chance both that *p* and that ¬*p*. Thus, hope belongs to the knowledge-precluding (or "epistemic") emotions. Turning to the question of what makes hope rational, Benton focuses on being hope*ful* that *p*, where being hopeful is stronger than merely hoping. One feature of hopefulness is that it disposes the person to act on her hope and makes her resistant to giving up her projects connected to this hope. Drawing on accounts by Martin (2013) and Blöser and Stahl (2017), Benton describes practical reasons—both instrumental and noninstrumental—for such hopefulness. Benton's central question is when hopefulness is rational over time given mounting counterevidence: at what point ought you to give up hope? His answer appeals to a combination of risk aversion and the rationality of updating one's credence.

Understanding the nature of hope also requires understanding hope in relation to its opposites. One attitude that is often seen as incompatible with hope is pessimism. In "Pessimism and the Possibility of Hope," however, Samantha Vice argues that this picture is too simple and that there is a sense in which hope and pessimism are compatible. She focuses on "anthropocentric moral pessimism," which is a perspective on the human world that is skeptical of the possibility of moral progress. This attitude is surely not excluded as irrational by empirical exploration. Neither is the pessimist making a moral mistake, as long as pessimism does not collapse into cynicism or nihilism. Vice argues that pessimism can coexist with hopefulness as long as it avoids collapsing into despair. Drawing on the work of Gabriel Marcel (1962), Vice understands the attitude of hopefulness as an orientation toward a future considered as open and receptive to our efforts. Despair, by contrast, sees the future as already determined. Despair involves a kind of capitulation that also threatens one's sense of integrity as a person. A pessimist need not view the future as closed to our efforts, however. As long as the pessimist keeps trying to bring about the good and retain a sense of integrity, pessimism is compatible with hopefulness. Vice closes her essay by exploring three speculative options of how to avoid despair and maintain the compatibility of the attitudes.

Nancy E. Snow systematically explores the question of whether hope is a moral virtue in "Is Hope a Moral Virtue?" Snow argues that the orthodox analysis of hope is not sufficiently informative for the question of how and whether we can acquire dispositions to hope that could count as a virtue and, in particular, for the question of how we can acquire a practical disposition to hope for moral ends. In order to answer this question, Snow turns to psychologist Erik Erikson and philosopher Victoria McGeer, who both discuss how capacities for action-guiding hope are formed in early childhood experiences, especially with caregivers, the best cases of which form a paradigm for the idea that hope can be cultivated as a disposition. Based on this psychological picture, Snow then discusses how hope fits into an Aristotelian picture of the virtues. Hope as a "natural virtue," as developed in early childhood, is only transformed into a moral virtue when it becomes informed by rational under- standing. Snow draws on McGeer to discuss two forms of defective hope to illustrate the requirements of this transformation: wishful hope (which is unrealistic) and willful hope (which is unreflectively attached to outcomes). She then extends the analysis to the moral qualities of hope by discussing how both immoral hopes and idle hopes can also constitute moral flaws.

Continuing the dialogue between philosophy and psychology, Matthew W. Gallagher, Johann M. D'Souza, and Angela L. Richardson systematically examine the conceptual foundations of empirical research into hope and their relevance for practice in their chapter "Hope in Contemporary Psychology." Following a historical overview, the chapter focuses on C. R. Snyder's in- fluential model of hope, which focuses on the perception of pathways and agency. Snyder's model, which sides with cognitivist understandings of hope in the philosophical literature and conceptualizes hope as relatively similar to optimism, has also served as the basis for several measures of hope. The final part of the chapter discusses a number of empirical findings, through which hope is connected to positive outcomes as well as the perspectives for inter- ventions based on an understanding of hope.

The final contribution to the systematic analyses, Rika Dunlap's "A Zen Buddhist Conception of Hope in Enlightenment," argues that there is a uniquely Buddhist conception of hope available in some of the texts of this tradition, even though it is not explicitly conceptualized this way. Dunlap starts from the observation that on many interpretations of the Buddhist conception of enlightenment, hope cannot serve as more than an intermediate instrument for reaching enlightenment but must be abandoned to fully achieve it. After a discussion of this problem based on the arguments offered by Nhat Hanh, Dunlap argues in three steps for the idea that there is a positive conception of hope available to Buddhists. First, she argues that we need to distinguish between two conceptions of hope, a present-oriented one and a future-oriented one, according to how they relate to *upāya* (emptiness). Second, only the present-oriented conception is compatible with Buddhist thought as it is directed not toward a fixed outcome but toward a hope that relates to the present practice. Based on arguments formulated by Dōgen, Dunlap argues that we can even reconstruct seemingly future-oriented hopes that Buddhism seems to recommend as forms of such present-oriented hope.

Adrienne M. Martin opens the section on the social and political aspects of hope with her analysis of "Interpersonal Hope." While most accounts of hope in the literature are individualist to the extent that they only incorporate a person's investment in outcomes that are relevant to her (even if brought about by other people), Martin argues that this tradition overlooks the way in which our agency can be extended when we place our hope in other people. A characteristic feature of such interpersonal hope—for example, the hope that one's children will take advantage of the opportunities provided to them—is that we can feel let down if the outcome does not materialize. This feeling of being let down—a "reactive attitude" of the Strawsonian kind—demands explanation. Martin supplies this explanation by suggesting that interpersonal hope arises from the ways in which our agency can be intersubjectively extended. By investing hope in others, we incorporate their acting fallibly into our own agency. Martin distinguishes such hope from trust and benefaction, which are more demanding as they involve agency in more specific ways than the relatively broad category of interpersonal hope. These distinctions have normative significance since they clarify when interpersonal hope is inappropriate or unwelcome and when it violates ethical norms.

Darrel Moellendorf investigates the question of the justification of hope under current conditions in his "Hope for Material Progress in the Age of the Anthropocene." He argues that hope is subject to rationality constraints and can only be justified if there are "hope-makers" that are constituted by evidence and explanation that allow reasons for hope to be shared. Concerning political progress, Moellendorf takes up a claim from the Marxist tradition that assumes that social justice can only be achieved under conditions of massively increased productive capacity. He discusses G. A. Cohen's version of this claim, in particular concerning the question whether there is evidence for a generalized tendency in human history for productivity to grow, but adds to Cohen's discussion an important new element: we can only hope for such increases if environmental circumstances are sufficiently favorable that when humans labor, improvements can be passed on to at least some successor generations—"the fact of climatic favorability." This fact is now in doubt since human progress seems to be self-undermining by threatening those very climatic conditions. This entails that our hopes must not only be founded in economic tendencies but also in evidence about humanity's abilities to solve social problems.

In his contribution "Political Hope and Cooperative Community," Titus Stahl moves from the interpersonal to the political level. Examining historical treatments of hope in the political theories of Hobbes, Spinoza, and Kant, he distinguishes between three functions that references to hope can play in political theory: An instrumental function, where hope is considered to be an attitude that is useful for political action; a constitutive function that relates to the fact that certain kinds of hope are necessary for the very emergence of the sphere of the political; and a justificatory function that concerns the way in which political arguments can draw on the desirability or reason-giving nature of hope. He then argues that the most famous accounts of hope in the history of political philosophy—those of Bloch and Rorty—and contemporary liberal theories about hope fail to develop a fully convincing picture of hope's potential as a basis for political justification. Drawing on an internal tension in Rawlsian theory, he argues that the justificatory function of hope is best captured by an account that sees ambitious forms of community as both something that is required by liberal justice and something that we cannot expect. As such, he argues, shared hope for such a community is both a desirable feature of a just society and a possible basis for reasonable political argument.

Finally, we need to acknowledge a regrettable gap in the setup of the last part. No discussion of hope in politics can be complete without an examination of the complex interplay between hope and pessimism in the Black philosophical and theological tradition in the United States, as recent debates about "afropessimism" and the legacy of the rhetoric of hope of the civil rights movement show (Lloyd 2017, Warren 2015, Bliss 2015). Our plans to include a contribution relating to these issues in the volume could unfortunately not be realized. This was entirely a result of bad luck, and we want to emphasize that the volume remains incomplete in this respect.

REFERENCES

Bliss, James. 2015. "Hope Against Hope: Queer Negativity, Black Feminist Theorizing, and Reproduction without Futurity." *Mosaic: A Journal for the Interdisciplinary Study of Literature* 48 (1): 83–98. https://doi.org/10.1353/mos.2015.0007.

Blöser, Claudia. 2019. "Hope as an Irreducible Concept." *Ratio*, May. https://doi.org/10.1111/rati.12236.

Blöser, Claudia, and Titus Stahl. 2017. "Hope." In *The Stanford Encyclopedia of Philosophy*, edited by Edward N. Zalta, Spring 2017. Metaphysics Research Lab, Stanford University. https://plato.stanford.edu/archives/spr2017/entries/hope/.

Blöser, Claudia, und Titus Stahl. 2017. "Fundamental Hope and Practical Identity." *Philosophical Papers* 46 (3): 345–71. https://doi.org/10.1080/05568641.2017.1400918.

Bovens, Luc. 1999. "The Value of Hope." *Philosophy and Phenomenological Research* 59 (3): 667–81. https://doi.org/10.2307/2653787.

Calhoun, Cheshire. 2018. *Doing Valuable Time: The Present, the Future, and Meaningful Living*. New York: Oxford University Press.

Döring, Sabine. 2014. "What May I Hope? Why It Can Be Rational to Rely on One's Hope." *European Journal for Philosophy of Religion* 6 (3): 117–29. https://doi.org/10.24204/ejpr.v6i3.166.

Downie, R. S. 1963. "Hope." *Philosophy and Phenomenological Research* 24 (2): 248. https://doi.org/10.2307/2104466.

Kwong, Jack M. C. 2019. "What Is Hope?" *European Journal of Philosophy* 27 (1): 243–54. https://doi.org/10.1111/ejop.12391.

Lamb, Michael. 2016. "Aquinas and the Virtues of Hope: Theological and Democratic: Aquinas and the Virtues of Hope." *Journal of Religious Ethics* 44 (2): 300–32. https://doi.org/10.1111/jore.12143.

Lloyd, Vincent W. 2017. *Religion of the Field Negro: On Black Secularism and Black Theology*. 1st ed. Fordham University Press.

Marcel, Gabriel. 1962. "Sketch of a Phenomenology and a Metaphysic of Hope." In *Homo Viator: Introduction to a Metaphysic of Hope*, translated by Emma Crauford, 29–67. New York: Harper and Brothers.

Martin, Adrienne M. 2013. *How We Hope: A Moral Psychology*. http://dx.doi.org/10.23943/princeton/9780691151526.001.0001.

McCormick, Miriam Schleifer. 2017. "Rational Hope." *Philosophical Explorations* 20 (sup1): 127–41. https://doi.org/10.1080/13869795.2017.1287298.

McGeer, Victoria. 2004. "The Art of Good Hope." *Annals of the American Academy of Political and Social Science*, Nr. 1: 100–27.

Meirav, Ariel. 2009. "The Nature of Hope." *Ratio* 22 (2): 216–33. https://doi.org/10.1111/j.1467-9329.2009.00427.x.

Milona, Michael. 2018. "Finding Hope." *Canadian Journal of Philosophy* 49 (5): 710–29. https://doi.org/10.1080/00455091.2018.1435612.

Milona, Michael, and Katie Stockdale. 2018. "A Perceptual Theory of Hope." *Ergo, an Open Access Journal of Philosophy* 5 (8). https://doi.org/10.3998/ergo.12405314.0005.008.

Moellendorf, Darrel. 2006. "Hope as a Political Virtue." *Philosophical Papers* 35 (3): 413–33. https://doi.org/10.1080/05568640609485189.

Ratcliffe, Matthew. 2013. "What Is It to Lose Hope?" *Phenomenology and the Cognitive Sciences* 12: 597–614. https://doi.org/10.1007/s11097-011-9215-1.

Segal, Gabriel, and Mark Textor. 2015. "Hope as a Primitive Mental State." *Ratio* 28 (2): 207–22. https://doi.org/10.1111/rati.12088.

Snow, Nancy E. 2013. "Hope as an Intellectual Virtue." In *Virtues in Action: New Essays in Applied Virtue Ethics*, edited by Mike Austin, 153–70. New York: Palgrave Macmillan.

———. 2018. "Hope as a Democratic Civic Virtue." *Metaphilosophy* 49 (3): 407–27. https://doi.org/10.1111/meta.12299.

Warren, Calvin L. 2015. "Black Nihilism and the Politics of Hope." *CR: The New Centennial Review* 15 (1): 215–48.

I

Hope in the History of Philosophy

Chapter Two

Hope in Archaic and Classical Greek

Douglas Cairns

To study hope in ancient Greek sources, we need a nonprescriptive account of what hope means in English. Many would be happy with the definition offered by Richard Lazarus (Lazarus 1999, 653): "To hope is to believe that something positive, which does not presently apply to one's life, could still materialize, and so we yearn for it." On this view, hope involves a desire for an outcome that one believes is possible, but not certain.[1] Yet philosophers are dissatisfied with the orthodox (Martin 2013) or "lowest common denominator" (Pettit 2004) account of hope.[2] Both Philip Pettit and Adrienne Martin find the distinctiveness of hope in its role as an antidote to despair, as a way organizing one's life in difficult and uncertain circumstances.[3] Thus hope is not just about desiring the end or about planning to achieve it. Indeed, there may be no clearly envisaged outcome, as in the "radical hope" explored by Jonathan Lear (2006, esp. 91–108, 113–17), in which hope for a future that one cannot as yet clearly imagine allows one to go on living in circumstances in which all old certainties have gone. The notion that hope sustains—that it involves not merely thinking that the desired outcome is possible, but also using that idea, motivationally, as a compensation for the outcome's uncertainty—explains why it is generally regarded as a "good thing." But it also explains why those who do not share the hopeful person's perspective may regard that person's hope as deluded or self-deceiving (Lear 2006, 105–7; Martin 2013, 98–101, 106–17).

The sense that hope sustains and motivates contributes greatly to its specificity in the English emotional lexicon. Optimism, being more closely linked with (what agents regard as) realistic assessments of outcomes, does not have these qualities (Gadamer 1991, 169–70; Lazarus 1999, 655, 672; Eagleton 2017). For similar reasons, hope differs from both confidence and expectation. Yet, though it is a normal feature of hope that it can remain in the

absence of confidence, and confidence in an outcome normally represents it
as probable enough to make hope unnecessary, still the hopeful person faces
life with more confidence than the desperate. Equally, if one expects a certain outcome (whether eagerly or dispassionately) that outcome is normally
seen as more likely than one that one hopes for.[4] Yet we also speak of the
"high hopes" that drive people to pursue outcomes that they believe to be
well within their grasp: such people expect to succeed and are confident that
they will do so. The possibility that they may not ties their hopes to the
prototypical case.

   These issues will recur when we come to discuss the moral psychology of
elpis in Greek. But in comparing the concepts and categories of different
historical cultures we need a descriptive rather than a prescriptive approach:
trivial formulations ("I hope you have a nice day," "I hope your headache
gets better") may have only limited contact with the core examples of the
concept, but they too have a claim on our attention. We cannot exclude as a
candidate for hope in Greek a scenario that would qualify as an instance of
hope in everyday English.

ELPIS AND HOPE

Elpis differs most obviously from hope in that it does not always focus on a
positive outcome. At *Odyssey* 21.314–16 Penelope's asks Antinous, "Do you
elpesthai that, if this stranger should string Odysseus' great bow, trusting in
the strength of his hands, he would take me home and make me his wife?"
Since the beggar's stringing the bow and winning Penelope as wife is precisely what Antinous and the other Suitors do not want, *elpesthai* here is not
"hope" (Lachnit 1965, 4; Schrijen 1965, 3). This is, as Penelope represents it,
an unlikely outcome that Antinous will not expect. But having dismissed the
possibility that Antinous might expect the beggar to string the bow and make
her his wife, Penelope then refers to the beggar's own perspective—"not
even he *elpesthai* that" (21.317). This is a remote hypothesis, with a negative
verb, and so the sense might be "expect"; but it is also, from the beggar's
point of view, a highly desirable outcome, and so we might want to translate
the verb as "hopes." In other cases, the sense "expect" seems to be excluded
by the context. In the same episode, the emphasis on the effort that it takes
for Telemachus to bend his father's bow, three times failing to draw it
(21.124–27), suggests that the *elpis* in "*epielpomenos* to stretch the string
tight and shoot an arrow through the iron" focuses on a remote goal that
Telemachus strives with difficulty to reach rather than a likely scenario that
he expects to see realized.

   Thus *elpis* can focus on bad outcomes as well as good and does not
always exhibit hope's motivational aspect. Yet hope is one of the senses of

elpis already in Homer (Schrijen 1965, 5–15), and Greek has all the resources it needs to express that concept.[5] Locutions such as Polyxena's reference to confidence that depends either on *elpis* or on belief (Euripides, *Hecuba* 370–71) and the Chorus' to an *elpis* that is beyond expectation (*Heracles* 771) help to confirm that native speakers are capable of distinguishing between "hope" and "expectation." Yet, as we see in investigating *elpis* in Plato and Aristotle, the term's semantic range is a significant fact that repeatedly causes difficulty in the search for ancient approaches to the moral psychology of hope.

PHILOSOPHICAL PERSPECTIVES I: PLATO

Elpis plays a central role in the *Philebus*'s argument that all pleasures involve some form of mental representation. Interpreters typically assume that this entails a role for what we call hope, but very few offer any argument for that position, and it is by no means self-evident.[6] The frame of the discussion includes incidental references to *elpis* that may well draw on traditional attitudes to what we call hope: at 12c–d the general premise that pleasure is not the good is supported with reference to a common opinion that "even the idiot who is full of idiotic opinions (*doxai*) and *elpides* feels pleasure"; at 61b Socrates opines that "there is more *elpis* that what we're looking for [i.e., the good] will be more apparent in the well-mixed life than in the one that is not well mixed." Similar traditional-sounding phrases ("we are always full of *elpides* throughout our whole lives," 39e; "every human being is full of many *elpides*," 40a) recur within the main relevant argument. The deployment of popular conceptions of *elpis* as fallible and misguided, both prior to and within the main discussion (12c–d, 39e, 40a) suggests that Socrates wants to draw on these common beliefs as a way of underpinning the overall argument that the pursuit of pleasure is an unreliable guide to life.

A specific element of this is the argument that, as all pleasures involve an element of mental representation, pleasures, like beliefs, can be false. This is an important discussion, especially for its exploration of what most would probably now call the "cognitive" aspects of pleasure and pain, but also for the links it draws between *aisthêsis* (sensory perception), *mnêmê* (memory), and the kind of projection of future states of affairs that Aristotle would go on to call *phantasia* (Moss 2012, 265–68). But it is also one that is full of difficulties, obscurities, and apparent contradictions. When the discussion of the mental aspects of pleasure gets underway, anticipation of future pleasure is first called *logismos*, calculation, at 21c. At 32b–c *elpis* enters the picture, but as one of two forms of expectation (*prosdokêma/prosdokia*): *elpis* is a pleasant and confident expectation of future pleasure,[7] as opposed to the painful expectation that gives rise to fear.[8] The association with confidence (*tharros*) and antithesis with fear might be thought to suggest hope. But fear and confidence can also be contraries, and confidence can derive from the mere expectation that success is likely. There is an affective aspect here, but hope is not unambiguously its focus.

Throughout the discussion, rather, *elpis* appears as a purely mental aspect of pleasure (32b–c) that involves pleasant anticipation of future pleasant experiences (32b–c, 36a–b, 47c–d). This entails an account of desire (*epithymia*) in which the *psychê* apprehends, by means of memory (*mnêmê*) the future condition of restoration, while the bodily condition supplies (to the *psychê*) the pain that underpins that apprehension (34d–35d, 41b–d), there being no purely bodily condition of desire (35c). Thus, as a projection of future states, *elpis* has a role to play in desire. But that role seems not to be in itself affective or desiderative—*elpis* simply conjures up, in a pleasant way, a narrative or picture of a future pleasurable state (38e–40b; see Davidson [1949] 1990, 344). Nor is *elpis* a name for that "one single mixture of pain and pleasure" (47d) in which pleasant anticipation of pleasant replenishment is combined with the pain of emptiness and so generates desire; rather, *elpis* names only one aspect of that experience, the pleasant anticipation of future pleasure (esp. 36b, 40a, 47c). Though the pleasant anticipation of realizing one's hedonic goals may generate desire, the actual descriptions of that anticipation are compatible not only with the kind of hope or longing for such future states that would motivate one to seek to realize them, but also with idle fantasy (as in the case of the man who sees images of himself enjoying the acquisition of abundant wealth at 40a).[9]

The difficulty in relating the role of *elpis* in the discussion to our concept of hope emerge clearly at 35e–36c. If, Socrates argues, someone remembers pleasures whose return might in future bring an end to the present pain, then that person is "in the middle of these affections" (*pathêmata*, 35e–36a). For Protarchus, such a person experiences a double pain—"in the body because he is in the grip of the *pathêma* and in the *psychê* because of a certain longing that derives from expectation" (36a). To this, Socrates offers a counterexample: some people who are empty are none the less in a state of "manifest (or vivid) *elpis*" of being replenished, while others are without *elpis* (36a–b). The latter, that is, someone who was empty and without *elpis* of replenishment, would fit Protarchus's case of "the double experience (*pathos*) of pain" (36b–c).

Socrates does allow that such cases exist. But if they do, it is difficult to fit them in to the psychology of the rest of the dialogue. The "double experience of pain" of the person who is "in an *elpis*-free condition" (ἀνελπίστως ἔχειν, twice in 36b) involves the pain that derives from emptiness and an additional element of mental pain at the absence of any prospect of replenishment. That thought, however, must surely entail a representation, deriving from memory, of what replenishment would feel like, even if it is unattainable (Gadamer 1991, 160–63; Delcomminette 2006, 346). The absence of any prospect of replenishment, moreover, does not exclude the possibility of desire for replenishment. So perhaps the person who is in an *elpis*-free condition has such a representation, but it is not *elpis*, and has a desire for replenishment, but that desire does not depend on *elpis*. Perhaps that person has what Protarchus called "a certain longing," albeit one that derives not from "expectation" but merely from the mental representation of replenishment. This might suggest that *elpis* is not merely the pleasant imagination of future pleasure that supplies the goal of desire, but precisely what is lacking in the person who ἀνελπίστως ἔχει—that is, hope or realistic expectation of relief. [10] Against that hypothesis, however, are (a) the implication (at 32b–c) that anticipation of future states takes only two forms, *elpis* and fear; (b) the clear statement of 41b–d that desire entails a mixture of pleasure and pain (not double pain); (c) the implication of the present passage (at 35e–36a) that all memory-based representations of future replenishment create this intermediate state of mixed pleasure and pain; and (d) a strong sense that Socrates's example of the pleasure that lies in the *elpis* of replenishment is meant to contradict Protarchus's view that the longing that derives from expectation might be painful—all desire, the argument suggests, involves the pleasure of anticipating its satisfaction. The argument at 36a–b does appear to suggest that there are two possible affective states with regard to the representation of future pleasant states—a pleasant feeling of *elpis* when fulfilment of one's desire appears as a distinct possibility (when one is "in manifest/vivid *elpis*," ἐν ἐλπίδι φανερᾷ, 36a) and a painful absence of *elpis* when there is no apparent prospect of fulfilment. If that were the case, we might describe the second of these stances as despair. What the person in "an *elpis*-free condition" has lost would be what we call hope; but what the person "in manifest/vivid *elpis*" has would remain ambiguous between hope and expectation. But this seems not to be the case: in itself, the passage appears to pit hope (or expectation) against despair; but the dialogue as a whole has no room for desires that do not depend on *elpis* or for representations of future pleasant states that are not themselves pleasant states. The problem lies in a tension between the immediate implications of this passage, the connotations of *elpis* as hope on which it seems to draw, and the wider role that *elpis* plays in the dialogue's account of the nature of pleasure and desire. This is a sign that the presentation of *elpis* in *Philebus* has little to tell us about the moral psychology of hope. The semantic range of *elpis* makes the specific phenomenon of hope more difficult to pin down than it might be for us; and pinning that phenomenon down is not in any case Plato's purpose in the dialogue.

The presentation of *elpis* in the *Laws'* celebrated image (*eikôn,* 644c) of the human being as a puppet with three strings is similarly located in a discussion of pleasure and pain. Here, *elpis* is the generic term for two varieties of opinion (*doxa*) about the future, *tharros* and *phobos*

(644c–645a).[11] The association with *doxa* reflects the most general sense of *elpis* as a matter of entertaining certain hypotheses. But these *doxai* are also *pathê*, affections[12]; *tharros* and *phobos* are correlated respectively with pleasure and pain, the two "opposite and senseless counsellors" that we each have within us (644c)[13]; and each of the three strings exercises motivational force, pulling us in opposite directions (644e).[14] Though *elpis* is a matter of *doxa,* its subspecies are affects. But though the negative motive of avoiding pain is called fear, the positive one, which pursues pleasure, is called not hope but confidence. It is possible that the choice of this term was at least partly influenced by a wish to avoid using *elpis* in both unmarked and marked senses, for it is clear that *tharros* performs a function, as the antonym of *phobos* (defined, as in *Philebus*, as expectation of harm, 646e) and as a motive for pursuing desired goals, that might be performed by *elpis* in its marked sense as a form of motivation focused on future good (England 1921, i.254).[15]

But the main reason for the choice of *tharros* rather than *elpis* as antonym of *phobos* is that it suits the Stranger's purpose in the next stage of the argument (646e–650b), where he presents the controlled drinking party as a means of inculcating shame (*aidôs/aischynê*), a positive form of fear that inhibits self-assertion and permits control of other emotions and desires.[16] This good fear is contrasted with the bad fear that leads to cowardice in martial contexts: alcohol promotes excessive confidence (called *tharros* at 647a, 649a–b) and overcomes *aidôs/aischynê* (647a–b, 649c), yet repeated exposure to such situations of overconfidence and shamelessness can inculcate an ingrained sense of shame and fear of ill-repute in the same way as repeated exposure to danger can develop courage (647b–649e). The affinity of the relevant sense of *tharros* here to traditional conceptions of *elpis* emerges at 649a–b, where excessive or misplaced confidence and "being full of a greater number of good *elpides*" are similar effects of drinking wine; just so (in *Laws* 2), it is the job of sympotic *nomoi* to step in when the drinker becomes "*euelpis*, confident (*tharraleos*), and more impudent than is fitting."[17] "Good *elpides*" and "being *euelpis*" designate that subclass of the generic *elpis* that is called *tharros* at 644d, and so *elpis* (in the sense at least of confident optimism, and perhaps even of hope) is drawn in to the *Laws'* extended discussion of law and education as means of fostering self-control and inhibiting self-assertion.[18]

Confidence, *tharros*, is thus a species of *elpis* in its neutral, generic sense, while "good *elpis*" is an element of the *tharros* that needs to be restrained by one's sense of honor and the fear of ill repute. The affective, desiderative side of *elpis* therefore does play a role in the argument, despite *elpis* being introduced as a kind of *doxa* of which fear is also a sub-species. While the use of *elpis* as the generic term reflects the fact that it may be neutral, a kind of belief or opinion, its division into subcategories both of which are affective states also reminds us that it encompasses forms of motivation that may not align with rational calculation (and thus may involve an element of moral danger). The designation of the subspecies of *elpis* that motivates us to pursue future pleasure as *tharros* invites us to consider in what ways *tharros* and *elpis* overlap, both as affects and as potentially harmful forms of motivation.

Elpis appears in conjunction with *doxa* again in Book 9's discussion of the forms of error that lead to injustice, but whereas Book 1 makes *elpis* a form of *doxa* that has two morally dubious varieties, fear and confidence, in Book 9 both *doxa* and *elpides* are associated with well-intentioned actions that nonetheless fail to achieve their aim (864b). Here, *elpis* may encompass a desire to achieve a good end and not merely an expectation that such an end will be achieved. Neither is sufficient, yet the possibility of failure entails the possibility of success, and so *elpis*, when its assessment of the ends to be pursued is correct, can also play a positive role in just action.

And in fact the *Laws* also makes room for positive conceptions of *elpis qua* hope. An association between *elpis* and the *aidôs* (698b, 699c) that overcomes negative *tharros* and promotes its positive counterpart emerges in Book 3, where Athenian resistance to the Persian invasions of 490 and 480 BCE is given as an example of a state's regulation of its mechanisms for allocating honor and disgrace with primary reference to the best conditions of the *psychê* (697b). The Athenians had only a slim prospect of salvation, yet were buoyed by a degree of *elpis* on the basis of their previous successes, which allowed them to find refuge in themselves and their gods. This fostered a spirit of cooperation among the citizens, in so far as their fear of annihilation was balanced by *aidôs,* the good fear that involves subjugating oneself to the city and its laws (699b–d).

Since the Athenians' chances of salvation seemed slim, it is clear that *elpis* in this passage refers to what we call hope, confirmed by the use of the metaphor of "riding at anchor" (*ocheisthai*). As far as the *Laws'* project is concerned, this positive *elpis* also resides in the suppression of individualistic motives in favor of cooperation, community, and deference to greater powers, the laws and the gods. The notion that positive forms of hope lie in understanding the limitations of one's powers as an individual human agent recurs. In Book 4, honoring the gods and one's parents, both before and after their deaths, permits one to live the rest of one's life "in good hopes (*elpides*)" that the gods will reward our efforts (718a).[19] But the strongest statement comes in Book 5, where all transgression is traced to its source in excessive self-love (731d–e), so that "every human being must shun excessive self-love, and always follow the person that is better than oneself, with no shame at so doing" (732b). In the same way, one should control one's emotions, both in good fortune and in bad,

in the hope (*elpizein*) that, for good people, at any rate, the god will confer his
gifts in such a way as to make the hardships that may befall us smaller rather
than greater and change for the better those that are currently present, while,
by contrast, the good things that fall to them should always come with good
fortune. It is with these hopes (*elpides*) and with reminders of all such things
that one should live, sparing nothing but always clearly reminding others and
oneself, both at play and in serious pursuits. (732c–d)

This passage is followed by an allusion to the puppet image (every mortal
animal is suspended from strings of pleasures, pains, and desires, 732e), but
here *elpis* avoids the *tharros,* the overconfidence, that is castigated in that
image and its sequel in Books 1 and 2, encompassing instead due recognition
of human fallibility, of the mutability of fortune, and of the role of the divine
in all human prosperity.[20] Divine favor is possible, but not certain; and so
this *elpis* is clearly hope,[21] here given a positive and sustaining role in a life
of self-restraint and religiously inspired humility—a keynote of the *Laws'*
ethical program.

PHILOSOPHICAL PERSPECTIVES II: ARISTOTLE

In Aristotle, *elpis* is to future events as memory (*mnêmê*) is to the past and
sensation (*aisthêsis*) to the present (*De Memoria* 1, 449b10–15, 449b25–8).
Each is a *pathos* of the *psychê*,[22] but though each can be implicated in
various ways in affective phenomena, in this basic sense, the affective aspect
of *elpis* is not phenomenologically salient—the "elpistic science" (i.e., divi-
nation) canvassed as 449b12 is simply about predicting future states of affairs. In a number of passages, *elpis* is oriented toward negative events in the
future[23]; when its orientation is positive, Aristotle occasionally makes this
clear by means of terms such as *euelpis* (see below) or "good *elpis*" (Gravlee
2000, 461–62 with refs). At the same time, *elpis* can be credited with a
pronounced affective aspect in passages such as *De Spiritu* 4, 482b36–483a5
(where it is one of the conditions that makes the pulse irregular) or *De
Partibus Animalium* 3.6, 669a17–23 (where the "leaping" of the heart in
elpis and expectation is described as a phenomenon that is more or less
confined to human beings). The addition of "and in expectation of the future"
suggests that "in *elpis*" refers to more than mere expectation here.

   The complementarity of *mnêmê* and *elpis* takes on particular affective
connotations when these phenomena are associated with pleasure and pain.
In the *De Motu* (8, 701b33–702a7), *elpides* (anticipations) and *mnêmai*
(memories) are causes of the changes in bodily temperature that are associated with the *pathêmata* in general (of which confidence, fear, and sexual
excitement serve as prototypical examples). The *elpides* underpin emotions
with negative as well as positive valence. More often, *elpis* appears as the

pleasant anticipation of future pleasure. It may thus be a marker of one's ethical character (*Physics* 7.3, 247a7–13):[24]

> All excellence of character is concerned with bodily pleasures and pains, and these depend on action, memory, or anticipation (*elpizein*). Now, those that depend on action relate to sensation, in the sense that they are aroused by something sensible, and those that depend on memory and anticipation derive from it too: for either they are pleased when they remember what has happened to them or when they anticipate (*elpizein*) the sort of thing that is going to happen to them. Thus, of necessity, all such pleasure is caused by sensible objects.

An extended discussion of pleasure in the *Rhetoric* (1.11) explores the psychology of this further. All pleasure depends on sensation, including that which depends on memory and *elpis*, because these require *phantasia* (imagination), which is itself a weak form of sensation (1370a26–35). The pleasures of *elpis* and memory derive from the same things as do present pleasures, though *elpis* in particular is focused on major sources of pleasure or (pain-free) benefit (1370b6–9). An element of pleasure of this sort informs "most" desires (1370b14–16), as when those whose fever makes them thirsty take pleasure in remembering or looking forward to (*elpizein*) drinking (1370b16–18).

Since it is pleasant to anticipate those things whose presence gives pleasure, anger, which involves the *elpis* of redress or revenge (*timôria*) also involves an element of pleasure (1370b9–14, 1370b29–32). While the *De Motu* passage cited above suggests a role for *elpis* in all *pathê* that focus on the future (and the *Rhetoric* concurs in giving it a role in desire more widely), Aristotle returns several times to its role in anger in particular, not only in the account of that emotion in *Rhetoric* 2.2 (1378b1–2), but also in discussions of courage and confidence in the *Rhetoric* and in the *Eudemian Ethics*, where the pleasant anticipation (*elpis*) of redress that anger entails can motivate people to face dangers in a way that is not truly courageous (*EE* 3.1, 1229b30–1)—the angry fear nothing and the element of *elpis* in anger makes them confident (*Rhet.* 2.12, 1389a26–8). Both in the discussion of pleasure at *Rhetoric* 1.11 and in the account of anger in 2.2, Aristotle emphasizes that anger's *elpis* focuses the possibility of the desired *timôria* (1370b12, 1378b3–4). This makes it natural to see this form of *elpis* as hope. Yet the second of these passages suggests that the element of pleasure lies in "thinking that one will obtain what one aims at" (1378b2–3), specified less in terms of yearning for a possible but uncertain outcome than as an obsessive fixation with the object of one's desires—the pleasure of anger rests both on the future pleasure of *timôria* and on dwelling on that outcome in the present, imagining oneself exacting revenge and so taking the kind of pleasure that one takes in dreams (1378b7–9). Distinctions that we might like to draw between hope, pleasant anticipation, and earnest desire are effaced by the semantic range of *elpis* in such passages; but the general thrust of Aristotle's approach clearly leans more toward anticipation and anticipatory pleasure than toward hope as such.

Elpis has a role in anger not only because it is future oriented but also because that orientation entails an element of desire that both motivates and can lead us to focus on the objects of our desires to the exclusion of all else. This also gives *elpis* a role in conditioning attitudes to risk—as we saw, the *elpis* that anger entails can accompany kinds of passion that look like courage, but are not (*EE* 3.1, 1229b30–1; cf. *Rhet.* 2.12, 1389a26–8). These points are expanded in Aristotle's discussions of courage (*andreia*) and his approach to the affective states of fear and confidence.[25]

The accounts of the virtue of *andreia* in the ethical treatises see it as a mean state with regard to both fear (*phobos*) and confidence (*tharrê*, *EN* 3.6, 1115a5–6, *EE* 3.1, 1228a26–b3).[26] Fear and confidence are treated in their own right in *Rhetoric* 2.5, where *elpis* has a role in both. *Tharsos* is analyzed in terms of *elpis* at 1383a16–19: "For confidence, *tharsos*, is opposed to [fear, and that which inspires confidence to] the frightening, so that the *elpis* [implied by *tharsos*] comes with a *phantasia* that salutary things are close, and that [or 'while'] fearful things do not exist or are far away." *Elpis* is regularly translated here as "hope,"[27] and no doubt hope can be a basis for confidence and may be elicited by the prospect of imminent salvation. But the forms of confidence in question here rest fundamentally on various ways of thinking that one is safe and having nothing to fear—the confident believe that nothing is likely to go wrong or that they can deal with it if it does (1383a20–b9); they are not simply people who have reasonable hopes of success. Even if they were, their *elpis* would be of a partial and limited sort— it would not encompass the hope that persists even when success is unlikely.

Yet it is precisely that brand of *elpis* that is at issue only lines before, at 1383a3–8, where *elpis* is said to be necessary for fear. The difference between those who fear nothing further, because they think that nothing worse can happen,[28] and those who are capable of fear is that the latter retain a degree of *elpis*:

> Nor do those [sc. experience fear] who think that they have suffered all the terrors that there are and who have become cold with regard to the future, like people who are already dying on the plank; there must be some *elpis* of salvation [from] the source of their agony [sc. if fear is to persist]. This is suggested by the fact that fear makes people inclined to deliberate, yet nobody deliberates about what is beyond hope.

The operative antithesis in these lines is between hope and hopelessness, not between confident expectation and hopelessness (Gravlee 2000, 468–71). Though *elpis* in Aristotle spans a range from anticipation of future states of affairs in general through the anticipatory pleasure that informs desire and confident expectation of success, it can also encompass hope. And this hope (like most if not all of the other forms of *elpis*, no doubt) can be a minimum condition for deliberation (Gravlee 2000, 471–73).

The conditions for fear and confidence outlined in the *Rhetoric* pertain to ordinary human beings rather than to the virtuous. In the ethical treatises, *elpis* features in the discussion of courage, but though in both the courageous person will manifest fear and confidence as the situation requires, only the Nicomachean explicitly credits that person with *elpis*. In the Eudemian, *elpis* is a feature only of one of the inferior forms of *andreia* (*EE* 3.1, 1229a18–20):

> Another [form of courage] is that based on *elpis,* in accordance with which those who have often been successful or those who are drunk face dangers; for wine makes people *euelpides.*

The condition of being *euelpis* (regularly translated "sanguine"), based on previous good fortune or the foolhardiness induced by alcohol, here signifies irrational forms of optimism and overconfidence that we might attribute to those with "high hopes"; but high hopes or great expectations differ from the hope that sustains us when we sets our hearts on a possible but uncertain outcome.

Being *euelpis* is a feature of states that resemble courage also in the *Nicomachean Ethics*. At 3.8 the *euelpides* are denied the status of *andreioi*, because their confidence rests on their experience of success in battle; they are confident because they think that their strength is sufficient and thus that nothing will go wrong. In so far as they are *euelpides*, they are like the inebriated.[29] Just as Dutch courage wears off, so does the confidence of the *euelpides* when they realize that circumstances are not as they had thought, while the truly courageous stand their ground, resisting real and apparent dangers because it is *kalon* to do so (1117a9–17). In this way, the *euelpides* are not far removed from those who underestimate the risks out of ignorance (1117a22–6). Again, one might say that the *eulpides* have "high hopes," but inasmuch as they believe that they are safe from harm and perfectly able to deal with the risks that face them, it would strain English usage to say that they are hopeful (Gravlee 2000, 463; Pearson 2009, 124 n. 4; Pearson 2014, 115).

At *EN* 3.6, however, Aristotle draws a similar contrast between the way that a courageous person and an experienced seafarer would face peril at sea: both would be without fear, but for the courageous this would rest on a belief that salvation was impossible and death in such circumstances deplorable, while seafarers are *euelpides* in relation to their experience; true courage is displayed where there is occasion for valor or where death is *kalon*, which is not true of death at sea (or from illness, 1115a35–b6). Here, *euelpis* refers to the confidence that derives from experience, but this passage raises the question of hope (in our sense) also in the case of the courageous. In "giving up on salvation'" (ἀπεγνώκασι τὴν σωτηρίαν) the courageous seem to have abandoned hope, and this is one of the reasons why they feel no fear; without hope (in our sense) they face an ignoble death at sea, one that gives them no occasion to demonstrate true courage, as courageously as they can. "Giving up on salvation" is a condition for the absence of fear, and so comparison with *Rhetoric* 1383a3–8 (above), where it is said "there must be some *elpis* of salvation" if there is to be fear, confirms that "giving up on salvation" entails abandoning *elpis*. But if *elpis* is necessary for fear, it is not sufficient: experienced sailors are both *euelpides* and fearless. *Elpis* can be a feature both of the kind of uncertainty in which fear might arise and of the conviction that risks are minimal that underpins (over)confidence. Since the courageous person is not entirely free from fear in those circumstances in which the virtue of courage is paradigmatically possible,[30] it seems likely that such a person will retain an element of *elpis* (*qua* hope) in such circumstances, whether that be hope of salvation or of achieving the nobility of action that is the aim of all virtue.[31]

But if *elpis qua* hope is a feature of courage in its prototypical sense so too is *elpis qua* confidence, as we see from *EN* 3.7, 1116a2–7:

> The coward is a hopeless/desperate (*dyselpis*) sort of person, for he is afraid of everything. As for the courageous person, the opposite is true: for confidence (*to tharrein*) is a mark of someone who is *euelpis*. The coward, the rash (*thrasys*) person, and the courageous person are concerned with the same things, but are differently disposed towards them: the cowardly and the rash exhibit excess and deficiency, while the courageous person is in the intermediate and correct state.

This passage seems to contradict those (*EN* 1115a35–b6, *Rhet.* 1383a3–8) that suggest that *elpis* is necessary for fear—here, the coward fears everything, but lacks *elpis*. Equally, the courageous person is contrasted, at *EN* 1115b3–4 and elsewhere, with the person who is *euelpis*; here, the courageous person is himself *euelpis*. But since *elpis* in Greek spans a wider semantic range than hope in English the apparent contradictions can be reconciled: we might say that the coward, excessively prone to fear, is *dyselpis* in so far as he is severely lacking in confidence; without confidence he has no belief that (as the *Rhetoric* puts it) safety is near; but one can be *dyselpis*—in the sense of expecting the worst—without abandoning hope altogether. Equally, the courageous person is neither overconfident nor excessively fearful, but feels both fear and confidence as is right in the circumstances: he can retain the *elpis* (of safety or of attaining the noble) that underpins fear of what is genuinely terrible *and* the *elpis* that underpins justified confidence, avoiding the extreme fearfulness that promotes deep pessimism without being *euelpis* to the extent of underestimating the danger or basing his confidence on reasons other than the pursuit of *to kalon*. The semantic range of *elpis* allows it to be mapped in a variety of subtle ways onto the continuum that encompasses fear and confidence and the various right and wrong ways of dealing with them. The multivalence of the terminology reflects both the extension of *elpis* as a concept in ordinary Greek and the functions that the notion is made to perform in Aristotle's system.

Many of the features of *elpis* in Aristotle come together in the *Rhetoric*'s account of the characters of the young and the old (2.12–13). The young are oriented toward *elpis* and the old toward *mnêmê*, because for the young the future is long and the past short, and vice versa for the old (1389a20–23, 1390a6–9). The old are *dyselpides* because of their experience of life's setbacks and because of their cowardice (1390a4–6); the young lack that experience, and so are *euelpides* (1389a18–20). This belongs with their gullibility (1389a17–18, 24–25), but also with the intensity of their passions: they are hot by nature, like the inebriated (1389a18). They tend toward courage, since they have characteristics associated with two of the imperfect varieties of courage identified in the ethical treatises, that is, they are spirited (*thymôdeis*) and they are *euelpides*: spiritedness implies anger, which drives out fear, while *elpis* is a source of confidence (1389a25–28). Equally, they tend to *megalopsychia,* not in the fully virtuous form expounded in the ethical treatises, but in its ordinary language sense,[32] in so far as "they have not yet been humbled by life, but are inexperienced in its stresses"; here again their being *euelpis* plays a role, in that being *euelpis* makes people think that they are worthy of great things, which is what *megalopsychia* entails (1389a29–32). The *elpis* of youth encompasses forms of optimism, boldness, and self-confidence that belong with the extravagance of young people's desires and ambitions (1389a1–14), but also with the apparently unlimited array of opportunities open to them (1389a23–24), even if this is only an illusion born of inexperience. This is an *elpis* with a strongly affective character, and so it is much more than mere anticipation or expectation of positive outcomes. It belongs with the "high hopes" that are attributed to the young in other authors, such as Plato and Bacchylides.[33] But in the way that it risks tipping over into overconfidence, failure to appreciate risk, and unwarranted optimism it excludes features that we might regard as typical of hope. As a future-oriented *pathos*, rooted in the *phantasia* that derives from sensory perception, focused on future pleasures, and enmeshed in affective phenomena such as anger and confidence, *elpis* has a role in a wide range of affective and desiderative phenomena, but that role only occasionally and in certain contexts encompasses hope as such. What we call hope is in there somewhere,[34] but one could hardly say that hope, in our sense, is thematized.[35]

NONPHILOSOPHICAL LITERATURE

From philosophical sources, one might get the impression that ancient Greeks had little interest in the moral psychology of hope. For the kernel of ancient Greek attitudes toward that phenomenon, we need to turn to poetry, where hope is a regular and indeed prototypical sense of *elpis*. Archaic and Classical Greek poetry is rich in reflexions on the nature of *elpis* as both a positive and a negative aspect of human motivation. These reflexions are expressed very largely in forms of imagery that underline *elpis*'s affective aspects, as well as the (often illusory) comfort that it can provide.[36]

Hesiod's myth of Pandora's jar (*Works and Days* 90–105) is antiquity's most celebrated account of *elpis*, but there is no end in sight to the controversy over its meaning.[37] The standard view is still that the jar contained both evils, whose escape allows them to afflict humankind, and one good, *elpis*, whose failure to escape paradoxically affords human beings some minimal and perhaps illusory comfort.[38] In the same spirit, but much clearer in sense, is an elegiac poem in the corpus attributed to the (probably sixth-century) Megarian poet, Theognis (1135–50):[39]

> Elpis is the only good deity among human beings: the others have abandoned us and gone to Olympus. Trust has gone, a mighty deity, and Moderation (Sophrosyne) has gone from men, and the Graces (Charites), my friend, have left the world. Oaths of justice are no longer trustworthy among people, and no one reveres the immortal gods. The race of pious men has perished, and they no longer recognize rules or acts of piety. But as long as a man lives and sees the light of the sun, let him be pious with regard to the gods and await Elpis; let him pray to the gods, and sacrifice to Elpis first and last, burning splendid thigh-bones. Let him always beware of the crooked speech of unjust men, who with no fear of the immortal gods always have their minds on others' goods, making shameful compacts for wicked deeds.

In the absence of other divinities representing positive commitments to moral, social, legal, and religious values, the deified Elpis of this poem is, we might say, human beings' only hope. Thus, as an emotion, *elpis* is a potential source of solace, yet its apotheosis as the only remaining protection against injustice emphasizes the precariousness of trust in circumstances of moral decline. Passages that present hope as at least potentially positive, as an antidote to despair, typically carry this implication of its limitations.

Other positive images reinforce this impression. *Elpis* is something one can cling to (Sophocles *Antigone* 235–36),[40] that can soothe (or "enchant") one in distress (*Homeric Hymn to Demeter* 33–37), or (most commonly of all) that can provide nourishment or comfort (Aeschylus, *Agamemnon* 1668; Euripides, *Phoenician Women* 396). Such comfort is often evanescent: trust in *elpis* is better than despair (Euripides, *Heracles* 105–6; Fisher 2018,

70–71), but the personified Elpis in whom we trust can lead us astray (Euripides, *Hecuba* 1032–33; Fisher 2018, 59) or betray us (*Heraclidae* 433–34),[41] for *elpis* is an unreliable thing (*Supplices* 479–80). The Messenger in Sophocles's *Antigone* "feeds on the hope" that Eurydice has simply gone to grieve in private (1246–50), but that hope is soon disappointed. The same locution in Euripides's *Bacchae* (617) in itself conveys the notion that Pentheus's hope of binding the god was illusory. Just so, Jocasta in *Phoenissae* follows her reference to hope's nurture of the exile (396) with another common metaphor, that hopes are frequently proved empty (398). Similarly, for Semonides of Amorgos, the sustenance that *elpis* offers plays all human beings false (1.1–10 West):

> My boy, Zeus the loud-thunderer holds the outcome of all that there is and arranges it as he wishes. There is no sense in human beings; they live from day to day like grazing beasts, knowing nothing of how the god will bring each thing to pass. *Elpis* and credulity nourish all as they strive for the impossible. Some wait for day to come, others for the turning of the years; there is no mortal who doesn't think that next year he will arrive as a friend to wealth and good things.

Here, the dubiety of *elpis* is subsumed in a typically "archaic" account of human ignorance and ephemerality (Fränkel 1960, 29–30; Theunissen 2002, 321–24). It is human beings' inability to foresee and determine the outcome of their actions that gives *elpis* this negative aspect, yet *elpis*'s shortcomings lie also in the false comfort that it offers and its misguided motivational force. In all or virtually all of the passages that present *elpis* as a source of sustenance, the notion has a strongly goal-directed, affective-desiderative, and motivational aspect. These are metaphors for hope (Cairns 2016).

Though, in this tradition, reason itself may be unreliable, *elpis* is also regularly reason's opponent. In Bacchylides *elpis* overcomes human reason,[42] while in the conclusion to Pindar's eleventh *Nemean* (38–48), the power of *elpis*, as a fetter that controls our movements, is embedded in a series of proverbial maxims on the principle of alternation, the power of fate, the contrast between divine knowledge and human ignorance, and the need for human beings to set limits to their desires and aspirations:

> Ancient excellences alternate in bringing strength to men's generations; the dark fields do not give fruit without interruption, and trees are unwilling to bear a fragrant flower of equal wealth in every annual cycle; they alternate. This is the way in which fate leads the mortal tribe. No clear sign from Zeus attends human beings, yet still we embark on deeds of proud manhood, yearning for many deeds; for our limbs are bound by impudent *elpis*, and the streams of foresight lie far off. As for gains, we must pursue due measure. From unattainable passions come more painful forms of madness.

Here, *elpis*'s failure to identify suitable goals belongs with an inability to foresee the outcome of the actions to which it gives rise and with forms of desire that, unchecked, can lead to madness (Theunissen 2002, 358–65; Johnston 2018, 36–41, 48–49).

These metaphors give us a sense of the way that ancient Greek culture valorizes *elpis* and represents its phenomenology. The representation of *elpis* is a facet of a traditional body of thought that emphasizes the limitations of human foresight, the vanity of human wishes, and the inability of human beings to secure their own happiness.[43] If Greek *elpis* differs from English "hope" in that its semantic extension is much wider, so even when *elpis* refers to what we call hope its valorization is very different from that which prevails in contemporary Western thought. Richard Lazarus (again) is not unrepresentative in expressing the view that hope "is in the Western world . . . usually regarded as a positive state of mind" (Lazarus 1999, 658).[44] This is true, he argues, even of "false hope" (655–56):

> To the extent that we need [hope] to sustain an appreciation of life, it makes poor sense to denigrate hope as false even when its realistic grounds are not attractive. I cannot believe it would be better to abandon hope and, therefore, succumb to despair. The only sound rationale I can see against hope are [*sic*] the occasions under which it would be better to give up hoping for a lost cause to turn to something more constructive.

Pessimistic formulations of the human condition, such as Achilles's parable of the jars of Zeus in *Iliad* 24, commend not despair, but action.[45] Greek has a large number of ways of referring to despair (*aporia, athymia/dysthymia, amêchania*, as well as *elpis*'s cognate antonym, *anelpistia*), none of which is commendatory. Despair "is the mark of a worthless man," according to Euripides's Amphytryon, whereas "the man who trusts *elpides* is best."[46] A classical Greek, then, might have agreed that hope is better than despair. But such a person might also have regarded Lazarus's formulation as excessively sanguine, saying, as it does, nothing about hope's delusional aspects or about the danger of its leading to error, overconfidence, and failure, both moral and practical. Greek attitudes reflect a greater sense that important aspects of human existence depend upon factors beyond the control of the individual and a corresponding skepticism about the power of positive thinking in itself to ameliorate one's lot.

Douglas Cairns (FRSE, FBA, MAE) is Professor of Classics in the University of Edinburgh. His most recent books are *Sophocles: Antigone* (2016), *Emotions in the Classical World: Methods, Approaches, and Directions* (with Damien Nelis, 2017), *Greek Laughter and Tears: Antiquity and After* (with Margaret Alexiou, 2017), *Seneca's Tragic Passions* (with Damien Nelis, 2017), *Distributed Cognition in Classical Antiquity* (with Miranda Anderson and Mark Sprevak, 2018), and *A Cultural History of the Emotions in Antiquity* (2019).

NOTES

1. For similar, more technical, formulations in clinical and social psychology, see Snyder, Irving, and Anderson 1991, 287; Snyder 2002; Rand and Cheavens 2009.
2. Cf. also Eagleton 2017.
3. Cf. already Gadamer 1991, 170 (first published 1931): "In hope, one does not simply leap toward something to come; rather, in being "out for" the hoped-for thing, one holds precisely to something present which gives one hope—be it only the straw at which the drowning person clutches." These remarks form part of a discussion (169–72) of Plato's failure to distinguish hope from desire and expectation in the *Philebus* (below).
4. On hope and expectation as different ways of feeling about (positive) outcomes with differing degrees of probability, see Martin 2013, 30–32.
5. Contrast Myres 1949; Lachnit 1965, 5–7, 21–22, and *passim*. Much of Lachnit's dissertation is devoted to explaining away evidence that hope is a distinct sense of Greek *elpis*. Schrijen 1965, by contrast, catalogues occurrences of that sense, mainly in terms of positive *versus* negative representations, from Homer to Plato. For a full account of *elpis*'s affective/desiderative aspects, see also Theunissen 2002, 307–95. Cf. the essays in Kazantzidis and Spatharas 2018. Useful remarks on *elpis* as hope also in Fulkerson 2015, 2016.
6. Frede 1985, for example, uses "hope" throughout, but in arguing that this hope focuses on what *will be* somewhat undermines the translation. Similarly, Forte 2016 devotes his article to "hope" in the dialogue, without setting out any criteria by which the dialogue's uses of *elpis* would qualify. Vogt 2017 also tends to use "hope" with only minimal explicit justification, though she does point (p. 40) to a link between pleasure and motivation that suggests a role for hope as we understand it. Moss 2012 translates *elpis* as "hope" throughout her discussion of *Philebus*, claiming that the argument for false pleasures is also intended to prove that affective states such as fear and anger can be false (2012, 263, on *Philebus* 40e), while also arguing for a (nuanced) form of cognitivism in the dialogue that "identifies passions with beliefs" (2012, 265). Gadamer 1991, 158–72, has a superb exploration of hope, but though he recognizes that the *Philebus* does not distinguish between hope and anticipatory pleasure (p. 169), he still attributes rather more of his insights on hope to Plato than the text warrants.
7. For *elpis* as a species of *prosdokia* (of good), cf. the Platonic *Definition* at 416a21. See also the definition of fear as expectation of bad at *Protagoras* 358d (picked up, but not necessarily endorsed, by Aristotle at *EN* 3.6, 1115a9).
8. At 39d–40a, on the other hand, *elpis* encompasses both pleasant anticipation of pleasure and painful anticipation of pain: all forms of "pre-pleasure" and "pre-pain" (39d–e) are said to be *elpides* that involve words and images (39e–40a). As Seeck 2014 notes (p. 86), Plato here uses *elpis* in the sense in which he had earlier used *prosdokêma/prosdokia*; most (e.g., Frede 1992, 446) overlook this. Even if this is merely a slip, the breadth of *elpis*'s semantic range asserts itself.
9. Cf. and contrast Moss 2012, 268–69. For a wider consideration of some of the issues here, see Martin 2013, 17–19, 25–29, 85–94.
10. Teisserenc 1999, 270–71, is right, as far as it goes, to note that "being in an *elpis*-free condition" here strongly suggests that the *elpis* that is lacking is hope. But he himself glosses that "hope" as that which "anticipe le plaisir proprement dit; il s'élance vers l'aspect agréable de l'avenir prévu"—that is, anticipatory pleasure, not *espoir*.
11. Cf. *phobos* and *elpis* at *Phil.* 32b (Schöpsdau 1994–2011, i.230).
12. As indeed is the element represented by the third, golden string, namely calculation (*logismos*), 644e, even though its job is to adjudicate on the goals pursued by the other two.
13. This draws on the language of the *Timaeus* at 69d, where the foolish counsellors are *tharros* and *phobos* themselves and *elpis*, which "readily leads us astray" appears alongside other terrible and compulsive *pathêmata* associated with the lower, mortal type of *psychê*.

14. With the added complication that the person him- or herself can also intervene to increase the pull on the golden string of *logismos* (644e, 645a–b); see England 1921, 256; Stalley 1983, 61; Bobonich 2002, 264, 266–67.

15. The *Laws'* deployment of *elpis*-words in unthematized, incidental contexts shows no real preference for "expectation" (853d, 893d, 898d, 923d, 954a) over "hope" (817c, 898d, 907d, 950d).

16. Cf. *Laws* 2, 666a–c, 671c–e, 672b–d, with Cairns 1993, 374–75.

17. For the *elpides* of the drinker, cf. Bacchylides fr. 20B Maehler, with Cairns 2016, 38.

18. See, for example, *Laws* 4, 715e–718a, 5, 782d–783a, with Cairns 1996, 28–31.

19. Cf. *elpis* used of the hopes that the virtuous may entertain of the afterlife at *Apology* 40c–41d, *Phaedo* 63b–c, 63e–64a, 67b–68a, 114c, where Socrates repeatedly affirms his *elpis* that the afterlife will be good and the confidence (*tharrein* as well as "being *euelpis*," 63d–64a) that this engenders. Confidence (*tharros*) in the face of death is a recurrent theme (78b, 87e, 88b, 95c, 114d, 115e). See also *Republic* 330d–331a, quoting Pindar fr. 214 Maehler on the "sweet *elpis*" that sustains the old.

20. For these as cornerstones of traditional Greek ethics, especially as reflected in epic and tragedy, see Cairns 2014.

21. Even if such *elpis* may be well founded (10, 950d).

22. Memory: *De Mem.* 1, 449b25; *aisthêsis*: see *DA* 1.1, 403a7. *Elpis* is not explicitly described as a *pathos*, but the *DA* passage in particular implies that everything that the soul does or undergoes is a *pathos*.

23. See, for example, *EE* 2.8, 1224b16–21, where the self-controlled are said to feel pleasure and the weak-willed pain "from *elpis*." Cf. *EN* 9.4, 1166b15–16, where bad people's memories of past and *elpis* of future difficulties contrast with the good memories and *elpides* of the good (1166a25–6).

24. Cf. *Metaph.* 12.7, 1072b17–18; *EN* 9.4, 1166a24–26, 9.7, 1168a13–14, 10.3, 1173b18–19; cf. *MM* 12, 1211b37–38.

25. On courage, see Pears 1980; Duff 1987; Leighton 1988; Curzer 2012, 19–63; cf. Lear 2006, 108–13; on confidence, see Garver 1982; Pearson 2009; cf. Pearson 2014; on the role of *elpis* in courage, see Gravlee 2000.

26. On courage as a mean, see Pears 1980; Leighton 1988, 98–99; Garver 1982; Duff 1987, 8–14; Curzer 2012, 30–32. For *tharros* and *phobos* as opposites, cf. *MA* 8, 702a3, *EN* 2.7, 1107a33, 3.6, 1115a6–7, 3.9, 1117a29.

27. For example, Grimaldi 1988, ii.99; Kennedy 2007; Waterfield 2018. The revised Oxford translation prefers "expectation" (cf. Leighton 1988, 95; Pearson 2009, 123; Pearson 2014, 114). Gravlee (2000, 467) translates "expectation" but explains in terms of hope.

28. Cf. *EN* 3.6, 1115a35–b6 with Curzer 2012, 30.

29. As at *EE* 3.1, 1229a20 (above), and in the case of the young at *Rhet.* 2.12, 1389a18 (below).

30. See *EN* 3.7, 1115b7–20; *EE* 3.1, 1228b4–1229a11.

31. On the issues here, see Pearson 2009, 124 n. 4, 126–32; cf. Leighton 1988, 93 n. 24; Curzer 2012, 30.

32. Gravlee 2000, 475, relates it to the "natural virtue" of *megalopsychia* at *EN* 6.13, 1144b4–7.

33. Plato, *Alcibiades* 1, 105a–e, Bacchylides fr. 20B Maehler.

34. At *EN* 1.9, 1100a3–4, children regarded as happy (*eudaimôn*) are counted blessed on account of *elpis*: given the context (that *eudaimonia* can be predicated only of a complete life, and life is beset by unpredictable changes of fortune, 1100a4–9) this *elpis* must be what we call hope.

35. Given the fragmentary state of our sources, and the fact that some of the best evidence is in Latin, I exclude Hellenistic sources from this survey. For a brief survey of Stoic approaches to *elpis* see Kazantzidis and Spatharas 2018, 10–14.

36. For more examples and further discussion see Cairns 2016.

37. For the various possibilities, with bibliography, see Musäus 2004, 13–30 (with 30–41 for his own suggested solution); cf. more recently Ercolani 2010, 156–58; Fraser 2011, 21–24 (both with further lit.).

38. A passage in Euripides (where Andromache laments that she does not "even have what is left to all mortals, namely *elpis*," *Trojan Women* (681–82) probably reflects the Hesiodic myth and suggests that the idea of *elpis* as the (only remaining and perhaps ineffectual) antidote to evils was an ancient commonplace. Cf. West 1978 on *Works and Days*, 96.
39. See, for example, Beall 1989. For the Theognidean elegy as the key to Hesiod's myth of Pandora, see Theunissen 2002, 339–40.
40. Cf. Aristophanes, *Knights*, 1244, fr. 156.10 K-A, with Slater 2018, 86–88.
41. Cf. Aristophanes, *Clouds* 1500; Slater 2018, 89.
42. Bacchylides 3.75–76: "winged *elpis* [undoes] the thought of people [of a day]"; 9.18: "*elpis* takes men's [thought] away."
43. For an exhaustive survey of *elpis* in archaic thought, see Theunissen 2002, 307–95.
44. Cf. the account of hope as biologically adaptive in Tiger 1995. Contrast Ehrenreich 2007, 2009, against the exaltation of hope and positive thinking (in U.S. culture).
45. See *Iliad* 24. 524 ("there is no purpose in icy lamentation"), 550 ("you will not achieve anything by grieving"); cf. Bacchylides 5.162–64 ("but since there is no purpose in bewailing these things, a man must speak of what he intends to accomplish").
46. Euripides, *Heracles* 105–6. Cf. Fisher 2018, 68–82, on the importance of hope and endurance in the play as a whole.

REFERENCES

Beall, Edgar. 1989. "The Contents of Hesiod's Pandora Jar: *Erga* 94–98." *Hermes* 117: 227–30.
Bobonich, Christopher. 2002. *Plato's Utopia Recast: His Later Ethics and Politics*. Oxford: Oxford University Press.
Cairns, Douglas. 1993. *Aidôs: The Psychology and Ethics of Honour and Shame in Ancient Greek Literature*. Oxford: Oxford University Press.
Cairns, Douglas. 1996. "*Hybris*, Dishonour, and Thinking Big." *Journal of Hellenic Studies* 116: 1–32.
Cairns, Douglas. 2014. "Exemplarity and Narrative in the Greek Tradition." In *Defining Greek Narrative*, edited by Douglas Cairns and Ruth Scodel, 103–36. Edinburgh: Edinburgh University Press.
Cairns, Douglas. 2016. "Metaphors for Hope in Early Greek Literature." In *Hope, Joy, and Affection in the Classical World*, edited by Ruth Caston and Robert Kaster, 13–44. New York: Oxford University Press.
Curzer, Howard. 2012. *Aristotle and the Virtues*. Oxford: Oxford University Press.
Davidson, Donald. [1949] 1990. *Plato's Philebus*. New York: Garland. Diss. Harvard.
Delcomminette, Sylvain. 2006. *Le Philèbe de Platon: Introduction à l'agathologie platonicienne*. Leiden: Brill.
Duff, Anthony. 1987. "Aristotelian Courage." *Ratio* 29: 2–15.
Eagleton, Terry. 2017. *Hope without Optimism*. New Haven: Yale University Press.
Ehrenreich, Barbara. 2007. "Pathologies of Hope." *Harper's Monthly*, February 1, 9–11.
Ehrenreich, Barbara. 2009. *Bright-Sided: How Positive Thinking Is Undermining America*. New York: Metropolitan Books.
England, Edwin, ed. 1921. *The Laws of Plato*. Manchester: Manchester University Press.
Ercolani, Andrea, ed. 2010. *Esiodo: Opere e giorni*. Rome: Carocci.
Fisher, Nick. 2018. "Hope and Hopelessness in Euripides." In *Hope in Ancient Literature, History, and Art*, edited by George Kazantzidis and Dimos Spatharas, 53–84. Berlin: De Gruyter.
Forte, Joseph. 2016. "Explaining Hope in Plato's *Philebus*." *International Philosophical Quarterly* 56: 283–95.
Fränkel, Hermann. 1960. *Wege und Formen frühgriechischen Denkens: Literarische und philosophiegeschichtliche Studien*. 2nd ed. Munich: Beck.
Fraser, Lilah Grace. 2011. "A Woman of Consequence: Pandora in Hesiod's *Works and Days*." *Cambridge Classical Journal* 57: 9–28.

Frede, Dorothea.1985. "Rumpelstiltskin's Pleasures: True and False Pleasures in Plato's *Philebus*," *Phronesis* 30: 151–80.

Frede, Dorothea. 1992. "Disintegration and Restoration: Pleasure and Pain in Plato's *Philebus*." In *The Cambridge Companion to Plato*, edited by Richard Kraut, 425–63. Cambridge: Cambridge University Press.

Fulkerson, Laurel. 2015. "Plutarch and the Ambiguities of Ἐλπίς." In *Emotions between Greece and Rome*, edited by Douglas Cairns and Laurel Fulkerson, 67–86. London: Institute of Classical Studies.

Fulkerson, Laurel. 2016. "Torn between Hope and Despair: Narrative Foreshadowing and Suspense in the Greek Novel." In *Hope, Joy and Affection in the Classical World*, edited by Ruth Caston and Robert Kaster, 75–91. Oxford: Oxford University Press.

Gadamer, Hans Georg. 1991, *Plato's Dialectical Ethics: Phenomenological Interpretations relating to the Philebus*. New Haven: Yale University Press. German original 1931. Second edition 1983.

Garver, Eugene. 1982. "The Meaning of *Thrasos* in Aristotle's *Ethics*." *Classical Philology* 77: 228–32.

Gravlee, G. Scott. 2000. "Aristotle on Hope." *Journal of the History of Philosophy*, 38: 461–77.

Grimaldi. William, ed. 1988. *Aristotle, Rhetoric II: A Commentary*. New York: Fordham University Press.

Johnston, Alexandre. 2018. "'Poet of Hope': *Elpis* in Pindar." In *Hope in Ancient Literature, History, and Art*, edited by George Kazantzidis and Dimos Spatharas, 35–52. Berlin: De Gruyter.

Kazantzidis, George, and Dimos Spatharas, eds. 2018. *Hope in Ancient Literature, History, and Art*. Berlin: De Gruyter.

Kennedy, George. 2007. *Aristotle, On Rhetoric: A Theory of Civic Discourse*. 2nd ed. New York: Oxford University Press.

Lachnit, Ottmar. 1965. *Elpis: Eine Begriffsuntersuchung*. Diss. Tübingen: Fotodruck Präzis.

Lazarus, Richard. 1999. "Hope: An Emotion and a Vital Coping Resource against Despair." *Social Research* 66: 653–78.

Lear, Jonathan. 2006. *Radical Hope: Ethics in the Face of Cultural Devastation*. Cambridge, MA: Harvard University Press.

Leighton, Stephen. 1988. "Aristotle's Courageous Passions." *Phronesis* 33: 76–99.

Martin, Adrienne. 2013. *How We Hope: A Moral Psychology*. Princeton: Princeton University Press.

Moss, Jessica. 2012. "Pictures and Passions in the *Timaeus* and *Philebus*." In *Plato and the Divided Self*, edited by Rachel Barney, Tad Brennan, and Charles Brittain, 259–80. Cambridge: Cambridge University Press.

Musäus, Immanuel. 2004. *Der Pandoramythos bei Hesiod und seine Rezeption bis Erasmus von Rotterdam*. Göttingen: Vandenhoeck und Ruprecht.

Myres, John. 1949. "Ἐλπίς, ἔλπω, ἔλπομαι, ἐλπίζειν." *Classical Review* 63: 46.

Pears, David. 1980. "Courage as a Mean." In *Essays on Aristotle's Ethics*, edited by Amélie Oksenberg Rorty, 171–87. Berkeley and Los Angeles, University of California Press.

Pearson, Giles. 2009. "Aristotle on the Role of Confidence in Courage." *Ancient Philosophy* 29: 123–37.

Pearson, Giles. 2014. "Courage and Temperance." In *The Cambridge Companion to Aristotle's Nicomachean Ethics*, edited by Ron Polansky, 110–34. Cambridge: Cambridge University Press.

Pettit, Philip. 2004. "Hope and Its Place in Mind." *Annals of the American Academy of Political and Social Science* 592: 152–65.

Rand, Kevin, and Jennifer Cheavens. 2009. "Hope Theory." *The Oxford Handbook of Positive Psychology* (2nd ed.), edited by Shane Lopez and Rick Snyder, 323–33. Oxford: Oxford University Press.

Schöpsdau, Klaus. 1994–2011. *Platon: Nomoi (Gesetze)*. 3 vols. Göttingen: Vandenhoeck und Ruprecht.

Schrijen, Joseph. 1965. *Elpis: De Voorstelling van de Hoop in de Griekse Literatuur tot Aristoteles*. Diss. Groningen: J. B. Wolters.

Seeck, Gustav Adolf. 2014. *Platons Philebos: Ein kritischer Kommentar*. Munich: Beck.

Slater, Niall. 2018. "Up from Tragicomedy: The Growth of Hope in Greek Comedy." In *Hope in Ancient Literature, History, and Art*, edited by George Kazantzidis and Dimos Spatharas, 85–110. Berlin: De Gruyter.

Snyder, Rick. 2002. "Hope Theory: Rainbows in the Mind." *Psychological Inquiry* 13: 249–75.

Snyder, Rick, Lori Irving, and John Anderson. 1991. "Hope and Health: Measuring the Will and the Ways." In *Handbook of Social and Clinical Psychology: The Health Perspective*, edited by Rick Snyder and Donelson Forsyth, 285–305. Elmsford, NY: Pergamon.

Stalley, Richard. 1983. *An Introduction to Plato's Laws*. Oxford: Blackwell.

Teisserenc, Fulcran. 1999. L'empire du faux ou le plaisir de l'image, *Philèbe* 37a–41a." In *La Fêlure du Plaisir: études sur le Philèbe de Platon 1*, edited by Monique Dixsaut, 267–97. Paris: Vrin.

Theunissen, Michael. 2002. *Pindar: Menschenlos und Wende der Zeit*. 2nd ed. Munich: Beck.

Tiger, Lionel. 1995. *Optimism: The Biology of Hope*. 2nd ed. New York: Kodansha Globe.

Tiger, Lionel. 1999. "Hope Springs Internal." *Social Research* 66: 611–23.

Verdenius, Willem. 1985. *A Commentary on Hesiod: Works and Days, vv. 1–82*. Leiden: Brill.

Vogt, Katja. 2017. "Imagining Good Future States: Hope and Truth in Plato's *Philebus*." In *Selfhood and the Soul*, edited by Richard Seaford, John Wilkins, and Matthew Wright, 33–48. Oxford: Oxford University Press.

Waterfield, Robin. 2018. *Aristotle: The Art of Rhetoric*. Oxford: Oxford University Press.

West, Martin, ed. 1978. *Hesiod: Works and Days*. Oxford: Oxford University Press.

Chapter Three

Hope in Christianity

Anne Jeffrey

The concept of hope enjoys a certain pride of place in the Christian doctrine and practice.[1] Christian Scriptures contain frequent exhortations to interpersonal hope—hope *in* God; and objectual hope—hope *that* God will, for instance, deliver his people from exile, suffering, and death. In the New Testament, "hope" often refers to hope in the gospel: that through Christ's atonement for human sin on the cross, Christians will enjoy eternal life in God's kingdom.

Christian teachings also emphasize the importance of having the theological virtue of hope—a stable disposition to desire union with God and see this as possible with God's assistance. In the Christian tradition, theological virtues like hope must be received from God rather than acquired through habituation. All the theological virtues aim at obtaining a transcendent good; however, hope distinctively regards this good as possible though difficult to obtain.

Christian hope extends beyond hope of and for individuals. Liturgical and social practices reflect that hope can be housed in the community of Christians—the church—and can be had for others. Because of hope's significance in Christianity, there is much to learn from rich philosophical work on hope that has been done within the Christian intellectual tradition. Yet the influence of the views developed within that tradition extends beyond it in important ways. Many contemporary secular accounts of hope bear traces of the Christian view in the way they treat the objects of hope, the kinds of attitudes hope can be, and what makes hope rational.

In this essay I aim to illuminate the nature of Christian hope by looking at the tradition's answers to three philosophical questions and then comparing them to those of contemporary secular accounts. First, *What are the possible objects of hope?* Next, *What are the psychological conditions a person must meet to have hope?* Finally, *What makes a hope rational and what makes it good for human life?* I conclude by suggesting that the role of hope in bringing about social goods (or evils) might be reconsidered in light of challenges presented by recent secular work on the social dimensions of hope.

1. THE OBJECTS OF HOPE

What sort of psychological attitude is hope on the Christian view? The answer to this question depends at least in part on hope's proper objects. This is true for lots of other moral psychological attitudes. Take indignation, for example. Indignation's typical object is a moral agent who has wronged someone else, not you. Knowing that indignation has this kind of object helps us understand that it is a reactive attitude and how it differs from other negative reactive attitudes, like resentment, where the object is someone who has wronged you (rather than someone else; Strawson 1962). So, too, getting a handle on what kind of objects are peculiar to Christian hope will help us better understand the nature of hope on this account. Further, we see a faint impress of the traditional Christian view about what hope's proper objects in contemporary secular accounts, but what is not transmitted is the critical idea that hope's two kinds of objects are intimately related.

1.1 Two Objects, Two Species of Hope: Interpersonal and Objectual Hope

On the Christian account, hope can take either future events or persons as its objects. In the primary case, Christian is hope *in* God, a personal being. I'll call the attitude that takes a personal object *interpersonal hope*.

We find the Christian Scriptures replete with references to hope in persons, especially (though not exclusively) hope in God. Hope in God should be distinguished from hope that merely implicates a person because the hoped-for outcome necessarily involves a person (e.g., hope that my roof will be fixed implicates the person who is working to repair the roof, but I may not hope in that person). One of God's epithets is "the hope of Israel," implying that they have—or at least ought to have—hope in God (e.g., Jeremiah 14:8, 17:3). The New Testament introduces the claim that Christ is the hope of Israel and that Christ "is our hope" (Acts 28:20, Colossians 1:27). The Psalms contain numerous exhortations to put hope in God, and we see the psalmist often saying that his hope is in God or that God is his hope (Psalm 43:5, 71:5). Some passages condemn the practice of placing hope in persons besides God, such as the gods of other nations (Jeremiah 14:22), a military army (Psalm 33:17, Isaiah 20:5), or oneself (Proverbs 11:7).

Christian theology echoes the idea that Christian hope is chiefly in the personal God. We see this most pronounced where theologians discuss the norms of hope—when it is proper to hope. For they argue that hope in Christ or in God must be primary and prior to hope for the various goods God might offer. Love of God and faith or trust in God should issue in hope in God; and that which we most desire is God's own presence and friendship (e.g., Aquinas, *Summa Theologiae* 1a2ae Q.40 Art.7).

The second kind of Christian hope is hope for certain future events. I'll call the sort of hope that takes events as objects *objectual hope*. (Some prefer "propositional hope," but this runs the risk of misconstruing the phenomenology of such hope; see Brewer 2009, 12–36.) Common objects of hope in Christian Scriptures include being healthy or living a long life, victory over enemies, and the forgiveness of one's sins (Fallon 1967, 98–107). Some Christian Scriptures contain expressions of hope for God, specifically, to bring about a future event, as when the Jews were hoping that they would overthrow the anti-Semitic persons in power in the story of Esther or when Job says that he hopes for God to take away his life because he is miserable (Esther 9:1, Job 3:11). In other passages, Biblical characters express disappointment in frustrated hopes for an outcome, such as deliverance from captivity, which they expected someone besides God to guarantee for them (Isaiah 20:5). Writers of the New Testament frequently write of the object of hope as the event of salvation. According to Christian teaching, Jesus Christ will appear on earth at what is called the Second Coming, and at that time those who have put faith in him will either experience bodily resurrection (if they have already died) or be given renewed bodies, and live forever in God's kingdom. In theological writings, "the Christian hope" becomes shorthand for this event of salvation, or resurrection from the dead and deliverance into God's kingdom, made possible by Jesus Christ's sacrifice for human sin on the cross and resurrection (Wright 2008).

Most authors in the contemporary philosophical literature on hope take for granted that hope's proper object is either an event or a person. Dominating the scene are debates about the nature of objectual (or propositional) hope (e.g., Benton forthcoming, Bovens 1999, Martin 2013, Milona and Stockdale 2018). Typically, philosophers dispute whether the attitude taken toward the object can be reduced to a desire for the outcome and a belief in its possibility, not whether an outcome or event is a proper object of hope. Even though objectual hope has enjoyed recent limelight, philosophers also discuss secular interpersonal hope, especially (unsurprisingly) in moral and political contexts. For instance, one can hope in another in the sense of trusting and relying on her "as one responsible for behaving in the way relied upon (Bobier 2017). Or, as Adrienne Martin's piece in this volume (chapter 13) explains, interpersonal hope may be a kind of investment in someone with whom you have a preexisting relationship and a desire to extend one's own agency by joining with them to produce some future together, with the belief that this is possible and another positive attitude toward the possibility.

It should not come as a surprise that contemporary secular accounts of hope have a good deal in common with the traditional Christian view regarding hope's objects. The Christian intellectual tradition is responsible for putting hope on the map in moral philosophy. In the ancient West, the term hope was used ambivalently, sometimes as clearly an unjustified or even painful emotion (thus more like despair), as when Aristotle describes the incontinent person whose hope (*elpidos*) in the pleasurable good he knows is wrong will produce painful feelings (*Nicomachean Ethics*, 1224b22). Christianity introduces hope as a virtue, unequivocally good when focused on the proper objects. Christian thinkers develop systematic theories of the psychology of hope as a virtue, passion or attitude, and action. Since the Christian view from the get-go acknowledges that people place interpersonal hope in agents besides the Christian God, and objectual hope does not always implicate God as an agent, it makes sense that secular theories could appropriate the view of the two kinds of objects of hope while leaving theism behind.

There are, however, important ways in which secular views depart from the traditional Christian account of hope's objects. The primary departures we will investigate below have to do with the relationship between time and hope's objects and the construal of the relationship between hope for events and hope in persons.

1.2 Hope for the Future

Traditional Christian accounts of hope typically assert that objectual hope must be for some future event. However, the rationale given for this assertion has to do with the nature of desire and the desiring component of objectual hope. It is worth briefly examining the reasoning here to see that the Christian account makes room for the same controversy that now exists in contemporary secular discussions about whether hope must regard the future, or simply what is epistemically possible (even if it is in the past; see Martin 2013, 68).

Origen and Augustine assert that hope must be about the future because if it were present or past, it would be needless (*Enchiridion*). In the medieval period, influential Christian thinkers like Bonaventure, Aquinas, and Scotus all affirm this position and treat hope as an attitude regarding future goods. The insistence that hope must regard the future persists in modern theology, both Catholic and Protestant. Protestant theologians who emphasize the future-directedness of hope include Emil Brunner (1952), Karl Barth (1994), and Jürgen Moltmann (1993). But this is not because hope must play a role in bringing about its object, and so must be prior in time to the object.

Instead, Christian authors assume that hope involves a desire to experience some event or to have some object present at hand. In their words, hope culminates from love and a desire for something not yet *possessed*. Those events that have already passed or are occurrent to the subject *are* possessed in that they have been or are experienced by the subject and so can be enjoyed either during the experience or through memory. Aquinas helpfully distinguishes hope from joy by explaining that joy may be about something that is presently occurring, whereas hope always anticipates and so is about what is to come (*Summa Contra Gentiles* 1 Q.89.9). As Augustine argues in his *Enchiridion*, this aspect of hope serves to distinguish it from faith, which can be about past, present, or future events. We have faith that Jesus Christ died, rose from the dead, and now sits at the right hand of God the Father. While hope and faith both regard a good, hope distinctively regards future goods only.

The argument then runs as follows: If desire always regards what is not yet experienced and cannot be remembered, then its object must be future; and as hope develops out of desire, so too with hope's object. But of course, this assumes that we have correct beliefs about what we desire. Perhaps proper hope with correct belief about the object must be for the future. However, if desire can be for what has already occurred objectively but is not yet enjoyed due to a subject's having a false or no belief about its occurrence, we can reject the inference that desire's objects must be in the future. Subsequently we can reject the claim that hope's objects must be future.

1.3 The Relationship between Objectual and Interpersonal Hope

Another significant difference between Christian and secular theories of hope regards the relationship between interpersonal and objectual hope. Early and medieval Christian theology places more emphasis on interpersonal hope and sees objectual hope as secondary. As we'll see later, this is in part because they consider hope a theological virtue when the attitude of interpersonal hope in God becomes a habit of will or memory. What distinguishes theological virtues from the moral virtues is that God is their appropriate end or object. In the Aristotelian vein of the Catholic tradition, it becomes common to refer to hope in God as having priority over hope for events precisely because the attitude (sometimes called the "motive") of interpersonal hope is more closely connected to the virtue of hope than the attitude of objectual hope.

At first glance, it looks like interpersonal hope cannot be understood without reference to objectual hope. Indeed, this is how a contemporary analysis often presents interpersonal hope. When I hope in a person, on this analysis, I hope for her to bring about some outcome, or to help one bring about an outcome jointly with me (Martin [this volume, chapter 13], McGeer 2004, Snow 2018). In many of the scriptural examples, hope in God is a sort of hope in a person (God) to bring about an outcome or event that is the object of an objectual hope. Perhaps hope in a person is only intelligible when one also has an objectual hope for some outcome, which the object of interpersonal hope is "hoped in" to bring about.

There are two problems with analyzing Christian interpersonal hope as reducible to, or even parasitic on objectual hope. First, it oversimplifies the relationship between the one hoping and the person hoped in, and something significant about the phenomenology of interpersonal hope is lost. Why care so much about a particular person bringing about an outcome? The natural answer is that one has a relationship with the personal object of hope that makes sense of one's desire that *she*, not anyone else, be the one to bring about some event. For instance, the apostles register the disappointment of their interpersonal hope in Jesus immediately after his death: "We had hoped that he was the one to redeem Israel" (Luke 24:21). The reason they hoped for Jesus to save Israel is their close relationship with him that involved trust, and their desire for reunion with him in God's kingdom. He had told them he would return and they would be together again. Their being together is not well described as a hoped-for event without first referencing the relationship of love.

On a reductive analysis, the subject of hope treats the personal object of hope as an instrument for obtaining the object of some other objectual hope. While there may be instances of God's people treating God in this way, those cases are certainly not put forward as *exemplary* on the Christian view. In fact, quite the opposite: the person who wants eternal life purely self-interestedly won't obtain it. Jesus says to the rich young ruler, "Whoever wants to save his life will lose it" (Matthew 16:25).

Moreover, church teaching makes clear that God himself is supposed to be the primary or principal object of hope. Hope in God is supposed to precede (both in time and importance) hope for the goods God may bring about. Christians are directed to hope in God for help in attaining God, that is, seeing and loving God in God's essence; but in order for the hope for help from God to be proper, the object of one's principal hope must be God— union with God in vision of God (*Summa Theologiae* 2a2ae Q.17-22). Theologians from Aquinas to Barth characterize hope in God as an expectation with desire for union with God, being in God's presence, and for God as the source of salvation (e.g., Barth 1994, X.47).

Finally, the strongest case against a reductive analysis of Christian hope is that many paradigm cases of hope in the Scriptures feature persons who simply do not have a determinate, static object of objectual hope they desire God to bring about. For instance, Abraham places hope in God when he leaves his home country on God's directive, but at that point he doesn't know what to expect from God. Certainly no desire and expectation for becoming the father of many nations has taken shape in him at that early point in his journey. Yet, we can accurately describe him as having interpersonal hope in God. Perhaps Abraham does hope in God to give him good things, whatever those may be; so the indeterminacy of his objectual hope doesn't preclude that Abraham's interpersonal hope is just a sort of objectual hope—that God bring about good things. Again, though, this doesn't capture the phenomenology of Christian interpersonal hope. On the reductive account, Abraham must just have a desire and expectation that God will bring about something vaguely good, and his attitude is about that particular state of affairs but not about the person of God or his relationship with God. This is implausible when there is no identifiable event for which one hopes, or when one's hope is in God to reveal what particular possible good is to be an object of objectual hope in the first place.

On the Christian account, then, interpersonal hope and objectual hope, in the best case, are intertwined and inseparable. The appropriate objects of Christian objectual hope always include divine action or a divine attitude, and they cannot be appropriate unless underwritten by a prior interpersonal hope in God. Once we already hope in God, we may develop hopes for God to bring about certain good outcomes; as Moltmann explains, "[o]ur hope in the promises of God, however, is not hope in God himself or in God as such, but it hopes that his future faithfulness will bring it also the fullness of what has been promised" (1993, 119). We will return to consider further questions about when objectual hope is good or normatively appropriate because based on hope in God.

2. THE SUBJECT OF HOPE

Christian teachings on hope also indicate that the attitude of hope is housed in a psychology with certain features (or, as it may be, lacking certain features). The Christian view includes a detailed picture of the subject of hope— the person who hopes. Can the person who hopes have knowledge of what she hopes for? Must she regard the thing hoped for as good? These canonical questions in the Christian intellectual tradition also make their way into secular contemporary literature on hope. A further question not typically considered, but whose answer is important for the Christian account, is whether other mental states or habits are required to buoy the subject's hope, not as parts of hope but as background conditions of hope. We will explore these questions below.

2.1 Hope, Faith, and Knowledge

The standard Christian view assumes that hope excludes a certain form of knowledge. For objectual hope, in order for a person to hope for p, she cannot already know p by acquaintance or experience. One Christian reason given for this view is based on the authority of Scripture. In the opening of the well-known chapter on faith in Hebrews, the writer says, "Faith is being sure of what we hope for, and certain of what we do not see" (Hebrews 11:1). New Testament frequently uses sight as a metaphor for knowledge, as when St. Paul writes in 1 Corinthians 13, "Now we see in a mirror dimly, then face to face. Now I know in part, then I shall know fully." So when the writer of Hebrews says that faith is certainty of what we do not see, interpreters standardly understand this to be a claim that faith supplies certainty of its object without knowledge—at least, knowledge by direct acquaintance. Christian authors argue that the Hebrews passage shows that hope and faith are similar in that they are both invisible and not known by direct experience or acquaintance. Aquinas defends the idea that hope is of what is unknown by appeal to its connection to faith: hope springs from faith and faith is of what is unseen and unknown, therefore hope must also be of what is unseen and unknown.

One scriptural passage that influences Christian views on the subject of hope's knowledge is St. Paul's claim in Romans 8:24–25: "Hope that is seen is not hope. For who hopes for what he sees? But if we hope for what we do not see, we wait for it with patience." Early Christian commentators like Origen and St. John Chrysostom interpret St. Paul as saying that hope's object is neither known nor acquired in the present life on earth. Origen explains that while the Christian can have confidence in her salvation because she believes in Christ, "that salvation is still in hope" until it is actually experienced by her. That is, her being saved is not something she knows by experience or present enjoyment of salvation. Unless the subject doesn't already know the object of her hope through direct experience, her hope doesn't make sense—why hope for what one sees? St. John Chrysostom (1889) argues that the person who hopes must not already be enjoying the good for which they hope, but visible things—things known by acquaintance or experience in the present life—can be enjoyed here and now, it will not do to hope for those things.

The Christian view claims that hope excludes knowledge and that hope involves *certainty*, simultaneously, while we see some resistance to this idea in contemporary secular views (Marcel 1951, Graper Hernandez 2011). Scholastic Christians define hope as a desire or appetite for a future good accompanied by certainty, or sure expectation (e.g., *Summa Theologiae* 2a 2ae Q.17 A.1). St. John Chrysostom says that hope is only needed for things that we don't yet have, and so hope has to be a feeling of "confidence in things to come." Medievals argue that hope disposes a person to daring precisely because of this confidence or certainty. Modern theologians, too claim that hope affords the subject of hope with special confidence in hope's objects (Barth 1994, IV).

Another reason Christians say hope requires confidence has to do with the Christian idea that hope should be preceded by another attitude that supplies confidence: faith. Just how faith relates to confidence in its propositional objects has been the subject of some recent debate (Howard-Snyder 2013,

Pace 2017). A Christian account, however, needs to explain (or explain away) scriptures such as Hebrews 11:1, "Faith is the assurance of things hoped for," Hebrews 10:22, "Let us draw near . . . in full assurance of faith," or Ephesians 3:12, "we . . . access with confidence through our faith in him."

Commonly, Christians hold that hope is an attitude found in the subject's will, not her intellect. But certainty appears to be a feature of the intellect. (This is a view developed and handed down by the Scholastics.) So, how does hope involve certainty on the Christian account? We should think of hope as depending on, rather than being constituted by, certainty in the hoped-for object through *faith*. Christian theologians from Aquinas to Calvin to contemporary authors affirm the idea that faith supplies the certainty associated with hope. In a memorable passage of *The Theology of Hope*, Moltmann writes,

> Faith is the foundation upon which hope rests, hope nourishes and sustains faith. For as no one except him who already believes His promises can look for anything from God, so again the weakness of our faith must be sustained and nourished by patient hope and expectation, let it fail and grow faint. . . . Faith in Christ gives hope its assurance." (1993, 20)

In faith, the intellect assents to some claim as true, such as "God will give us eternal life." Faith consists in confident adherence to a proposition with certainty but without full understanding (e.g., *Summa Theologiae* 2a 2ae Q.1 Art.5 ad.4). Only when the subject of hope *already has faith* that this is true can her desire for obtaining eternal life qualify as hope (Jeffrey 2017). Desire for some difficult good with no assurance that it will obtain might be better labeled optimism than hope.

This helps us sort out an important difference between Christian and secular accounts. Often, the secular theorist will say propositional (or objectual) hope is incompatible with assigning epistemic probability of 1 or 0 to the object (Bovens 1999, Martin 2013). If they draw the conclusion that hope is incompatible with epistemic certainty, then their view conflicts with the Christian view, where hope requires faith that includes certainty. If they draw the conclusion that hope excludes knowledge, what then? It depends on how "knowledge" is understood. If knowledge is inclusive of all forms of knowledge, propositional and knowledge by acquaintance, then there is no reconciling the secular and Christian views. If, however, a secular view claims that hope excludes propositional knowledge only, then it need only accept that one can acquire certainty without propositional knowledge to concur with the Christian view.

2.2 Hope and the Guise of the Good

We can also differentiate (objectual) hope from faith based on the way the subject perceives of the object. While a person can have faith in something they do not desire, or even desire not to be the case—like that someone will be condemned to hell—a person cannot hope for what they do not desire (Augustine, *Enchiridion*, II).

The traditional Christian account of hope, recall, is that hope is for a "possible but arduous good." The connection between hope and the good lies first, in an assumption about the nature of desire. Everything a person desires, she must desire under the aspect or "guise" of the good. Further, when something shows up to be good in some respect or other—when I desire it— this moves me. Medieval theologians argue that the part of me called appetite is positively moved by desires through the perception of particular goods. My being moved could consist in a positive appreciation of p (though it's important to note that the appreciation can't be intellectual like assent), motivation to bring about p, or a positive feeling about someone else bringing about p.

Hope thus falls into the psychological category of a passion or emotion. On the traditional Christian view, heavily influenced by Augustine (who was impacted by Stoics like Cicero), passions are positively—or negatively— valenced affects. These affects actually are accompanied by bodily changes (*Summa Theologiae* 1a 2ae Q.22, Art.3). Hope as a passion consists in a kind of approach toward the object of hope. It can be a help to action, it can make actions done for the sake of the object more pleasant because of the positively colored anticipation of the object, and it can keep up the person's strength needed to pursue the object (Lamb 2016a).

Hope differs from ordinary desire in that the person hoping must see the object as both good *and* difficult. Christian writers argue that it would not make sense to say we hope for "trifles, which are in one's power to have at any time" (Summa Theologiae 1a 2ae Q.40 Art.1). Contemporary accounts have not made much of the idea that the object of hope needs to appear to the subject as an arduous good—some, in fact, will disagree with this assessment. But it fits particularly well with the more general Christian moral psychology on which contrary passions have the same object and different emotional takes on the object. The opposite passion of hope, in this view, is despair, and what makes despair what it is depends on the person despairing seeing something they want as *too* difficult to obtain, and thus keeps her from pursuit or positive appreciation of the object (ibid. Art. 4). Both the despairing and hopeful person may have a desire and see a good as difficult to obtain, but the hopeful person regards it as to be pursued because of the possibility of obtaining it, while the despairing person takes the small chance of obtaining it to be a reason to give up on pursuit of it.

2.3 The Virtue of Hope

As mentioned earlier, the Christian tradition is first in the West to promote hope to the ranks of the virtues. Hope the virtue doesn't simply require lots of hopes *qua* passions, nor is it simply a transformation of the emotion of hope that entrenches it in the mind through habituation. Instead, hope historically is one of three theological virtues, along with faith and charity, that God gives to persons as a gift. Here, the Christian account of hope starkly differs from secular accounts.

Within the Christian tradition, views about virtue in general vary. Christian authors disagree about the definition of virtue and the connection of the virtues with each other, with some (like Aquinas) holding that the virtue of practical wisdom necessarily and formally unifies all the moral virtues, and others (like Scotus, *Lectura* 3 D.36 Q.1 N.98) denying the formal unity of the virtues, some holding that there are degrees of virtue and others denying this, some claiming virtues are in the intellect, others arguing that they are in the will or memory (Doyle 2011).

It is thus perhaps surprising to see substantial agreement in the Christian intellectual tradition when it comes to treatments of the theological virtues (except, see Niebuhr 1974). For one thing, theological virtues like faith prompt action and modulate perception, but they are given by God rather than acquired by habituation. Second, theological virtues perfect not a person's emotions or desires, but her intentions—what medieval philosophers call the "internal acts of a person's will" (Lamb 2016b). Third, all of these virtues must have God as their object in some respect. Because we can't achieve union with or vision of God on our own, these virtues have to be given through grace. Hope, like charity and faith, must be infused by God in a person's psyche. Further, even authors who disagree about the unity of the moral virtues all seem to acknowledge the unity of the theological virtues; for anyone to have one, she must also have the others to some degree. Someone without charity or love of God doesn't have hope as a theological virtue, for she lacks the precondition of hope, namely, stable desire for God and union with God (Jeffrey 2017). And hope, remember, requires the certainty of faith (Pinckaers 1958).

The Christian account makes clear that for a habit to be a theological virtue of hope, it must dispose the subject to rely on God in thinking the object is obtainable, and the object must be an actual transcendent good— God or union with God. Someone has the disposition to desire for God to help her obtain an apparent difficult good and regard it as possible, but the good she wants is not a true good because she has a false belief, then she doesn't have the theological *virtue* of hope (Lamb 2016a). As we learned in discussing the objects of Christian hope, a desire for goods that can't be possessed on earth—for the unseen—often characterizes hope. Moreover, interpersonal hope in God is supposed to precede and ground objectual hopes. Without this aspect of reliance, a habit cannot qualify as the theological virtue of hope (Aquinas, *Disputed Questions on the Virtues*, 1 ad.1). If a person hopes for union with God but desires to achieve this on her own, she too will lack the virtue.

While Scholastic thinkers emphasize the importance of relying on God for help, some modern and contemporary Christian philosophers expand the sphere of auxiliaries to include fellow humans. Aaron Cobb and Adam Green (2017) attempt to bring out the social dimension of the virtue of hope from the periphery, where it is in traditional accounts, to the center. They argue that members of the community shore up the theological virtue of hope not just by creating fertile conditions for it—teaching the individual to see her own agency and worth in the right ways—but also by relying on others to hope for this good when one's own hope wanes or wavers. What is relevant to our current question—what is the psychology of the subject of hope?—is that it involves reliance on someone else to bring about the expected good in the paradigmatic case, whether that other is a community of Christian believers or God.

Recent secular theories that count hope as a virtue typically highlight the social dimensions and benefits of hope. But more often than not, they retain the kind of ambivalence we see in Greek thought about hope's normative status, claiming that while it can be a virtue, it is also easily distorted. In large part this difference between secular and Christian views on hope as a virtue owes to the fact that the Christian view assumes a substantive account of the moral good, and attaches the virtue of hope to that good. Many secular accounts refrain from pronouncing on what precisely is the good a person must desire to have the virtue of hope. Hope can equip a person to be realistic about her chances at an outcome in a way that tempers our beliefs and actions—even giving us courage in the face of challenges (Kadlac 2015). But it could lead a person to have courage to do the wrong sorts of things or to develop camaraderie and solidarity for the wrong cause.

The question of what makes hope a virtue, or what makes certain hopes (qua emotion) appropriate, takes us into normative territory. Here we will see that the Christian view contrasts more starkly with secular accounts, in part because of the Christian account of the good underwriting the moral psychology.

3. NORMATIVE DIMENSIONS OF HOPE

Now that we have an idea of what hope is, we are in a position to ask what makes a hope reasonable and what makes it good for human beings to have on the Christian view.

3.1 The Normative Grounds of Interpersonal Christian Hope

Christian theologians often answer the rationality question by citing the "grounds of hope" or "foundation of hope." The grounds of hope will be a person or event or evidence that form an appropriate basis for the person's hope. Typically in the Christian view, the character of a person in whom one hopes, some past event like a promise, or a fact about a future event serves as the grounds that makes hope not just intelligible but gives a normative reason for one's Christian hope.

Begin with the most fundamental hope: interpersonal hope in God. What grounds do we have to invest such hope in God? Our perception of God's absolute goodness and divine attributes, such as God's mercy, power, and faithfulness, says the standard view. In recognition of God's goodness, we subsequently realize that it is good for us to be united with an unqualifiedly good being. In fact, it is better than anything else we could want.

Some scholars argue that this point drives a wedge between Catholic and Protestant thought. Protestants worry that if we come to desire God because God is good for us, we do not love God with the love of charity. Catholics take it that love for oneself (*amor concupiscentiae*) is not morally tainting; rather, with Aristotle, they recognize proper love of self (*amor amicitiae*) as a requisite for love of others, and so the residual care for one's own good while loving others (*amor concupiscentiae*) is fitting (Delany 1910). Supposing we can characterize self-love without reducing it to egoism, it would seem perfectly reasonably to place hope in God based on knowledge that one would benefit from relationship with God. In fact, we might echo Aristotle here in saying that we should pray that what is good unqualifiedly good is good for us (*Nicomachean Ethics* 1129b5–6).

God's mercy and power constitute proper grounds for reasonable hope in God's help. We can expect God's mercy, desire to refrain from giving us punishments we deserve, to occasion extension of assistance in our pursuit of union with God. And because God is regarded as Almighty, helping to bring us into union with God is something God is able to do (Aquinas, *Summa Theologiae* 2a 2ae Q.18 Art.4 Ad.2). If God has both these features then the expectation that union with God is possible seems reasonable. Here, the reasonability of the hope owes to the reasonability of the probabilistic belief, given the way one has conditionalized on beliefs one has about God's character.

3.2 The Rationality of Objectual Hopes

Starting in the medieval period, hopes identified as passions, or emotions, are considered morally neutral (Miner 2009). This is because they are in the appetite, rather than the will—that is, not a direct product of choice or responsive to reason. Further, they are fleeting rather than stable so long as those hopes are only passions.

Nonetheless, objectual hope—the emotional attitude—can be related to reason in more or less fitting ways, making it more or less rational (Miner 2009, 219). One way hope may be irrational indirectly is if the hope comes about due to an inaccurate estimation of the difficulty of achieving the hoped-for object (ibid., 224). A person who hopes to become a professional soccer player, not adequately attending to the time, effort, and luck it will take to train and be picked up by a league, may have irrational objectual hope.

A second way objectual hope might fail to be rational is when the subject overestimates her own powers or underestimates her limitations. The person who hopes to earn eternal life through good works suffers from an irrationality of this kind, and the habit of hoping in this manner is traditionally called presumption—not wanting or seeking help where it is needed. She discounts her own limitations and thinks she can merit salvation.

Finally, hope can inherit unreasonableness from an unreasonable judgment about what would be good for oneself. Someone might be convinced that now is the right time to quit her job and seek a more fulfilling career, when in fact, because of a recent downturn in the market, this is imprudent. Her subsequent hope to find more meaningful work in the immediate future is irrational.

The Christian tradition's account of how objectual hopes, as emotions, can come under rational criticism has analogues in contemporary secular accounts. Especially where theorists support the standard view of hope as consisting in a belief and desire, the rationality of hope has to do with its cognitive basis rather than its cognitive element. Michael Milona, for example, introduces the idea of a cognitive base of a hope-constituting desire—a belief in the possibility of the outcome one hopes for and desires (Milona 2018). A person could have a belief that the outcome is possible, and also have a belief that the likelihood of the outcome occurring is low. If a desire for the outcome is cognitively based on the probability estimate rather than the mere possibility belief, what results might be despair rather than hope, since the focus is on the negative belief about the outcome rather than the positive belief about its possibility. Milona acknowledges that this makes hope quite vulnerable to irrationality, since hope can become entangled in a feedback loop feeding the belief in the probability of the hoped-for outcome or encouraging the person to side with, or focus on, her judgment about its possibility over her judgment about the high likelihood of its not coming about.

While the Christian account of rational norms for objectual hope certainly includes a subjective element, we should be careful not to understand the view as purely subjective or coherentist. Even Luther, who is accused for giving a thoroughgoing subjective theology in earlier work, ends up arguing that Christian objectual hopes are rational only because of truths that objectively ground them (Cooper 2012). Christian theologians take care to emphasize that it is not simply beliefs about what God has done or promised that rationalizes belief in the possibility of future goods like victory over enemies or resurrection from the dead. Actual events or promises do the grounding as well. Theologians will claim that Christ's resurrection of Lazarus from the dead, or the fact that Christ resurrected from the dead, is the ground of our hope for bodily resurrection, for instance. Barth says, "because this event took place" (not simply because we believe it did or have faith it did) . . . "there is every reason to hope" (Barth 2009, 30).

Beyond bodily resurrection, there are many Christian objectual hopes that have an event or promise of God as their objective rational ground, on the Christian account. Hope for deliverance from enemies rests on the actual event of God rescuing Israel from enemies in the past and God's faithful character, which invites trust for future deliverance. We can rationally hope for God's kingdom to come, and the new heavens and the new earth, both because Christ promises to come again and bring with him the kingdom of God, and because God has already accomplished the condition for this occurring by defeating death (1 Corinthians 15:55–57). What makes Abraham's hope to become a father of many nations reasonable is God's promise to him, not merely that it appeared to him that God made such a promise. Christian authors often speak of the "already but not yet" to indicate that what we hope for is something that is already actual but not yet possessed by us subjectively. For instance, the Christian who has been saved will enjoy union with God, and her eternal fate is sealed though she doesn't yet experience it. So objectual hope's rationality depends on the coherence of the beliefs that hope is based on as well as the evidence for that belief or the truthmaker for the truth one believes or in which one has some credence.

3.3 Why Hope Is Good for Human Beings

Christian accounts evaluate hope along another normative dimension, namely, moral goodness. Here the concern is not so much the cognitive base or ground of the hope, but the role of hope in well-being or the achievement of the human good. The emotions of objectual and interpersonal hope, when not yet stable dispositions, are a mixed bag unless their object is itself good, as we explored earlier. So in this final section we will consider how hope as a virtue is good for human beings.

Different Christian authors give varying accounts of what makes hope a virtue. Early and medieval accounts emphasize that without hope, we fall into one of two vices—despair or presumption. Despair comes about when we desire the great good of union with God, which constitutes our own ultimate good, but see it as too difficult to attain. Aquinas argues that this kind of despair is sinful because it willfully ignores God's offer of help. We saw earlier that for hope to be a theological virtue it must rely on another for help in achieving what it desires. Despair occurs when we fail to rely on another, namely God, as well as the community God has given us—the Church—to sustain our hope. The vice of presumption also threatens when we lack hope. Presumption consists in aiming at our ultimate good while assuming we do not need help or can achieve it on our own. Hope strikes a balance between these two psychological states regarding the final end of union with God.

Whether a person has theological hope has practical ramifications for present life as well. It can affect the kinds of emotions she forms, whether hope or despair, about goods attainable on earth. For instance, if I lack the theological virtue of hope and I witness a severe evil, like the starvation of children in Yemen due to conflict, I will likely fall into despair not just about my achieving an ultimately good life, but about whether any of these children will be rescued, whether what I donate will securely reach emergency organizations, and whether this suffering can be redeemed or defeated. Despair like this can undermine successful pursuit of practical goals. If hope guards against despair, then one way hope acts as a virtue in this life is by supplying the conditions to continue to have objectual hopes important for our present practical aims.

Another way that theological hope can rectify our emotional lives, encouraging appropriate objectual hopes, is by providing a perspective on the importance of their objects. Robert Roberts explains, "What devastates the eternal self is not that it has earthly hopes, but that it ascribes to them a significance they can't bear" (Roberts 2007, 151). This happens when the objectual hopes aren't grounded in a basal hope in God. Hopes we acquire for finite goods while having a disposition of hope in God avoid this pitfall because inevitably, the estimate of how much the object of hope matters will be governed by the belief that one's ultimate good consists solely in union with God.

The modern existentialist Christian thinkers like Kierkegaard and Marcel hold that hope has a distinctive role in fostering our practical agency. Kierkegaard places hope at the center of the process of becoming a self—that is, a person whose life is unified, makes sense, and is shaped by ethical commitments (Bernier 2015, 29). We face constant threats of fragmentation, loss of meaning, and deviance from the ethical; without hope, this can lead us to despair of the very project of forming a self or deep practical identity (ibid., 144). By fixating on a singular hope, we avoid dispersing ourselves into the world through disparate commitments that end up in practical conflict. The virtue of hope also gives one's life meaningful tasks. When we have hope in ultimate union with the person loved above all, God, the life activities subsumed under that goal take on meaning.

3.4 Social Dimensions of Hope

For Marcel, virtues are "those traits through which we are able to see beyond ourselves and our own limits," and hope draws our attention to what is possible, especially what is possible with the help of others (Graper Hernandez 2011, 59). In fact, hope turns our focus from the objects we seek to the *other,* not as an object but as a person with whom one is in meaningful relationship.

This pivot to discussing the social aspect of hope in Christian thought has increased in the last half a century. Famously, Martin Luther King, Jr., invites the Christian to hope for racial justice as part of the hope for the kingdom of God to come (King 2007; see Lloyd 2016). The hope in the infinite good of union with God is "the only way we will be able to live without fatigue of bitterness and the drain of resentment" (ibid., 522). Hope has played a prominent role in sociopolitical Christian movements such as those growing out of liberation theology and Black theology. These movements hearken back to the scriptural passages about hope in God to defend the oppressed and rectify injustice here on earth, and ultimately to complete this work in the life to come. More recently, Cobb and Green argue that hope can be a virtue of communities, through extended agency. The virtue of hope, they say, can be "enacted within and scaffolded by a community whose collective practices are ordered toward a shared conception of human flourishing" (2017, 231).

Parallel to developments in Christian accounts of hope as socially productive and a social virtue, we see secular increasing discussion of the social dimensions of hope in secular theories. Here, objections of Christian accounts of hope in light of social harms, such as Vincent Lloyd's critique of hope as perpetuating white supremacy, call due attention to the social philosophical issues related to hope (Lloyd 2016). Katie Stockdale (2019) develops a social theory of hope; Nancy Snow (2018) defends hope as a democratic virtue, and Adam Kadlac (2015) argues that hope is a virtue because it can produce solidarity with others.

In many respects, these accounts present new questions and challenges that Christian accounts going forward will need to address. Whether hope for humanity, generally, is warranted will bring Christian thinkers right back to controversial questions about salvation and universalism raised by theologians like Van Balthasaar and Barth. But perhaps contemporary Christian thinkers will see these debates in a new light as secular theories press us to think about the historical oppression of peoples related to Christian religious institutions and messages.

NOTE

1. I am grateful to the editors of this volume, Claudia Blöser and Titus Stahl, for their insightful and constructive comments on a prior draft, as well as to Matt Benton, Andrew Chignell, Aaron Cobb, and Sam Newlands for earlier discussions on the Christian account of hope.

REFERENCES

Aquinas, Thomas. 2005. *Disputed Questions on the Virtues*, edited by E. M. Atkins and Thomas Williams. Cambridge: Cambridge University Press.
———. 1947. *Summa Theologica*, edited by Fr. Joseph Kenny. Benzinger Brothers edition. https://dhspriory.org/thomas/summa/.
Aristotle. 1999. *Nicomachean Ethics*. Translated by Terence Irwin. 2nd ed. Indianapolis: Hackett Pub. Co.
Augustine. 1887. "Enchiridion on Faith, Hope, and Love." In *Nicene and Post-Nicene Fathers*, edited by Philip Schaff, translated by J. F. Shaw, vol. 3. Buffalo, NY: Christian Literature Publishing Co.
Barth, Karl. 1994. *Church Dogmatics*. Translated by Helmut Gollwitzer. 1st American ed. Louisville, KY: Westminster John Knox Press.
———. 2009. "Easter." In *Insights: Karl Barth's Reflections on the Life of Faith*, edited by Eberhard Busch, translated by O. C. Dean. Louisville, KY: Westminster John Knox Press.
Benton, Matthew. In press. "Knowledge, Hope, and Fallibilism." *Synthese*.
Bernier, Mark. 2015. *The Task of Hope in Kierkegaard*. New York: Oxford University Press.
Bobier, Christopher A. 2017. "Hope and Practical Deliberation." *Analysis* 77, no. 3: 495–97.
———. 2018. "Why Hope Is Not a Moral Virtue: Aquinas's Insight." *Ratio* 31, no. 2: 214–32.
Bovens, Luc. 1999. "The Value of Hope." *Philosophy and Phenomenological Research* 59, no. 3: 667. https://doi.org/10.2307/2653787.
Brewer, Talbot. 2009. *The Retrieval of Ethics*. Oxford: Oxford University Press.
Brunner, Emil. 1952. *Dogmatics II: The Christian Doctrine of Creation and Redemption*. Cambridge: James Clark & Co.
Chrysostum, St. John. 1889. "Homilies on Romans." In *Nicene and Post-Nicene Fathers*, edited by Philip Schaff and Kevin Knight, translated by J. Walker, J. Sheppard, and H. Browne, New Advent. Vol. 11.1. Buffalo, NY: Christian Literature Publishing Co.
Cobb, Aaron D., and Adam Green. 2017. "The Theological Virtue of Hope as a Social Virtue." *Journal of Analytic Theology* 5, no. 1: 230–50.
Cooper, Adam G. 2012. "Hope, a Mode of Faith: Aquinas, Luther, and Benedict XVI on Hebrews 11:1." *The Heythrop Journal* 53, no. 2: 182–90. https://doi.org/10.1111/j.1468-2265.2008.00461.x.
Delany, J. 1910. "Hope." In *The Catholic Encyclopedia*. New York: Robert Appleton Company. http://www.newadvent.org/cathen/07465b.htm.
Doyle, Dominic. 2011. "From Triadic to Dyadic Soul: A Genetic Study of John of the Cross on the Anthropological Basis of Hope." *Studies in Spirituality*, 219–41. https://doi.org/10.2143/SIS.21.0.2141951.
Fallon, J. E. 1967. "Hope." In *New Catholic Encyclopedia*, VII: 98–107. New York: McGraw-Hill.
Graper Hernandez, Jill. 2011. *Gabriel Marcel's Ethics of Hope: Evil, God, and Virtue*. London; New York: Continuum.
Howard-Snyder, Daniel. 2013. "Propositional Faith: What It Is and What It Is Not." *American Philosophical Quarterly* 50, no. 4: 357–72.
Jeffrey, Anne. 2017. "Does Hope Morally Vindicate Faith?" *International Journal of Philosophy of Religion* 81, no. 1–2: 193–211. https://doi.org/10.1007/s11153-016-9603-0.
Kadlac, Adam. 2015. "The Virtue of Hope." *Ethical Theory and Moral Practice* 18, no. 2: 337–54.

King, Jr., Martin Luther. 2007. *The Papers of Martin Luther King, Jr.* Volume VI, edited by Susan Carson, Susan Englander, Troy Jackson, and Gerald L. Smith. Berkeley and Los Angeles: University of California Press.

Lamb, Michael. 2016a. "A Passion and Its Virtue: Aquinas on Hope and Magnanimity." In *Hope*, edited by Ingolf Dalferth and Marlene Block, 67–88. Tubingen: Mohr Siebeck.

———. 2016b. "Aquinas and the Virtues of Hope: Theological and Democratic." *Journal of Religious Ethics* 44, no. 2: 300–32. https://doi.org/10.1111/jore.12143.

Lloyd, Vincent. 2016. "For What Are Whites to Hope?" *Political Theology* 17, no. 2 (March): 168–81. https://doi.org/10.1080/1462317X.2016.1161302.

Marcel, Gabriel. 1951. *Homo Viator*. Translated by Emma Craufurd. Victor Gollancz Ltd.

Martin, Adrienne M. 2013. *How We Hope: A Moral Psychology*. Princeton: Princeton University Press.

McGeer, Victoria. 2004. "The Art of Good Hope." *The Annals the American Academy of Political and Social Science* 592, no. 1 (March): 100–27. https://doi.org/10.1177/0002716203261781.

Milona, Michael. 2018. "Finding Hope." *Canadian Journal of Philosophy*, 1–20. https://doi.org/10.1080/00455091.2018.1435612.

Milona, Michael, and Katie Stockdale. 2018. "A Perceptual Theory of Hope." *Ergo* 5. https://doi.org/10.3998/ergo.12405314.0005.008.

Miner, Robert. 2009. *Thomas Aquinas on the Passions*. Cambridge: Cambridge University Press.

Moltmann, Jürgen. 1993. *Theology of Hope*. Translated by James W. Leitch. Minneapolis: First Fortress Press.

Niebuhr, H. Richard. 1974. "Reflections on Faith, Hope, and Love." *Journal of Religious Ethics* 2, no. 1: 151–56.

Pace, Michael. 2017. "The Strength of Faith and Trust." *International Journal for Philosophy of Religion* 81, no. 1–2 (April): 135–50. https://doi.org/10.1007/s11153-016-9611-0.

Pinckaers, Servais. 2007. "La Nature Vertuese de L'esperance." *Revue Thomiste* 54 (1958).

Roberts, Robert C. 2007. *Spiritual Emotions: A Psychology of Christian Virtues*. Grand Rapids, MI: William B. Eerdmans Publishing.

Scotus, John Duns. *Lectura*. Editio Vaticana 10. Rome.

Snow, Nancy E. 2018. "Hope as a Democratic Civic Virtue." *Metaphilosophy* 49, no. 3: 407–27. https://doi.org/10.1111/meta.12299.

Stockdale, Katie. 2019. "Social and Political Dimensions of Hope." *Journal of Social Philosophy* 50 (1): 28–44.

Strawson, P. F. 1962. "Freedom and Resentment." *Proceedings of the British Academy* 48: 1–25.

Wright, N. T. 2008. *Surprised by Hope*. 1st ed. New York: HarperOne.

Chapter Four

Hope in Kant

Claudia Blöser

Kant famously states in the Canon of the *Critique of Pure Reason* that "What may I hope?" (A805/B833) is one of the fundamental questions of reason.[1] However, it is not easy to pin down Kant's full answer to the question. One puzzle concerns the question of what hope is: Kant does not explicitly discuss the nature of hope, which may explain in part why interpreters have often conflated hope and faith (e.g., Flikschuh 2010). Another difficulty is that Kant talks about hope in a number of different writings, and it is not immediately clear whether there is a unified account of hope in the background. In this contribution, I want to shed light on these issues. In section 1, I sketch a framework for understanding what hope is, according to Kant, and for understanding what makes it rational. I then show how this abstract picture helps to describe the role of hope in different writings: in the first and second *Critiques*, in *Religion within the Boundaries of Mere Reason*, and in the historical and political writings. Finally, I briefly discuss the role of hope in moral motivation.

1. A FRAMEWORK FOR KANT'S ACCOUNT OF HOPE

In order to better understand what hope is, it is helpful to distinguish it from wishing. The following passage from the *Doctrine of Virtue* gives a valuable hint. This passage is taken from the "Doctrine of the Method of Ethics," where Kant is concerned with how to teach the doctrine of virtue. One way is through what he calls "moral catechism," in which the "teacher elicits from his pupil's reason, by questioning, what he wants to teach him" (6:480). If the teacher does not correct the pupil's answer, we can assume that Kant regards it as the correct one.

> Teacher: But even if we are conscious of such a good and active will in us, by
> virtue of which we consider ourselves worthy . . . of happiness, can we base on
> this a sure hope of sharing in happiness?
> Pupil: No, not on this alone. For it is *not always within our power* to provide
> ourselves with happiness, and the course of nature does not of itself conform
> with merit. Our good fortune in life . . . depends, rather, on circumstances that
> are far from all being in our control. So our happiness always *remains a wish
> that cannot become a hope, unless some other power is added.* (6:482, my
> emphasis)

I will discuss central elements of this passage in the next section. Here, I
want to emphasize that Kant draws attention to the limitations of our power:
Absent further assumptions, we cannot have "sure hope" of becoming as
happy as we deserve to be because it is "not always within our power" to
bring this about. This does not mean that we can only have hope if it is in our
own power; rather, hope for happiness requires the addition of some *other*
power. Hence, hope presupposes the idea that our own powers do not (or
might not) suffice regarding the realization of the hoped-for outcome.[2] This
presupposition may serve on the one hand to distinguish hope from choice
[*Willkür*], which is accompanied by "one's consciousness of the ability to
bring about the object by one's action" (6:213). On the other hand, it reveals
a similarity between hope and wishing, where the latter "is not joined with
this consciousness" (6:213). Like wishing, hope is characterized by a lack of
consciousness of the ability to bring about the object by one's action.

In order to see the difference between hope and wishing, consider Kant's
claim that a wish may *become sure hope* if "some other power is added." In
line with his account in the *Critiques* (section 2), Kant identifies this other
power with god in the lines following the quote above (6:482). Thus, in
contrast to wishing, hope requires a *ground*, namely a power that is able to
bring about the hoped-for object.

Kant's question "What may I hope?" is a question about the rationality of
hope. As we will see, the rationality of hope depends on the question of
whether we may rationally assume its grounds.[3] In all cases of hope that
Kant considers, our epistemic situation regarding the grounds is that we *lack
knowledge* about it. How can it still be rational to assume that the grounds of
hope obtain? This is where Kant's conception of faith or "moral Belief"
[*moralischer Glaube*] (A828/B856) comes in.[4] Another term that is closely
linked to faith and Belief in Kant's account is *trust*: as Allen Wood points
out, Kant often characterizes faith or moral Belief in terms of trust (Wood
1970, 162). A succinct formulation can be found in the *Lectures on Ethics*, in
a section titled "Trust in God under the Concept of Faith": "So faith means
the confidence that, so long as we have done everything possible to us, God
will supply what does not lie in our power" (27:320 f.).[5] As I will describe in
the next section, Kant argues that we can assume that the grounds of hope

obtain and can hence have moral Belief or trust in them if this assumption is empirically undecidable and a necessary presupposition of a practical necessity, i.e. connected to the moral law.

In sum, hoping, like wishing, presupposes lack of certainty regarding one's own powers to realize the object in question; unlike wishing, however, it also requires the assumption of grounds—typically another power that is necessary for realizing the object, in addition to one's powers.[6] We may hope for something if we can rationally assume that those grounds exist. The grounds for rational hope are such that we lack knowledge, although we may have an attitude of moral Belief or trust toward them. This framework also sheds light on the question of why Kant considers "What may I hope" to be necessary, in addition to "What should I do" and "What can I know": Hope enters the picture in light of the *limitations* of what we can do (it presupposes an awareness of the limits of our powers) and of what we can know (it presupposes grounds that we cannot know to exist).

2. HOPE IN THE FIRST AND SECOND *CRITIQUES*

Kant's starting point for answering the normative question concerning what we may hope is a descriptive claim about what we *de facto* hope for: "all hope concerns happiness" (A805/B833). Kant's focus on hope for *happiness* suggests that he starts from a hope that every human being already naturally has, since "happiness is an end that every human being has (by virtue of the impulses of his nature)" (6:386). Happiness fulfills the presupposition of being partly beyond our powers, as its future realization comprises aspects that are not within our control.

Subsequently, Kant presents a second version of the hope question: "If I do what I should, what may I then hope?" (A805/B833). The antecedent points to the fact that Kant is concerned with hope that human beings have insofar as they are moral beings. A first step toward an answer must take into account the fact that Kant maintains that there is a conceptual connection between moral behavior and *worthiness* to be happy: The moral law "commands how we should behave in order . . . to be worthy of happiness" (A806/B834). If we need to make ourselves worthy of happiness, it is plausible that we may also only hope for morally deserved happiness.

A full answer to the specification of the morally appropriate object of hope leads to Kant's account of the highest good.[7] According to Kant, the answer to the hope question hinges on "whether the principles of pure reason that prescribe the law a priori also necessarily connect this hope with it" (A809/B837). Even though Kant has not yet presented his mature moral philosophy in the first *Critique*, he leaves no doubt that the "law a priori" to which he refers is the moral law (A807/B835). Thus, hope for happiness must be necessarily bound up with the moral law. Kant claims (without further argument) that our hope for happiness must assume a certain form, namely "hope for happiness in the same measure as he has made himself worthy of it in his conduct" (A809/B837). Kant calls this conjunction of morality and happiness for everyone the "highest good" (A814/B842). This suggests that the object of rational hope is the highest good. While this is a legitimate way of putting it, note that, strictly speaking, it is still one's *own happiness* that is the object of one's hope. This becomes especially clear when Kant speaks of the "*hope* of being happy" and the "*effort* to make oneself *worthy* of happiness" (A810/B838, my emphasis) as the two elements that come together in the highest good. In sum, Kant's position thus far is that insofar as we are moral, we hope for our own happiness as part of the highest good.

Whereas this answers the question of what the appropriate object of hope is according to *moral* standards, the third version of the hope question turns to the question of *theoretical* standards for rational hope, that is, how we may hope for the *attainment* of happiness: "Now if I behave so as not to be unworthy of happiness, *how* may I hope thereby to partake of it?" (A809/B837, my emphasis). For Kant, the "how may I hope" question concerns the *grounds* of our hope: He assumes that we need to have an account of the "ground of the practically necessary connection of both elements [i.e., happiness and morality, CB] of the highest . . . good" (A810/B839f.). The question of the grounds of hope is pressing because it is questionable whether the highest good is possible at all: The necessary connection between happiness and morality can neither be ensured by us nor be due to mere nature (A810/B838).

According to Kant, the *only* answer to the question of the grounds is that we need to assume god as the cause of nature. Further, we need to assume a "future life" because the sensible world "does not offer such a connection [i.e., of happiness and morality] to us" (A811/B839). Here, I am not concerned with the precise form and persuasiveness of Kant's specific arguments for god and a future life. Instead, let us look at his conclusion:

> Thus God and a future life are two presuppositions that are not to be separated from the obligation that pure reason imposes on us in accordance with principles of that very same reason. (A811/B839)

Perhaps surprisingly, this conclusion does not present god and a future life as presuppositions of *hope*. However, as mentioned above, Kant holds that there is a necessary connection between moral obligation and hope for the highest good. Thus, if god and a future life are presuppositions of moral obligation, they are also presuppositions of hope.

In the third section of the Canon, "On having an opinion, knowing, and believing," Kant develops the general theoretical framework for seeing how the assumptions of god and a future life can be rational. In a nutshell, Kant's idea is that even if the assumptions of god and a future life cannot be backed up by sufficient evidence and thus never amount to knowledge, we have *practical* reasons for these assumptions, such that we may rationally assume god and a future life as objects of faith or "moral Belief" (A828/B856). The following passage contains Kant's argument:

> [In the case of moral Belief], it is absolutely necessary that something must happen, namely, that I fulfill the moral law in all points. The end here is inseparably fixed, and according to all my insight there is possible only a single condition under which this end is consistent with all ends together and thereby has practical validity, namely, that there be a God and a future world. . . . But since the moral precept is thus at the same time my maxim (as reason commands that it ought to be), I will inexorably believe in the existence of God and a future life. (A828/B856)

The point here is that if an end is practically necessary, it is rational to believe that the conditions necessary for the "practical validity" of the end obtain. Kant claims that the end that is "inseparably fixed" is that "I fulfill the moral law in all points," and that this end is only "consistent with all ends together" (i.e., constitutes the highest good) if we assume god's existence and a future world.

Kant's reasoning seems problematic on the assumption that he wants to establish either the rationality of hope or the rationality of moral Belief independently of each other. On this reading, the argument is circular: On the one hand, in the passage of the Canon, he argues that the assumptions of god's existence and a future life are rational because they are necessary presuppositions of the highest good. The highest good is presented as a necessary end, and so the rationality of *hope* for the highest good seems to be presupposed in this argument. On the other hand, in answering the question "What may I hope?," it seems that we may rationally hope for the highest good *only if* we may assume god and a future life—where the rationality of hope is established only if we may presuppose the rationality of these assumptions. However, an alternative reading is that we should not expect either (hope for) the highest good or the assumptions of god and a future life to be rational independent of each other. Rather, Kant presents a picture in which the rationality of hope for the highest good and the rationality of moral Belief reciprocally imply each other; they stand and fall together. What seems to be an open question is whether there is really a rational necessity for moral beings to hope for the highest good.

Kant's new assumption in the *Critique of Practical Reason* is that it is a "duty for us to promote the highest good" (5:125). In light of the preceding discussion, this might be seen as an attempt to put the justification of the assumptions of god and immortality on more solid grounds: The assumptions are not presented primarily as presuppositions of hope, but of a duty, and this clarifies the connection between the moral law and the highest good. One difficulty is that Kant does not address the question of why the promotion of the highest good is a duty.[8] However, let us assume for the sake of argument that Kant can legitimately claim such a duty. From "ought-implies-can," he then infers that the highest good must be practically possible (see 5:125). As in the first *Critique*, Kant draws attention to the fact that the possibility of the highest good is questionable if one restricts oneself to the empirical realm.[9] Kant argues that we can indeed think of the highest good as possible, albeit only if we consider the "supersensible relation of things" (5:119). As in the first *Critique*, Kant wants to give an account of the "grounds of that possibility" (5:119).

Kant introduces a distinction that is not explicit in the first *Critique*: the distinction between the grounds of possibility insofar as they are "within our power" and insofar as they are "not in our power" (5:119). What *is* in our power is our own moral behavior. It is precisely with regard to those aspects that are *not* within our power that an account of the grounds of possibility leads to faith in god and immortality; in the second *Critique*, Kant presents this in the framework of the postulates. Kant defines a "postulate of pure practical reason" as "a *theoretical* proposition, though one not demonstrable as a such, insofar as it is attached inseparably to an a priori unconditionally valid *practical* law" (5:122), which is obviously the moral law. It is not difficult to see the similarity to Kant's account of moral Belief in the first *Critique*: Moral Belief and the postulates concern theoretically undecidable objects or propositions, which are presuppositions of a practical law (and in this sense practically necessary).[10]

One aspect beyond our power, familiar from the first *Critique*, is the necessary relationship between happiness and morality, which leads to the postulate of god's existence (5:125). Further, in contrast to the conception of the highest good in the first *Critique*, Kant requires "holiness" (5:122) as part of the highest good. This requirement leads to the assumption of infinite progress and thus to the postulate of immortality.

Only after introducing the postulates does Kant mention hope: One object of hope is one's own happiness (to the extent that one is virtuous) (5:130). Further, the realization of the highest good is itself an object of hope (5:129), along with one's own moral progress (5:123, 5:128) and the stability of one's moral disposition (5:123, fn.). The feature that unites these objects is that they are all aspects of the highest good that are not within our power (or the highest good itself in virtue of those aspects).[11]

In the second *Critique*, Kant characterizes our attitude toward the highest good in terms of both duty and hope. This adds up to a coherent picture if we understand duty and hope as referring to complementary aspects of the highest good. Kant typically specifies the content of the duty as *promotion* of the highest good in accordance with our powers (see, e.g., 5:143f. note). Thus duty, strictly speaking, refers only to those aspects that are within our power, while hope, strictly speaking, refers only to aspects that are not under our control.

On this picture, it becomes apparent that the assumption of a duty (instead of hope) as the basis for the justification of god and immortality has its own problems: It seems that we can rationally obey the duty to *promote* the highest good without assuming that another power will help us, because there is nothing in the demand of the duty that goes beyond our powers. To be sure, the duty to *realize* the highest good would motivate the need for divine assistance because the realization is beyond our powers—but it is then unclear how there can be a duty for us that we are unable to fulfill. What needs to be shown is that in order to promote the highest good (i.e., to approximate it), we also need to believe in its realizability or hope for it. However, what would seem to be relevant to our ability to promote a goal is not our believing in its realizability, but rather our *not* believing in its *impossibility* (see Willaschek 2016, 232). This attitude may involve "hope" (in some sense) that the goal can be realized, but this hope would not imply an (even implicit) assumption of the existence of grounds that are necessary to realize it. Hence, it would not be rational hope in the Kantian sense. [12]

3. HOPE IN *RELIGION WITHIN THE BOUNDARIES OF MERE REASON* (1793/94)

Kant discusses hope in all three parts of *Religion within the Boundaries of Mere Reason*. In the first part, Kant treats hope in the "[g]eneral remark concerning the restoration to its power of the original predisposition to the good" (6:44). The central problem concerns individual moral improvement, which requires that one change one's fundamental maxim from a bad one to a good one. A person with a good fundamental maxim will prioritize the moral law before all maxims of self-love; a person with a bad fundamental maxim will obey the moral law only if it does not contradict maxims of self-love. The problem with moral improvement is the following: on the one hand, there is a "command that we *ought* to become better human beings . . . , consequently, we must also be capable of it" (6:45). On the other hand, "if a human being is corrupt in the very ground of his maxims, how can he possibly bring about this revolution by his own forces?" (6:47). The thesis of fundamental corruption corresponds to Kant's thesis that the human being is "radically evil": There is a propensity in human nature to reverse "the moral order of his incentives in incorporating them into his maxims" (6:36). This evil is "radical, since it corrupts the ground of all maxims," and "it is also not to be extirpated through human forces, for this could only happen through good maxims—something that cannot take place if the subjective supreme ground of all maxims is presupposed to be corrupted" (6:37).

Kant distinguishes between the "possibility" of moral improvement and the "comprehensibility" of this possibility (6:50). On the basis of "ought-implies-can," the possibility of moral improvement is not put into question. However, "*[h]ow* it is possible . . . surpasses every concept of ours" (6:44f., my emphasis). In this situation of lack of insight into the possibility of a morally required end, hope becomes relevant. Kant draws attention to two hopes with different objects. The first is as follows:

> [H]e must be able to *hope* that, by the exertion of *his own* power, he will attain to the road that leads in that direction, as indicated to him by a fundamentally improved disposition. For he ought to become a good human being yet cannot be judged *morally* good except on the basis of what can be imputed to him as done by him. (6:51)

Kant sums up the object of this hope as "expectation[13] of self-improvement" (6:51), which incites reason "under the pretext of natural impotence" to come up with various religious ideas. Kant introduces the second kind of hope as a kind of religious hope. He distinguishes between "religion of rogation (of mere cult)" and "moral religion, that is, the religion of good life-conduct" (6:51). The latter implies a kind of hope:

> [T]o become a better human being, everyone must do as much as it is in his powers to do; and only then, . . . if he has made use of the original predisposition to the good in order to become a better human being, can he hope that what does not lie in his power will be made good by cooperation from above. (6:52)

The crucial difference between the religious hope that Kant seems to approve of and the "mere wishing" of a religion of "mere cult" is that hope requires doing "as much as it is in [one's] powers to do."

Kant does not present the first kind of hope—the hope to improve things by using one's own power—as irrational. However, would this be a hope without grounds? It seems that the ground of the hope is *one's own powers*. Still, it fits the framework presented in section 1, since we lack certainty regarding our powers (in light of radical evil). It is promising to give an argument in analogy to the postulates: Even though we cannot *know* that our own powers suffice, we are entitled to have (moral) Belief or trust in them, since they are a necessary means for a required end: moral self-improvement. We encounter a similar thought in the second book of the *Religion*.

If the first kind of hope is rationally possible, this means that the second kind of hope—hope for divine assistance—is not rationally necessary.[14] Why, then, does Kant present this religious hope? He seems to admit that the "expectation of self-improvement" might strike some (even reason itself!) as too ambitious; that human beings perhaps suffer from a "natural impotence" cannot be ruled out. Calling this a "pretext," however, devalues the following line of reasoning, at least to a certain degree. Still, Kant's aim could be to show that *if* one finds oneself hoping for divine assistance, this hope is legitimate as long as one does everything in one's power to become a morally better person.

In the second section of the *Religion*, Kant presents an "idea" that "resides in our morally-legislative reason" (6:62) and that is a "universal human duty" (6:61): "to *elevate* ourselves to this ideal of moral perfection, i.e. to the prototype of moral disposition in its entire purity" (6:61). Kant equates this ideal of moral perfection with the idea of a "human being, alone pleasing to God" (6:60), following the example of the "Son of God" (6:62). Kant leaves no doubt that it follows from the principle "ought-implies-can" that this idea refers to a really possible object (see 6:62). However, just as in the case of the highest good (the antinomy of practical reason) and moral improvement (radical evil), there are "difficulties that stand in the way of the reality of this idea" (6:66). I will focus here on the second difficulty: due to epistemic limitations, we cannot be "conscious of [our] moral disposition" and therefore do not seem to be entitled to "self-assuredly trust" that we are and will be following our moral ideal: "[W]e cannot base this confidence [in the perseverance and stability of our disposition] upon an immediate consciousness of the immutability of our disposition, since we cannot see through to the latter" (6:71).

Kant thinks that absolute assurance about one's own disposition is impossible, but he also assumes that we cannot act on mere ignorance and uncertainty about the quality of our disposition: "[W]ithout *any* [trust][15] in the disposition once acquired, perseverance in it would hardly be possible" (6:68). This suggests an argument along the lines of the postulates: We cannot *know* our disposition, but it is practically necessary to assume that it is good; therefore, we are entitled to postulate or trust that it is good. This line of argument is in the background, but there is an important disanalogy to the postulates of god and immortality. God and immortality are transcendent objects that cannot be objects of experience. One's own disposition, by contrast, manifests itself in experience. Therefore, empirical evidence cannot be entirely ignored when assessing one's own disposition. Kant acknowledges this point by emphasizing that we take into account a person's actions. On this basis, Kant distinguishes between reasonable and unreasonable hope:

> [Take] a human being who, from the time of his adoption of the principles of
> the good and throughout a sufficiently long life henceforth, has *perceived* the
> efficacy of these principles on what he does, i.e. on the conduct of his life as it
> steadily improves, and from that has cause to *infer, but only by way of conjec-*
> *ture*, a fundamental improvement in his disposition: [he] *can yet also reason-*
> *ably hope* that in this life he will no longer forsake his present course but will
> rather press in it with ever greater courage. . . . By contrast, one who has
> always found himself unable to stand fast by his often repeated resolutions to
> be good but has always relapsed into evil, or who has been forced to acknowl-
> edge that in the course of his life he has gone from bad to worse . . . [such a
> one] *can reasonably entertain no hope of improving.* (6:68, my emphasis)

Kant says here that on the basis of empirically observable behavior, we can have *reasonable* hope that our disposition to approach the moral ideal will be stable. Here, the *ground* of hope is our own disposition (which we cannot know), and our hope is reasonable if we can reasonably assume such a ground *in accordance with* (even though not conclusively proven by) empirical evidence. Those who do not take into account empirical evidence in such cases succumb to "the sweetness or the anxiety of enthusiasm" (6:68). Note that although hope and trust go hand in hand and have similar objects, they are distinct attitudes: Hope refers to the *future*, that is, its object is our future moral development, whereas trust refers to the quality of the already-adopted disposition. This trust is the ground of hope as an attitude toward the future.

In the third section of the *Religion*, Kant is concerned with the founding of an "ethical community," which is an "association of human beings merely under the laws of virtue" (6:94). Kant also calls this the "highest good as a good common to all" (6:97), claiming in addition that there is a duty to promote it (ibid.).[16] Even though the ethical community does not involve proportionate happiness, Kant argues that the duty to establish an ethical community presupposes the idea of god. A central point again turns on the limitations of our powers:

> [S]ince this highest moral good will not be brought about solely through the
> striving of one individual person for his own moral perfection but requires
> rather a union of such persons into a whole toward that very end, . . . yet the
> idea of such a whole, as a universal republic based on the laws of virtue,
> differs entirely from all moral laws (which concern what we *know to reside*
> *within our power*), for it is the idea of working toward a whole of which *we*
> *cannot know whether as a whole it is also in our power*: so the duty in question
> differs from all others in kind and in principle.—We can already anticipate that
> this duty will need the presupposition of another idea, namely, of a higher
> moral being through whose universal organization the forces of single individ-
> uals, *insufficient on their own*, are united for a common effect. (6:97f., my
> emphasis)

As in the case of one's own moral improvement, it is ambiguous whether we *cannot be sure* whether it is beyond our power to realize the required end (i.e., that we might be able to realize it alone) or whether we definitely *need* the presupposition of a divine power that complements our insufficient powers. For our practical life, however, we do not need to decide between the two options: As in all cases of hope that require the cooperation of human agency with external powers, Kant emphasizes that one condition of rational hope is that we do our part to *promote* it: "Each must . . . so conduct himself as if everything depended on him. Only on this condition may he hope that a higher wisdom will provide the fulfillment of his well-intentioned effort" (6:101).

4. HOPE IN KANT'S POLITICAL PHILOSOPHY

In Kant's writings on history and politics, the object of hope is moral (and legal) progress:[17] In the *Idea for a Universal History* (1784), Kant envisages a "steadily advancing but slow development of man's original capacities" (8:17); in *On the Common Saying* (1793), Kant asks whether "the race will always progress towards what is better" (8:307) and defends "hope for better times." In *Perpetual Peace* (1795), he closes by affirming "grounds for hoping that we succeed" to "bring about in reality a state of public right (albeit by an infinite process of gradual approximation)" (8:386), and in *The Contest of the Faculties* (1798) he asks under which conditions "we can expect man's hopes of progress to be fulfilled" (7:93). Since the ultimate future goal of all progress is perpetual peace, the "highest political good" (6:355), it is fitting to say that political hope, for Kant, is hope for perpetual peace.

Invoking the notion of the highest political good suggests that we ought to look for parallels with Kant's account of hope for the highest good in the *Critiques*. Indeed, the key features of Kant's account of hope described thus far apply to the political context as well: hope is understood, first, as a response to (partial) powerlessness and, second, as requiring *grounds* in order to amount to more than a wish. The ground of hope for progress, according to Kant, is nature (understood as a teleological order) or providence (see, e.g., 8:361). Third, we lack knowledge of whether this ground really exists. Still, it is rational to assume such a ground, and hence we may hope for progress and peace.

Kant explicitly claims that progress is (partly) beyond our powers only in *Theory and Practice* (8.311f.), while he seems to assume it implicitly in the other political writings. One problem that I can only mention briefly is that Kant introduces the idea that nature pursues its *own* goals and (inevitably) brings about progress. In *Perpetual Peace*, for example, Kant claims that nature "guarantees" perpetual peace (see 8:360), "whether we are willing or not" (8:365). There is a tension between viewing progress as a *moral* end and viewing progress as the end of nature, brought about without the contribution of intentional human actions. Kant tries to mitigate this tension by claiming that human reason and freedom are themselves part of the teleological order of nature (see 8:19 and 8:313).

What is the rational status of the claim that providence is necessary to bring about progress?[18] Throughout his historical and political writings, Kant seems to regard the assumption of providence as a presupposition of progress and the realization of peace.[19] Thus, the assumption of providence is a candidate for moral Belief: A necessary assumption for a moral end, which cannot be known (but also cannot be proven impossible) on the basis of empirical evidence. As we saw in section 1, Kant closely connects moral Belief and *trust* in the case of god. Thus, Kant's expression of *"trust . . . in the nature of things, which constrains one to go where one does not want to go"* (8:313, my emphasis), is further support for the parallel between the assumption of god and a teleological order of nature.

In order to show that the assumption of providence is an object of moral Belief, it must be shown that it cannot be proven or falsified by empirical evidence. Providence is the ground for hope for the highest political good, just as god is the ground for hope for the highest good. However, there is an important disanalogy, which we encountered earlier with regard to one's disposition in the *Religion*. Whereas there cannot be any empirical evidence for god's existence, moral progress toward peace is to be realized in *this* world; therefore, empirical evidence cannot be entirely ignored in assessing whether there has been such progress, and hence whether we may hope for progress in the future. Kant never directly justifies the assumption of *providence* as an object of moral Belief, but he shows that the possibility of *progress* cannot be proven or falsified by empirical evidence. If this is so, the assumption of a teleological order of nature as the "motor" of such progress is also immune to empirical evidence. With regard to progress, Kant says in the *Contest* that the reason why progress cannot be *proven* is that "we are dealing with freely acting beings . . . of whom one cannot *predict* what they actually *will* do" and who are endowed with a "mixture of evil and goodness in unknown proportions" (7:83), such that both change for the better and change for the worse are always possible. It remains to be shown that evidence (from the past) does not show that moral progress is *impossible*. One serious obstacle against affirming progress is the existence of war. Kant, however, gives an interpretation of war that aims to show how it can even *contribute* to progress: Wars "and the resultant distress . . .—these are the means by which nature drives nations to . . . take the step which reason could have suggested to them even without so many sad experiences—that of . . . entering a federation of peoples" (8:24f.). Let us assume for the sake of argument that Kant succeeds in giving a convincing interpretation of the function of wars. If so, he has removed the main obstacle to believing that progress is possible. Hence, progress and the assumption of a teleological order of nature as what drives it can be objects of moral Belief.

In order to further clarify the relation between Belief in providence, hope for progress and peace, and the duty to promote it, it is helpful to look at the *Doctrine of Right*, where Kant does not invoke the assumption of providence at all. He states that perpetual peace is a moral end "even if there is not the slightest theoretical likelihood that it can be realized" (6:354). What matters is the "continual approximation to the highest political good" (6:355). In order to acknowledge this duty to *promote* and thereby *approximate* perpetual peace, Kant claims that it suffices to assume that its "impossibility cannot be demonstrated" (6:354). We do not need to believe in a providence that complements our limited powers. This is because the duty to *promote* an end requires nothing beyond our powers. Note that in this passage of the *Doctrine of Right*, not only does Kant omit the invocation of providence, but he does not mention hope at all. Hope for peace requires more than the duty to promote peace. Hope for peace requires grounds, namely an assumption of powers that complement our own. In the *Doctrine of Right*, Kant confirms this reading by saying that "even if the complete realization of this objective [realizing peace] . . . always remains a pious *wish*, still we are certainly not deceiving ourselves in adopting the maxim of working incessantly towards it" (6:354, my emphasis). Without the assumption of providence, the *realization* of peace can only be a wish, not a hope.

If this picture is accurate, there is a problem analogous to the problem in the second *Critique*: the assumption of providence is only justified if it is a necessary presupposition of a practical necessity. The duty to promote peace is a practical necessity, but it does not necessarily presuppose providence. The hope for the *attainment* of peace presupposes providence (because hope presupposes grounds), but it is not clear that this hope is a practical necessity.

5. HOPE AND MORAL MOTIVATION

Many interpreters have discussed the question of whether, on Kant's view, hope is relevant to moral motivation (e.g., Wood 1970, Ebels-Duggan 2016, Insole 2008). To be sure, if hope turned out to be a sensible incentive that is *necessary* for moral motivation, this would threaten Kant's thesis that pure reason can be practical, i.e. that we can be motivated to act morally out of duty, merely out of respect for the moral law.[20] In light of this, some interpreters attribute to Kant the view that hope *can* be supportive of our moral motivation, without being necessary for it.[21]

Andrew Chignell holds that understanding the role of hope requires attributing to Kant a "consequence-dependent moral psychology" (Chignell

2018, 299). Kant is sensitive to the empirical fact that human beings can be demoralized by "perceived inefficacy" (ibid.): "a morally good person will reasonably care about the goodness of the consequences of her actions" (Chignell 2018, 300), and losing hope that the intended goal will eventually be realized can slowly undermine our resolve. Chignell bases his interpretation on a passage in the third *Critique*, where Kant describes the case of a "righteous man (like Spinoza)" (5:452) who does not believe in god. Kant sees two options for Spinoza in light of the evils of the world: either he will give up the end (the highest good) and "weaken the respect, by which the moral law immediately influences him to obedience, by the nullity of the only idealistic final end [the highest good, CB]" or "assume the existence of a moral author of the world, i.e., of god, from a practical point of view, i.e., in order to form a concept of at least the possibility of the final end that is prescribed to him by morality."

It is worth noting that Kant does not talk about hope in this passage. Kant's claim is that Spinoza's moral resolve would be weaker if there were no ultimate moral *end*. It is the assumption of a *final purpose* that is described as necessary for full moral resolve. A passage in the *Religion* confirms this reading:

> This idea [of a highest good, CB] is not (practically considered) an empty one; for it meets our natural need, which would otherwise be a hindrance to moral resolve, to *think* for all our doings and nondoings taken as a whole some sort of *ultimate* end. (6:5, my emphasis)

Kant does not talk about hope in this passage, which points to the fact that it is the *thought* that some ultimate end is possible, and not specifically our hope for it, which fulfills a "natural need" that, if it were to remain unfulfilled, would be an obstacle to moral resolve. Thus there are questions that, although I cannot address them here, must be considered more fully: first, in what sense do we have a "natural need" to conceive of an ultimate end? Second, what is the role of hope regarding this ultimate end?

As to the first question, a problem with Chignell's interpretation is that a concern for the *efficacy* of my actions normally does not imply concern for an ultimate end or final purpose of "all our doings and nondoings taken as a whole." The problem is one of efficacy only if we describe our actions as having the goal to promote the highest good. That is a possible description, but not the typical one in everyday life. Normally, we describe the goal of our actions in a less encompassing way, for example, as "helping this person in need" or "charging the stranger a fair price." In my view, the "natural need" that Kant talks about in the *Religion* should be described not as the need for the efficacy of individual actions (which normally concerns success in their *particular* ends) but as a need for rational *meaning* or for an encompassing moral *sense* of our life as a whole, and perhaps even the life of the species (i.e., contribution to some *ultimate* end). Without hope that the highest good is attainable, we face the possibility that our moral actions may in fact fail to contribute to a larger, reasonable whole.

As to the second question, I want to close by merely pointing in a direction that I find worth exploring: Kantian hope might not be an extra motivational aid on the level of sensible incentives. Rather, it may perhaps be understood as a psychological mode in which we represent the ultimate end, or the future where goodness is realized.[22] Just as respect is the way in which we relate to the moral law and are motivated by it, hope can perhaps be understood as the way in which we relate to the highest good and are motivated to promote it.

6. CONCLUSION

In this contribution, I offer an overview over all contexts that are relevant to Kant's answer to the question "What may I hope?" It turns out that Kant's different treatments of hope share a common structure. Hope, like wishing, presupposes an awareness of the (possible) limitations of our power to bring about the hoped-for end. In contrast to wishing, hope also presupposes trust (or moral Belief) in *grounds* that are necessary for the attainment of the end. Kant envisages hopes for *moral* objects, that is, for states of affairs that are morally required, where even though we lack knowledge of the grounds, we are entitled to have moral Belief in them, and hence may hope. Hope for the highest good and the ethical community presupposes moral Belief in god (and the former also in immortality). Hope for one's own moral improvement is based on trust in one's own powers or in divine assistance and hope for the stability of one's disposition is based on trust in one's disposition, if the evidence (one's life conduct) allows. Hope for progress toward perpetual peace presupposes trust in providence or in nature's plan. In all of these cases, hope anticipates a future in which moral goodness and happiness will eventually be realized. This view of the future fulfills our need to conceive of the world as a place that is hospitable to our most important ends.[23]

NOTES

1. Kant's works are cited using volume and page numbers (volume:page) of the standard Academy edition of Kant's writings (Berlin. 1900–), except for the *Critique of Pure Reason*. The latter is cited using the A- and B-editions (A/B). I use the following translations: *Critique of Pure Reason*, trans. Paul Guyer and Allen Wood, Cambridge: Cambridge University Press, 1998. *Critique of Practical Reason*, trans. Mary Gregor, in Mary Gregor (ed.): *Practical Philosophy*, Cambridge: Cambridge University Press, 1996, 133–271. *Religion within the Boundaries of Mere Reason*, trans. Allen Wood and George di Giovanni, Cambridge: Cambridge University Press, 1998. *Critique of the Power of Judgment*, trans. Paul Guyer and Eric Mat-

thews, Cambridge: Cambridge University Press. *Metaphysics of Morals*, trans. Mary Gregor, Cambridge: Cambridge University Press, 1996. *On the Common Saying: That May Be Correct in Theory, but It Is of No Use in Practice* and *Toward Perpetual Peace* in Mary Gregor (ed.): *Practical Philosophy*, Cambridge: Cambridge University Press, 1996. *Idea for a Universal History with a Cosmopolitan Purpose* and *The Contest of the Faculties* in: H. S. Reiss (ed.): *Kant. Political Writings*, second Edition, 1991. *Lectures on Ethics*, Peter Heath and J. B. Schneewind (ed.), trans. Peter Heath, Cambridge: Cambridge University Press, 1997.

2. It is plausible that the assumption of some degree of powerlessness applies not only to hope for deserved happiness, but to hope in general. Rachel Zuckert also emphasizes that Kant assumes that we hope for outcomes "over which we do not have (total) control" (Zuckert 2018, 247). In the contemporary debate, see Han-Pile (2017) for the thesis that hope presupposes some degree of powerlessness.

3. Günther Zöller (2013, 254), who refers to Grimm's Dictionary, points out that "may" [*dürfen*], in Kant's time, was used not only in the sense of permission but also in the sense of "need" [*bedürfen*], or "having grounds" [*Grund haben*]. In line with the latter meaning, I understand the question as "What do I have grounds to hope for?"

4. In the third section of the *Canon* in the first *Critique*, Kant describes faith [*Glaube*] as a special kind of assent or "*Fürwahrhalten*," which literally means "taking-to-be-true." Translating the term *Glaube* into English is difficult; I will call it "faith" or, following Andrew Chignell (2013), "Belief" with a capital "B."

5. Both "trust" and "confidence" are translations of the German "*Zutrau*," which is perhaps closer to "trust." (The German original reads: "Vom Zutraun auf Gott unter dem Begriff des Glaubens. [. . .] Der Glaube bedeutet also das Zutraun, daß Gott das, was nicht in unsrer Gewalt stehet, wenn wir auch alles, was uns möglich ist, warden gethan haben, ersetzen werde.") In cases of hope that Kant discusses in the *Religion*, it becomes apparent that the assumption of some *external* power is not strictly necessary for hope. What is necessary is the assumption of grounds of which we lack knowledge but in which we are still entitled to trust, and these grounds may be one's *own* powers.

6. In cases of hope that Kant discusses in the *Religion*, it becomes apparent that the assumption of some *external* power is not strictly necessary for hope. In cases where one *doubts* whether one's own powers suffice, what is necessary is the assumption of grounds (one's own powers) of which we lack knowledge but in which we are still entitled to trust.

7. "Morally appropriate" is ambiguous between "morally permitted" and "required." Surely, the highest good is a *permitted* object of hope. One might even think that it is a required object of hope, not least since the highest good turns out to be the object of a duty (in the second *Critique*). However, this does not make it a required object of hope, or, in other words, this does not require us to hope for it. Kant nowhere claims that hope can be required, and I think that his rejection of a duty to *Believe* (in god) (5:125) amounts to a rejection of a duty to hope. Rather, Kant seems to assume that insofar as we are rational and sensible beings, we hope for our own happiness, and insofar as we are moral, we hope and strive for the highest good.

8. Whereas some interpreters are skeptical about whether Kant has the resources to successfully justify the duty, there have been attempts to help him on that point. See especially Marwede 2018, 210–23.

9. In the second *Critique*, Kant makes this point in the form of an antinomy. See Watkins (2010, 152) for a formally valid reconstruction of the antinomy.

10. I borrow the terminology "theoretical undecidability" and "practical necessity" from Willaschek 2010, 169.

11. Just how Kant conceives of the element of powerlessness regarding one's own moral progress and the stability of one's good disposition only becomes fully clear in *Religion within the Boundaries of Mere Reason* (see, e.g., 6:71 and section 3 in this text).

12. Chignell argues in detail that Kant operates with a stronger condition on (rational) hope than that which results from "armchair analysis" (Chignell 2013, 209).

13. A better translation of the German "Zumutung" would be "imposition."

14. Here I disagree with Chignell (2013), who claims that "throughout *Religion* Kant says that we may and even must hope for external assistance in this task [i.e., moral improvement]" (Chignell 2013, 210).

15. I changed the translation from "confidence" to "trust" because this better corresponds to the German "Vertrauen." Further, it highlights the point made in section 1: Kant sometimes uses "trust" to describe our attitude toward the grounds of hope.

16. Wimmer identifies three reasons for this duty: (1) living in community leads to vices; (2) we have to exit the ethical state of nature just as we have to exit the juridical state of nature; and (3) we have to realize the highest good (Wimmer 1990, 187–93).

17. Kant suggests that there is an intimate connection between legal and moral (or ethical) progress. In *Theory and Practice*, Kant describes "the foundation of a right of nations as a condition in which alone the predispositions belonging to humanity that make our species worthy of love can be developed" (8:307n.).

18. To be sure, Kant offers a detailed framework for the status of a teleological view of nature in the third *Critique*. In §83, he takes up the philosophy of history, arguing that the assumption that nature has a teleological order is a principle "for the reflecting power of judgment, that . . . is regulative and not constitutive, and that by its means we acquire only a guideline for considering things in nature" (5:379). That is, in line with my interpretation offered in the main text, Kant clearly denies *knowledge* with regard to the assumption of a teleological order.

19. In *Perpetual Peace*, for example, Kant claims that "we can *and must* supply it [the agency of nature] mentally" (8:362, my emphasis) and that "while this idea is indeed far-fetched in *theory*, it does possess dogmatic validity and has a very real foundation in *practice*, as with the concept of *perpetual peace*, which makes it our duty to promote it by using the natural mechanism described above" (ibid.).

20. In the first *Critique*, Kant does make several remarks that suggest that hope and Belief in god and immortality are necessary for moral motivation (e.g., A813/B841). He later clearly retracts this position, for example, when he emphasizes that through the moral law "our reason commands us compellingly, without however either promising or threatening anything thereby" (6:49).

21. This suggestion leads Zuckert to call the role of hope "quasi-motivational" (Zuckert 2018, 255). Similarly, Insole (2008) holds that hope can have motivational influence but that moral motivation can exist independently of hope.

22. In the *Religion*, hope that one's disposition will exhibit stable goodness is not obviously hope for a final end, but still it is hope for a future state of affairs that will be (or remain) good and rational.

23. I would like to thank Jakob Huber, Dieter Schönecker and his colloquium, Marcus Willaschek and the *Frankfurter Kant-Arbeitskreis* for helpful comments on earlier versions of this text.

REFERENCES

Chignell, Andrew. 2013. "Rational Hope, Moral Order, and the Revolution of the Will." In *Divine Order, Human Order, and the Order of Nature: Historical Perspectives*, edited by Eric Watkins, 197–218. Oxford: Oxford University Press.

Chignell, Andrew. 2018. "Religious Dietary Practices and Secular Food Ethics; or, How to Hope that Your Food Choices Make a Difference Even When You Reasonably Believe That They Don't." In *Oxford Handbook on Food Ethics*, edited by Anne Barnhill, Mark Budolfson, and Tyler Doggett, 287–312. Oxford: Oxford University Press.

Ebels-Duggan, Kyla. 2016. "The Right, the Good, and the Threat of Despair. (Kantian) Ethics and the Need for Hope in God." In *Oxford Studies in Philosophy of Religion*, Volume 7, edited by Jonathan Kvanvig, 81–110. Oxford: Oxford University Press.

Flikschuh, Katrin. 2010. "Hope or Prudence: Practical Faith in Kant's Political Thinking." In *Faith and Reason. International Yearbook of German Idealism* (7/2009), edited by Jürgen Stolzenberg and Fred Rush, 95–117. Berlin/New York: de Gruyter.

Han-Pile, Béatrice. 2017. "Hope, Powerlessness, and Agency." *Midwest Studies in Philosophy* XLI: 175–201.

Insole, Christopher. 2008. "The Irreducible Importance of Religious Hope in Kant's Conception of the Highest Good." *Philosophy* 83 (325): 333–51.

Marwede, Florian. 2018. *Das Höchste Gut in Kants Deontologischer Ethik*. Berlin/New York: de Gruyter.

Watkins, Eric. 2010. "The Antinomy of Practical Reason: Reason, the Unconditioned and the Highest Good." In *Kant's Critique of Practical Reason: A Critical Guide*, edited by Andrews Reath and Jens Timmermann, 168–96. Cambridge: Cambridge University Press.

Willaschek, Marcus. 2010. "The Primacy of Practical Reason and the Idea of a Practical Postulate." In *Kant's Critique of Practical Reason. A Critical Guide*, edited by Andrews Reath and Jens Timmermann, 168–96. Cambridge: Cambridge University Press.

Willaschek, Marcus. 2016. "Must We Believe in the Realizability of Our Ends? On a Premise of Kant's Argument for the Postulates of Pure Practical Reason." In *The Highest Good in Kant's Philosophy*, edited by Thomas Höwing, 223–44. Berlin/New York: De Gruyter.

Wimmer, Reiner. 1990. *Kants kritische Religionsphilosophie*. Berlin/New York: de Gruyter.

Wood, Allen. 1970. *Kant's Moral Religion*. Ithaca/London: Cornell University Press.

Zöller, Günther. 2013. "Hoffen—Dürfen. Kants kritische Begründung des moralischen Glaubens." In *Glaube und Vernunft in der Philosophie der Neuzeit*, edited by Dietmar H. Heidemann and Raoul Weicker, 245–57. Hildesheim/New York: Olms.

Zuckert, Rachel. 2018. "Is Kantian Hope a Feeling?" In *Kant and the Faculty of Feeling*, edited by Kelly Sorensen and Diane Williamson, 242–59. Cambridge: Cambridge University Press.

Chapter Five

Kierkegaard on Hope as Essential to Selfhood

Roe Fremstedal

Kierkegaard differs from his contemporaries Schopenhauer and Nietzsche by emphasizing the value of hope and its importance for human agency and selfhood or practical identity. In *The Sickness unto Death*, Kierkegaard argues that despair involves a loss of hope and courage that is extremely common. Moreover, despair involves being double-minded by having an incoherent practical identity (although it need not be recognized as such if the agent mistakes his identity). A coherent practical identity, by contrast, requires wholehearted commitment toward ideals *and* the hope that our ideals are realizable.[1]

Although Kierkegaard's analysis of despair in *The Sickness unto Death* is well known, his equally important analysis of hope is largely neglected.[2] There seems to be two reasons for this neglect. First, Kierkegaard's account of hope is spread out over a number of lesser-known writings such as *For Self-Examination*, *Upbuilding Discourses in Various Spirits*, *Christian Discourses*, and *Eighteen Upbuilding Writings* in addition to the better-known *Works of Love*. Whereas *The Sickness unto Death* analyses despair systematically, these lesser-known writings give a somewhat fragmented account of hope that is largely overlooked by commentators.[3] (Partially as a result, Kierkegaard is known as the melancholic Dane.)

Second, Kierkegaard's *via negativa* methodology approaches hope (as well as selfhood and practical identity) indirectly by focusing on despair.[4] However, despair itself is described as hopelessness both by *The Sickness unto Death* and various commentators (SKS 11, 133f., 153 / SUD, 18, 37f.) (Grøn 1997, 151; Hannay 2006, 142). Kierkegaard even argues that hope proper, that is hope against hope, presupposes despair while overcoming it at every instant (see section 5).

On Kierkegaard's account, hope and despair are therefore so closely connected that it is difficult to separate them without ignoring his dialectical and negativistic approach to selfhood. In the following, we will start by introducing Kierkegaard's influential account of despair and then show how it not only points toward moral commitment but also toward hope and religiousness. Instead of giving a full account of despair, the present text limits itself to elements of despair that are directly relevant for Kierkegaard's account of hope.

1. DESPAIR AS LOSS OF HOPE AND COURAGE

Kierkegaard characterizes despair both as hopelessness and as double-mindedness. Here we will start by discussing the former, while the next section will discuss double-mindedness.

It is often the case that despair is contrasted with hope, since despair seems to entail hopelessness. In *The Sickness unto Death*, Kierkegaard follows this common usage of the terms by characterizing despair as hopelessness (SKS 11, 133f., 153 / SUD, 18, 37f.) (Bernier 2015, 58ff.; Gouwens 1996, 155ff.; Theunissen 2005). More specifically, he takes despair to involve an act whereby the agent actively gives up hope and courage (Grøn 1997, 152f.).

On the one hand, despair involves *passivity* by virtue of resulting from an experience of loss or disappointment. By suffering (what he takes to be) a fatal loss or disappointment, the agent gives up all hope and courage. As a result, he is stuck in a desperate situation and can neither cope with the loss nor accept himself (SKS 11, 176ff. / SUD, 60ff.). The demonic, for example, is deeply disappointed over the impossibility of self-creation and defiantly rejects all help to overcome despair (SKS 11, 182–87 / SUD, 67–74).

On the other hand, despair involves *activity* since the agent takes the loss (or disappointment) to be significant enough to give up hope and courage. Kierkegaard is particularly interested in radical despair that gives up all significant hope and courage by attributing infinite value or importance to the loss or disappointment (Grøn 1997, 143–53). Despair is then not merely something one suffers passively, since it always involves actively abandoning hope and courage. It is not only a psychological phenomenon but also a moral notion that refers to an unwillingness to accept human agency in general and moral responsibility in particular (Kosch 2006, 142f., 154, 206–8).

On this account, despair presupposes that the agent has ideals, values, or at least something he identifies with, which he takes to be actually impossible to realize. For instance, the agent values his personal freedom and identifies fully with it but takes it to be impossible to realize because it is conditioned by states of affairs that do not obtain (e.g., due to imprisonment). Hope, by contrast, sees the good as possible to realize. Kierkegaard describes hope as expectancy of the possibility of good (SKS 9, 249 / WL, 249), as an anticipation that what one hopes for can be realized. The object of hope then represents the ideals or values of the agent.

Both despair and hope seem to involve a fundamental tension, or conflict, between ideals and reality. Both presuppose that the world is not as it should have been. Still, despair and hope represent fundamentally different attitudes toward the conflict between ideals and reality. Hope takes this conflict to be resolvable, whereas despair takes it to be irresolvable. Despair therefore overlaps with forms of nihilism and pessimism, which hold that the world as it is ought not to be, whereas the world that ought to be does not exist.[5]

Pessimism was developed by Schopenhauer, who Kierkegaard read in 1854–1855. Although Kierkegaard shares Schopenhauer's view that the world is unacceptable in its actuality, he nevertheless affirms a hopeful perspective by viewing the world as acceptable in its potentiality. Merely accepting the world as it is—as Nietzsche suggests—would amount to a fatalistic acceptance of evil and injustice in the world. Hope, by contrast, involves a protest that makes it possible to try to overcome evil and injustice by enabling progress toward ideals in the future. Nietzsche, by contrast, argues that we must either accept the world unconditionally (by saying yes to the eternal recurrence of the same) or be pessimists or nihilists who condemn it as being incompatible with our ideals or values. To Kierkegaard, this represents a false dilemma, since hope represents a third option that offers the possibility of reconciling ideals and reality.

2. DESPAIR AS DOUBLE-MINDEDNESS: INCOHERENT PRACTICAL IDENTITY

The above account of despair, points to a further idea—emphasized by Kierkegaard—that despair takes the form of double-mindedness. Just like the German *Verzweiflung*, the Danish word for despair—*Fortvivelse*—is based on the numeral "two" (Danish *tvi* or *tve*; German *zwei*), suggesting that despair involves a split or duality. Based on this, Kierkegaard writes, "[E]veryone in despair has two wills, one that he futilely wants to follow entirely, and one that he futilely wants to get rid of entirely" (SKS 8, 144 / UD, 30). Despair involves being double-minded by having an incoherent will. However, rather than merely referring to volition, it involves an incoherent practical identity with different motives (Davenport 2008, ch. 3; Rudd 2012, 42ff.). To despair is simply to lack a coherent practical identity.

On Kierkegaard's account, despair results from a tension that is fundamental to human agency and selfhood. More specifically, our agency and selfhood are characterized by both facticity and freedom. Facticity represents a given, inescapable sociohistorical context as well as embodiment that limits or constrains human agency. Freedom, by contrast, represents the human ability to transcend limitations by gradually and partially reforming and modifying facticity. Hence, Kierkegaard stresses the interplay (or dialectics) between facticity and freedom. Human freedom is always situated in a particular context or situation that limits it. The result is a fundamental tension between freedom and facticity that is constitutive of human nature, since both freedom and facticity represent constitutive features of our nature.[6]

For that reason, any attempt to identify only with facticity or freedom is self-defeating and will result in double-mindedness. Unless freedom and facticity are reconciled, the tension between freedom and facticity results in double-mindedness that exaggerates either freedom or facticity. Someone who identifies with only one of these two constitutive features is double-minded, since he is split between what he identifies with and what he wants to avoid.

The Sickness unto Death argues that despair is dominated either by weakness or by defiance (SKS 11, 162 / SUD, 47). The "despair of weakness" does not want to be the self it is, whereas the "defiant" "desperately wants to be . . . a self that he is not (for the will to be the self that he is in truth is the very opposite of despair)" (SKS 11, 136 / SUD, 20). The "despair of weakness" understates the possibilities represented by freedom, while exaggerating limitations. The "defiant," by contrast, exaggerates possibilities, while understating limitations. Neither of them want to be themselves wholeheartedly, since both forms of despair identify with—or value—something they are not. Overcoming despair then requires accepting oneself completely by taking full responsibility for one's whole life here and now.[7] Without unconditional willingness to be itself, the self is double-minded, since it is split between ideals, which it identifies with, and reality, which it does not fully accept or endorse. Despair therefore refers to an unwillingness to accept human agency (cf. Kosch 2006, 142f., 154, 208).

3. WHOLEHEARTEDNESS AS CONSTITUTIVE OF SELFHOOD: COHERENT PRACTICAL IDENTITY

Kierkegaard thinks that despair is extremely common, since it results from a tension that is constitutive of human nature (i.e., freedom vs. facticity; defiance vs. weakness; activity vs. passivity). This tension will result in double-mindedness, unless the two opposites, such as freedom and facticity, are reconciled. In order to avoid double-mindedness, the agent therefore needs to actively shape and unify his entire practical identity so that it becomes coherent.

However, this shaping requires a self with higher-order motives. *The Sickness unto Death* maintains that the potential for selfhood is latent in human nature, although the self cannot be identified either with human nature or with any of its constitutive features (facticity or freedom) (SKS 11, 129 / SUD, 13). Instead, selfhood requires higher-order motives that identifies with some lower-order motives, while distancing itself from other motives (Davenport 2012, 117). For Kierkegaard, the self is a reflexive self-relation that relates actively to human nature (and others) by forming higher-order motives and volitions. It is therefore conceived of in hierarchical and relational terms (Stokes 2015, 145; Davenport 2008, 239n).

However, nonideal selves that despair consciously differ from ideal, wholehearted selves. The former are double-minded, although they are aware of both despair and selfhood. The latter, by contrast, actively overcome despair at every instance by unifying their identity. (Human beings who are not selves, by contrast, lack higher-order motives.)

Kierkegaard emphasizes that only a wholehearted or unified self avoids double-mindedness (SKS 8, 138ff. / UD, 24ff.). However, in order to become wholehearted, the self needs an unreserved orientation toward the good that defines its whole identity. The self cannot shape and unify its whole identity if it is only conditionally, occasionally, or partially committed to some project. Instead, a coherent self, which unifies freedom and facticity, needs categorical commitment toward the good. Only such commitment always makes it possible to unify one's whole identity coherently and to coordinate different roles and various other projects. Without unreserved commitment to good, agency therefore lacks coherence and unity (Rudd 2012, 139f., 187f.).

There are two different problems here. One problem is that agency could be fragmented into different projects and roles that are not integrated as parts of a single life. Such a life would lack coherence and unity but it need not be contradictory. Another problem, however, is that agents may pursue projects and roles that are incompatible with each other, either in principle or in fact.

An underlying orientation toward good prevents these problems by being a meta-project that shapes, unifies, and coordinates all other projects and roles that we engage in. As such, it underlies the specific projects and roles that we have. However, not any categorical commitment to a project or cause will do if double-mindedness is to be avoided. Rather, we need a normative standard that makes it possible for agency to either fail or succeed in shaping and unifying its identity. This requires a fundamental form of normativity that is basic to human agency and selfhood. However, this normativity cannot be unique to each individual but must rather be shared by all agents, since our very self-relation is intertwined with our relation to others (cf. SKS 3, 250 / EO2, 262). In general, becoming a self requires ethics that is other-regarding rather than egoistic or eudaimonistic (cf. SKS 7, 121ff., 385ff. / CUP1, 129ff., 423ff.). More specifically, proper self-love requires neighbor-love; and hope for ourselves requires hope for all others (SKS 9, 227ff., 246ff. / WL, 225ff., 246ff.; SKS 10, 127–32 / CD, 116–22).

Both our self-relation and our relation to others then involve a shared normative constraint, which Kierkegaard identifies with the good and the divine (SKS 9, 111–24 / WL, 107–21).[8] Kierkegaard holds the good to be inescapable (SKS 8, 123 / UD, 7). He writes, "[T]he person who in truth wills only one thing *can will only the good*. . . . The person who wills one thing that is not the good is actually not willing one thing; . . . he must be, double-minded" (SKS 8, 138–40 / UD, 24f.). Only categorical moral dedica-tion, therefore, allows wholeheartedness; anything else involves double-mindedness (Davenport 2012, chs. 3–4; Rudd 2012, chs. 2, 6–7; Fremstedal 2019, 326f.).

4. PRACTICAL COMMITMENTS REQUIRE HOPE

However, unconditional moral commitment do not suffice to rule out despair. Like anyone else, moral agents may experience loss, disappointment, or hardship and feel stuck in situations that appear hopeless. Moral agents may even suffer from depression or unhappiness that makes them self-preoccu-pied and therefore less responsive to the—morally decisive—needs of others (cf. Martin 2012, 109). Worse still, morality often requires sacrificing pru-dential interests. Conflict between morality and prudence can even lead to despair that weakens or deteriorates moral motivation. In situations that may involve either serious normative conflict or the experience of loss, disap-pointment, and hardship, there therefore is a tendency toward despair and—partially because of this—demoralization (i.e., a psychological loss of re-solve to continue to be moral) (cf. Adams 1987, 151ff.).

In many situations, it seems impossible or improbable to realize our ideals. Unless we manage to reconcile ideals and reality, by hoping (or be-lieving) in realizability, the result is a double-mindedness that is split be-tween the ideals it identifies with and the reality it is stuck with. Hope seems necessary, since moral commitments often transcend available evidence, making it necessary to act in the face of uncertainty and put up with difficul-ties. Indeed, moral agency often involves being committed toward projects whose feasibility cannot be known by us (cf. O'Neill 1997). Since evidence is insufficient, we then need hope that our projects can be realized.

Kierkegaard here accepts the broadly Kantian idea that our practical com-mitments clearly go beyond available evidence (cf. SKS 9, 229ff. / WL, 227ff.). Like Kant, he appeals to the hope that we can realize our moral (and prudential) interest, even though it is not warranted by evidence.[9] Onora O'Neill makes a similar point, writing,

> [W]e must assume that . . . our future is one in which we can act, and in which the aim of moral action is not absurd: it must be possible to insert the moral action into the world. . . . [W]e are committed to moral aims whose feasibility we cannot prove theoretically; to make sense of this we need to postulate, assume, or hope for a human future that allows room for human progress. . . . [T]hese hopes for the future of humankind cannot be renounced if we are committed to morality. (O'Neill 1997, 282, 287f.)

The point is not that it psychologically hard to live without hope. Rather, it is that it is incoherent to live without hope, unless we also give up moral agency (O'Neill 1997, 284). Morality requires action, but this does not make sense unless the moral agent takes moral action to be possible. Moral agency that does not have any hope of making good by acting seems incoherent, since its ideals and values do not cohere with its perception of reality. Without hope, it cannot reconcile ideals and reality, and therefore finds itself stuck in a hopeless situation.

5. DIFFERENT TYPES OF HOPE: CHRISTIAN AND HUMAN HOPES

Kierkegaard describes hope as an expectation of the possibility of good (contrasting it with fear as an expectation of the possibility of evil—SKS 9, 249 / WL, 249). He seems to assume that what we hope for must be *possible* yet *uncertain*, if there is to be room and need for hope (cf. SKS 10, 117–24 / CD, 106–13; SKS 11, 153f. / SUD, 38f.). In addition, it must be *difficult* to attain, since there is hardly any need for hope if what we hope for is easily attainable (SKS 10, 117–24 / CD, 106–13).

The argument so far indicates that a unified practical identity requires hope of realizing moral commitments. However, Kierkegaard goes even further by arguing that hope and charity are insufficient, since Christian faith is also needed. Kierkegaard therefore distinguishes between Christian and non-Christian hopes (SKS 8, 214ff. / UD, 112ff.; SKS 13, 99, 103f. / FSE, 77, 82f.; Pap. VI B 53, 13 / JP 2, 1668). Non-Christian hope is not based on divine revelation and divine grace as Christian hope is. Kierkegaard therefore describes it as "natural hope" and "human hope." In the following, we will discuss human hope first and then turn to Christian hope and its justification.

Human hope takes many different forms. Kierkegaard here distinguishes between a pre-reflexive and reflective hope (Pap. VI B 53, 13 / JP 2, 1668). The former expects the possibility of good when the outcome is *objectively* uncertain, but it does not realize that it hopes for something that is uncertain or difficult to attain, since it lacks reflection. This hope involves a pre-reflexive expectation similar to immediate trust or confidence (cf. Fremstedal 2014, 179). It appears identical or closely related to, the hope that Kierke-gaard elsewhere claims "expects victory in everything" "without a struggle" (SKS 5, 29 / EUD, 20). It lacks reflection and experience, and assumes that everything is (humanly) possible (Lippitt 2015, 125).

Reflexive hope, by contrast, realizes that it hopes for something uncertain that is difficult to attain. The notions of possibility and uncertainty here are subjective notions, referring to how things appear to the agent. Kierkegaard claims that this hope is based on the calculations of the understanding (*For-standen*—Pap. VI B 53, 13 / JP 2, 1668). Although he hardly explains what the understanding is, it nevertheless seems to involve the following elements:

1. It represents a natural human faculty, elsewhere described as reason (cf. Burgess 1994, 109–28).
2. It involves a rational capacity for calculation and manipulation, at least for practical purposes. It only allows risks that are likely to pay off.
3. It does not represent moral rationality, but rather prudential and instru-mental rationality that is informed by experience.
4. It involves a naturalism that excludes reference to the supernatural and eschatology (Westphal 2014, 91ff.; Fremstedal 2014, 97, and ch. 7; Davenport 2008, 196–233).
5. It is concerned with what is humanly possible, not with what is divine-ly possible. More specifically, it is concerned with practical possibility in which an agent contributes to the realization of an end by acting. Mere metaphysical or divine possibility is not sufficient.
6. It seems to involve evidentialism about belief, according to which rational beliefs require sufficient evidence.

Based on this concept, Kierkegaard assumes that non-Christian hope is typi-cally concerned with the pursuit of personal happiness. Moreover, he asso-ciates reflexive non-Christian hope with finite worldly wisdom that offers prudential advice based on experience, under the motto that everything only holds "to a certain degree" (SKS 5, 30 / EUD, 21).

However, Kierkegaard insists that non-Christian hope leads to hopeless-ness (cf. SKS 5, 100f. / EUD, 94f.). On the one hand, he argues that hope-lessness results from misfortune, hardship, and distress (SKS 10, 117–24 / CD, 106–13). As we have seen, the idea seems to be that by suffering a loss or experiencing normative conflict, the agent gives up hope (see sections 1 and 4). On the other hand, Kierkegaard claims that one must despair or give up hope, since one fails to realize the infinite ethical requirement (SKS 9, 252, 261 / WL, 252, 262).[10] The latter claim suggests that the one despairs (or that one *ought* to despair) because of one's moral shortcoming. But it could also mean that despair itself results from not just any moral failure but from the failure of unifying one's identity. Rather than presupposing immoral actions, despair then results from an incoherent identity that is morally objectionable.

Morality, hope, and despair are then interconnected. Like hope and despair, morality can be approached from both a non-Christian and a Christian perspective. Kierkegaard's "first ethics" represents non-Christian ethics, whereas the "second ethics" represents Christian ethics. Kierkegaard argues that the first ethics constitutes the natural starting point, although it collapses internally due to human guilt and sinfulness (SKS 4, 323ff. / CA, 16ff.). It fails to live up to its own ideals (and is therefore split between ideals and reality), something that involves despair (double-mindedness) that prepares the transition to Christian ethics.[11] Kierkegaard's argument here emphasizes the moral gap between our moral obligations and our natural capabilities.[12] This gap is closed by Christian ethics that relies on forgiveness of sins and divine assistance (SKS 4, 323ff. / CA, 16ff.). In addition, we will see that it involves hope against hope that radically transcends ordinary hopes.

To support his views, Kierkegaard relies on the classical idea that our final end is the highest good (Fremstedal 2014, chs. 5–6). Although he does not identify it with eudaimonia, he still takes the highest good to include virtue and happiness, describing it as eternal happiness (*Salighed*), which Christians may hope for or expect (SKS 5, 214, 250ff. / EUD, 214, 253ff.) (cf. Bernier 2015, 115; Lippitt 2013, 147ff.). In addition, he follows the Augustinian tradition by interpreting the highest good as an ethico-religious community—"the kingdom of God"—that cannot be realized by any individual alone (SKS 5, 255 / EUD, 258f.; SKS 7, 356 / CUP1, 391; SKS 8, 303–6 / UD, 208–12). It is the highest good in this collective form that represents the ultimate object of justified hope for Kierkegaard (as for Kant and much of the Augustinian tradition).[13]

However, this end cannot be realized by human effort alone. First, moral virtue is undermined by moral failure and evil. Second, we could end up being unhappy even if we were morally perfect. Finally, the highest good takes the form of a kingdom that cannot be realized by an individual alone. As a result, human agents cannot possibly realize the highest good even collectively, unless divine assistance is introduced. Secular hopes for the highest good must then be disappointed (Fremstedal 2014, ch. 9).

However, Kierkegaard maintains that Christian hope is only possible as a response against human despair (Pap. VI B53, 13 / JP 2, 1668). The reason for this is that Kierkegaard follows Paul in taking Christian hope to be "hope against hope," that is, as hope in a hopeless situation (SKS 13, 102–4 / FSE 81–83). The idea is that when everything breaks down due to despair, God offers new hope as divine gift that, once accepted, makes it possible to overcome all human (non-Christian) despair (SKS 13, 102–4 / FSE, 81–83, cf. SKS 5, 100f. / EUD, 94f.; Pap. VI B 53, 13 / JP 2, 1668). It is only God, for whom everything is possible, that can guarantee that there is always hope (cf. SKS 11, 185 / SUD, 71). Only Christian religiousness overcomes all despair by hoping against hope.

Kierkegaard thinks that this hope is found in our innermost being, although we only become aware of it when we despair over our whole situation. Despair abandons human hope while procuring Christian hope (SKS 10, 121–23 / CD, 110–12, cf. SKS 8, 214ff. / UD, 112ff.). To procure this hope, we need to give up human hopes and to accept the gift of divine assistance (which is given universally).[14]

Kierkegaard maintains that the Christian hope for the highest good cannot be disappointed, since it is based on eschatology and patiently expects something that transcends our finite schedules and probabilities.[15] It is not a specific hope for a particular event (which may be disappointed) but something that lies beyond human calculation and all time limits (Lippitt 2015, 136ff.). As such, it may be realized in another form and at another time than expected. The assumption is that it will be realized somehow, sometime.

Like faith and charity, Christian hope is not based on evidence or knowledge. Rather, it goes beyond available evidence (cf. SKS 9, 229ff. / WL, 227ff.). Still, this does not amount to a blind leap of faith, since it is based on practical or pragmatic considerations. More specifically, religiousness fits a natural human need for coherent selfhood by offering a way out of despair and demoralization. Instead of being justified epistemically, religious hope and faith is then justified practically. Like Kant, Kierkegaard therefore seems to be a pragmatist (non-evidentialist) about belief and hope.[16] However, Kierkegaard goes beyond Kant by accepting not only (moral) natural theology but also divine revelation. The idea seems to be that Christian doctrine fits a natural need, although it cannot be reduced to human needs or natural theology since it relies on revelation, which has its own language and perspectives.

6. FAITH, HOPE, AND CHARITY

In *Works of Love*, Kierkegaard emphasizes that Christian hope requires charity that expects good for both oneself and one's neighbor alike. Kierkegaard claims that charity mediates between hope for oneself and hope for all others. He writes, "[L]ove is . . . the middle term: without love, no hope for oneself; with love, hope for all others—and to the same degree one hopes for oneself, to the same degree one hopes for others, since to the same degree one is loving" (SKS 9, 259 / WL, 260).

Kierkegaard first claims that justified hope requires charity, since there are moral restrictions on hope.[17] He therefore holds that hope is nothing without love (SKS 9, 258 / WL, 259). He then claims that charity itself is "built up" (*opbygges*) and nourished by Christian hope (SKS 9, 248 / WL, 248). That is, hope cultivates and strengthens love and prevents us from giving it up by despairing. *Works of Love* therefore contrasts despair not only with hope but also with charity (SKS 9, 248–59 / WL, 248–60).

However, *The Sickness unto Death* contrasts despair with Christian faith, whereas *For Self-Examination* contrasts it with Christian hope (SKS 11, 195f. / SUD, 81; SKS 13, 99, 103f. / FSE, 77, 82f.). This suggests that only the theological virtues avoid despair (cf. SKS 8, 204f. / UD, 100f.; SKS 9, 227ff., 248ff. / WL, 225ff., 248ff.; SKS 10, 127–32 / CD, 116–22). Although these virtues represent character traits, it is still the case that they must be actively maintained and renewed if we are to be wholehearted agents. Despair must therefore be constantly overcome by hoping, believing, and loving. Gene Fendt comments:

> There is a unity of the theological virtues, but they are not the same thing. Insofar as faith believes God, believes in God, and believes that God makes good, it is distinct from hope which is an expectation of the good for both oneself and one's neighbor. But insofar as faith believes that God makes good it is inseparable from the hope which expects the good for both oneself and one's neighbor. If the first (faith) is given up, then the second (hope for both oneself and others) is *ipso facto* given up. If, on the other hand, one does not expect the good for both oneself and one's neighbor, then one lies if he says he has faith. (Fendt 1990, 168)

In a work influenced by Fendt, Mark Bernier concludes,

1. (1) [D]espair can be characterized as an unwillingness to hope an in authentic way;
2. (2) authentic hope [hope for eternal happiness, the highest good] constitutes the primary task of the self; and
3. (3) faith is a willingness to hope, wherein the self secures a ground for the possibility of hope. (Bernier 2015, 212)

However, (1) it is only complete despair over one's situation in general that involves an unwillingness to hope (in a hopeless situation) by rejecting Christian hope against hope. (2) It is not only hope but the theological virtues that constitutes the primary task of the self. These virtues represent intrinsic, non-instrumental goods essential to selfhood (cf. SKS 10, 129 / CD, 118). Finally, (3) faith is not identical to "a willingness to hope," but the theological virtues are interconnected. Kierkegaard emphasizes that hope is nothing without charity, although charity is nourished by hope (SKS 9, 248, 258 /

WL, 248, 259). Moreover, hope in God requires faith and trust in God and *vice versa* (Gouwens 1996, 157). The religious believer expects that good is possible for himself and his neighbor alike, since he believes that God makes good for all.

7. CONCLUSION AND COMPARISON WITH SCHOPENHAUER AND NIETZSCHE

Despite the fact that it is often neglected, Kierkegaard's account of hope lies at the very heart of his theory. Bernier therefore concludes, "[H]ope is a fundamental theme in Kierkegaard's narrative, connecting despair, faith, and the self. Indeed, we cannot adequately understand Kierkegaard's view without drawing out this theme of hope" (Bernier 2015, 212). As we have seen, Kierkegaard argues that hope is necessary in order to overcome double-mindedness. Wholeheartedness requires not only categorical moral dedication but also hope and faith that supports moral agency. However, even Christians become double-minded if they lack hope, faith, and charity. This means that shaping and unifying human identity is highly demanding on Kierkegaard's account. Double-mindedness is therefore far more common than wholeheartedness.[18]

Kierkegaard's account of hope deserves attention for the following reasons: it represents an existential account of hope that emphasizes the interrelation between hope and despair, seeing both as crucial for human agency and selfhood. More specifically, Kierkegaard defends the strong view that we should always hope for the good, no matter how bad the situation might be. Put differently, Kierkegaard therefore sees hope against hope as necessary for human agency and selfhood. His emphasis lies not so much on a description of what hope is as an analysis of what justified hope is. More specifically, he argues that justified hope is interrelated with charity and religious faith, and has the highest good as its proper object. As such, it belongs not only to a Judeo-Christian tradition that focuses on the Pauline triad of faith, hope, and charity but it also belongs to a philosophical tradition from Augustine and Kant that views the highest good (the *summum bonum*), a synthesis of virtue and happiness, as the ultimate object of hope. However, Kierkegaard goes beyond his forerunner by developing a *via negativa* approach to hope that starts with hopelessness and despair before it proceeds to hope. Indeed, Kierkegaard holds that proper hope, hope against hope, both presupposes and overcomes despair.

Kierkegaard differs from his contemporaries Schopenhauer and Nietzsche not only by viewing hope as valuable but also by viewing it as indispensable for human existence. Without hope, human selfhood and identity involves despair (and self-deception), Kierkegaard argues. Still, Kierkegaard does not rule out the possibility of false hopes that may involve self-deception or irrationality. However, it is crucial to Kierkegaard that not all hopes are false, since there are justified hopes that are central to human existence. This means that Schopenhauer and Nietzsche may be justified in criticizing false hopes as long as this critique does not undermine hope altogether.

Schopenhauer argues that it natural for humans to hope, since hope expresses the will to life that lies at the ground of everything (cf. Schopenhauer 1974, vol. 2, §313). However, this will is not only blind and irrational but the source of all suffering. Schopenhauer therefore describes hope as a "folly of the heart" that confuses what we wish for with what is probable (Schopenhauer 1969, vol. 2, §313). Hope distorts our thinking by engaging in wishful thinking that increases suffering. On this pessimistic view, hopes inevitably lead to disappointment and suffering, since genuine, lasting satisfaction is impossible for us. Even if we are lucky and get what we hope for, this will not cause real happiness but only increase striving and suffering.[19] Ultimately, this view rests on the pessimistic claim that neither individual happiness nor moral improvement is humanly possible. Schopenhauer argues that comprehensive happiness involves final satisfaction, which is impossible, since our life oscillates between pain and boredom (Schopenhauer 1969, vol. 1, 312, 360; §§57, 65).

Still, Schopenhauer thinks that the experience of hopelessness—and not hope—is beneficial, since it facilitates an ascetic denial of the will to live. Only asceticism provides a permanent liberation from suffering, since it negates the will to life that causes suffering in the first place (aesthetic experience, by contrast, only provides a temporal escape from suffering) (Schopenhauer 1969, vol. 1, books 3–4). Although there is a tendency toward asceticism and pessimism in the late Kierkegaard as well, he still does not accept Schopenhauer's pessimism. Yet, he agrees with Schopenhauer that the experience of hopelessness is beneficial, since it rejects false hopes. However, whereas Schopenhauer uses hopelessness to deny the will to life, Kierkegaard uses it to highlight the Pauline idea of hope against hope, which promises hope in a hopeless situation. Whereas Kierkegaard advocates Christian hope, both Schopenhauer and Nietzsche reject religious hopes.

Nietzsche tends to share Schopenhauer's negative evaluation of hope as a form of self-deceived escapism. In *Human, All Too Human*, he describes hope as "the worst of evils because it prolongs the torments of man" (Nietzsche 2008, 53; *Human, All Too Human* §71). This claim, which is from his comment on the myth of Pandora, is reminiscent of Schopenhauer's view that hope leads to suffering. But in his later writings from the 1880s, Nietzsche offers a reason for rejecting hope that differs strongly from Schopenhauer's reason. The problem with hope is not that it increases suffering but rather that it involves nihilism (or pessimism). To hope is generally to hope for some perceived good that seems lacking in one's current situation. Hope thereby depreciates reality, and values something else (e.g., the future) instead. It finds reality insufficient and the object of hope valuable. It thereby involves a nihilistic conflict between ideals and reality. Nietzsche writes, "A nihilist is a man who judges of the world as it is that it ought *not* to be, and of the world as it ought to be that it does not exist" (Nietzsche 1999, vol. 12, 366; Nietzsche 1968, §585A). Nihilism presupposes that we hope for (or expect) values that is not found in the world (and that alternative values are lacking). The problem arises because our values or ideals are unrealistic and impossible to realize, both now and in the future. They cannot be realized in this world, and there is no other world in which they can be realized either (Reginster 2008, 8).

Nietzsche therefore associates hope with otherworldly escapism. This is the reason why he warns against those who speak of extraterrestrial hopes and dismisses hope in "hidden harmonies, in future blessedness and justice" (Nietzsche 1999, vol. 4, 15, and vol. 5, 74; Nietzsche 2006, 6; Nietzsche 2008, 560, *Beyond Good and Evil*, §55). Nietzsche's eternal recurrence of the same represents an influential alternative to the Platonico-Christian tradition that Kierkegaard represents. Nietzsche argues against this tradition and against escapism, other-worldliness, and transcendence that belittles or depreciates this world. From this perspective, Schopenhauer's atheistic pessimism is just as nihilistic as the religious tradition that Kierkegaard represents. Indeed, Schopenhauer belongs to the very same tradition from Nietzsche's perspective.

It is this tradition that Nietzsche wants to overcome by criticizing nihilism. Somewhat paradoxically, he describes the overcoming of nihilism (and pessimism) in terms of hope. He writes, for instance, "the bridge to the highest hope" is "that mankind be redeemed from revenge," something that refers to revenge as a reactive and nihilistic emotion (Nietzsche 1999, vol. 4, 128; Nietzsche 2006, 77). Nietzsche can thus be said to hope for the end of hope, by hoping to overcome the nihilism and hope of the tradition. He finds the tradition unacceptable, judging that it ought not to be, whereas the *Übermensch* that accepts the eternal recurrence of same does not yet exist. He thereby stands in danger of repeating the nihilism that he tries to overcome.

Somewhat surprisingly, Kierkegaard anticipates Nietzsche's warning against religious nihilism and escapism. In 1844, he writes,

> [T]he expectation of an eternal salvation is able (which otherwise seems impossible) to be two places at the same time: it works in heaven and it works on earth, "it seeks God's kingdom and his righteousness and gives the rest as an over-measure" (Matthew 6:33). If the expectancy does not do this, then it is fraudulent, the craftiness of a sick soul that wants to sneak out of life, and not the authentic presence of a healthy soul in the temporal; then it is not the

expectancy of the eternal but a superstitious belief in the future. (SKS 5, 255 / EUD, 259)

Unlike Nietzsche, Kierkegaard develops an anti-nihilistic, existential approach to religion, which makes it possible to orient oneself in this life (SKS 5, 256 / EUD, 259). Nothing seems to capture this better than the notion of hope against hope, which lies at the heart of Kierkegaard's theory.

NOTES

1. Whereas Rudd and Davenport argue that a coherent practical identity requires unconditional moral commitment, the present text argues that it also requires hope. More specifically, the text reconstructs Kierkegaard's argument for hope as essential to practical identity. The latter is understood as "a description under which you find your life to be worth living and your actions to be worth undertaking" (Korsgaard 1996, 101). See also Rudd 2012; Davenport 2012.

2. Notable exceptions include McDonald 2014; Fremstedal 2014, chapter 9; Bernier 2015; Sweeney 2016. To some extent, the present text draws on Fremstedal 2014, 2016, and 2019.

3. *The Sickness unto Death* is published under the pseudonym Anti-Climacus. However, Kierkegaard introduces Anti-Climacus only because he does not claim to live up to the latter's ideals, although he fully accepts these ideals and the views of Anti-Climacus. For this reason, we attribute the views of Anti-Climacus to Kierkegaard. See SKS 22, 130, NB 11:209 / KJN 6, 127.

4. For Kierkegaard's negativistic methodology, see Theunissen 2005 and Grøn 1997.

5. Cf. Friedrich Nietzsche, *Kritische Studienausgabe*, vols. 1–15 (Berlin: de Gruyter, 1999), vol. 12, 366; Friedrich Nietzsche, *The Will to Power* (New York: Random House, 1968), §585A. There is substantial overlap between nihilism and despair (see Fremstedal 2016). Still, pessimism may only overlap partially with Kierkegaardian despair, since pessimism lacks hope but retains courage, whereas despair lacks both hope and courage. For pessimism, see Beiser 2016, 282.

6. Rudd 2012, 31ff.; Davenport 2008. At this point, Kierkegaard influenced continental philosophy from Heidegger to Sartre and Habermas. However, Rudd and Davenport also show that it is relevant to Anglophone philosophy after MacIntyre and Frankfurt. Davenport argues that Kierkegaard's account of human nature is either a two-aspect account of body and mind or some form of Aristotelean hylomorphism. See Davenport 2013, 234.

7. Stokes argues that selfhood in Kierkegaard concerns not only practical identity but also a naked (minimal) self that takes full responsibility for itself in the present. Exactly how the naked self relates to practical identity is a contested issue that I do not discuss here. See Stokes 2015, 167.

8. Lippitt 2013, 56f., 90ff., 121f. Kierkegaard *identifies* the good and the divine. See SKS 4, 160 / FT, 68; SKS 7, 133, 143 / CUP1, 142, 153f.; SKS 8, 151–53, 364, / UD, 39–41, 268. See also note 10 below.

9. Fremstedal 2014, chapter 9. In the context of religion, Kierkegaard repeatedly contrasts Kant's "honest way" with the dishonesty of post-Kantian philosophy (notably Hegelianism). See SKS 6, 142 / SLW, 152; SKS 19, 170, Not4:46 / KJN 3, 167; SKS 20, 229, NB2:235 / KJN 4, 229; SKS 22, 215, NB12:121 / KJN 6, 216f.; SKS 27, 390, 415, Papir 365:2, 369 / JP 1, 649, 654. For Kierkegaard's reference to Kant on hope, see SKS 19, 140, Not 4:11 / KJN 3, 139, 539; SKS K19, 198f.

10. In this context, "infinite" seems to mean "divine" and "inexhaustible," although it might also suggest that the ethical task is categorically overriding and highly demanding.

11. From the Christian perspective, Kierkegaard identifies despair with sinfulness. See part II of *The Sickness unto Death*, which has the title "Despair Is Sin."

12. Hare uses the moral gap to defend religious ethics, partially by basing his argument on Kant and Kierkegaard. See Hare 2002. For Kierkegaard's interpretation of original sin and radical evil, see Fremstedal 2014, chapter 2.

13. However, Kierkegaard accepts a Kantian critique of eudaimonism, denying that virtue should be motivated by the prospect of happiness. Cf. SKS 7, 367, 387 / CUP1, 403, 426; SKS 20, 223, NB 2:211 / JP 2, 1510; SKS 27, 277, Pap. 283:1 / JP 3, 2349.

14. Bernier has a long, critical discussion of Theunissen but he does not discuss Grøn's development of Theunissen's reading. Grøn claims that despair gives up hope, whereas Bernier claims that it rejects hope. However, Kierkegaard's point seems to be that despair abandons human hope *and* rejects Christian hope against hope. See Bernier 2015, chapter 4; cf. Grøn 1997, 142ff.; Theunissen 2005.

15. Cf. Roberts 2003, 192f., 200f. Kierkegaard endorses Paul's statement that someone who only hopes for this life is the most miserable of all. SKS 8, 329 / UD, 228, cf. CUP1, 389 / SKS 7, 355.

16. For Kierkegaard's pragmatism about belief, see Evans 1982; Emmanuel 1996; Fremstedal 2014, chapter 6. Kierkegaard does not distinguish between belief and faith, since the Danish *"Tro"* covers both terms, just like the German *"Glaube."*

17. Hope depends on *commanded* love: "Only when it is a duty to love, only then is love . . . eternally and happily secured against despair" (SKS 9, 36 / WL, 29).

18. Indeed, it is possible to be in despair without knowing it. This is a form of self-deception Kierkegaard calls "inauthentic despair." See SKS 11, 138–57, 209, 212 / SUD, 22–42, 96, 99f.

19. A similar point is made by Martin, who writes, "[T]here is no tight correlation between satisfying your desire and being satisfied with what you get. Hence the saying: Be careful what you wish for, lest you get it. . . . Even when realization brings satisfaction, the satisfaction is short lived, as we adjust and take for granted what we gained" (Martin 2012, 98).

REFERENCES

Kierkegaard's Writings

CA: *Concept of Anxiety*. Princeton: Princeton University Press, 1980.
CD: *Christian Discourses*. Princeton: Princeton University Press, 2009.
CUP1: *Concluding Unscientific Postscript to Philosophical Fragments*, vol. 1. Princeton: Princeton University Press, 1992.
EO2: *Either/Or*, Part II. Princeton: Princeton University Press, 1990.
EUD: *Eighteen Upbuilding Discourses*. Princeton: Princeton University Press, 1990.
FSE: *For Self-Examination*. Princeton: Princeton University Press, 1990.
JP: *Søren Kierkegaard's Journals and Papers*, 7 vols. Bloomington: Indiana University Press, 1967–1978.
KJN: *Kierkegaard's Journals and Notebooks*. Princeton: Princeton University Press, 2007ff.
Pap.: *Søren Kierkegaards Papirer*. 2nd. edition, 16 vols. Copenhagen: Gyldendal, 1968–1978.
SKS: *Søren Kierkegaards Skrifter*, 28 vols. Copenhagen: Gad, 1997–2013.
SUD: *The Sickness unto Death*. Princeton: Princeton University Press, 1983.
UD: *Upbuilding Discourses in Various Spirits*. Princeton: Princeton University Press, 2009.
WL: *Works of Love*. Princeton: Princeton University Press, 1998.

Other Works

Adams, Robert. 1987. *The Virtue of Faith and Other Essays in Philosophical Theology*. Oxford: Oxford University Press.
Beiser, Frederick. 2016. *Weltschmertz: Pessimism in German Philosophy 1860–1900*. Oxford University Press.
Bernier, Mark. 2015. *The Task of Hope in Kierkegaard*. Oxford: Oxford University Press.

Burgess, Andrew. 1994. "*Forstand* in the Swendson-Lowrie Correspondence and in the 'Metaphysical Caprice.'" In *Philosophical Fragments and Johannes Climacus*, edited by Robert Perkins (*International Kierkegaard Commentary*, vol. 7), 109–28. Macon, GA: Mercer University Press.

Davenport, John. 2008. "Faith as Eschatological Trust in *Fear and Trembling*." In *Ethics, Love, and Faith in Kierkegaard*, edited by Edward Mooney, 196–233. Indianapolis: Indiana University Press.

———. 2012. *Narrative Identity, Autonomy, and Mortality: From Frankfurt and MacIntyre to Kierkegaard*. London: Routledge.

———. 2013. "Selfhood and Spirit." In *The Oxford Handbook of Kierkegaard*, edited by J. Lippitt and G. Pattison, 230–51. Oxford: Oxford University Press.

Emmanuel, S. E. 1996. *Kierkegaard and the Concept of Revelation*. Albany: State University of New York Press.

Evans, C. S. 1982. *Subjectivity and Religious Belief: An Historical, Critical Study*. Washington, DC: University Press of America.

Fendt, Gene. 1990. *For What May I Hope? Thinking with Kant and Kierkegaard*. Bern: Peter Lang.

Fremstedal, Roe. 2014. *Kierkegaard and Kant on Radical Evil and the Highest God: Virtue, Happiness, and the Kingdom of God*. Basingstoke: Palgrave Macmillan.

———. 2016. "Kierkegaard and Nietzsche: Despair and Nihilism Converge." In *Modernity— Unity in Diversity? Essays in Honour of Helge Høibraaten*, edited by K. K. Mikalsen, Erling Skjei, and Audun Øfsti, 455–77. Oslo: Novus.

———. 2019. "Kierkegaard's Post-Kantian Approach to Anthropology and Selfhood." In *The Kierkegaardian Mind*, edited by Patrick Stokes, Eleanor Helms and Adam Buben (*Routledge Philosophical Minds*), 319–30. London: Routledge.

Gouwens, David. 1996. *Kierkegaard as a Religious Thinker*. Cambridge: Cambridge University Press, 1996.

Grøn, Arne. 1997. *Subjektivitet og negativitet: Kierkegaard*. Copenhagen: Gyldendal.

Hannay, Alastair. 2006. *Kierkegaard and Philosophy: Selected Essays*. London: Routledge.

Hare, J. E. 2002. *The Moral Gap: Kantian Ethics, Human Limits, and God's Assistance*. Oxford: Clarendon Press.

Korsgaard, Christine. 1996. *The Sources of Normativity*, edited by Onora O'Neill. Cambridge: Cambridge University Press.

Kosch, Michelle. 2006. *Freedom and Reason in Kant, Schelling, and Kierkegaard*. Oxford: Oxford University Press.

Lippitt, John. 2013. *Kierkegaard and the Problem of Self-Love*. Cambridge: Cambridge University Press.

———. 2015. "Learning to Hope: The Role of Hope in *Fear and Trembling*." In *Kierkegaard's* Fear and Trembling: *A Critical Guide*, edited by Daniel Conway, 122–41. Cambridge: Cambridge University Press.

Martin, M. K. 2012. *Happiness and the Good Life*. Oxford: Oxford University Press.

McDonald, William. 2014. "Hope." In *Kierkegaard's Concepts: Envy to Incognito*, edited by S. M. Emmanuel, William McDonald, and Jon Stewart (*Kierkegaard Research: Sources, Reception and Resources*, vol. 15, tome III), 163–68. Farnham: Ashgate.

Nietzsche, Friedrich. 1968. *The Will to Power*. New York: Random House.

———. 1999. *Kritische Studienausgabe*, vols. 1–15. Berlin: de Gruyter.

———. 2006. *Thus Spoke Zarathustra*, edited by Adrian del Caro and Robert Pippin. Cambridge: Cambridge University Press.

———. 2008. *Human, All Too Human and Beyond Good and Evil*, edited by H. Zimmern and P. V. Cohn. Hertfordshire: Wordsworth.

O'Neill, Onora. 1997. *Kant on Reason and Religion*. The Tanner Lectures on Human Values, 1995–1996. Salt Lake City: University of Utah Press.

Reginster, Bernard. 2008. *The Affirmation of Life: Nietzsche on Overcoming Nihilism*. London: Harvard University Press.

Roberts, R. C. 2003. "The Virtue of Hope in *Eighteen Upbuilding Discourses.*" In *Eighteen Upbuilding Discourses*, edited by Robert Perkins (*International Kierkegaard Commentary*, vol. 5), 181–203. Macon, GA: Mercer University Press.

Rudd, Anthony. 2012. *Self, Value, and Narrative: A Kierkegaardian Approach*. Oxford: Oxford University Press.

Schopenhauer, Arthur. 1969. *The World as Will and Representation*, vol. 1. New York: Dover,1969.

———. 1974. *Parerga and Paralipomena*, vol. 2. Translated by E. F. J. Payne. Oxford: Clarendon, 1974.

Simmons, J. Aaron. 2017. "Living Joyfully after Losing Social Hope: Kierkegaard and Chrétien on Selfhood and Eschatological Expectation." *Religions* 8, no. 3, 33: 1–15, https://doi.org/10.3390/rel8030033.

Stokes, Patrick. 2015. *The Naked Self: Kierkegaard and Personal Identity*. Oxford: Oxford University Press.

Sweeney, Terence. 2016. "Hope against Hope: Søren Kierkegaard on the Breath of Eternal Possibility." *Philosophy and Theology* 28, no. 1: 165–84.

Theunissen, 2005. Michael. *Kierkegaard's Concept of Despair*. Princeton: Princeton University Press.

Westphal, Merold. 2014. *Kierkegaard's Concept of Faith*. Grand Rapids, MI: Eerdmans.

Chapter Six

Pragmatist Hope

Sarah M. Stitzlein

Pragmatism offers one of the most sustained accounts of hope in any philo-sophical tradition; yet, many key pragmatists have not discussed hope expli-citly or in depth. Instead, hope is a concept that arises out of central elements of pragmatism, including its accounts of truth, inquiry, meliorism, growth, and habits. While it may seem odd to write a chapter locating hope within the history of philosophy using philosophers who have not actually said much about it, I intend to reveal how integral hope is to classic pragmatism and how it plays a more overt role within neo- and contemporary pragmatism.

In this chapter, I will trace the origins of hope within early American pragmatism. Even though often implicit within classic pragmatist writings, I will tease out a pragmatist account of hope as a set of habits that lead one to act to improve one's life and that of others. For pragmatists, to hope is to recognize the difficulty of current circumstances, but approach them with thoughtful action, emphasizing effort, and believing that things can be im-proved. That is not to say that there are not significant differences among the views of pragmatists, but I focus largely here on what unites them in their understanding of hope. I will then show how this view further developed within the more explicit writings on social and political life penned by recent pragmatists.

COMMON WAYS OF UNDERSTANDING HOPE

Pragmatist hope is distinct in that it grows out of and is closely tied to real world circumstances, plays out through habits, and is richly social, rather than individualist. In order to begin to distinguish this unique character of pragmatist hope, it's worthwhile to first clarify ways in which hope is more commonly understood. Doing so offers a useful foil for revealing key differences in pragmatist understanding. For many people, hope is seen as an emotion, a feeling we have that motivates us to have certain outlooks on the world. Many philosophers, however, argue that hope is a combination of desire and belief, where one desires a certain outcome, but is uncertain about whether it may be obtained (Martin 2014). These desires are for things that we want to occur or be fulfilled, but are sufficiently uncertain, such that we cannot count or plan on them. Many theologians, however, locate hope in an individual's faith in a deity who will act on his or her behalf (Godfrey 1987 and Mittleman 2009). Finally, some psychologists describe hope as an individual's use of willpower and "waypower" to achieve clearly stated goals (Snyder).

While the theologians direct our attention to deities and psychologists emphasize that we should hope regardless of real world constraints, pragmatist hope, as I will show, is firmly rooted in the real circumstances of life on Earth. And while theologians, psychologists, and many philosophers operating in the desire-belief paradigm describe hope in individualist terms, pragmatists work to encompass the larger social process of hoping. I will show how pragmatist hope connects individuals to other people and can be used to not only pursue our individual goals, but also to enrich our experiences in communities.

A NEW UNDERSTANDING OF HOPE ARISES FROM CLASSICAL PRAGMATISTS

Even though early American pragmatists said little directly about hope, their writings are richly connected to central aspects of hope through discussions of truth, inquiry, meliorism, and imagination. Classical pragmatists, including Peirce, James, and Dewey, began to more fully articulate pragmatism in the late 1800s and early 1900s. Pragmatism, more than an *-ism*, is at heart a method—a way of going about the world, inquiring into problems, and reconstructing our world to enable us to better flourish. In James's words, pragmatism "does not stand for any special results. It is a method only" (James 1907). Relying upon man's intellect, empirical experimentation, and imagination, pragmatism is anti-foundational. Notably, the resulting implication for hope is that it is not based in fixed truths, theological sources, or messianic political figures; rather, it is a human creation.

Truth

A pragmatist account of truth begins with Peirce who offered a maxim that his followers picked up and expanded upon: "Consider what effects, that might conceivably have practical bearings, we conceive the object of our conception to have. Then, our conception of these effects is the whole of our conception of the object" (Peirce [1878] 1992, 124). Here we see the beginning of a call to determining truth via consequences insofar as Peirce emphasizes how those consequences shape our conception of an object. For classical pragmatists who built off the initial work of Peirce, ideas become true insofar as they "work" for us, fruitfully combine our experiences, and lead us to further experiences that satisfy our needs. Unlike truth more commonly understood as a corresponding match between proposition and reality, pragmatist truth is something that occurs when the goals of human flourishing are satisfied, at least temporarily. Notably, determining truth is typically a social endeavor, rather than an independent one. Truth as "what works" is that which helps us navigate the world, avoid difficulties, and get out of problematic situations. In James's words, "Truth *happens* to an idea" as we trace and determine its practical consequences, often through inquiry and experimentation that validates our hypotheses and experiences (James 1907).

Determining truth is not an independent practice. Pragmatists argue that we must consider how to grow and flourish alongside others as we craft our goals and determine what is truthful in the world. As such, the hope that arises from our resulting truth claims is not merely individualist, but rather social. This is one component of the more richly social nature of pragmatist hope.

Inquiry

Classical pragmatists were committed to scientific inquiry and empirical experimentation, grounded in naturalism and held open to revision through fallibilism. Such an approach tends to break down simplistic dualisms dividing theory and practice, though pragmatists have varied in their adherence to one end of the spectrum or the other, with Peirce emphasizing the theoretical, neopragmatist Richard Rorty emphasizing the practical, and Dewey attempting to collapse the dichotomy altogether. Shared inquiry is a way to solve problems, whether they be personal or social, and a way of living democratically together, thereby further tying together pragmatism with the origins and goals of early America. Within inquiry, the focus is less on what we can know for certain and more on how we can learn and how we can change— both ourselves and the world around us. Classical pragmatists were especially interested in habits as the key platform for such learning and changing, which I will say much more about later.

For Dewey, hope sometimes arises within the midst of despair, when we have lost our way and are struggling to move forward. Dewey describes these moments as "indeterminate situations." He uses "despair," for example, to characterize the mood following World War I, as people around the world struggled to determine how to recover from the war, how to deal with significant loss of life and property, and more (Dewey [1929] 1988, 276). He turns to the process of inquiry via the empirical method to help us explore those situations, consider possible courses of action, and test out various solutions. It is inquiry that helps us to understand, act upon, and reconstruct our environments and our experiences so that we are able to move forward out of the indeterminate situation. In a richly cognitive and often social practice, inquiry invokes curiosity and problem solving to move us out of ruts. While some people may be prone to lingering in despair, it is inquiry and experimentation that moves pragmatists from despair to hope.

Meliorism

Most significant to the notion of hope, classical pragmatists upheld meliorism as, in Dewey's words, "the idea that at least there is a sufficient basis of goodness in life and its conditions so that by thought and earnest effort we may constantly make things better" (Dewey [1916] 1980, 294). Pragmatism acknowledges the complexities and challenges of our circumstances, yet aims to approach them practically, with intelligent inquiry and thoughtful action, believing that those conditions can be improved. Thus, pragmatism doesn't believe, as an optimist might, in inevitable progress, but rather issues a call to action. Dewey explains that it would be foolish to believe that there is "an automatic and wholesale progress in human affairs," insisting instead that betterment "depends upon deliberative human foresight and socially constructive work" (Aronson 2017, 92).

Neither is pragmatism aligned with pessimism, insofar as pragmatism asserts the possibility of improving our world and our experiences in it, rather than accepting those conditions as fixed or effort as futile. Because simple optimists may believe the situation will necessarily work out for the best and the pessimist may believe that intervention is futile and the outcome is doomed, both optimism and pessimism can be paralyzing. Meliorism, however, demands action in order to fulfill the possibility of bettering the world (Dewey [1920] 1982, 181–82).

Such efforts are rarely undertaken alone, instead they are tied to others who are working together to solve problems. Pragmatists believe people should work together, focusing on the ways that their actions can improve the world. Future-directed meliorism, then, also serves to encourage critique and dissent into currently problematic ways of being and, through exploring hypotheses about those circumstances, gives rise to action to change them. Contemporary pragmatist Cornel West distinguishes hope from optimism and gets at its more active spirit when he says, "Optimism adopts the role of the spectator who surveys the evidence in order to infer that things are going to get better. Yet when we know that the evidence does not look good. . . .

Hope enacts the stance of the participant who actively struggles against the evidence" (West 2004, 296).

The current of meliorism and its call to hopeful action runs strongest in the work of Dewey. Robert Westbrook goes so far as to call it "radically democratic meliorism" (Westbrook 2005, 205). It holds that our hope must be cautious and contingent, open to criticism and validation (Green 2008, 78–79). Because of this, meliorism fits well with democracy as a way of life where our hopes can be nurtured together and where inquiry tests and revises what we believe to be true or desirable. Additionally, meliorism is aligned with a belief in the agency of people, trusting that they can have significant impact on the world and may improve it (Stitzlein 2018, 229–50). Yet, Dewey also recognized that action can be inhibited by stagnant and entrenched habits of individuals and culture in a democracy. As a result, Dewey turned to education, arguing that new and more flexible habits can be cultivated to welcome and fulfill the call to action to improve the world. But critics warn that pragmatism may acquiesce too much to the status quo, failing to recognize the need for change, and even then, only changing gradually (Berman 2016, 173–88). Moreover, action may be impeded by political power dynamics that make change difficult or impossible (Westbrook 2005, 208). Nonetheless, meliorism is central to pragmatist hope because it urges action in order to fulfill the possibility of bettering the world, suggesting that hope is active and effort-driven.

CONTRIBUTIONS OF THE CLASSICAL PRAGMATISTS

Method, truth, inquiry, and meliorism developed across the writings of the classical pragmatists and can be constructed into an account of hope today. Along the way, each of the three key classical pragmatists, Peirce, James, and Dewey, contributed to the understanding of hope in significant ways.

Charles Sanders Peirce

Peirce primarily discusses hope within his account of inquiry. There, hope is a condition where we believe that inquiry is worthwhile and will contribute to new ideas and truth. It leads us to view the world as intelligible to us. He says, "We are therefore bound to hope that, although the possible explanations of our facts may be strictly innumerable, yet our mind will be able in some finite number of guesses, to guess the sole true explanation of them" (Cooke 2005, 651–74, and Peirce [1878] 1992, 106). For, without hope that our questions can be answered, we may never initiate inquiry (Cooke 2005, 651). And we must have hope in order to view the slow progress of scientific inquiry and experimentation as eventually warranting worthwhile results.

Peirce describes hope as a sentiment and yet celebrates its role in logical thinking:

> So this sentiment is rigidly demanded by logic. If its object were any determinate fact, any private interest, it might conflict with the results of knowledge and so with itself; but when its object is of a nature as wide as the community can turn out to be, it is always a hypothesis uncontradicted by facts and justified by its indispensableness for making action rational. (quoted in Cooke 2005, 654)

He further says,

> We are, doubtless, in the main logical animals, but we are not perfectly so. Most of us, for example, are naturally more sanguine and hopeful than logic would justify. We seem to be so constituted that in the absence of any facts to go upon we are happy and self satisfied; so that the effect of experience is continually to contract our hopes and aspirations. Yet a lifetime of the application of this corrective does not usually eradicate our sanguine disposition. Where hope is unchecked by any experience, it is likely that our optimism is extravagant. (Peirce [1878] 1992)

Elizabeth Cooke rightfully interprets this passage to show that hope alone is not enough, but rather its value depends on how well it is informed by experience and not simply wishful thinking. And, while hope is not rational, it is an impulse that can be put to good use to urge us forward in inquiry. Hope is useful because it predisposes us to inquiry and to the testing of ideas in experience. It works, in part through imagination and hypothesis formation, to come up with guesses and ideas that extend beyond the current state of affairs or what we know. Peirce concludes, "Despair is insanity. . . . We must therefore be guided by the rule of hope" (Misak 2013, 59). Peirce notes that when we lack hope, we invite the despair that comes from insane practices. Despair is understood differently by several key pragmatists, which is notable given that despair is often viewed as the opposite of hope. While I will not go into those distinctions here, I will note how some of the scholars have used despair in order to illuminate their views on hope.

It may be argued that Peirce maintains a greater distinction between theory and practice than his later colleagues (Bergman 2012, 125, 48). This distinction leads him to be less interested in the real problems of our social and political lives that later fascinated and motivated Dewey. And it leads him to be less of a meliorist because he is less focused on the outcomes of bettering reality on the lives of people and communities. Nonetheless, like Mats Bergman, I also hold that Peirce does have some meliorist tendencies. Namely Peirce is the first pragmatist to emphasize the role of habits, which he rather counterintuitively posits as fluid, noting "the power of readily taking habits and of readily throwing them off" (quoted in Shade 2001, 189).

This unusual notion of habit is further developed by later pragmatists and is key to the sense of pragmatist hope that I lay out here. Peirce sees habits as learned and acquired, allowing opportunity to influence and change them. He points to imagination and intellectual experimentation as ways to call our habits into question and to change them for the better, suggesting a form of applied meliorism. Indeed, he says, "continual amelioration of our own habits . . . is the only alternative to a continual deterioration of them" (Bergman 2013, 749). Peirce largely stays at this level of personal change however, while Dewey and later pragmatists describe meliorism in terms of changing and improving social and political problems as well as the world itself (Bergman 2012). Peirce retains a more individualist view of hope, but his use of hope in his understanding of inquiry and habits paves the way for later pragmatists to develop a more social and political view of hope.

William James

James significantly contributed to the pragmatist account of truth. To get at truth, James turned traditional, foundational thinking on its head. He claimed that pragmatism is "[t]he attitude of looking away from first things, principles, 'categories,' supposed necessity; and of looking towards last things, fruits, consequences, facts" (James 1907, 32, and Stuhr 2010, 198). Like Peirce before him, James emphasized consequences, arguing that "[t]he whole function of philosophy ought to be to find out what definite difference it will make to you and me, at definite instants of our life, if this world-formula or that world-formula be the true one" (James 1906). Yet, James recognized that in order to bring about desired ends, we require certain material conditions as well as a meliorist spirit to act in the world and on imaginative ideas.

Ruth Anna Putnam locates three propositions of James's meliorism:

1. The world is not perfect, or evil is real.
2. The future is not determined; human beings cooperating can make the world better.
3. A finite deity is their helper, *primus inter pares*, in this endeavor. (Putnam 2010, 187)

She sees the first two as constituting meliorism in general and the third as James's particular theistic meliorism, which generally has not been adopted by other pragmatists, so I will set it aside here.

Focusing on the first two propositions reveals that meliorism depends on trusting that others will also make effort to improve the world. Moreover, while the world is not perfect, we can form ideals in our minds that better equip us to undertake such work, whether it be together or parallel. James explains that the more conscious we are of those ideals, the more they can motivate action (Stroud 2009, 382). Through these two propositions, James moves beyond Peirce, who largely constrained his talk of hope to its role within scientific inquiry, into everyday human struggles in the real world and our ability to meet and alleviate them with effort. And he emphasizes the role of cooperation in working toward change and thereby achieving objects or objectives of hope.

James turns to schools as a site of building awareness of ideals: "Education, enlarging as it does our horizon and perspective, is a means of multiplying our ideals, of bringing new ones into view" (James 1912, 83, and Stroud 2009, 382). Schools not only nurture ideals, they also cultivate habits that enable us to enact and pursue them by attuning us to the present so that we can adapt it for the future we desire. And they can offer a space where we learn how to trust one another in our efforts to make the world better, thereby building a culture of support for our endeavors. In the meantime, that world "still in the process of making" requires a certain sort of fortitude and hardiness on our part, for while we must trust each other, we cannot rely on supposed abiding foundations (James 1906 and Koopman 2009, 20). This persistence plays out as habits that enable us to pursue ideals as the content of our hopes, hopes which have notably been constructed and shared in the social context of schooling.

John Dewey

Even more so than James, it is Dewey who turns to education as a way to support hope. For Dewey, the process of education begins with his account of growth. When we encounter indeterminate situations where we aren't sure how to proceed, we have to figure out how to reconstruct our world and ourselves so that we can begin to move smoothly from activity to activity once again. Growth describes the process of using inquiry to reconstruct ourselves and our environment, enabling our experiences to continue in a chain so that one can live satisfactorily.

Many people assume that growth should be directed toward a fixed goal, but Dewey warns that this way of thinking emphasizes the static end, rather than the process of growing, one he sees as itself educative and worthwhile. Giving up the focus on a clear end point, Dewey's account of growth tends not to march in a clear and linear path. Instead, he describes trajectories that are more complicated, often shifting as we encounter obstacles in the environment. Moreover, Dewey shows that holding out a fixed goal may inadvertently close off possible versions of our future, thereby limiting us and our potential. Instead, Dewey argues that we must continually inquire into our changing circumstances, develop new hypotheses about them, and revise the aims that result.

Rather than overarching goals or final end points, Dewey operates with what he calls "ends-in-view," which are relatively close and feasible, even if difficult to achieve. Those ends-in-view guide us as we conduct inquiry along the way and help to make us resourceful and open to change. Each fulfilled ends-in-view helps to sustain our hope by highlighting meaningful headway and directing our future actions. Ends-in-view later become means to future ends, working in an ongoing continuum. This sustenance of hope differs from theological accounts which are difficult to sustain on faith alone and may leave believers frustrated at an apparent lack of improvement. It also differs from psychological accounts, include recent positive psychology and calls for grit, which focus on large, far-off, and challenging goals that one must hold tenaciously and approach directly.

Many people think of hope as goal-directed and future-oriented. While objects of hope for pragmatists may temporarily serve as ends-in-view, the practice of hope moves us forward through inquiry and experimentation as we pursue our complicated trajectory. It helps to unify our past, present, and future. Hope, then, is not just about a vision of the future, but rather a way of living in the present that is informed by the past and what is anticipated to come. Whereas utopian views of what could be may actually immobilize one and may exhaust one in the present, pragmatist hope is always tied to what one *is* doing and feasibly *can do* in the present, especially when equipped with knowledge of the past (Stitzlein 2018). Dewey, then, focuses more on how we live in hope and openness to opportunity and change, rather than the particular ultimate hopes that we may hold.

Summarizing Dewey's account of growth and its related contributions to hope, Richard Rorty concludes, "Hope—the ability to believe that the future will be unspecifiably different from, and unspecifiably freer than, the past—is the condition of growth" (Rorty 1999, 20).

Habits

A concept running throughout the work of the classical pragmatists, and which becomes central to a pragmatist account of hope, is that of habits. Habits begin with impulses, basic and often unintelligent natural urges to act. Dewey even locates hope initially within those basic impulses when he says, "But man as man still has the dumb pluck of the animal. He has endurance, hope, curiosity, eagerness, love of action" (Dewey [1922] 1983, 199–200, and Fishman and McCarthy 2007, 15). And Peirce sees a natural bent toward hope in how we are prone to approach inquiry, even though it is not well refined.

Over time our impulses tend to collect and be shaped by our experiences with the world and with cultural norms, eventually molding those impulses into habits. People tend to have many habits in common because of their similar transactions with the world and some of those habits then become recognized as customs, for they are typical ways in which people in a community act. These habits are often learned indirectly throughout our lives, but their cultivation is most overt in schools, where certain habits are directly taught, some are implicitly shared, and others develop through our imitation of teachers and peers. Within classrooms, we reflect upon our impulses and overtly subject them to intelligent critique.

Notably, pragmatists offer a version of habits that differs from that understood by most people who think of habits as dull routines that we repeat exactly and indefinitely. For pragmatists, especially Dewey and those who followed him, habits are predispositions to act and we enact them with ease and familiarity because they have proven to help us live fruitfully in the past. Dewey adds, "Any habit marks an *inclination*—an active preference and choice for the conditions involved in its exercise. A habit does not wait, Micawber-like, for a stimulus to turn up so that it may get busy; it actively seeks for occasions to pass into full operation" (Dewey [1916] 1980, 53). Habits for pragmatists, seek to be put into action. They are not mere defaults that we thoughtlessly rely upon.

Because habits are urges to act, they give rise to desires. Importantly, habits also offer a way to pursue those desires, often through thought or bodily movement. For Dewey, habits "do all the perceiving, recognizing, imagining, recalling, judging, conceiving and reasoning that is done" (Dewey [1922] 1983, 124). They organize our perceptions based on past experiences so that we can form ideas about the world that we test out in order to overcome indeterminate situations. As we encounter new stimuli, habits help us to filter and make sense of those encounters, enabling us to develop ideas about them. Habits then provide the know-how to act in the world because they entail our working capacities. Finally, we reflect on our experiences and our inquiries to determine which habits bring about our growth by promoting smooth and just transactions with the world and with other people (Stitzlein 2018).

Dewey explains, "All habits are demands for certain kinds of activity; and they constitute the self" (Dewey [1922] 1983, 21). So, we *are* a collection of habits. Habits shape who and what we are, including how we understand ourselves and how others see us. Whereas many people see habits as fixed and unchanging, pragmatists see considerable flexibility. This begins with the fluid description of habits offered by Peirce and continues into Dewey's account of habit formation and change in *Human Nature and Conduct*. When we engage in inquiry, we aim to not only change our world, but also often change ourselves, including our habits that may no longer be serving us well. Rather than being unthinking actions, it is the intellectual aspect of habits that gives them meaning and keeps people flexible and capable of growth. When we are facing despair, we may find that our habits are no longer meeting our needs. One option is to succumb to bad habits that lack flexibility, such as cynicism or apathy, but those result in stagnation and fail to keep up with the changing world. Pragmatists depict flexible habits as an avenue for reorienting ourselves in those moments, for making ourselves anew, and for moving forward in hope (Stitzlein 2008).

Hope, understood as a set of habits, brings together proclivities and intelligent reflection to motivate one to act while providing a sustainable structure for doing so. Hope is a way of projecting ourselves toward a better future, positioning us toward action. In Dewey's words, pragmatist habits of hope are "active attitudes of welcome" (Dewey [1916/1917] 1983, 50). They are ways we greet the world and are disposed toward action in it. Unlike common understanding of habits as mere thoughtless, repeated action, pragmatist habits of hope are attitudes and dispositions that shape how we transact with the world. They often lead us to seek out or create possibilities when we face challenges. Differing from individualist accounts of hope in terms of desire for a self-serving goal or faith in other savior figures, habits of hope entail action that moves us toward better ways of living. Hope helps us envision a desired future that arises practically out of our conditions and with knowledge of the past. Yet, we move beyond those conditions through assessing possibilities, determining whether outcomes are desirable, and imagining how we might rearrange our circumstances to achieve new and better conditions (Godfrey 1987, 169). Hope, working as habits, encourages us to seek out or imaginatively create possibilities when we encounter roadblocks.

BRIDGING CLASSICAL AND CONTEMPORARY PRAGMATISM WITH HOPE AS HABITS

While the notion of hope as a set of habits is not directly named within the writing of classical pragmatists in the late nineteenth and early twentieth centuries, it derives from their work and has been picked up by more recent pragmatists in the late twentieth and early twenty-first centuries, including myself. Building on this trajectory, I have argued that hope, as a set of habits and their enactment, is a disposition toward possibility and change for the betterment of oneself and/or others (Stitzlein 2018). Such habits unite our proclivities and intelligent reflection to motivate us to act, while at the same time providing us pathways to do so. Hope, then, is a way of positioning us toward action and projecting ourselves toward an improved future. And, as with other pragmatist habits, habits of hope can be cultivated and nurtured through education.

Habits of hope are dispositions that influence how we transact with our environments. In particular, they tend to provoke us to seek out or create imaginative possibilities when we encounter roadblocks. Unlike other accounts of hope that put hope in a savior figure or in a distant and unchanging goal, pragmatist habits of hope respond to the problems of the present using knowledge of the past so that we can craft a better future ourselves. These habits support us as we test hypotheses and imagine alternative ways that we might reconstruct our circumstances in order to better our lives.

This understanding of habits of hope brings together pragmatist notions of truth, inquiry, growth, and meliorism. Each of those elements unites us with the other people, insofar as our well-being is intimately connected to other people who are inquiring into and acting upon the world. Collectively, habits of hope operate more like hoping, an ongoing activity. Notice how that differs from saying that one "has hope," as though hope is an object that can be passively possessed, held, or lost. Such active doing of hope bolsters courage and agency amongst hopers, helping them to identify opportunities to improve their circumstances and to impact the world. Contemporary Peirce commentator, Elizabeth Cooke concludes that hope "functions as a habit of openness, a willingness to act, despite a lack of expectation—to take a leap" (Cooke 2005, 664).

As this notion of hope has been developed by recent pragmatist philosophers, we see their accounts following in the spirit of Dewey, bridging the individual with the social and political. Rather than hope being something that we hold internally and may direct toward a deity or something that we privately engage as we pursue our individual goals, hope emerges in the midst of social and political contexts. While habits of hope are housed within and compose individuals, hope is not individualist. Habits are shaped by our communities and our experiences with others. Habits of hope employ the resources of our community and our relationship with others in it to provide means for us to pursue our desires, many of which themselves have been influenced by those around us. Insofar as our own growth must often account for living fruitfully with others, our habits of hope must account for, and often engage with, others. As a result, we often enact habits of hope through collective work that seeks to improve our world physically, socially, or politically.

To achieve our ends frequently requires collaboration and, especially, listening to the needs and ideas of others. Dewey describes this as "an attitude of mind which actively welcomes suggestions and relevant information from all sides" ([1916] 1980, 182). While listening often is confined only to our most immediate relationships or communities, the increasing interconnectedness of our decisions and implications on others, should urge us to listen to and include others—something contemporary pragmatist Judith Green dubs "a global network of social hope" (Green 2008, 129). Hoping connects us to other people. Inquiry and meliorism connects us to an understanding of the past and a vision of the future. These connections between people, ideas, and imagination, provide us with resources needed to pursue our ends-in-view and enable us to see that we can, indeed, improve the world. But this comes with recognition of our contingency and mutual dependence, as well as the limits of our own agency. Pragmatist hope relies on trusting other people and trust in the possibility of bettering the world.

CONTRIBUTIONS OF
NEO- AND CONTEMPORARY PRAGMATISTS

Hope has gained an increasingly prevalent role in the works of neo- and contemporary pragmatists, especially within the work of Richard Rorty, Judith Green, Cornel West, Patrick Shade, and Colin Koopman. I will briefly summarize some of the key ways in which each of these scholars has contributed to and furthered a pragmatist concept of hope.

Richard Rorty

Unlike his predecessors who rarely mentioned hope, Rorty gives hope more explicit attention and even includes it in one of his book titles. His writing ushered in a new generation of pragmatist commentary on and employment of the notion of hope. He introduces hope largely as a foil to the quest for truth that other philosophers have supported. He said, "[S]ubstituting hope for knowledge, substituting the idea that the ability to be citizens of the full-fledged democracy which is yet to come, rather than the ability to grasp truth, is what is important about being human" (Rorty 2000, 3). So, rather than pursuing truth, Rorty insists upon the more radical project of aiming for hope in America. This is, in part, because, like earlier pragmatists, he values beliefs insofar as they are useful to us and he sees beliefs based in narratives of hope as especially useful for shaping our lives. Those narratives lack foundations, rather are based in the contingency of human lives and experiences, often providing descriptions of past suffering, an opportunity to build solidarity with others, and a vision of an improved future. They can be used to guide meliorist efforts through employing courage and imaginative experimentation, perhaps a bit more boldly and freely than suggested by some of his pragmatist peers.

Judith Green

Like Rorty, Green relinquishes what Dewey called, "the quest for certainty," yet she does not go as far as Rorty in letting go of truth entirely. Instead, she champions a

> a democratic social epistemology that inclusively yet critically recombines and mutually corrects all the perspectival knowledges that flow from differing,

often rival social locations, deepening these provisional knowledges with those existential truths-in-living on which each of us is betting our lives, and balancing its live intellectual "water quality" by adding the often reliable though always revisable generalizations of open, collaborative, future-oriented sciences and other cross-disciplinary inquires. (Green 2008, 107)

In this regard, Green reflects a more traditional pragmatist account of truth.

Whereas Green believes that Rorty focuses a bit too much on hopeful narratives that provide solidarity amongst Americans and a vision of better American life, Green follows the tragic optimism of Viktor Frankl and James Baldwin (Winters 2016, 213). She grounds her hope more firmly in an accounting for the widespread suffering of multiple groups and the bringing of those people together to work toward a new future in light of that past. She then issues a call to her pragmatist peers to be public philosophers who take up the aim of supporting and embodying democratic social hope.

For Green, social hope arises out of experience, endures struggles, brings feelings of safety, and entails creative imagination. As social, hope involves being concerned for and engaged with others. Green believes today's circumstances require not just the national call for hope that Rorty voiced, but a global vision of deeply democratic living. This is because when one group (America) puts its efforts toward hope without regarding the hopeful visions of other people, anti-American frustration grows, perpetuating cycles of hatred and fear (Stitzlein 2009, 657–63).

Cornel West

Cornel West provides a unique contribution to the pragmatist account of truth by tracing the roots of his musically-inspired "blues" version of hope to the struggles of Black folks in America. Like Green, he attends carefully to the harms of the past as he considers hopeful visions of the future. He contends that despair and hope are often intimately connected. He explains, "It is impossible to look honestly at our catastrophic conditions and not have some despair—it is a healthy sign of how deeply we care. It is also a mark of maturity—a rejection of cheap American optimism" (West 2008, 216). Rather than a mere rose-colored glasses outlook on life, West recognizes that things are, in many ways, not getting better and he points to the history of his race for evidence.

Instead, his call to meliorism is one that upholds a belief that other people can do better and an historically informed and wary trust in others. He says, "I never give up on any human being no matter what color, because I believe they all have potential" (West 2008, 41). Moreover, his meliorism is driven by virtues that enable one to flourish as one faces despair, a drive "to try to keep struggling for more love, more justice, more freedom, and more democracy" (2008, 217). Such a hope—one that is closely connected to a painful history and ongoing suffering—is, as he says, "always blood-stained and tear-soaked" (2008, 217). Whereas his pragmatist predecessors established that hope must always attend to and grow out of the real conditions of our lives, West drives home the point that those conditions are often quite horrid and that hope is closely related to the despair that those conditions cause. But his call to effort in spite of and because of those conditions is strong: "Real hope is grounded in a particularly messy struggle and it can be betrayed by naïve projections of a better future that ignore the necessity of doing the real work. So what we are talking about is *hope on a tightrope*" (2008, 6).

West's version of hope is situated within his account of prophetic pragmatism. While I will not detail prophetic pragmatism here, it is worthwhile to point out that it entails the sort of critical outlook discussed earlier. It arises from an informed understanding of the atrocities of the past as well as frustrations revealed when our world falls short of visions of what could be. Such a "critical temper," as he calls it, takes despair head on with an "experimental disposition" and a faith in the ability of people to work democratically together (West 2008, 125). "The critical temper motivated by democratic faith yields all-embracing moral and/or religious visions that project credible ameliorative possibilities grounded in present realities in light of systemic structural analyses of the causes of social misery (without reducing all misery to historical causes)" (2008, 125). As a result, West calls for hope as a sort of cultural criticism that reveals injustice, pushes us to act on it, and sustains us through our experiments to alleviate it. For West, this prophetic, blues hope is bolstered by habits of courage and Christian love, which is focused less on a savior figure and more on how people can support each other (2008, 22).

Patrick Shade

Perhaps the pragmatist to contribute most overtly to the notion of hope is Shade. His twenty-first-century writings have articulated how hope operates as an activity—hoping—between a person and her social and natural environments, rather than as a private mental state (Shade 2001, 14). He explains how hope works as habits. Shade offers a three-part account of hope: particular hopes, habits of hope, and the habit of hopefulness. First, particular hopes are of the more familiar and widely understood sort insofar as they are specific ends that we seek to achieve. But "understanding particular hopes requires more than simple reference to an end; what is distinctive about them is that the involve a *commitment to the desirability and realizability of an end in the face of some obstacle which marks the limits of our agency*" (2001, 19). Such an end, then, must be feasibly realizable for the particular individual; hence, it must be practical. They are ends-in-view in the Deweyan sense and therefore help to guide our experiments and our actions. They may be challenging to attain, but they are never entirely out of reach.

Second, habits of hope are the means we use to pursue those ends-in-view, our particular hopes. They enable us to pursue our particular hopes and help us stay committed to doing so. "Chief among them are persistence, resourcefulness, and courage. Habits of persistence sustain us, while habits of resourcefulness guide our active exploration and attempts to transcend our limitations. Courage undergirds our ability to persist and to explore by enabling us to face arduous tasks" (Shade 2001, 77). Like pragmatists before him who valued the plastic and educative nature of habits, Shade adds, "Habits of hope that we do not possess, and yet need, can become ends developed through the process of hoping. The ability to persist, for example, can be acquired or expanded commitment to a hoped-for-ends requires it; hoping provides the opportunity for the development (or, more often, the further development) of each of its dimensions" (2001, 21). His writings provide great detail about how the habits of hope relate to and build upon each other and such a description has opened the door for education-based pragmatists like myself to consider how we might nurture those habits through intellectual reflection and experience (Foote and Stitzlein, 2016, 32–40, and Hytten 2011, 1–3). This most recent work in the field suggests that pragmatist hope has moved from general philosophical idea to applied educational settings, where it can be tested and refined by teachers and students.

Finally, the habit of hopefulness is an orientation to possibility. Hopefulness does not have a specific end, but rather is an openness to living life differently. It is a disposition that sustains us when we have not achieved our particular hopes. Yet, hopefulness is itself supported through engaging with others in nurturing this way of life, thereby revealing its social nature. Hopefulness energizes us to keep trying, even in the face of despair and suffering. Pulling together a hopeful life within democracy,

> hopefulness, especially in the degree to which it is developed through the *coordination* of habits of hope, can itself become a habit of hope. As such a habit it sustains us in pursuing particular hopes. Moreover, hopefulness can become the dominant habit of the self, in which case it functions as a further means to the life of hope; it then provides the basis for a hopeful person and, in turn, for a hopeful community. (Shade 2001, 21–22)

Rather than just being an optimist, like pragmatists before him, Shade turns to meliorism to argue that hopefulness is a proclivity toward making a better future through effort.

Seeing hope as practical, intelligent, and generative activity, Shade concludes that hope entails what he calls "conditional transcendence," where hope has two modes: "being grounded in real conditions and being productive of new and better ones" (Shade 2001, 6–7). Hope enables us to move past our history and the limitations of our environment to create new ways of living, but never to escape those conditions entirely. Pragmatist hope focuses on the agency of people in realistic settings, rather than resorting to supernatural forces or optimistic pipe dreams. But it also recognizes that hope must be realistic and generative, otherwise, as in the case of the poor and racial minority citizens urged to keep on hoping in spite of a long history of seeming insurmountable injustices (perhaps in the spirit of West's blues hope), "[i]f hoping exhausts our resources, it is better not to hope" (2001, 6–7).

Like Rorty and Green, Shade turns to storytelling and communities to nurture hope. Stories engage our imagination, helping us envision alternatives and sometimes urging us to act. Stories also sharpen our skills of inquiry and hypothesis formation, teaching us to attend to what has worked in the past and what might work when tested in our imagination. Storytelling is typically a social endeavor, bringing people together to share in critiquing the past and envisioning the future. Shade recognizes that hope, as habits, is best nurtured in communities where hope is practiced. There, we can learn from and model others. Obviously, this happens within schools, but Shade also points to volunteer organizations. Within such settings, we also come to see how our agency is connected to and sometimes dependent upon that of others.

Colin Koopman

Koopman argues that it is hope that unites the philosophies of the otherwise diverse pragmatists: James, Dewey, Emerson, and Rorty. Indeed, he locates hope at the heart of pragmatism, saying, "I understand pragmatism, and find it at its best, as a philosophical way of taking hope seriously. Pragmatism develops the philosophical resources of hope" (Koopman 2006, 106). His work focuses on how philosophically robust hope operates as meliorism, bringing together the contingent pluralism of James and the humanist effort of Dewey. "As such, meliorism resonates with the central ethical impulse at the heart of pragmatism: democracy. Democracy is the simple idea that political and ethical progress hinges on nothing more than persons, their values, and their actions" (2006, 107). This spirit lingers from the founding days of America described earlier. And, like Rorty and Green before him, Koopman calls for citizens to work together today, using their radical imaginations, to create a new and better nation and world. Reflecting the early roots and corollary growth of pragmatism and democracy, Koopman warns "that a loss of hope is a loss of America itself" (2006, 112). For Koopman, it is meliorism that builds our skills of cultural criticism and sustains the confidence needed to proceed in continually recreating our democratic way of life.

CONCLUSION

From its earliest formations, pragmatism has been engaged with understanding and acting upon hope. Classical pragmatists honed their accounts of truth, inquiry, meliorism, and habits, collectively helping to shape an initial pragmatist notion of hope. This was further developed many decades later by contemporary pragmatists who carefully situated hope within social and political contexts. There, they shed light on the relationship between hope, education, imagination, and agency, while relying upon approaches such as storytelling and solidarity building to bolster hoping. Pragmatist hope is a set of habits that predispose one to possibility and working with others to make the world a better place.

REFERENCES

Aronson, Ronald. 2017. *We: Reviving Social Hope*. Chicago and London: The University of Chicago Press.

Bergman, Mats. 2012. "Improving Our Habits: Peirce and Meliorism." In *The Normative Thought of Charles S. Peirce*, edited by Cornelis De Waal and Krzysztof Piotr Skowroński, 125–48. New York: Fordham University Press. http://dx.doi.org/10.5422/fordham/9780823242443.003.0006.

Bergman, Mats. 2013. "Fields of Rhetoric: Inquiry, Communication, and Learning." *Educational Philosophy and Theory* 45, no. 7 (2013): 737–54.

Bergman, Mats. 2016. "Melioristic Inquiry and Critical Habits: Pragmatism and the Ends of Communication Research." *Empedocles: European Journal for the Philosophy of Communication* 7, no. 2 (2016): 173–88.

Cooke, Elizabeth. 2005. "Transcendental Hope: Peirce, Hookway, and Pihlström on the Conditions for Inquiry," *Transactions of the Charles S. Peirce Society* 41, no. 3 (Summer 2005): 651–74.

Dewey, John. (1916) 1980. "Democracy and Education." In *The Middle Works, 1899–1924*, Volume 7, edited Jo Ann Boydston, 294. Carbondale: Southern Illinois University Press.

Dewey, John. (1916/1917) 1983. "The Need for a Recovery of Philosophy." In *The Middle Works, 1899–1924*, Volume 10, edited by Jo Ann Boydston, 50. Carbondale: Southern Illinois University Press.

Dewey, John. (1920) 1982. "Essays, Miscellany, and Reconstruction in Philosophy." In *The Middle Works, 1899–1924*, Volume 12, edited by Jo Ann Boydston, 181–82. Carbondale: Southern Illinois University Press.

Dewey, John. (1922) 1983. "Human Nature and Conduct." In *The Middle Works, 1899–1924*, Volume 14, edited by Jo Ann Boydston, 199–200. Carbondale: Southern Illinois University Press.

Dewey, John. (1929) 1988. "What I Believe." In *The Later Works, 1925–1953*, Volume 14, edited by Jo Ann Boydston, 267–78. Carbondale: Southern Illinois University Press.

Fishman, Stephen M., and L. McCarthy. 2007. *John Dewey and the Philosophy and Practice of Hope*. Urbana: University of Illinois Press.

Foote, Lori, and Sarah M. Stitzlein. 2016. "Teaching Hope: Cultivating Pragmatist Habits." *Journal of School and Society* 32, no. 2 (2016): 32–40.

Godfrey, Joseph. 1987. *A Philosophy of Human Hope*. Boston: Martinus Nijhoff Publishers.

Green, Judith M. 2008. *Pragmatism and Social Hope: Deepening Democracy in Global Contexts*. New York: Columbia University Press.

Hytten, Kathy. 2011. "Building and Sustaining Hope: A Response to 'Meaningful Hope for Teachers in a Time of High Anxiety and Low Morale.'" *Democracy & Education* 19, no. 1 (2011): 1–3.

James, William. 1906. "Lecture II—What Pragmatism Means." In *Pragmatism: A New Name for Some Old Ways of Thinking*. Project Gutenberg EBook, 2013. Available online at http://www.gutenberg.org/files/5116/5116-h/5116-h.htm.

James, William. 1906. "XI: The Absolute and the Strenuous Life." In *The Meaning of Truth: A Sequel to "Pragmatism."* Project Gutenberg EBook, 2013. Available online at http://www.gutenberg.org/files/5116/5116-h/5116-h.htm.

James, William. 1907. "Lecture II: What Pragmatism Means." In *Pragmatism: A New Name for Some Old Ways of Thinking*. Project Gutenberg EBook, 2013. Available online at http://www.gutenberg.org/files/5116/5116-h/5116-h.htm.

James, William. 1907. "Lecture VI: Pragmatism's Conception of Truth." In *Pragmatism: A New Name for Some Old Ways of Thinking*. Project Gutenberg EBook, 2013. Available online at http://www.gutenberg.org/files/5116/5116-h/5116-h.htm.

James, William. (1907) 1995. *Pragmatism*, edited by Thomas Croft and Philip Smith, 32. New York: Dover Publications.

James, William. 1912. *On Some of Life's Ideals: On a Certain Blindness in Human Beings; What Makes a Life Significant*. New York: Henry Holt and Company, p. 83; here Stroud, "William James on Meliorism," 382.

Koopman, Colin. 2006. "Pragmatism as a Philosophy of Hope: Emerson, James, Dewey, Rorty." *Journal of Speculative Philosophy* 20, no. 2 (2006): 106–16.

Koopman, Colin. 2009. *Pragmatism as Transition: Historicity and Hope in James, Dewey, and Rorty*. New York: Columbia University Press.

Martin, Adrienne. 2014. *How We Hope: A Moral Psychology*. Princeton, NJ: Princeton University Press.

Misak, Cheryl. 2013. *The American Pragmatists*. Oxford: Oxford University Press.

Mittleman, Allan. 2009. *Hope in a Democratic Age: Philosophy, Religion, and Political Theory*. Oxford: Oxford University Press.

Peirce, Charles Sanders. 1934/1935. *Collected Papers of Charles Sanders Peirce Volumes 5–6*, edited by Charles Hartshorne and Paul Weiss, 222. Cambridge, MA: The Belknap Press of Harvard University Press.

Peirce, Charles Sanders. 1958–1966. *Collected Papers of Charles Sanders Peirce*, Volumes I and II: *Principles of Philosophy and Elements of Logic*, edited by Charles Hartshorne and Paul Weiss, 405. Cambridge, MA: Belknap Press of Harvard University Press.

Peirce, Charles Sanders. (1878) 1992. *The Essential Peirce*, Vol. 1: *Selected Philosophical Writings (1867–1893)*, edited by N. Houser and C. Kloesel. Peirce Edition Project. Bloomington: Indiana University Press.

Peirce, Charles Sanders. (1878) 1992. *The Essential Peirce*, Vol. 2: *Selected Philosophical Writings (1893–1913)*, edited by N. Houser and C. Kloesel, 106. Peirce Edition Project. Bloomington: Indiana University Press.

Peirce, Charles Sanders. (1878) 1992. "How To Make Our Ideas Clear." *The Essential Peirce*, Vol. 1: *Selected Philosophical Writings (1867–1893)*, edited by N. Houser and C. Kloesel, 124–41. Peirce Edition Project. Bloomington: Indiana University Press.

Putnam, Ruth Anna. 2010. "Reflections on the Future of Pragmatism," In *100 Years of Pragmatism*, edited by John Stuhr, 185–93. Bloomington: Indiana University Press.

Rorty, Richard. 1999. *Philosophy and Social Hope*. New York: Penguin Books.

Rorty, Richard. 2000. "Universality and Truth." In *Rorty and His Critics*, edited by R. Brandom, 1–30. Oxford: Blackwell.

Shade, Patrick. 2001. *Habits of Hope: A Pragmatic Theory*. Nashville, TN: Vanderbilt University Press.

Stitzlein, Sarah M. 2008. *Breaking Bad Habits of Race and Gender: Transforming Identity in Schools*. Lanham, MD: Rowman & Littlefield.

Stitzlein, Sarah M. 2009. "Reviving Social Hope and Pragmatism in Troubling Times." A review article for *Journal of Philosophy of Education* 43, no. 4 (2009): 657–63.

Stitzlein, Sarah M. 2018. "Hoping and Democracy." *Contemporary Pragmatism*, 15, no. 2 (2018): 229–50.

Stroud, Scott R. 2009. "William James on Meliorism, Moral Ideals, and Business Ethics." *Transactions of the Charles S. Peirce Society: A Quarterly Journal in American Philosophy* 45, no. 3 (2009): 378–401.

Stuhr, John J. 2010. "Looking toward Last Things: James's Pragmatism beyond Its First Century." In *100 Years of Pragmatism*, edited by John Stuhr, 194–208. Bloomington: Indiana University Press.

West, Cornel. 2004. "Prisoners of Hope." *The Impossible Will Take a Little While*, edited by Paul Rogat Loeb, 296. Cambridge, MA: Basic Books.

West, Cornel. 2008. *Hope on a Tightrope*. Carlsbad, CA: SmileyBooks.

Westbrook, Robert B. 2005. *Democratic Hope: Pragmatism and the Politics of Truth*. Cornell University Press.

Winters, Joseph. 2016. *Hope Draped in Black: Race, Melancholy, and the Agony of Progress*. Durham, NC: Duke University Press.

II

The Nature of Hope

Chapter Seven

Emotional Hope

Katie Stockdale

Philosophers have come to a general consensus that there are at least two, and quite likely more, components of hope: hope involves the desire for an outcome and the belief that the outcome's obtaining is at least possible.[1] Debate has centered around the question of what, beyond desire and belief, the attitude of hope consists in. Luc Bovens (1999) argues that hope involves "mental imaging," or conscious thoughts about what it would be like if the desired outcome were to obtain. Philip Pettit (2004) has proposed an account of hope as "cognitive resolve," according to which substantial hopes, or hopes in which we are significantly invested, involve acting as if the desired outcome is likely to occur. Adrienne M. Martin (2013) has deepened our understanding of hope yet further, proposing an incorporation analysis of hope that unifies the belief, desire, modes of perception, and feeling components of hope as a syndrome. Michael Milona (2018) and I argue that hope is a perceptual-like experience of practical reasons to pursue the hoped-for outcome that patterns similarly to the emotions. The literature on the nature and value of hope has received much deserved attention in recent years.[2]

My aim in this chapter is not to offer another theory of hope, but to reorient the discussion about the nature of hope to focus on hope's place in our hearts: on how, exactly, hope makes us feel. Although philosophers writing on hope have certainly paid attention to hope's affective dimensions to some extent, when affect is discussed, it is often assumed that hope is positively valenced. I want to argue that descriptions of the phenomenology of hope as positively valenced paint hope as brighter and cheerier than many hopes tend to be, and that hope is not always pleasant to experience (even in part). In making this argument, I focus specifically on hopes we form in response to nonideal conditions, hopes that are tainted by the negatively valenced emotion of fear. Reflecting on the dark side of hope, I explore more deeply the phenomenon of fearful hope that challenges us to remove fear as one of hope's potential opposites. I then consider the relationship between fearful hope and *basal* hope: a form of hope that is an "experiential back-drop" on which some philosophers have proposed our particular hopes depend (Ratcliffe 2013, Calhoun 2018). I argue that basal fear, which causes agents to experience the world as threatening, is also an experiential back-drop on which particular hopes arise. I then consider implications of this discussion for the relationship between hope and motivation and raise the question of whether hope itself is an emotion.

1. THE AFFECTIVE DIMENSIONS OF HOPE

Episodes of hope can be charged with affect. There is debate about what "affect" essentially is, but it is typically thought to be a conscious, felt experience of emotion characterized by either a positive (pleasant) or negative (unpleasant) tone, or what philosophers and psychologists refer to as "valence" (Charland 2009). Emotions with a pleasant affective tone (e.g., joy and happiness) are associated with feelings such as comfort, tranquility, and elation; and emotions with a negative affective tone (e.g., anger and jealousy) are associated with feelings such as discomfort, anxiety, and disorientation. Although all hopes might themselves be emotions (I see this as an open question), not all hopes *feel* emotional, or affect-laden. This distinction might seem strange at first; but notice that it captures many emotions. I might be angry about an injustice yet not feel angry right now (even if I'm thinking about the injustice). Similarly, I might be grieving the loss of a loved one yet feel neutral at this moment in time.

Emotions often make us feel and feel deeply; but they do not always do so. In many cases, our emotions do not have a strong affective tone because we are only slightly invested in their objects. For example, if I read about the unjust working conditions at Amazon, I may experience indignation, perhaps sighing in frustration about the exploitation of employees at the company. But the exploitation of Amazon employees is not an injustice in which I have a personal stake, or personal investment; I do not work for Amazon or know anyone who works for Amazon. So, when I read a news story about this issue, my distance from the injustice affects the intensity of my emotion.[3] My emotion is present, but it is not accompanied by strong feelings. On the other hand, if I discover that a friend of mine has been sexually assaulted, my indignation will be deeply, painfully felt. I might go home and scream the story to my partner, connecting it to the systemic injustice of sexual violence against women, tearing up and experiencing strong feelings: a racing heart and surge of energy; and feeling scattered and disoriented, as though the world is spinning. My closeness to the victim and personal investment in the elimination of sexual violence against women would shape, and deepen, the painful tone of my emotion.

What of hope? Often, like anger, hope does not feel like much to us because we are only slightly invested in the outcome for which we hope. If I remark to a stranger on an airplane before we exit, "I hope you enjoy your stay in Halifax," my hope might very well be genuine; but it will feel quite neutral. I might forget about my hope and never wonder if it was fulfilled within minutes (even seconds) simply because I am not invested in a stranger's enjoying their stay in Halifax. Other hopes, hopes in which we are significantly invested, tend to be charged with strong feelings: hoping that a candidate wins the election as the election results filter in, or hoping that one is awarded a research grant the day the results will be announced, or hoping that the weather cooperates on one's wedding day. These are hopes that feel like something to the person hoping. In these cases, the strength of one's desire or the degree to which one cares about or is invested in the outcome's obtaining intensifies the affective tone of hope.

Beyond the degree to which we are invested in the outcome's obtaining, our estimated closeness to the time at which we will find out whether our hope will be realized can also intensify how hope feels. As Ernst Bloch observes, "The more imminent this future is, the stronger, 'more burning' the expectant intention as such; the more extensively the content of an expectant intention affects the intending self, the more totally the person throws himself into it, and the 'deeper' it becomes a passion" (Bloch 1986, 157).[4] For example, if I am hoping that a family member's surgery goes well, then my hope will be accompanied by strong feelings—especially when the time arrives at which I anticipate finding out about how the surgery has gone. I might be in the waiting room feeling consumed with hope: anxiously imagining a positive result, watching the clock attentively, and anticipating that any second, the surgeon will come out of the operation room with news about the outcome of the surgery.

Hope, then, might be strongly felt for two reasons (or both together): (1) because of a strong desire or investment in the hoped-for outcome, and/or (2) because the experience of hope is occurring close to the estimated time at which one will find out about whether the hoped-for outcome materializes.

I want to focus on hopes that are accompanied by strong feelings. They are the "significant" or "substantial" hopes in which many philosophers have been interested, hopes that involve strong desires for outcomes we very much care about. In the spirit of my previous work, I take some inspiration from literature in the philosophy of the emotions in which the relevance of feelings to emotions has been examined in significant depth. There is debate about whether, and to what extent, feelings of any kind are necessary to emotions,[5] but there is consensus that many emotional experiences are felt in some way. Emotions might be accompanied by bodily feelings such as a racing heart,

Katie Stockdale

shaking hands, or sweaty palms. But bodily feelings do not allow us to distinguish *between* different emotions, since, for example, a racing heart might accompany both fear and anger. Thus, some philosophers have suggested that in addition to bodily feelings, emotions involve emotional or evaluative feelings which contribute to the affective tone of each emotion (Goldie 2002, Helm 2009). Peter Goldie argues that emotions are intentional feelings toward their objects: there is something that it is like to feel jealous, angry, joyful, or afraid. Bennett Helm suggests that, through the emotions, we feel as though things are good or bad in some way, with a corresponding pleasant or unpleasant affective tone (Helm 2009).[6]

Philosophers working on hope have typically characterized hope as an attitude that is accompanied by a positive tone or pleasant feelings. For example, Aquinas argues that hope causes pleasure and contributes to action (*Summa Theologica*, I–II.40.8) and Hobbes classifies hope as a "pleasure of the mind" (*Leviathan* I.6; Blöser and Stahl 2017; Martin 2013, 12). Bovens, more recently, argues that the mental imaging constitutive of hope "provides for the pleasures of anticipation," which he argues is especially important in difficult times (Bovens 1999, 675). In such cases, Bovens says, "the mental play that is constitutive of hoping provides a satisfaction that one cannot attain from attending to one's actual circumstances" (675). Margaret Urban Walker argues that our hopeful ideas and plans "awaken anticipation, excitement, or pleasure about what its realization or consequences will be like" (Walker 2006, 50). Common-sense views of hope, and the way in which we talk about hope in everyday life, also suggest that hope is positively valenced. Images associated with hope are of rainbows, light, open arms indicating freedom, and plants surviving in unlikely places.[7]

The pleasant feelings of anticipation associated with hope are part of why hope is supposed to be good for our well-being, health, and motivation.[8] Since hope is thought to consist in, or is often accompanied by, pleasure, it seems better to have than to not have all things considered. But hope can also be accompanied by unpleasant feelings of *anxiety*: a feeling that is commonly felt in the presence of a threat alongside the emotion of fear (e.g., Descartes *Passions of the Soul* 2.58). This is because hope consists in uncertainty, which is a state that itself can give rise to feeling anxious about the future or about what one does not yet know. To take a specific example: the uncertainty constitutive of my hope to win a competitive research grant will likely be accompanied by feelings of anxiety about *not* winning the research grant. In this case, I have hope and fear about the same outcome simultaneously: because I am only slightly hopeful, the absence of a strong hope allows fear to sneak in. When I focus on the possibility that I might actually be awarded the grant, I feel hope and thus pleasant anticipation; and when I focus on the possibility that I might not be awarded the grant, I feel fear and thus unpleasant anxiety.[9]

I want to argue that, in some cases, fear actually *constitutes* hope and does not just exist alongside it. In particular, when we hope that *p* and the content of *p* is perceived as threatening, we experience fearful hope. Fearful hope is not, at all, pleasant. And fearful hope is not pleasant because fear constitutes hope in a way that changes the phenomenological character of the emotional attitude. As I will argue, what distinguishes pleasant hopes from unpleasant (fearful) hopes is the *object* of hope: pleasant hopes are for happy outcomes, whereas fearful hopes are about escaping a threat.

This analysis implies that it is not something inherent in the attitude of hope which determines whether hope has a positive or negative valence. Instead, what we hope for shapes how our hopes feel. It is possible that, beyond fearful hope, other cases of negatively valenced hopes exist. For example, there might be shameful hopes in which agents are so ashamed of their hopes (e.g., that an innocent successful person suffers) that shame colors the phenomenological character of hope when it arises. Or, there might be grief-stricken hopes (e.g., that a loved one did not suffer too much when they died). I present fearful hope as a case study from which we might begin to understand other complex hopes.

2. FEARFUL HOPE

Many philosophers have theorized the relationship between hope and fear. Seneca suggests that hope and fear are "bound up with one another . . . the two march in unison like a prisoner and the escort he is handcuffed to" (*Letters* 5.7–8). This provocative description makes sense of the idea that both attitudes look to an uncertain future. Hume writes that uncertain outcomes give rise to either fear or hope, where which passion experienced is determined by the person's degree of uncertainty (*Treatise* 2.3.9.6). Spinoza presents a similar picture of the relationship between hope and fear. Whereas hope is a form of pleasure that arises from a picture of an uncertain outcome, fear is an "*un*pleasure" that arises from the picture of an uncertain outcome one desires as doubtful (*Ethics* III.P18). Because hope responds to contexts of perceived uncertainty, "there is no hope without fear, and no fear without hope" (*Ethics* III.P50). He states,

> For someone who is in suspense, hoping for something while being unsure that he will get it, is assumed (from his unsureness) to be imagining something that would exclude the existence of the thing he hopes for; to that extent he has unpleasure; and so while he is in his suspenseful hope he fears that the thing that he imagines will happen and thus that the thing he hopes for won't happen. (*Ethics* III. Definition of the Affects 13)

J. P. Day, following Spinoza, argues that hope and fear "are inseparable propositional attitudes" (Day 1998, 122). Similarly, James Averill suggests that "a person cannot hope for something unless he or she also fears that the hoped-for event might not happen. Hope and fear are two sides of the same coin" (Averill [1996] 2000, 36). Martha Nussbaum describes her own experience of "feeling of being buffeted between hope and fear, as if between two warring winds" (Nussbaum 2001, 26). Aaron Ben-Ze'ev defends a way of classifying emotions that appeals to the positive or negative nature of the emotions, in which hope (a positive emotion) and fear (a negative emotion) are used as paradigm examples (Ben-Ze'ev 2001). Positive emotions like hope "express a favorable evaluation, a positive desire, and an agreeable feeling" and in contrast, negative emotions like fear express "an unfavorable attitude, a negative motivation, and a disagreeable feeling" (94). Bennett Helm and Christine Tappolet, too, list fear amongst negatively valenced emotions and hope amongst positively valenced ones in their analyses of the emotions more generally (Helm 2009, 252; Tappolet 2016, 25–26). On this picture, hope involves pleasure in imagining, or thinking about, a desired outcome obtaining; and fear involves displeasure or pain in imagining, or thinking about, a desired outcome not obtaining.

The pleasant feelings commonly associated with hope and the painful feelings commonly associated with fear has even led some theorists to propose that hope and fear are *opposites*. For example, O. H. Mowrer, working within a stimulus-response paradigm, argues that fear is the "antithesis" of hope because "hope is aroused by the onset of a stimulus that indicates the imminent occurrence of a pleasurable experience. To the contrary, fear . . . is aroused by the onset of a stimulus that indicates the imminent occurrence of a noxious experience" (Oettingen and Chromik 2018). Patricia Greenspan suggests that hope and fear are "contrary emotions . . . with comfort and discomfort seen as directed towards contrary evaluations of the same object" (Greenspan 1988, 110); and Trudy Govier argues that hope and fear are opposites with respect to their affective tones (Govier 2011). These descriptions illustrate that much of the philosophical and psychological literature has theorized hope to be an opposite of or at least in contrast to fear.

These theorists are, in one sense, right about the relationship between hope and fear: the two attitudes take the same object and focusing on or attending to the possibility that a desired outcome will occur tends to be accompanied by pleasurable feelings; whereas focusing on or attending to the possibility that the same desired outcome will *not* occur tends to be accompanied by unpleasant feelings. It is also common to feel pleasant feelings of anticipation or excitement alongside unpleasant feelings of anxiety—even at the same time. One might simultaneously feel excitement and anxiety about getting a job, or one's child performing well in a play, hoping that these outcomes occur and simultaneously fearing that they will not occur. And it is the uncertainty about whether the desired outcome will obtain that gives rise to the experience of these mixed affective states. Sliding between fear and hope, and sometimes experiencing them together, is an instance of emotional ambivalence.[10]

But in addition to the experience of mixed affective states arising from the presence of hope and fear, I want to argue that there are other important cases in which fear constitutes hope and is not merely experienced alongside it—what I call fearful hope. What distinguishes fearful hope from cases in which a person is emotionally ambivalent in their hope and fear is that, in fearful hope, the affective tone of hope is *entirely* negatively valenced. I suggest that

> when a person hopes that p and the content of p is perceived as threatening, she experiences fearful hope.

What might this look like? Here is one example:

> When a woman, Suzie, hopes that a man aggressively cat calling her on the street corner does not assault her, she experiences fearful hope.

In this case, Suzie hopes that the proposition "the man aggressively cat calling me on the street corner does not assault me" obtains.[11] But the content of the proposition, the outcome for which she hopes, is the nonrealization of a threat: she sees the man aggressively cat calling her as a threat to her safety from potential harm. Because the hoped-for outcome is avoiding that which she fears, fear is both the basis for, and shapes the phenomenological character of, Suzie's hope. Suzie will likely feel very anxious and panicky as she thinks to herself, "I really hope this man leaves me alone." But she will not feel pleasant feelings of anticipation about her hope's obtaining. Suzie's hope is thus not positively valenced in the way that many philosophers have supposed hopes to be.

Here is another case:

> When a Black woman, Kayla, hopes that the police officer who has pulled her over for no apparent reason and is walking toward her vehicle acts without violence toward her, she experiences fearful hope.

In this case, Kayla hopes that the proposition "the police officer I am about to encounter does not use violence toward me" obtains. The content of the proposition, the outcome for which she hopes, is the nonrealization of a threat. In particular, she sees the police officer as threatening in light of her racial identity and knowledge about the disproportionate levels of violence perpetrated by police officers against people of color. Police officers are, reasonably, seen as fearsome to people of color like Kayla. Just like in

Suzie's case, Kayla's hoped-for outcome is about a perceived threat that is the basis for, and shapes the phenomenological character of, her hope. What these cases illustrate is that there is no sense in which women or people of color experience anything like pleasant feelings of anticipation in hoping to escape violence. Instead, their fear colors their hopes in such a way that hope itself is negatively valenced. [12]

Although I want to remain neutral with respect to what theory of hope is correct, it is notable that the phenomenon of fearful hope challenges any account of hope according to which hope involves, beyond belief and desire, something like positively valenced anticipation about the hoped-for end's obtaining. But one might object that fearful hope is a non-paradigmatic instance of hope. Fearful hope is a fringe case of hope, one that does not capture the majority of our significant hopes. Perhaps, then, paradigmatic hope really is pleasantly toned. But it is notable that fearful hope is ubiquitous, and even part of our everyday experiences. One might, for example, find oneself fearfully hoping to make it out of the bathtub safely if one is suffering from a mobility impairment; or fearfully hoping that the water dripping from one's ceiling is not a sign of serious, expensive damage; or fearfully hoping that one's dog's limp is not a sign of a fracture. [13] It is not just rare cases in which individuals find themselves in terrifying situations that fearful hope arises. Although it is more deeply felt in cases in which we are strongly invested in an outcome, and/or are closer to the time at which we anticipate the outcome might occur (just as in cases of non-fearful hopes), fearful hope is part of the everyday, mundane experiences of diverse sorts of human lives.

The phenomenon of fearful hope reminds us that human agents live in a nonideal world, a world in which the desires we form do not only orient us toward things we evaluate as good. Hope is quite often a response to these nonideal conditions in which we find ourselves, conditions in which feeling good is out of the question. All of us likely have found ourselves with fearful hope at some point or another, whether one has fearfully hoped to escape violence, arrest, betrayal, rejection, embarrassment, or exposure. But what about people whose safety or well-being is under *persistent* threat in virtue of their membership in certain social groups?

My own interest in hope emerged from a concern about the existence of pervasive, multi-faceted, and intersecting oppressions that structure certain individuals' lives: oppression based on gender, race, class, ability status, and other features of social difference. I have sought to understand the ways in which hope can be affected by one's relative position within systems of privilege and oppression (Stockdale, in progress). For example, how might oppression diminish, shape, or distort people's hopes, and how might privilege bolster possibilities for hope? Elsewhere, I have argued that oppression is a threat to hope (Stockdale 2019); but I also think that oppression can shape the character of people's hopes, making more ubiquitous the experience of fearful hope.

If fearful hope is systematic for people whose safety and well-being are under persistent threat because they are women, people of color, disabled, and so on, then one might wonder how such an experience shapes their emotional lives beyond the formation of particular fearful hopes. Our emotions are not just slices of affective experience that respond to individual situations and prospective events. They are avenues of engagement with our surroundings more generally, contributing to a felt sense of how we *find* ourselves in the world.

3. HOPE, FEAR, AND BEING IN THE WORLD

I want to suggest that hope and fear as very general affective states can color agents' experiences in ways that influence episodes of hope. In the context of women's shame, Sandra Bartky argues that beyond the episodes of shame we all experience, women are prone to shame as a way of *being in the world* in Heidegger's sense of the term; in other words, women see and navigate the world through shame (Bartky 1990). Whereas all of us might experience the emotion of shame, which involves feelings of defectiveness, a "cringing withdrawal" from others, the physical sensation of being pulled downward, and a disposition to hide, women's shame is not just an emotional "blip" at particular moments in time. Women's shame is, instead, a way in which they inhabit the world and respond to events within it. And there are numerous examples that illustrate how shame colors the entirety of women's experiences. Bartky reflects on cases in which women exhibit shame behaviors from the classroom to the workplace. She observes her women students' shame in their apologies for the quality of their work, their hesitancy when handing in assignments, their tendency to remain quiet in classroom discussions, and through the display of low degrees of confidence in their ability to master course material. Bartky explains that she wonders "when or whether any of these women truly felt confident and free, indeed, unashamed" (Bartky 1990, 90). Sexist oppression causes women to *live in shame*.

I wonder to what extent oppression might shape women's and other members of oppressed groups' *hopes* as a way of being in the world. There is increasing discussion of a kind of hope that might mirror women's all-encompassing shame as Bartky describes it. Matthew Ratcliffe points out that hope, like other emotions, is not always about a specific outcome but is sometimes an "existential feeling": a felt sense of how one finds oneself in the world (Ratcliffe 2013, 600). Ratcliffe argues that the ability to form particular hopes depends on having this existential feeling of hope. Cheshire Calhoun (2018), drawing upon Ratcliffe, calls this form of hope *basal hope* and argues that agents with such hope have a qualitative sense of the future as being hospitable to their agency. Basal hope is what is lost in depression, a state that involves a loss of one's "globally motivating interest in The Future" (Calhoun 2018, 117). Milona and I (Milona and Stockdale 2018) suggest that basal hope is similar to Robert Solomon's notion of happiness as a meta-emotion. In Solomon's view, happiness is an "ongoing evaluative judgment about our being in the world. It is a kind of all-embracing emotion, one that is not just about any particular aspect of our lives but about our lives as a whole" (Solomon 2007, 265).

Basal hope, or hope as a meta-emotion, is thus a very general affective state. It derives, as Calhoun points out, from a multiplicity of psychological sources including reflectively held beliefs, the emotions, habituation, and socialization (Calhoun 2018). It also derives from one's relative position within systems of privilege and oppression. Since oppression confines, restricts, or immobilizes certain people in virtue of their membership in certain social groups (Frye 1983, Young 1990, Cudd 2006), oppression constrains agency; it makes the world less hospitable to our agency in ways that might cause a loss of basal hopefulness. Hilary Abrahams, for example, discusses the emotional effects of living under domestic violence that twelve women she interviewed reported. She explains that some women were traumatized to such an extent that "they were unable to formulate any concept of a future," and could only take one day at a time (Abrahams 2010, 18). This is a loss of basal hope. And the women Abrahams interviewed described their feelings associated with this experience. One woman, Gemma, reported feeling "dazed and helpless" and as if she was "bleeding" from the abuse she endured (18).

Ratcliffe and Calhoun defend the need for basal hope to form significant, particular hopes. If one loses basal hope, one might lose the ability to form and pursue hopes to begin with. I mostly agree with Ratcliffe and Calhoun on this point, but I also think that damages to basal hope, and perhaps even a *loss* of basal hope, are consistent with the formation of many quite powerful *fearful hopes*. The women Abrahams interviewed, for example, testified to living in basal fear. I understand basal fear as the felt experience of living in fear, of inhabiting and navigating a world that seems generally threatening to oneself. Abrahams explains how the women's fear under domestic violence became an "undercurrent to their existence," resulting in their everyday lives becoming "increasingly unpredictable and frightening" (Abrahams 2010, 22). One woman, Sally, said that she "was so frightened of everything" (22). Fear, for these women, was not merely an episodic response to particular situations, but an emotion that structured the entirety of their experiences.

Even though these women's testimony suggests that they were living in basal fear (and in the absence of basal hope), it is notable that basal fear did not necessarily prevent, but sometimes shaped, the formation of their particular hopes. Another woman, Sylvia, described "living in this kind of walking egg shell scenario . . . of just hoping that every day is going to be okay and don't say anything, don't tell anybody" (Abrahams 2010, 20). Alongside this hope, Sylvia explained feeling as though the world was closing in on her and shrinking, feelings that are unpleasant to experience. And I imagine that Sylvia's hope that "every day will be okay" was fearful. Although her hope was not articulated as a proposition involving a perceived threat, Sylvia's hope cannot be adequately understood without reference to her testimony of living in fear. We might recast the hope, then, in the following way:

> Sylvia hopes that *despite the violence with which she persistently lives*, every day will be okay.

Thus, living under the persistent threat of domestic violence can cause women to form fearful hopes, hopes that arise from the experiential backdrop of fear.[14] As Abrahams explains, "In listening closely to the early hopes and dreams about their new lives[,] . . . they wanted to live without fear, to be free to act for themselves, and to be treated with respect and valued" (Abrahams 2010, 19). Their hopes "centre on a new life free from violence" (Abrahams 2010, 17). These are hopes that are shaped by basal fear, and possibly (for some) formed in the absence of basal hope.

Whereas basal fear might give rise to the formation of fearful hopes, there are other cases in which basal fear prevents the formation of any hopes. Ta-Nehisi Coates, for example, points out that fear is "one of the dominant emotions of the black experience" (Public Broadcasting Service 2015). Coates is referring to fear as a way in which Black people experience a world in which their bodies are under persistent threat of violence. He is not referring merely to episodic fear, or what Bartky would call an emotional blip at a particular moment in time. As Coates explains, "To be black in the Baltimore of my youth was to be naked before the elements of the world, before all the guns, fists knives, crack, rape, and disease. The nakedness is not an error, nor pathology. The nakedness is the correct and intended result of policy, the predictable upshot of people forced for centuries to live under fear" (Coates 2015, 18).

Coates contrasts his experience of living in basal fear with "other worlds where other children did not have to fear for their bodies" (Coates 2015, 20), worlds inhabited by white bodies. His fear is a result of living under racial oppression, similarly to how women's fear is often a result of living under sexist oppression. And fear, for Coates, was part of how he and other Blacks perceived, interpreted, and engaged with their environments. It "ruled everything around" him (29) and colored his experiences; it was not an emotion that he experienced only in brief episodes involving clear threats. Coates describes, for example, making a friend in Paris and sharing wine and a meal with him, but mistrusting the new friend and wondering whether the encounter would turn violent. He concludes, "I felt that I had missed part of the experience because of my eyes, because my eyes were made in Baltimore, because my eyes were blindfolded by fear" (Coates 2015, 126).

I read Coates's *Between the World and Me* as almost entirely unhopeful, and it is helpful to understand Coates's absence of hope as connected to a loss of basal hopefulness and the presence of basal fear. But Coates also connects his absence of hope to a lack of religious faith. He remarks, "I thought of my own distance from an institution that has, so often, been the only support for our people. I often wonder if in that distance I've missed something, some notions of cosmic hope" (Coates 2015, 139). Whereas basal fear might cause agents like Coates to lose basal hope and the ability to form particular hopes, other agents might sustain basal hopefulness and the ability to form particular hopes because of their religious faith.

Like particular hopes and fears, basal hope and fear as feelings of being in the world can manifest as affective states. They are felt experiences that influence the particular hopes we come to form, the character of those hopes, and our thoughts, feelings, patterns of attention, and actions. I now turn to some implications of the present discussion to the relationship between hope and motivation. Although various philosophers have discussed the question of how hope motivates (e.g., Pettit 2004, Martin 2013, Calhoun 2018, Milona 2018), I suggest that explicitly treating hope as an emotion, with a focus on the relationship between *affect* and motivation, might lead to new lines of inquiry into the connection between hope and motivation.

4. IS HOPE AN EMOTION? AND IMPLICATIONS FOR UNDERSTANDING HOW HOPE MOTIVATES

Philosophers have not yet grappled with the question of whether hope is an emotion in any great depth. This is somewhat puzzling, especially when we focus on the relationship between hope and fear: an attitude that many philosophers and psychologists consider to be a basic or paradigm emotion (e.g., Damasio 2003, 44; Tappolet 2016, 4). Ben-Ze'ev (2001) reflects on the strangeness of treating fear as a paradigm emotion but not hope. As he says, "It is interesting to note that although fear is also directed at a future situation, no one has claimed that fear is not an emotion; on the contrary, fear is often described as the most basic and typical emotion. This difference expresses the greater emotional impact we attach to negative events as compared with positive ones" (Ben-Ze'ev 2001, 475). The idea is that because philosophers and psychologists have focused more on negative emotions, in part because they seem to affect us more deeply than positive ones, the thought that *hope* is an emotion has been overlooked.

This is an interesting psychological explanation, but I think the lack of engagement with the question of whether hope is an emotion is best explained by the methodologies at work in theorizing hope. Some philosophers have avoided the question of whether hope is an emotion because answering it seems to require committing to a theory of the emotions. Martin (2013) notes that she does not engage with this question because philosophical theories of emotion are themselves controversial, and it's not clear which (if any) theories of the nature of emotion are correct. This is certainly an obstacle to thinking about whether hope is an emotion, and by setting aside the question, philosophers have been able to advance our understanding of the nature of hope significantly. But there are key similarities between hope and emotions, similarities which might enable us to rethink our classifications. Drawing out these similarities is also helpful in seeing how hope might be a source of motivation beyond the desire constitutive of the attitude.

I find five plausible similarities between hope and emotions:

1. Hope, and emotions, are *intentional*. They are directed toward objects.[15]
2. Hope, and emotions, are *evaluative*. They involve a normative representation of a situation, or the world more generally, as being a certain way.[16]
3. Hope, and emotions, are *affective*. They have a distinctive phenomenology, or "what it is like" experience.
4. Hope, and emotions, are often accompanied by *bodily feelings*.
5. Hope, and emotions, are *motivational*.

One of the central questions in the philosophy of hope has been about the relationship between hope and motivation: whether the desire constitutive of hope does all of the motivational work in motivating action, or whether there is something else in addition to desire that gives hope its motivational power. Calhoun warns against what she calls the "energizer bunny" view of hope, where it is tempting to assert hope's special motivating power ("a kind of fuel, like super-charged batteries") without any explanation of where that motivating power comes from (Calhoun 2018, 112). Calhoun argues that it is easier to see how other emotions provide additional motivation in agents' practical pursuits. For example, the experience of anger in response to an opponent's derogatory remarks toward you in a competition is a source of motivation in the form of new motivating reasons to win the competition (130). But this is different from hope, which Calhoun says, "does not seem to provide a new motivating reason beyond your original reasons for desiring success and thinking it possible" (131).

But I think it's worth reflecting on *why* anger seems to provide additional motivational fuel in these sorts of cases. Anger motivates not only because the agent acquires an additional reason for winning—to show up the opponent—but because emotions motivate action. When I see a situation as unjust or offensive, my seeing-as experience is affective in character: I *experience* the situation as wrong, unjust, or offensive; and such an experience might be accompanied by bodily feelings such as a racing heart and surge of physical energy. And these feelings move us to act, whether the emotion is positively valenced, negatively valenced, or both. Anger can be entirely negatively valenced, as in when one feels hurt by a wrong. In these cases, anger might motivate the agent to correct the perceived injustice, where the particular actions they undertake will depend on the nature of the injustice. But anger might also be both negatively and positively valenced, as when experiencing anger feels good and, indeed, can serve as a protective shield against other negatively valenced emotions such as shame. When a male colleague told me in graduate school that I held a moderate position in epistemology because "women hold moderate positions," my fitting anger in response to the wrong shielded me from my underlying shame about being potentially unfit for philosophy because I am a woman. Whereas shame may have motivated me to leave the profession, my anger motivated me to publish feminist work.

There are a number of views about just how emotions motivate, and I cannot do justice to the rich philosophical and scientific literature here. But a brief survey suggests that competing views do agree that the affective and bodily feeling dimensions of emotions help to explain their role in motivation.[17] In Bennett Helm's view, emotions are motivational because they are "emotional feelings of import," where "import" refers to what one *cares* about that is worthy of attention and action (Helm 2009, 252). If we apply this insight to hope, then hope is an evaluative feeling that, given whatever probability assessment one gives to a desired outcome, the outcome is worthy of attention and action. On Julien A. Deonna and Fabrice Teroni's attitudinal theory of the emotions, emotions are inherently motivational states because they are, by their nature, "bodily experiences of being disposed or tending to act in a differentiated way" whether away from, toward, or against some object; or to contemplate, submit, or be attracted to the object; or to disengage from the object (Deonna and Teroni 2015, 302–3). Hope, on this theory, would be a bodily experience of being disposed to act to bring about the desired outcome. The field of affective science has also developed sophisticated theories of how emotions motivate through their affective dimensions (Scarantino and de Sousa 2018).

Treating hope as an emotion and engaging more explicitly with literature on the emotions will likely lead to new insights about the role of hope in human motivation. I also think that an adequate understanding of the role of hope in motivation must appeal to both basal and episodic emotions. Calhoun's (2018) answer to the question of how hope motivates requires both an understanding of basal hope and practical hope. She suggests that basal hope is critical for motivation in "leading the life of an agent" (Calhoun 2018, 117). And, in the case of particular practical hopes, "those who hope use the desired successful future to fill in the content of the determinate future" (134). They have a phenomenological idea of the future in which one's desire has been fulfilled, a phenomenological idea which has motivational effects independent of the agent's initial motivating reasons (e.g., committing to the project of aiming to bring about the desired end). This is an important start to understanding hope's role in motivation.

But as I have argued, basal *fear* is often compatible with, and can shape, the objects and character of agents' hopes; and such basal fear can affect how hope motivates as well. For example, a queer student living in a rural community in Texas might live in basal fear, a fear that motivates them to flee from threats to their safety and well-being. The student may come to form particular, practical hopes from this experiential backdrop of fear: to be accepted to law school in a different state, for example. The student's phenomenological idea of the future in which their desire is fulfilled does, as Calhoun suggests, have motivational effects. The student might work extremely hard to ensure that they receive straight As, doing everything in their power to increase the probability that their hope will be realized. But there might be additional emotional sources of motivation at work, too. The student might be motivated by *anger* at their caregivers for being unaccepting (motivating retaliation against the different life their parents wanted them to lead), and/or *shame* about who they are in their current community (motivating withdrawal from the community). Basal fear, anger, and shame together influence the formation of the particular, practical hope the student formed; and they are all sources of motivation in the student's pursuit. Understanding hope's role in motivation requires an analysis of hope alongside and interacting with other basal and episodic emotions.

These reflections are meant to complement, rather than challenge, the existing philosophical literature on the relationship between hope and motivation. But they suggest that (1) attending to key similarities between hope and the emotions, and understanding how emotions motivate human action, might lead to a richer or perhaps new account of how hope motivates; and (2) attending to other sources of motivation, including basal and episodic emotions, is important to sort out whether hope or another state is doing the motivational work, or whether motivation results from the interaction of hope with other emotions.

5. CONCLUDING THOUGHTS

This chapter has aimed to bring the affective dimensions of hope, and the relationship between hope and the emotions, into fuller view. There is, as we have seen, a dark side of hope. Hope is not always pleasant or cheery, an attitude oriented toward achieving happy outcomes. It is often a response to nonideal, even horrific conditions, in which agents live. And its role in these conditions is not always to provide a release for the mind, giving us space away from our difficulties to imaginatively inhabit more pleasant circumstances.[18] When agents hope to escape a perceived threat, hope itself is negatively valenced and not at all pleasant to experience. And just as agents can live in basal hope, so too they can live in basal fear: a general affective state that influences the formation and character of particular hopes. By attending explicitly to the complex ways in which hope interacts with other emotions, and is perhaps itself an emotion, we will gain a richer understanding of the nature of hope and its role in human life.[19]

NOTES

1. There are a few notable exceptions. One is Gabriel Segal and Mark Textor (2015), who argue that hope is a primitive mental state and not a combination of belief, desire, and potentially other elements. Another is Michael Milona (2018) who argues that the belief-desire model of hope is right once we understand the nature of hope-constituting desires. For the purpose of this article, I begin from the more common view that hope involves belief, desire, and likely other elements; but I acknowledge that there is much room to explore different ways of classifying hope.

2. For a comprehensive overview of the history of hope and current debates, see Claudia Blöser and Titus Stahl (2017).

3. And, we might add, the fact that news stories about horrific events are constant dilutes the affective tone of our emotions in response to them.

4. See also Ben-Ze'ev 2001, 475.

5. On some views, emotions just are experiences of bodily feelings (James 1884, Prinz 2004). Other philosophers agree that emotions are often accompanied by bodily feelings but argue that feelings are not necessary to emotions (Nussbaum 2001).

6. The positive/negative emotion dichotomy is common in characterizing emotions in the philosophical and psychological literature. For discussion of the ambiguity around this distinction, see Robert C. Solomon and Lori D. Stone (2002). For the purpose of this chapter, I am understanding positive in terms of pleasure and negative in terms of pain. But I agree with these authors that the dichotomy can be ambiguous.

7. These are selected descriptions of images one finds by searching "hope" in Google.

8. There is growing empirical literature on the benefits of hope to well-being, health, and motivation. See, for example, Matthew W. Gallagher and Shane J. Lopez (2018) for a number of psychological perspectives on these benefits of hope.

9. Maria Miceli and Cristiano Castelfranchi argue that the presence of anxiety itself indicates that both hope and fear are present (Miceli and Castelfranchi 2010).

10. For discussion of emotional ambivalence, see Philip J. Koch (1987).

11. I do not think that hopes must be experienced as thoughts in the form of propositions; but articulating hopes in this way is helpful in illustrating how the presence of a perceived threat shapes the character of hope.

12. One might be tempted to reduce fearful hopes to fear. But doing so fails to capture the complexity of our emotional experiences. When a woman thinks anxiously, "I really hope that man does not pursue his aggressive behavior further," she is not *merely* in a state of fear and mistaken that she has a hope. She sees a desired outcome that is possible but not certain as one that might obtain, and these are the key ingredients of hope.

13. Thanks to Michael Raven for helping me to see more clearly just how ubiquitous fearful hope really is.

14. Basal fear still seems consistent with the formation of some non-fearful hopes, such as Sylvia's hope to see her children "safe, secure, and happy" and for her to be in "peace" (Abrahams 2010, 18). Such hopes might even have been positively valenced, involving pleasant thoughts about what it would be like if these outcomes were to occur.

15. Although some philosophers think that basal hope is preintentional (Ratcliffe 2013, Calhoun 2018), Milona and I (2018) have argued that basal hope is intentional but highly general.

16. There are different ways of describing hope's evaluative dimension. For example, Martin (2013) argues that, in hope, the agent incorporates one's desire into one's rational scheme of ends, seeing oneself as having sufficient reason to engage in hopeful activities. Milona and I (2018) argue that the normative representation involved in hope is best understood as a perceptual-like experience, whereby the agent perceives oneself as having practical reasons to aim for the hoped-for outcome or to ready oneself for it to obtain.

17. One objection to strong judgmentalist theories of the emotions, according to which emotions are evaluative judgments (e.g., resentment is an evaluative judgment that one was wronged) is that it is unclear how such a view can explain how emotions motivate (Scarantino and de Sousa 2018).

18. This is how I read much of the literature on the role of hope in dark times.

19. Thanks to Claudia Blöser, Dave Dexter, Matt Hernandez, and Titus Stahl for very helpful feedback on previous drafts.

REFERENCES

Abrahams, Hilary. 2010. *Rebuilding Lives after Domestic Violence: Understanding Long-Term Outcomes*. London: Jessica Kingsley Publishers.

Aquinas, Thomas. 1265–1274. *Summa Theologica (Part 2.1)*. Authentic Digital Classic Series, 2012.

Averill, James. (1996) 2000. "Intellectual Emotions." In *The Emotions: Social, Cultural and Biological Dimensions*, edited by Rom Harré and W. Gerrod Parrott, 24–38. London: Sage Publications.

Bartky, Sandra. 1990. *Femininity and Domination: Studies in the Phenomenology of Oppression*. New York: Routledge.

Ben-Ze'ev, Aaron. 2001. *The Subtlety of Emotions*. Cambridge: MIT Press.

Bloch, Ernst. 1986. *The Principles of Hope: Volume I*. Cambridge: MIT Press.

Blöser, Claudia, and Titus Stahl. 2017. "Hope." *The Stanford Encyclopedia of Philosophy* (Spring 2017 Edition), edited by Edward N. Zalta. https://plato.stanford.edu/archives/spr2017/entries/hope/.

Bovens, Luc. 1999. "The Value of Hope." *Philosophy and Phenomenological Research* 59, no. 3: 667–81. doi: 10.2307/2653787.

Calhoun, Cheshire. 2018. *Doing Valuable Time: The Present, the Future, and Meaningful Living*. New York: Oxford University Press.

Charland, Louis. 2009. "Affect (Psychological Perspectives)." *Oxford Companion to Emotion and the Affective Sciences*, edited by David Sander and Klaus Scherer, 9–10. New York: Oxford University Press.

Coates, Ta-Nehisi. 2015. *Between the World and Me*. New York: Penguin Random House.

Cudd, Ann E. 2006. *Analyzing Oppression*. New York: Oxford University Press.

Damasio, Antonio. 2003. *Looking for Spinoza: Joy, Sorrow, and the Feeling Brain*. New York: Harcourt.

Day, J. P. 1998. "More about Hope and Fear." *Ethical Theory and Moral Practice* 1: 121–23. doi: 10.1023/A:10099411.

Deonna, Julien A., and Fabrice Teroni. 2015. "Emotions as Attitudes." *Dialectica* 69, no 3: 293–311. doi: 10.1111/1746-8361.12116.

Descartes, Rene. 1649. *Passions of the Soul*, in the version presented at http://www.earlymoderntexts.com, 2017.

Frye, Marilyn. 1983. *The Politics of Reality: Essays in Feminist Theory*. Trumansberg: Crossing Press.

Gallagher, Matthew W., and Shane J. Lopez. 2018. *The Oxford Handbook of Hope*. New York: Oxford University Press.

Goldie, Peter. 2002. "Emotions, Feelings and Intentionality." *Phenomenology and the Cognitive Sciences* 1: 235–54. doi: 10.1023/A:1021306500055.

Govier, Trudy. 2011. "Hope and Its Opposites." *Journal of Social Philosophy* 42, no. 3: 239–53. doi: 10.1111/j.1467-9833.2011.01532.x.

Greenspan, Patricia. 1988. *Emotions and Reasons: An Inquiry into Emotional Justification*. New York: Routledge.

Helm, Bennett. 2009. "Emotions as Evaluative Feelings." *Emotion Review* 1: 248–55. doi: 10.1177/1754073909103593.

Hobbes, Thomas. 1651. *The Leviathan*. Oxford: Clarendon Press, 1965.

Hume, David. 2009. *A Treatise of Human Nature*, edited by David Fate Norton and Mary J. Norton. New York: Oxford University Press.

James, William. 1884. "What Is an Emotion?" *Mind* 9, no. 34: 188–205. doi: 10.1093/mind/os/IX.34.188

Koch, Philip J. 1987. "Emotional Ambivalence." *Philosophy and Phenomenological Research* 48, no. 2: 257–59. doi: 10.2307/210768.

Martin, Adrienne M. 2013. *How We Hope: A Moral Psychology*. Princeton: Princeton University Press.

Miceli, Maria, and Cristiano Castelfranchi. 2010. "Hope: The Power of Wish and Possibility." *Theory and Psychology* 20: 251–76. doi: 10.1177/0959354309354943.

Milona, Michael. 2018. "Finding Hope." *Canadian Journal of Philosophy* 49, no. 5: 1–20. doi: 10.1080/00455091.2018.1435612.

Milona, Michael, and Katie Stockdale. 2018. "A Perceptual Theory of Hope." *Ergo* 5, no. 8: 203–22. doi: 10.3998/ergo.12405314.0005.008.

Nussbaum, Martha C. 2001. *Upheavals of Thought: The Intelligence of Emotions*. Cambridge: Cambridge University Press.

Oettingen, Gabriele, and Malin Patricia Chromik. 2018. "How Hope Influences Goal-Directed Behavior." *The Oxford Handbook of Hope*, edited by Matthew W. Gallagher and Shane L. Lopez, 69–79. New York: Oxford University Press.

Pettit, Philip. 2004. "Hope and Its Place in Mind." *Annals of the American Academy of Political and Social Science* 592, no. 1: 152–65. doi: 10.1177/0002716203261798.

Prinz, Jesse. 2004. *Gut Reactions: A Perceptual Theory of Emotion*. New York: Oxford University Press.

Public Broadcasting Service. 2015. "Ta-Nehisi Coates on Fear and the Black Experience." November 20, 2015. https://www.pbs.org/wnet/religionandethics/2015/11/20/ta-nehisi-coates-fear-black-experience/27488/.

Ratcliffe, Matthew. 2013. "What Is It to Lose Hope?" *Phenomenology and the Cognitive Sciences* 12: 597–614. doi: 10.1007/s11097-011-9215-1.

Scarantino, Andrea, and Ronald de Sousa. 2018. "Emotion." *The Stanford Encyclopedia of Philosophy* (Winter 2018 Edition), edited by Edward N. Zalta. https://plato.stanford.edu/archives/win2018/entries/emotion/.

Segal, Gabriel, and Mark Textor. 2015. "Hope as a Primitive Mental State." *Ratio* XXVIII 2: 207–22. doi: 10.1111/rati.12088.

Seneca. 2003. "Letters to Lucilius." *The Many Faces of Philosophy: Reflections from Plato to Arendt*, edited by Amelie Oksenberg Rorty, 8–13. New York: Oxford University Press.

Solomon, Robert C. 2007. *True to Our Feelings: What Our Emotions Are Really Telling Us*. New York: Oxford University Press.

Solomon, Robert C., and Lori D. Stone. 2002. "On 'Positive' and 'Negative' Emotions." *Journal for the Theory of Social Behavior* 32: 417–35. doi: 10.1111/1468-5914.001986.

Spinoza, Benedict. 1655. *Ethics Demonstrated in Geometrical Order*, in the version presented at www.earlymoderntexts.com, 2017.

Stockdale, Katie. 2019. "Social and Political Dimensions of Hope." *Journal of Social Philosophy* 50, no. 1: 28–44. doi: 10.1111/josp.12270.

———. *Hope under Oppression.* Manuscript in progress.

Tappolet, Christine. 2016. *Emotions, Values, and Agency.* Oxford: Oxford University Press.

Walker, Margaret Urban. 2006. *Moral Repair: Reconstructing Moral Relations after Wrongdoing.* New York: Cambridge University Press.

Young, Iris Marion. 1990. *Justice and the Politics of Difference.* Princeton: Princeton University Press.

Chapter Eight

Epistemological Aspects of Hope

Matthew A. Benton

Hope is an attitude that typically has a proposition as its content, where propositions represent possibilities or events or states of affairs, that is, the world as being a certain way.[1] Thus when one has such propositional hope, one hopes that the world is (or will turn out) a certain way. For example, one may hope that it not rain for the upcoming outdoor party, or one may hope that one's team won their recent game. One's hopes are fulfilled when one learns that the propositions one hopes for are (or become) true; one's hopes are frustrated or dashed when one learns that they are (or turn out) false.

Hope clearly has a desire element to it, for one only hopes for those propositions that one wants to be true. But hope also has an interesting epistemological element to it, namely, it is an attitude that is somehow incompatible with knowledge: we do not hope for propositions that we know, or take ourselves to know, to be either true or false. When one comes to know that what one hoped for obtains, one's attitude changes from hope to satisfaction, or even joy, at learning that one's hope was fulfilled. Yet when one comes to know that what one hoped for does not obtain, one's attitude changes from hope to mere wish, or even regret, at learning that one's hope was dashed. In both cases it would be somehow irrational, perhaps even psychologically impossible, to retain one's hope upon coming to know the outcome. The present essay focuses on these epistemological aspects of hope.

Because our main concern will be hope as it relates to knowledge, probabilities, and inductive generalizations, we shall keep an eye on the epistemic constraints that can make hope either impossible, or, when hope remains possible, how one's epistemic situation might make hope rational rather than irrational. I shall begin, in section 1, by rehearsing some data that reveal the incompatibility of hope with knowledge. Then in section 2, I consider a range of propositional emotive attitudes, and compare the epistemological dimension of hope with that of other attitudes. Next, in section 3, I examine whether there are any norms of rationality invoking epistemological concepts that govern being hopeful, and whether there are related norms concerning when hope may permissibly figure in practical deliberation over a course of action. Finally, in section 4, I consider second-order inductive reflection on when one should, or should not, hope for an outcome with which one has a long record of experience: in other words, what is the epistemology behind when one should, if ever, stop hoping for outcomes that have failed one many times in the past?

1. KNOWLEDGE AND HOPE

In addition to our intuitive judgments about cases, a range of linguistic data provides grounds for regarding propositional hope as somehow incompatible with knowledge. Our language offers a window into the rules for how we may deploy the concepts of hope and knowledge, and thus these data reveal not only how we speak about these notions, but how we reason with them and rely on such reasoning socially. Thus examining such data enables us to discover important aspects of our cognitive lives.[2]

Suppose you and a colleague, Tim, are at a park for lunch, away from your workplace. You are getting ready to head back to the office when you get information about a dangerous emergency situation at work: your notification indicates that you should stay away from the office. You begin discussing the whereabouts of your coworkers, including your mutual friend, Janice, whom you both know sometimes works from home. Tim says,

(1) I hope that Janice is at home.

You. agree with Tim, of course, since you prefer that Janice not be at the scene of the emergency, where she could be in danger. Notice that Tim might just as easily have said,

(2) I hope that Janice is at home, but she might not be.

Your agreement with Tim's having said either (1) or (2) consists not simply in your both desiring that Janice be safe. It also consists in neither of you knowing whether Janice is at home.

But now suppose that an hour later, you come to learn that Tim knew all along that Janice was in fact at home.[3] You will likely regard Tim's having said (1) as being highly misleading, perhaps even insincere. For if Tim knew that Janice was at home, why would he say that he *hopes* that she is?[4] If he knew, Tim arguably claimed something false by asserting (1). At the very least, by saying (1), Tim invited the inference that he did not know Janice's whereabouts (and similar reactions would attend to Tim's having said (2) instead). What is more, Tim's knowing Janice's whereabouts when he told you (1) throws into question the idea that you *agreed* with Tim. While you might have agreed, in some sense, with what he said in asserting (1), you will likely now judge that you both didn't actually hope that Janice was at home, even if you both desired that she be there. Yet Tim, in knowing she was home, knew that what he desired was true; rather than hoping she was home, he surely instead felt relief that she *was* home. So Tim didn't hope that Janice was home. And if he didn't hope, then the idea that you agreed with Tim in hoping for this seems to vanish.

These reactions strongly suggest that hope that p is incompatible, in some strong sense, with knowing whether p (that is, with either knowing that p, or with knowing that $\neg p$). And these evaluations surface again in the availability of other conversational moves. Consider the following exchange, where A's question prompt to B involves whether B hopes for a particular outcome about a match known to have already been settled:

A: Do you hope that she won?
B: # Yes, I know that she won. [5]

B's response beginning with "Yes" to the question, about whether B (now) hopes, is bizarre given that B claims to know. If B had intended to convey that B desired her to win, and had earlier hoped for this, it would have been much more appropriate to reply with "I did, and then I learned that she won." Yet the propriety of claiming that B *did* hope, but now knows, points to the fact that it is somehow impermissible, or psychologically impossible, to continue to hope when one now knows whether the hoped-for event has come to pass. [6]

Such judgments are reinforced by noting our reactions to various attempts to conjoin self-ascriptions of hope in some proposition with self-ascriptions of knowledge concerning that proposition (or its negation). Consider how bad each of the following sound:

(3) # I know that John is in his office, but I hope that he is not.
(4) # I hope that John is in his office, but I know that he is not.
(5) # I hope that John is in his office, and/but I know that he is.

Note that the example of (5) shows that it is even strange to consider hoping for what you know, where your hope and knowledge "agree" on their propositional object (as B's response in the above dialogue showed). Taken together, our judgments of (3) through (5) provide further evidence that hoping that p is incompatible with knowing whether p. [7]

Similar judgments attend to conjoining hope self-ascription with outright assertion of that proposition (or its negation), which suggests that the difficulty is not simply due to explicitly claiming knowledge:

(6) # John is in his office, but I hope he is not. [8]
(7) # I hope that John is in his office, but he is not there.
(8) # I hope that John is in his office, and/but he is.

An alert reader may notice that the knowledge conjuncts of (3) through (5) entail their outrightly asserted conjuncts of (6) through (8), respectively, because knowledge is "factive": one can only know facts or true propositions. So a speaker of (3) through (5) would be committed to (6) through (8), which they entail. Yet this latter triad of sentences seem problematic even though we can clearly envision how their conjuncts could both be true together: to take (6) for example, it is quite possible for John to be in his office while I hope that he is not in his office. So (6)'s conjuncts, as well as (7)'s and (8)'s, are semantically consistent (in contrast to (3) through (5), which seem semantically inconsistent). [9] Thus (6) through (8) are, even if not semantically inconsistent, somehow pragmatically inconsistent: the attempt to assert the conjunction generates a felt infelicity.

But importantly, (6) through (8) reveal that there is something epistemic about features we normally evaluate in an outright assertion, and that epistemic dimension plausibly concerns knowledge. As many philosophers have argued, properly asserting that something is so requires knowing that it is so: knowledge is in this sense the *norm* of assertion, such that one ought not assert unless one knows. [10] The knowledge norm explains, among other things, why our assertions represent ourselves as knowing what we assert. Given the knowledge norm, we may explain what is incoherent about asserting any of (6) through (8), as follows. Asserting their hope conjuncts has the effect of representing the speaker as not knowing whether John is in his office. But by asserting the other conjuncts, which claim outright that John is (or is not) in his office, the speaker represents herself as knowing whether John is there. So the infelicity attending to each of (6) through (8) is aptly explained in terms of knowledge: each conjunct represents something contrary to the other conjunct, with respect to the speaker's knowledge.

So far we've seen data that is well explained by the idea that hope in a proposition is itself somehow incompatible with knowledge of that proposition or of its negation. And this is exactly how most philosophers have recently theorized about hope. For example, two earlier theorists put it this way: "one cannot hope that something will occur if one already knows that it will; knowledge overshoots the criterion of probability" (Downie 1963, 249); and "one cannot, logically, want, and so hope for, what he already knows that he has . . . [nor] hope for, what he . . . knows he cannot have" (Day 1969, 95).

Robert Gordon argues that "a person hopes that *p* only if he *does not know* that *p*" (1969, 412; 1987, 26). And Adrienne Martin suggests that "hope entails uncertainty . . . e.g. lack of knowledge" (Martin 2011, 154).[11] Yet many of these same philosophers tie the possibility of hope in part to the subject's credences, that is, their subjective probabilities. Day says that in order to hope that *p*, a subject must "think that *p* has some degree of probability, however small" (Day 1969, 89). Luc Bovens insists that "one cannot hope for some state of the world, unless one has a degree of credence that it will come about that ranges between some threshold value close to 0 for confidence that it will not come about and some threshold value close to 1 for confidence that it will come about" (Bovens 1999, 673). Or, as Adrienne Martin recently puts it, "the subject must assign a probability between and exclusive of 0 and 1 to the outcome" (Martin 2014, 62).

These formulations strongly support an intuitive Chances License Hope principle (CLH) for a proposition *p* which one, all things considered, desires to be true:

> (CLH) If there is a chance for one that *p*, and a chance for one that ¬*p*, then one may hope that *p*.

CLH provides an epistemic norm of permissibility on hope. Yet how might we square CLH's bare probabilistic conditions on hoping with the above claims, and the substantial evidence, suggesting that hope is also incompatible with knowledge? One approach is to endorse infallibilism about knowledge, namely, to accept that when one knows a proposition *p*, there is no (epistemic) chance or possibility for one that *p* is false. Infallibilism straightforwardly handles the incompatibility of hope and knowledge given CLH.[12] But infallibilism about knowledge has been quite unpopular in recent epistemology, in no small part because it seems to many that we can have propositional knowledge without being certain of what we know, or without our evidence eliminating all chances of error. So fallibilism has instead been the dominant view; but fallibilism plus CLH seems to predict the compatibility, rather than the incompatibility, of knowledge and hope. For such theorists, one approach might be to articulate a theory of the conditions under which one's epistemic chances become psychologically salient to one's deliberations, and reframe CLH in terms of only those epistemic chances that are salient to one's context (whether that context concerns practical deliberation, attitude formation, or both). This latter approach could perhaps fit with fallibilism about knowledge,[13] but it may run the risk of divorcing the possibility of hoping from the possibility of knowing, such that it may not predict the incompatibility revealed by the above data after all. For if CLH is reframed so as to focus on what the subject considers the epistemic chances concerning *p* to be, it conceives of such chances along broadly internalist lines[14]; yet most in epistemology have sided with externalists about the sorts of evidence or cognitive processes that produce knowledge. For those theorists pulled in both directions, a challenge for this approach will be to formulate suitable bridge principles connecting their internalism about the chances relevant to hope with the externalist conditions on knowledge, in such a way that their incompatibility is still upheld. I shall leave such explorations to others.

It should be clear from the foregoing that hope possesses significant epistemic dimensions that render it incompatible[15] with knowledge. In the next section we consider several other emotive propositional attitudes with connections to knowledge.

2. EMOTIVES: FACTIVE AND EPISTEMIC

Hope is among several emotive attitudes that are propositional in structure, that is, they take propositions as their objects; their paradigmatic linguistic schema of expression is "S emotes that p." For example, one can be happy that p, pleased that p, thankful that p, excited that p, proud that p, surprised that p, embarrassed that p, disgusted that p, sorry that p, angry that p, can regret that p, and so on.[16] As Gordon (1987, ch. 3–4) demonstrates, these emotions divide into two classes: those on the former list, and more besides, are *factive* emotions that take facts as their objects. Because we bear these emotions toward what we regard as facts, we are psychologically disposed to feel them only when we take ourselves to know the relevant facts. Thus Gordon argues that these factive emotions are *knowledge-requiring*: for these emotions, one emotes that p only if one knows that p (see also Unger 1975, 151–52, 171ff.; and Dietz 2018). Of course, one can also fear or be afraid that p, be worried that p, and, as we've seen, one can hope or be hopeful that p. By contrast with those emotions from the longer list, those on this latter list involving hope and fear are *knowledge-precluding*: one hopes (or fears) that p only if one does not know that p. Gordon calls these "epistemic" emotions.

Some evidence for the knowledge requirement on factive emotions comes from the following. As Gordon notes (1987, 38), with factive emotives, one can first assert what one emotes about, then as a separate claim, ascribe the emotion:

(9) They lost. I regret that (fact).
(10) She got the job. I'm surprised about that (fact).

If, as I've noted above, knowledge is the norm of assertion, one represents oneself as knowing by asserting the initial conjunct. The anaphoric use of "that" in the second claim, to refer back to the object of one's emotion, along with the availability of adding "fact" after it, complements the idea that one's expected epistemic position is that of knowing the fact that one regrets or is surprised about: knowing that fact, which is required to assert that it is a fact, also positions one epistemically to emote about that fact. But the relevance of knowledge here is reinforced by attempts to deny knowledge once one has self-ascribed the factive emotion:

(11) # I regret that they lost, but I don't know whether they did.
(12) # I am surprised that she got the job, but I don't know that she did. [17]

Unsurprisingly, these two sets of data, when explained in terms of the requirement of knowledge, combine to enable us to predict that asserting, then disavowing knowledge immediately in the next sentence, will sound quite strange:

(13) # They lost. I regret that, but I don't know whether they lost.
(14) # She got the job. I'm surprised about that, but I don't know that she did.

Thus while (9) and (10) implicate the speaker in knowing and sound fine, the infelicity of (11) through (14) support the idea that knowledge is *required* for self-ascribing such factive emotions. For if it were not required, we should expect that one could disavow knowledge of the fact emoted about.

Additional evidence emerges from similar linguistic data as that considered in section 1, concerning self-ascription of hope and self-ascription of a factive emotion, each with the same propositional object. Infelicity judgments comparable to (3) through (5) apply to the following:

(15) # I regret that John is not in his office, but I hope that he is.
(16) # I hope that John is in his office, and/but I am grateful that he is.
(17) # I hope that John is in his office, and/but I am surprised that he is.

And it likewise sounds strange to self-ascribe hope using anaphoric "that" after having asserted the fact:

(18) # They lost. I hope that (fact).
(19) # She got the job. I hope that she did.

Similar results ensue for (18) or (19) self-ascribing fear instead of hope. [18] If we can make any sense of what such a speaker of (18) or (19) would be trying to say, the interpretation would seem to require a retreat from their commitment in having first asserted the claim, as in "They lost, I hope." (Thus one may, perhaps awkwardly, convey the idea behind (18) with "They lost. That is what I hope.") But such constructions would, of course, amount to a hedging of one's assertion rather than an outright assertion with a discrete hope ascription added subsequently; and hedged assertions are most plausibly understood as hedging against the requirement that one know what one asserts.[19]

So while many emotions are naturally held when and only when we think we know some facts, the epistemological aspects of hope, like fear, involve not knowing that for which one hopes or that which one fears. Events or outcomes that we regard as epistemically possible and not already known are eligible to hope for (or to fear), depending on our desires and their importance to us. But this is a rather thin constraint on the possibility of hope. In the next section we consider some additional epistemological considerations that bear on the rationality of being hopeful, and of acting on the basis of such hope.

3. RATIONALLY HOPEFUL

For all that has been said so far, one may hope that p so long as one does not know whether p, and one prefers or desires that p over $\neg p$. But this is a somewhat bare notion of hope, describing a set of merely necessary conditions. There are great many propositions that I do not know that I desire to be (or become) true, but I plausibly do not hope for all of them. Furthermore, this thin conception of hope will be unable to distinguish between people with the same low probability that p and the same strength of desire for p, but where only one of them hopes that p while the other despairs that $\neg p$.[20] What more can be said about why one may or should hope, and how this might matter to one's practical life? Many of these considerations will invoke non-epistemic norms on hope but articulating these allow us to examine some epistemically relevant features, especially once we get to section 4.

Let us move beyond merely hoping that p to being hope*ful* that p, where being hopeful labels something stronger. I might, for example, hope that I win the lottery, or that the vastly outmatched underdog team win through to become eventual tournament champions. But should I be *hopeful* for these things? To be hopeful about something being or becoming true presumably involves being disposed to refrain from anxiety and despair at the first signs that what one hopes for will not turn out true. If I am to be hopeful as opposed to merely having hope, I would need to be somewhat resistant to giving up my projects aimed at, or otherwise linked to, the outcomes for which I hope. In addition, I would need to be disposed, within limits, to act in ways that suggest some minimal measure of confidence that these outcomes will turn out as I desire.

Such hopefulness is the target of analyses given by Martin 2014 and Blöser and Stahl 2017.[21] Martin's influential Incorporation Analysis recognizes the relevance of desire and probability (insufficient for knowledge), but also appeals to the idea that the hopeful person integrates their hope into their motivational scheme, such that it plays a crucial role in justifying their plans and actions:

> [H]opeful people stand ready to *justify* dedicating certain kinds of attention and thought to the outcome, as well as hedged reliance on the outcome in their plans; moreover, they stand ready to appeal to the outcome's probability as part of their justification for these activities. (Martin 2014, 24)

When we are hopeful, she says, "we *incorporate* our attraction to an uncertain outcome into our agency by treating it as a reason for hopeful activities and feelings" (2014, 25). For Martin, this incorporation element involves two parts. First, "the hopeful person takes a 'licensing' stance toward the probability she assigns the hoped-for outcome," where this stance involves her "seeing that probability as licensing her to treat her desire for the outcome" and its desirable features "as reasons to engage in the forms of planning, thought, and feeling" characteristic of one who is hopeful for that outcome. Second, the hopeful person goes beyond this "seeing as" characteristic of said licensing stance to actually treat her attraction to that outcome and its desirable features as reasons to engage in such planning, thinking, and feeling. These two parts involve ways in which the subject represents their probability assigned to, as well as their attraction to, the hoped-for outcome; together they elucidate what it is for the hopeful person to stand ready to offer a justifying rationale for their actions (2014, 35–36; cf. also 62).

For Martin, while theoretical norms exclusively govern one's probability assignment to an outcome, the norms governing the hopeful person's two-part representation of the probability and the desired outcome are practical rather than theoretical in nature. Taking a licensing stance toward that outcome's probability, and treating one's attraction to it as a reason for such thoughts, plans, or feelings, are governed solely by practical rationality in terms of rational-ends-promotion, that is, whether doing so coheres with and promotes the hopeful person's rational ends. On this approach, part of what makes hopefulness rational,[22] is that the reasons that figure in the justification that one stands ready to offer of one's thoughts, plans, or feelings, serve to promote the ends at which they are aimed. Because some of such doings can involve simply thoughts or feelings related to fantasizing about the outcome, it is possible on Martin's analysis for one to be hopeful even for outcomes over which one's actions have no control (Martin 2014, 66–68).

One possible shortcoming of Martin's account is that the reasons for hopefulness might seem to be merely instrumentalist in nature: the reasons that make hopefulness rational do so because they are instrumental to securing the ends of either the hoped-for outcome or the practical and mental activities characteristic of desiring that outcome. As such, Martin's account may fail to capture certain sorts of hope grounded in one's practical identity, where what makes it rational to continue being hopeful that p is not that one's probability for and attraction to p license one in incorporating that attraction into one's rational scheme of ends, but rather, that such a hopeful attitude is partly constitutive of the agent's identity and so in some sense is intrinsically valuable to them. Blöser and Stahl 2017 argue that such "fundamental hopes can be noninstrumentally rational if they are essential to the hopeful person's being who she is": the rationality of such hopefulness is not grounded in "that of end promotion but that of upholding one's personal integrity, such that the relevant hope is a constituent part of a scheme of ends that one has reason to uphold" (2017, 354–55). Examples of such practical identities might be "the cancer patient who continues to hope despite the low probability of her recovery, and the political activist who hopes for the end of global inequality in full knowledge of its unlikeliness" (356).[23] For such cases,

> the crucial condition is that the identity of the agent must be partly constituted by a certain *perspective on the world* in which certain considerations count as reason-giving, and that giving up hope would entail the unavailability of those lines of reasoning. . . . If it is true that being responsive to certain reasons is constitutive of an individual's practical identity, then adopting a perspective of resignation endangers parts of their identity. To the extent that they want to maintain their identity, they have reason to resist such a change of perspective and to maintain hope. . . . [T]he fact that the hopeful activities form part of a person's practical identity provides a reason to continue to hope that may outweigh the reasons given by cost-benefit analysis. (357)

For these fundamental hopes tied to one's practical identity, a natural question will be what could make it rational for one to give up these sorts of hope. Blöser and Stahl (2017, 364ff.) consider some of the ways this might become rational, due to a revision of one's probability (or whether the original probability no longer suffices a licensing stance), or due to a revision of their practical identity (by no longer viewing the practical identity as being constitutively connected to such hopeful activities, or because of a devaluing of that practical identity). Such revisions are instructive and are arguably related to a concern about what might make it rational, or irrational, to continue on in hopefulness under certain circumstances. In particular, it will help to consider the epistemic dimension of inductive cases that can seem to threaten the rationality of persisting in hopefulness.

4. INDUCTIVE CONSIDERATIONS

Suppose that you have studied and received many years of training to be employed in a certain profession, which you regard as ideal for you given your passions and your considerable skills. Perhaps you even regard such work as somehow fundamental to your identity, the sort of work you were "born to do." But this profession is very competitive and there are far too few full-time positions for how many qualified applicants there are applying to any given post. You are able to support yourself presently through employment related to your intended career, all while submitting numerous applications for positions in your profession. Despite a few interviews and some encouragement here and there, you never get to the final interview stage, nor have you been offered a full-time position. And this discouraging pattern goes on for *years*. While you began hopeful that you would eventually secure such a post, it is beginning to look more and more unlikely, and you cannot continue to apply for such jobs indefinitely. The evidence, inexact as it is, appears to be mounting that you will not get such a post no matter how long you try. At what point should you decide not to pursue this career anymore and move on to something else?[24] At what point, that is, ought you to give up hope?[25]

In some cases like these, we may regard one who persists in hopefulness, against very strong evidence that their hope will be fulfilled, as exhibiting a series of *virtues*: being steadfast, brave, faithfully and unwaveringly committed to the increasingly unlikely but hoped-for outcome. Yet in other (perhaps very similar) cases, we will view such a hopeful person as exhibiting a kind of intellectual *vice* or irrationality: we may regard them as stubborn, unrealistic, or even delusional. What, if anything, might mark the difference between such divergent judgments? Is there any principled way to draw the line between virtuous and vicious hopefulness, which tracks some fact of the matter about the right or best conditions in which to be hopeful and act hopefully?

A skeptic about the possibility of such a principled account might insist that there can be no such account, because all there is to our divergent judgments is the following. Perhaps, on the one hand, we are disposed to label retrospectively as virtuous people who are hopeful, in the face of strong inductive counterevidence, for outcomes that we also desire (or might desire were we in their shoes) that end up turning out as they desire. Whereas on the other hand, we are disposed to label retrospectively as vicious people who are hopeful, in the face of strong inductive counterevidence, for outcomes that either we do not similarly desire (or would not desire were we in their shoes) or that, unfortunately for them, do not turn out as they desire. On this rather natural idea, our hypological judgments of praise and blame in these cases of hopefulness simply track how we ourselves would like things to turn out for us were we in their shoes: we will praise as virtuous the person who is hopeful against all odds when it turns out well for them, whereas we will scorn as irresponsible the person who is hopeful against all odds for something that we either do not ourselves want, *or* that, if we also want it, does not turn out well for them (or us).[26] In other words, such a skeptic urges us to accept that our virtue-theoretic evaluations just amount to a kind of affective counterfactualizing, informed by our moral psychology regarding how we ourselves would prefer to act in similar circumstances, which include the circumstances of how things turned out.[27]

Yet the skeptic's natural explanation[28] cannot, it seems, be correct as it stands. For we often admire those who in hopefulness persevere even when we do not desire what they do, marveling at their pluck even if in the end they never achieve or arrive at their desired outcome. We can applaud the hopeful efforts by the losing team even as the possibility of winning appears to be increasingly out of reach. Somewhat differently, but perhaps relatedly, the atheist can admire the hopefulness of the faithful, even to the point of wishing they had such faith themselves. On the other hand, we can regard as irrational one who takes an unacceptable risk out of hopefulness even when we desire what they do and it turns out, against all odds, well for them. So, against the skeptic, perhaps instead there *is* a principled way of demarcating virtuous from vicious hopefulness, at least in cases of mounting counterevidence, which appeals to a combination of risk aversion and the rationality of updating one's credences. Here I shall only provide the briefest sketch, but my hope is that it can still be profitable for understanding a line between rational and irrational hopefulness.[29]

In Martin's terminology, whether one ought to continue to treat one's attraction to the increasingly unlikely but hoped-for outcome as a reason for engaging in one's efforts, plans, thoughts, or feelings, depends on whether adopting the licensing stance (toward the probability of the desired outcome) and engaging in the hopeful activities (of thinking, feeling, and planning for the outcome) ends up promoting one's rational ends. Whether doing both of these does promote one's rational ends is in part a function of how probable it is for one that the outcome will obtain, but also of how strong one's desire is for that outcome. And in the face of mounting inductive counterevidence, one will (if one is being rational) be lowering the probability of the desired outcome *while also* reevaluating whether the strength of one's attraction to it suffices, under such circumstances, to justify one's ongoing intentional and affective investment in it. In particular, if the wait for the desired outcome takes long enough, and coincides with enough counterevidence, the hopeful person will have to add into her considerations the undesirability of prolonged and ongoing frustration of her hopes: not only must she contend with the increasing unlikelihood of the desired outcome, but also the concern that even if her desired outcome obtains, gaining it only after years of disappointment may make the total situation less desirable. Sunken costs (among other factors) may push her to continue on in hopefulness, but opportunity costs and being risk averse with respect to continued failure, given the lowering probability, may make her feel that she can no longer justify her intentional and affective investment in her hope.[30] Yet such risk aversion is not simply a product of how strongly one wants to avoid continued disappointment; how probable such episodes of disappointment are is also relevant, and this probability appears to increase with the mounting counterevidence.[31]

My suggestion then is that the rationality of persistence in hopefulness, despite mounting counterevidence, will depend on how resilient one can anticipate being in the face of further likely disappointments. But whether one can anticipate being this resilient depends on how probable it is, given one's evidence, that it will be worth it for one to persist through more disappointment. And whether it will be worth it so to persist is related to (a) how hard such disappointments have been on one in the past (a practical judgment), as well as (b) how likely, and how often, one's hopes will be frustrated in the future (a theoretical/probabilistic judgment). One persists rationally in such hopefulness if one continues to incorporate one's probability and attraction to the outcome into one's rational agency, while also not neglecting how the counterevidence has affected both one's continuing desire for the outcome under these circumstances (concerning the probability and affective impact of future frustrations) *and* the probability that it will occur. One persists irrationally in such hopefulness if one neglects how the mounting counterevidence has affected both one's desires for both the outcome and for avoiding future disappointment, and the probability that one can be resilient to further frustrations.

5. CONCLUSION

We have encountered a variety of epistemological dimensions related to hope. In particular, our conceptual and linguistic judgments suggest very strongly that bare hope that *p* is somehow incompatible with knowledge whether *p*, and one is licensed in such hope when there is an epistemic chance for one both that *p* and that ¬*p*. Given their incompatibility with knowledge, first-personal propositional claims to *hope that*, or to *fear that*, distinguish themselves from a wide range of emotive predicates that plausibly require that one know, or at least take oneself to know, in order to satisfy the emotive relation. Yet such bare hope may be distinguished from hope*fulness*, which brings several of its own epistemological features. These include the ways in which one's assessment of the probability of the outcome to which one is attracted bears on the rationality of persisting in the thoughts, feelings, and actions characteristic of hopefulness. And cases of mounting inductive counterevidence in the face of that for which one seeks to maintain hopefulness, particularly when such hopefulness is grounded in one's practical identity, provide further interesting cases for investigating the evaluative aspects which might make for rational, as opposed to irrational, hopeful persistence.[32]

NOTES

1. There are other sorts of hope, which arguably have a different structure: for example, one may place hope *in* a person, or perhaps an institution (e.g., hope in democracy), or even a life project. For work on the interpersonal version of such hope, see Adrienne Martin's contribution to this volume.

2. For a more thorough treatment of such data see Benton 2018. Here I only consider linguistic data from English, but I am assured by native speakers of Spanish, French, German, and Korean that such data is cross-linguistic. (Note that in some languages like Mandarin, there is no word comparable to the English word *hope*; the closest word only means something like *wish* or *desire*. In such languages, there is no linguistic data like those discussed here, because they have no word expressing the same concept of *hope*.)

3. Or, alternatively, that Tim had known all along that Janice was *not* at home.

4. This reaction might be undergirded by an *assert the stronger* rule: see especially Grice and White 1961, 132 (though he omits this from its reprinting in 1989: see 229–30); cf. also DeRose 2009, 87, and (related to hope) Chignell 2013, 198 and 200. For more general considerations on how such language can hedge our assertions, see Benton and van Elswyk 2019.

5. I use # to mark sentences or responses that clearly clash, suggesting some inconsistency or incoherence.

6. Such examples should also make clear that, although we often think of hope in *forward-looking* terms about the future, one can clearly hope for already settled outcomes: what is forward-looking is the time at which one comes to know the outcome.

7. That data discussed here (and more thoroughly in Benton 2018), show that propositional hope is not, *contra* Ninan 2012, a counterfactual attitude like imagining, which we may take toward propositions we know to be false.

8. Some may be able to hear (6), and perhaps also (3) above, as (somewhat) felicitous. But such an interpretation appears to track only the desire aspect of hope, and thus such claims would be better put in terms of a mere *wish*: and indeed, substituting *wish* (plus its subjunctive mood) for *hope* in these examples makes them sound much more apt for such an interpretation.

9. In Benton 2018, I discuss embedding tests that provide strong evidence that they are semantically inconsistent.

10. This is sometimes called the Knowledge Norm of Assertion. See Williamson 2000, ch. 11; Hawthorne 2004, 23ff.; Turri 2011, 2014, 2016; Benton 2011, 2016; and Benton and van Elswyk 2019, among many others. Rival norms of assertion are offered by Weiner 2005, Douven 2006; Lackey 2007; McKinnon 2015; and Gerken 2017, among others. For an overview of this literature, see Benton 2014, section 1.

11. For some related ideas, cf. Eagleton 2015; Pasnau 2015 and 2017, chapter 6.

12. See Benton 2018 for more.

13. Fantl and McGrath 2009 develop a related account of the practical relevance of such chances and their relation to (fallibilist) knowledge; but they do not consider hope or a principle like CLH.

14. Such chances might then be identified with credences or subjective probabilities, rather than objective probabilities or what Williamson 2000, ch. 10, calls *evidential* probabilities, namely the probability on one's evidence. Note that on Williamson's E = K view of evidence, which identifies one's evidence with all and only one's knowledge, CLH's chances could be evidential probabilities; and on E = K a version of infallibilism is upheld since whenever one knows p, the probability of p on one's evidence is 1.

15. The incompatibility could be logical, or psychological, or rational in nature; I take no stand on this here. But see Benton 2018 for arguments that it cannot simply be explained by conversational pragmatics.

16. For a more thorough list, see Gordon 1969, 410, and 1987, 26–27.

17. Note also that many of such conjunctions sound bad even in third-person form: # She is surprised that she got the job, but she doesn't know that she did.

18. See Gordon 1980; and 1987, chapter 4. Gordon acknowledges that there are some conventional uses of "I fear" that seem like exceptions to the knowledge-precluding requirement: like when one says "I fear I will have to get another job," or "I fear going to the dentist

this afternoon." Gordon insists that these are parasitic on the standard use (1987, 68). But also, these cases seem more like stative attributions than propositional attitudes: one fears the state or process of having to find a new job, or going to the dentist, and so on.

19. See Benton and van Elwsyk 2019.

20. See Gordon's case of the two farmers (1987, 8 and 33); Meirav's (2009) Shawshank Redemption case (2009); and Martin's Cancer Research case (2014, 14–15).

21. Martin explicitly states that her Incorporation account aims to capture hope "in its fullest sense" (2014, 62), that is, when it is "full-fledged," and here she is mainly concerned with hopefulness even though she also acknowledges the more bare notion of hope such as we have discussed above. Note that Martin also uses the language of "hopeful" throughout her presenta-tion of it, as cited below.

22. Given a theoretically rational probability assignment between 0 and 1 on one's evidence.

23. They also cite the case of "a religious person's hope for life after death" (350).

24. Note that comparable (sometimes tragic) cases abound: for example, how long should a couple who wants a baby try to conceive before turning to adoption or other options? How long should one hold out for finding a life-partner before deciding to remain single? How long should loved ones search for a missing person? And so on.

25. Such a case seems related to Martin's examples of people who "hope against hope" (2014, 14), as in her cancer research case. But the above case varies in that the strong counter-evidence in question is gained diachronically and applies to the subject's own situation, where-as in a cancer research case, the strong statistical evidence is gained from others' experiences with an experimental drug. See also Blöser and Stahl 2017, section 3.2 for related cases on when to give up hope.

26. These ideas bear some similarities to what Williams 1981, 30–37, suggests may ground retrospective judgments of our own actions.

27. Such affective counterfactualizing, if this is what we do, might be related to work on affective forecasting in psychology (e.g., work by Wilson and Gilbert, esp. 2003 and 2005, among others). I shall leave it to the interested reader to draw any relevant comparisons or contrasts.

28. This story would justify skepticism about a principled account of rational hopefulness because the skeptic has offered a deflationary relativism to explain why different individuals will make the hypological judgments that they do: relative to a certain individual A's prefer-ences, plus B's evidence, plus how things turn out for B, we have the whole story about why A would judge B's hopefulness as (say) rational/virtuous, without needing any underlying princi-ple that accurately represents some facts that make B rational to be hopeful in B's case. This skepticism would be borne of a kind of relativism insofar as it leads the skeptic to insist that there is no fact of the matter which makes for rationality here; and without such facts, no principled account can accurately represent them.

29. I am assuming here that virtuous hopefulness must at least involve some sort of rational-ity or responsibility, and that vicious hopefulness at least involves a corresponding irrationality or irresponsibility. Of course, our focus here is on the epistemic or evidential dimensions; it could be possible, however, to be rational along these dimensions while nevertheless exhibiting a different sort of vice, for example, by valuing and desiring certain (immoral or evil) ends. But for present purposes I put those vices aside.

30. Buchak's 2013 risk-weighted expected utility (REU) theory might shed some light on such cases, though her theory is not framed in terms of hopefulness; however, I suspect that one will be rational in persisting in hopefulness in at least those cases where her REU theory sanctions as rational the relevant actions done from hopefulness.

31. Calhoun 2018, chapter 5, explores some related matters concerning hope's role in moti-vation when one contemplates the possibility that one's present and past efforts will have been wasted: see, especially, pp. 77–80.

32. For helpful comments, many thanks to Claudia Blöser, Adrienne Martin, Titus Stahl, and Peter van Elswyk, as well as Patrick McDonald, Rebekah Rice, and Leland Saunders; thanks also to many helpful conversations with Anne Jeffrey. This paper was supported by a Faculty Research and Scholarship grant (Seattle Pacific University, 2018), and by a grant from the John Templeton Foundation (the Hope and Optimism: Conceptual and Empirical Investiga-

tions project, based in part at the University of Notre Dame, 2016–2017). The opinions expressed in this publication are those of the author and do not necessarily reflect the views of the John Templeton Foundation.

REFERENCES

Benton, Matthew A. 2011. "Two More for the Knowledge Account of Assertion." *Analysis* 71 (4): 684–87.
Benton, Matthew A. 2014. "Knowledge Norms." *Internet Encyclopedia of Philosophy*. ISSN 2161–0002. http://www.iep.utm.edu/kn–norms/.
Benton, Matthew A. 2016. "Gricean Quality." *Noûs* 50 (4): 689–703.
Benton, Matthew A. 2018. "Knowledge, Hope, and Fallibilism." *Synthese*. Early View. https://doi.org/10.1007/s11229-018-1794-8.
Benton, Matthew A., and Peter van Elswyk. 2019. "Hedged Assertion." In *The Oxford Handbook of Assertion*, edited by Sanford Goldberg. Oxford: Oxford University Press.
Blöser, Claudia, and Titus Stahl. 2017. "Fundamental Hope and Practical Identity." *Philosophical Papers* 26: 345–71.
Bovens, Luc. 1999. "The Value of Hope." *Philosophy and Phenomenological Research* 59 (3): 667–81.
Buchak, Lara. 2013. *Risk and Rationality*. Oxford: Oxford University Press.
Calhoun, Chesire. 2018. *Doing Valuable Time: The Present, the Future, and Meaningful Living*. Oxford: Oxford University Press.
Chignell, Andrew. 2013. "Rational Hope, Moral Order, and the Revolution of the Will." In *Divine Order, Human Order, and the Order of Nature: Historical Perspectives*, edited by Eric Watkins, 197–218. Oxford: Oxford University Press.
Day, J. P. 1969. "Hope." *American Philosophical Quarterly* 6 (2): 89–102.
DeRose, Keith. 2009. *The Case for Contextualism*. Oxford: Clarendon Press.
Dietz, Christina H. 2018. "Reasons and Factive Emotions." *Philosophical Studies* 175 (7): 1681–91.
Douven, Igor. 2006. "Assertion, Knowledge, and Rational Credibility." *The Philosophical Review* 115 (4): 449–85.
Downie, R. S. 1963. "Hope." *Philosophy and Phenomenological Research* 24 (2): 248–51.
Eagleton, Terry. 2015. *Hope without Optimism*. Charlottesville: University of Virginia Press.
Fantl, Jeremy, and McGrath, Matthew. 2009. *Knowledge in an Uncertain World*. Oxford: Oxford University Press.
Gerken, Mikkel. 2017. *On Folk Epistemology*. Oxford: Oxford University Press.
Gordon, Robert M. 1969. "Emotions and Knowledge." *Journal of Philosophy* 66 (July): 408–13.
Gordon, Robert M. 1980. "Fear." *Philosophical Review* 89 (4): 560–78.
Gordon, Robert M. 1987. *The Structure of Emotions: Investigations in Cognitive Philosophy*. Cambridge: Cambridge University Press.
Grice, H. P., and Alan R. White. 1961. "Symposium: The Causal Theory of Perception." *Proceedings of the Aristotelian Society, Supplementary Volumes* 35 (1): 121–68. Portions reprinted in Grice 1989.
Grice, Paul. 1989. *Studies in the Way of Words*. Cambridge, MA: Harvard University Press.
Hawthorne, John. 2004. *Knowledge and Lotteries*. Oxford: Clarendon Press.
Lackey, Jennifer. 2007. "Norms of Assertion." *Noûs* 41 (4): 594–626.
Martin, Adrienne M. 2011. "Hopes and Dreams." *Philosophy and Phenomenological Research* 83 (1): 148–73.
Martin, Adrienne M. 2014. *How We Hope: A Moral Psychology*. Princeton, NJ: Princeton University Press.
McKinnon, Rachel. 2015. *Norms of Assertion: Truth, Lies, and Warrant*. London: Palgrave Macmillan.
Meirav, Ariel. 2009. "The Nature of Hope." *Ratio* 22 (2): 216–33.

Ninan, Dilip. 2012. "Counterfactual Attitudes and Multi-Centered Worlds." *Semantics and Pragmatics* 5, article 5: 1–57. https://doi.org/10.3765/sp.5.5.

Pasnau, Robert. 2015. "Snatching Hope from the Jaws of Epistemic Defeat." *Journal of the American Philosophical Association* 1 (2): 257–75.

Pasnau, Robert. 2017. *After Certainty: A History of Our Epistemic Ideals and Illusions*. Oxford: Oxford University Press.

Turri, John. 2011. "The Express Knowledge Account of Assertion." *Australasian Journal of Philosophy* 89 (1): 37–45.

Turri, John. 2014. "Knowledge and Suberogatory Assertion." *Philosophical Studies* 167 (3): 557–57.

Turri, John. 2016. *Knowledge and the Norm of Assertion: An Essay in Philosophical Science*. Cambridge: Open Book Publishers.

Unger, Peter. 1975. *Ignorance: A Defense of Skepticism*. Oxford: Clarendon Press.

Weiner, Matthew. 2005. "Must We Know What We Say?" *The Philosophical Review* 114 (2): 227–51.

Williams, Bernard. 1981. *Moral Luck: Philosophical Papers 1973–1980*. Cambridge: Cambridge University Press.

Williamson, Timothy. 2000. *Knowledge and Its Limits*. Oxford: Oxford University Press.

Wilson, Timothy D., and Daniel T. Gilbert. 2003. "Affective Forecasting." *Advances in Experimental Social Psychology* 35 (35): 345–411.

Wilson, Timothy D., and Daniel T. Gilbert. 2005. "Affective Forecasting: Knowing What to Want." *Current Directions in Psychological Science* 14 (3): 131–34.

Chapter Nine

Pessimism and the Possibility of Hope

Samantha Vice

There are good reasons to think that hope is necessary for a life worth living and that there are not only prudential reasons to value it, but ethical ones too. Pessimism about the possibility of moral progress, on the other hand, is optional, and unless one is already temperamentally inclined toward attending to the human world's gloomier aspects, there seem to be no obvious moral or prudential reasons in its favor. The pessimistic outlook may not be morally iniquitous, but is there anything to warrant it? Furthermore, are pessimism and hope not clearly incompatible? They are both forward-looking attitudes, but their views of the future are opposed: Hope anticipates a future that is open to our efforts and which promises to be good, or at least better than the present. Pessimism anticipates a future much like the present, which is much like the past, which, given our record, is not an uplifting prediction. Seen like this, they are incompatible attitudes. And given that hope seems indispensable for a worthwhile life, it is tempting to set the one against the other and recommend the clearly more felicitous option.

I will argue, however, that this picture is too simple and that there is a sense in which the two attitudes are compatible. Moreover, the world gives us ample evidence that pessimism is not unreasonable and is often warranted, and it is difficult to accuse the pessimist—as opposed to the cynic or nihilist or misanthropist—of moral corruption. Common responses toward pessimism as a character trait are usually negative, but this is often because they reduce pessimism to these close, but morally distinct relatives. In this paper, I neither defend pessimism and its moral credentials directly, nor present a full account of hope and its ethical significance, but rather explore whether these two attitudes are, in some interpretation, compatible. If they are, and if hope is as ethically and psychologically important as is often suggested, this would render pessimism less problematic. My suggestions are sketchy, but if there is anything in their favor they could leave open the fortunate possibility that those inclined toward pessimism might yet retain some hope.

Both hope and pessimism can be variously described, of course, so I begin in section 1 by describing the kinds that interest me—and here, on the whole, I stipulate rather than defend them. In section 2, I then explore three considerations in favor of their compatibility.

1. PESSIMISM AND HOPE

Pessimism

The kind of pessimism I am interested in I call "anthropocentric moral pessimism" (hereafter, "Pessimism"). It is a perspective or attitude on the human world that is skeptical of the possibility of significant moral progress, and that considers the harm that humans cause to be morally more salient and weighty than the good they bring about. It is an *attitude*, so it encompasses beliefs, perceptions, behavior and modes of valuing. The object of the attitude is fundamentally moral, rather than for instance, prudential. That is, it concerns moral progress and moral failures, on the part of human moral agents. It is *anthropocentric* because it focuses on human beings and makes no claims about the nature of the nonhuman world, except that it is adversely affected by the presence of humans. And it is "moral," for a number of reasons that I will explore further below: it is an evaluative attitude, which, as noted above, takes moral progress and failure as its object; it accepts the objectivity of (some) value; and it is distinguished from morally problematic attitudes like cynicism and misanthropy.

There are many ways of filling in this basic position, and the authors I draw on below do so variously, but to be distinctive and not to reduce to other, morally problematic, attitudes, I would argue that the following aspects are essential to any more substantial conception: First, Pessimism contains a view about human beings, that something in their nature makes them more susceptible to going morally wrong, either intentionally or unintentionally, than to loving and being guided by the good. Pessimism is therefore concerned with human-originating disvalue, rather than with disvalue in the world generally.[1] Religious views might offer original sin as an explanation; Kant (1960) would point to our propensity to "radical evil"; secular accounts might point to aggressive or selfish instincts, or to motivational and deliberative structures that reliably send us in the wrong moral (and often prudential) direction. Whatever the reason, the position is not one of hard determinism, and it describes tendencies and susceptibilities rather than certainties. We therefore maintain responsibility and can fairly be blamed to some significant degree for our failings, whether through our actions or our omissions and indifference. We should try to be better, even knowing that we might very well fail.

Second, Pessimism does not deny that humans can do what is good and right, nor that we do create and properly respond to value. It is not cynicism, nihilism, or misanthropy.[2] It does, however, deny that the value we create and realize generally outweighs or "counts for more" than the bad that we more reliably bring about. It is difficult to make this point in a way that does not immediately make it empirical—that is, does not reduce the discussion to the calculation of consequences and effects. We can argue about that to no conclusion, because optimists and pessimists will differ about what evidence is salient, what time frame to consider, or what weight to give the different considerations. Marshalling of facts on either side will not settle the debate. So we should resist being pushed to the quantitative and should instead think in terms more like "redemption," "triumphing over," or "making up for." The good we do, then, does not redeem or make up for the bad. The pessimist thinks that values are intelligible and possible to realize, but that it is unlikely that they will be realized by humans to a significant degree, in a way that outweighs the bad. In Paul Prescott's terms (throughout 2012), Pessimism claims that it is unrealistic to expect the good to prevail over the bad; or in Stewart Sutherland's (1981, 538) terms, to expect the triumph of good over evil.

Third, if the good cannot prevail, then, drawing on Stuart Hampshire (1978, 22) now, moral progress is not to be expected except within very narrow limits, and social and historical changes are expected to be only superficial in their consequences. If this sounds too strong, we can note how undoubted gains in one area of human life (e.g., rights for women; more protection for animals and children) can be offset by losses in another (the gender "glass ceiling"; the inequality and persecution of transgender people; the continuation of factory farming; ongoing war in the Middle East and Africa). Globally, progress does not seem stable, and the expected effects of climate change now threaten most social and political gains. In any case, Pessimism makes a prediction only, and therefore remains a position of some epistemic and moral humility.

Finally, Pessimism is distinguished from attitudes like cynicism or misanthropy because it does not imply or require a particular response to human beings; it does not, for instance, claim that because the human world is disappointing, we should therefore hate it or disengage from or mistrust people. There is a real question whether such pessimism is sustainable, or whether it would naturally fall into more negative attitudes. Would our disappointment in ourselves not rankle? What could sustain love of human beings in the face of our harmful record? I cannot address this adequately in this paper, but much of what I say in section 2 is relevant to addressing it. It is important to note, however, that there is conceptual space for such a morally benign attitude—one that is skeptical of the possibility of progress and impressed by human failures, but which does not prescribe a hateful attitude toward people in response.

Although one may be pessimistic about particular issues, events and people—a point toward which I shall return—it is fundamentally a broader attitude toward the moral failings and prospects of human existence in general. Pessimists see the world in a certain light, or perhaps it is more phenomenologically accurate to say that the world *comes to them* already qualitatively somber. (Here, of course, it mirrors the optimistic attitude, and it is worth noting that we do not think the optimist *prima facie* irrational merely for seeing the world cheerfully.) In light of current political conditions across the world, ongoing wars, and anthropogenic climate change, the urgent effects of which we are starting to feel, Pessimism does not seem obviously irrational. Despite attempts like those of Steven Pinker's (2011) to show that the world is in a better state than it has ever been, it is difficult to believe that this is really the case for those in the midst of famine, wars, or rising sea levels. Perhaps levels of violence are indeed down, as he argues, but given the levels that still remain, taking comfort in this sets the bar pretty low. Given the inevitability of major climate upheaval, we seem to have bequeathed our children a brutally difficult future, regardless.

While it would be churlish to encourage Pessimism, it seems no less rational and as warranted as optimism and—in certain moods—more so. The supporting views of human nature given by varieties of Pessimism may of course be up for discussion and be more or less plausible, but the basic Pessimism about human effects and the implausibility of expecting significant moral progress in the future is on the table as much as an optimistic belief in a better future. Given that empirical exploration will not settle the matter, a critic would need to show that the Pessimist is making a *moral* mistake, rather than unfortunately missing out on a more comforting or prudentially valuable outlook. One way of showing this would be to argue that it is destructive of or incompatible with clearly morally admirable or necessary attitudes and values, like hope. I now explore hope to see if this is, indeed, the case. Much is at stake, because a life bereft of hope would be a version of hell.[3]

Hopefulness

The standard account of hope, going back to Aquinas and Hume, understands it as consisting of a desire and a belief that the desire can be satisfied.[4] Hope on this account involves deliberating about possibilities and it always has a definite object: we hope that something particular and identifiable will be the case. Hope requires both that we be uncertain about the future and think that it is at least possible that what we desire will come about. If the probability is very low or zero, to hope would be irrational and turns into mere wishful thinking.

I will leave detailed analyses of this standard account of hope to other contributors in this collection, and broaden my focus beyond these discrete hopes, to being a certain kind of person with a certain kind of perspective on the world. The *hopeful* person will have particular hopes, certainly, but the world also comes to her as promising; she tends to notice the good more than the bad and expects some goodness in the future. Hopeful people in this sense are hopeful about the present and future, and hopeful not only about their present and future, but about those of human beings in general. They need not always expect something *better*, but they expect something good or good enough. This may be an expectation of moral or nonmoral value, and it is in the former instances that it is most in tension with Pessimism. However, while it is possible to restrict one's expectation to the nonmoral, it does seem artificial. If the world is experienced by the hopeful person as promising value in the future, and as revealing value now, it is odd to think of the experience as selectively revealing only nonmoral value. In either case, hope is not restricted to the human world, for one may hope for God's intervention or for nature's resilience, but in the morally significant cases something is personally at stake for the person hoping; in crucial hopes, our sense of self is implicated in their realization, and we will not be simply disappointed if they fail.

Pessimism and hopefulness are therefore both attitudes, including particular beliefs, predictions, and desires, but which go beyond that to a way of living in and perceiving the world. They both admit of degrees and eschew certainty—neither pessimism nor hope offer proofs or assurances for their predictions. While Pessimism is defined in terms of *moral* progress, the hopeful person may restrict her hopes to nonmoral value. They are not yet logically incompatible. However, in the absence of certainty, hope expects the good, while pessimism expects states of affairs the same or worse, or perhaps only inconsequentially better. It does therefore seem difficult to see how a person could be both attitudinally hopeful and pessimistic, though of course they could have hopes for particular objects while being pessimistic about others. If hope and pessimism are understood in this way, they do, indeed, seem to be practically incompatible, for how can the world come to a person in both a gloomy and a bright aspect, and how can a person doubt that humans are progressing morally while being hopeful that they might? Logical compatibility seems far less than we would want and leaves the possibility of the two attitudes cohabiting still highly unlikely. If they are to be possible together, we need a different orientation.

Drawing on the work of Gabriel Marcel (1962), I shall therefore further understand the attitude of hopefulness as an orientation toward a future considered as open and receptive to our efforts. The hopeful person, then, is one reliably inclined to view the future in this way, to see her will and actions (or those of others) as being effective in making the world better. The world is not resistant to our efforts and the future may turn out significantly better than the present because of our agency. On this account, there is still a tension with Pessimism, but I will now suggest that Marcel's account of hope as a contrast to despair shows us what Pessimism must avoid if it is to be compatible with hope.

On Marcel's account, hope is a response to a situation that tempts one to despair—what he calls a "trial"—like severe illness, the death of a loved one, captivity, and oppression. Importantly, hope and despair have different relations to the self and to time, and it is on these relations that I will focus.

First, despair threatens our relation to our self. When we despair, we *capitulate*—we identify with the person the situation threatens to make of us, and this, Marcel thinks, threatens our integrity:

> To capitulate . . . is not only . . . to accept the given sentence or even to recognise the inevitable as such, it is to go to pieces under this sentence, to disarm before the inevitable. It is at bottom to renounce the idea of remaining oneself, it is to be fascinated by the idea of one's own destruction to the point of anticipating this very destruction itself. (Marcel 1962, 37–38)

In contrast, to hope is to refuse to capitulate:

> Because I am condemned never to recover from this illness, or not to come out of this prison I do not mean to give up, I do not consent, from this very moment, to be the useless creature which illness or my captivity may finally make of me; I will counter the fascination which the idea of this creature might have for me with the firm determination to remain what I am. (1962, 38)

Again, to refuse despair is to safeguard one's integrity,[5] and it is an advantage of Marcel's account of hope that by linking it to integrity, it can explain why hope is a virtue of character and why we value it.[6] Earlier, I said that in morally significant hopes, one's sense of self and identity is at stake, and the link to integrity brings this out. Cheshire Calhoun (2019) picks up on the personal aspect of hope that Marcel makes central:

> Most importantly, having hopes for ourselves involves the capacity to take our own future seriously. In having hopes for myself . . . the future possibilities from which I pick are desirable, or not, because of the qualities they have as *my* future state. It is some version of me, of my life, that I am picking when I hope for one future rather than another.[7]

Further, the refusal to capitulate is understood as a form of *patience*, rather than a strenuous and anxious struggle against fate. As Philip Stratton-Lake (1999, 143) explains, "to be patient with another is to place our confidence in a certain process of growth, or development, be it our own, or that of another," "in the face of the evidence which tempts one [to] give up on oneself, or another." We do not try to force a result or change a person's natural rhythm; there is a suppleness and grace to our refusal to capitulate to the trial (Marcel 1962, 38). I will return to these ideas, and to their aesthetic suggestiveness.

Second, despair and hope have different relations to the experience of time. In despair, one experiences time as determined, as closed off and mechanical, whereby everything which will occur is represented as already determined by what has occurred (Stratton-Lake 1999, 141). Time is thus conceived of as enclosing or imprisoning us (ibid.). Despair then carries a temptation to turn within and withdraw from the world: "I shall always be exposed to the temptation of shutting the door which encloses me within myself and at the same time encloses me within time," Marcel (1962, 60) writes. The despairing self is imprisoned in the claustrophobia of an unchanging world. In contrast, to hope is to experience time as open with possibilities despite one's trial, and the hopeful self resists the temptation to withdraw into the isolation of despair.

Others writing on hope also characterize it as involving a sense of an open future. Margaret Urban Walker (2006, 45), for instance, describes "the *futurity* of hope"—the sense that hope "goes to what hovers before us with a sense that all is not decided *for us*; what is not yet known is 'as if' open to chance and action, for all one knows." Similarly, Walter Brueggemann (1987, 80) writes,

> *Hope keeps the present arrangement open and provisional.* Hope reminds us that the way things are (and all the extrapolations we make from that), is precarious and in jeopardy. Hope reminds us not to absolutize the present, not to take it too seriously, not to treat it too honourably, because it will not last.

It is certainly tempting for pessimists to view the future as already determined, but the attitude as I understand it does not require this and doing so presents a clear obstacle to hopefulness.

My suggestion now is that pessimism can coexist with hope if it avoids collapsing into despair. Despair sees the future as already determined; time "imprisons" us within a present that determines who we are and how the future will be. Agency is ineffectual and the present or past trial provides the only evidence and information relevant for assessing the future and ourselves. We "capitulate" to this vision, not testing our agency's power to change it, or our self's resilience. In contrast, pessimism does not require capitulation, quietism, or determinism about the future. The pessimist can hope that the good will occur, despite her pessimistic predictions. She can act to try to bring it about, while ruefully accepting the high probability of less than complete success. The future is still open, though the odds may be against its proving significantly better than the present. If she is committed to the good, her efforts will support her integrity and protect her from the prison of despair.

This conjunction of attitudes may be possible, but is it likely, and how would it be sustained? If pessimism is an encompassing attitude, delivering the world to the pessimist already clouded, occluding if not ruling out the possibility of seeing what is good, is hope psychologically possible? I would like to explore three very speculative options of how to avoid despair and keep the attitudes compatible: The first is to consider the role of axiological commitments in rendering the two attitudes compatible; the second is to consider the scope of hope and pessimism; and the third is to consider the role of creativity in maintaining integrity and hope.

2. THE COMPATIBILITY OF HOPE AND PESSIMISM

2.1 Value Commitments

The first line of thought is that the two attitudes may practically coexist against a particular axiological framework. That is, if we see humans as attracted (however imperfectly) to a value that is independent of each one of us, we can retain the hope that this attraction could prove fruitful despite our past record. We can hope that in a particular instance the attraction of value might prove stronger than our moral weakness. If the faults of the human world originate in us and not in there being no value in a robust sense to realize or stand in relation to, we may yet orient ourselves around value. It may act as an "idea of perfection," in Iris Murdoch's (2000) words, which opens the future to our efforts and lights the way. This too can prevent despair—the world and people are not bereft of goodness, the future may yet have goodness in it, even if we feel that it cannot outweigh the bad. The future, the world, our selves, are not monolithic, and goodness does exert its force.

The pessimist need not deny that human beings are valuable in some crucial way despite their faults. Most moral traditions allow for this, and pessimism as described is neutral regarding them. The pessimist may yet be a Kantian, or a consequentialist, religious or atheist, as well as a pessimist. The value of our rational nature is without price, and must be respected, regardless of the moral quality of our actions, says Kant and those traditions influenced by him. Utilitarians, eschewing the metaphysical flights of Kant, still take there to be some quality of undeniably fallible human (though not necessarily only human) experience that makes it morally considerable. Most mono-theistic traditions ascribe supreme value to humans, as the creations of a God who loves and forgives us despite our numerous sins. Virtue ethics considers the flourishing of imperfect human lives to be the proper concern of ethics. Each one of us, then, is in the same moral boat—valuable, error-prone, destructive, and value-seeking all at once—and so there are no good reasons to be self-righteous or harshly judgmental toward each other. We may, instead, take up an attitude of rueful disappointment toward our mistakes and commit ourselves to being better. Still, the human world reveals plenty to love and protect. And the nonhuman world is the source of deep and abiding joy and guidance. By remaining mindful of this, even while the bad looms, the pessimist may avoid despair.

That pessimism as a distinctive attitude is not nihilist or misanthropist, nor denies the many values available to us, therefore provides space for the work of hope. Sometimes we will surprise each other in our goodness, and we can hope for this. If we care about value, then our integrity will be tied to our efforts to achieve it; the recognition of value thus has the potential to protect us from despair's obdurate prison.

These suggestions can be developed in various ways, depending on the metaphysical and ethical framework one finds conducive. While pessimism is compatible with most normative theories, at the level of meta-ethics, as my discussion would have suggested, a nonsubjectivist framework is probably most conducive to the required work. If you think that people tend to get things wrong more than they get them right, or have perverse or irrational desires, or are attracted more to what is bad than what is good, grounding morality on our attitudes, emotions, or desires seems unpromising as an antidote to pessimism. I will not, however, canvass the options here, but instead concentrate on two other (even) more speculative ideas, that of the morally appropriate scope of pessimism, and of creativity as a means of maintaining hope.

2.2 The Scope of Hope and Pessimism

Hopeful people can have generalized hopes—that "things will turn out ok," for instance—without being able to specify them more concretely. Hopes can also be directed toward specific objects, as the standard model best describes, as in "I hope that your health improves." Fundamentally, pessimism is a general attitude toward a group—humans. Of course, one may also be pessimistic about particular people or states of affairs or possibilities, but it is as an attitude toward "human beings" that it interests me and that makes it distinctive. My suggestion is that as long as pessimism remains on the whole general, directed toward "human beings" rather than particular, identifiable people and behavior, it can avoid despair and thus be compatible with hope. This thought requires some exploration, however, as there are at least two senses in which our attitude could have the group, "human beings," as its object.

We can—and often do—take up an objective, "God's-eye" view of our-selves as a group and consider our record. Pessimists come to a conclusion that we—humans—have much to be ashamed of and that it seems unlikely that our record will improve significantly. This is one, and the most funda-mental, sense in which pessimism is a general attitude toward humans. How-ever, taking up this perspective can also encourage us to consider individuals *as* members of the human species—as representative specimens—and then we can be pessimistic about particular people, including ourselves, insofar as we are considering them in the light of their species membership. Pessimism can have both of these foci, although as I have said, the first is fundamental to the distinctive attitude. Once we have accepted that pessimism is a reason-able view of the group, human beings, which is the primary task in defending it, pessimism can then seem to require that we consider each person in the light of this stance, as a member of the human species. Doing this then opens the way to a harshly judgmental view of people, and pessimism would slide into morally less defensible attitudes. However, it is open to us to defend the first "group-focused" version and yet find the second "individual-focused" version problematic and optional, and this is my position.

The view of a whole group that abstracts from particularity and difference is paradigmatically thought of in terms of an "objective" or "impersonal" observer, or as a distanced and impersonal point of view from outside the human world. The view of human existence *sub specie aeternitatis* is, as Joshua Seachris (2013) reminds us, characteristically thought to generate pessimism about meaning and, I would add, about our capacity for creating and protecting what is good.[8] Sometimes value is taken to disappear from the world seen at a distance; sometimes—as in pessimism of various kinds—the bad seems more *visible*, more *significant*, than the good we do.[9] However, as many writers on the meaning of life have also argued, the view from eternity is not the only reasonable view and meaning and value need not evaporate within the human world, however it seems from without.[10] Similarly if not precisely, one's view of particular others can escape the pessimistic view of human beings; in fact, meaningful and rewarding relations require this occlu-sion of pessimism, and then pessimism toward particular loved ones may be the more demanding attitude to sustain. It is difficult to be a loving friend, partner, or parent, or a committed colleague, without seeing the other person as in some sense good and receptive to value, and expecting good from them. A sense of inevitable disappointment in others, especially oneself, is a sign of distress and depression, corrosive cynicism, or the strategic adoption of a distancing and objectifying attitude.[11]

When evaluating or emotionally responding to individual people, or sim-ply being with them in our everyday life, we can choose what to focus on and find salient and most of the time it will be their particularity that is ethically and personally relevant.[12] If I am evaluating or responding to *this* person, then it is her uniqueness that is relevant, even if we discover that her qualities and the explanations for her behavior are similar to those of others. That similarity is superficial and to be expected given our common species, but it is the unique configuration of shared features which makes her the particular and irreplaceable person she is. Here, we might think, adding "and she is a human being and we know what *that* means" to the information we consider when evaluating someone is otiose. Our being human provides the very framework from which any evaluation and any moral life is possible at all.

That ethics requires from us an attention to the particular is a familiar view since Aristotle. Murdoch (2000, 28), for instance, argues that love is knowledge of the particular, that the moral task is to attend to the reality of *this* person before me, with love, justice, and humility. The moral task of attending to people and maintaining loving relationships, and probably any good relationships at all, is then possible only if one's general, shared features—one's membership of a group, for instance—is not taken to exhaust one's identity and moral qualities. This is a common thought in race and gender studies and just as apposite here. [13] The thought applies as much to our relation with ourselves as to others: it is a condition of integrity and self-respect that one not feel reduced to what one thinks problematic about oneself, whether one's race, species, or more particular faults. Though "being human" is fundamental in a way other characteristics of us are not—we are always and inescapably speaking of and with human beings (although not only about them)—it is usually unnecessary to remind ourselves of this fact. I say "usually" because there are important occasions in which mercy and compassion might be aided by thinking of a person in a pessimistic mode, as a human being—that is, not perfect, morally frail, one of a problematic species. A gentler judgment may occur from this thought, and this possibility provides another reason for thinking that pessimism need not inevitably lead to cynicism or misanthropy. Pessimism about moral progress and human nature can incline one to mercy rather than to harshness. [14]

If I am hopeful about a particular person—that a student will show resilience in the face of difficulties and make a success of her studies, for example—then (given a relevantly similar description of her and the situation) I cannot be pessimistic to the same degree about her and at the same time. Both attitudes are future-directed and have the same object. I may find hope difficult to maintain about my student *because* I see her as just an instance of "human beings" and therefore bound to be disappointing. Or I can be pessimistic about human beings and our capacity to make the world significantly better, while being hopeful about this student, as long as I do not consider her only in light of my pessimism. Living from both perspectives—the impersonal and the embedded or particular—is characteristic of moral agency, sometimes required by morality, sometimes optional, sometimes thoroughly inappropriate. That we move between perspectives is also a familiar thought.

We *can* and sometimes *ought to* take the step back; there are times when morality requires such impartiality of us, just as there are times (more times) when the meaning of our lives depends on partial attention to particular, special others.[15] It seems, therefore, that the more we are immersed in the human world that we are pessimistic about, the less our pessimism will corrode into cynicism or despair about the particular people we live with. And it is helpful here to return to Marcel. Integrity requires not capitulating and becoming the self a trial threatens to reduce one to. I would add that it also requires us to protect and value the relationships that give meaning and substance to our lives, and to thus refuse to capitulate to an entirely hopeless vision of them.

What, however, of a generalized hopefulness about the prospects of human beings to improve morally, rather than hopes about particular people and events? Would this be compatible with a generalized pessimism? If hopefulness is understood in Marcel's terms, as noncapitulation to a trial, the maintenance of integrity, and the experience of a future that is open to our efforts, then it does seem possible to be both pessimistic and hopeful about humans in general. Because pessimism is not a deterministic view of the world and self, and because it is not the morally and personally corrosive attitudes of misanthropy or cynicism, it would be possible not to expect significant moral progress, while still taking efforts to achieve it and staking one's integrity on the effort; not to count on success, while trying one's best to approximate it. Furthermore, because Pessimism and hopefulness are not essentially *feelings*—of depression or optimism or lightheartedness, which would indeed be incompatible with hope—then one may hope for a morally better future, see the future as open to one's efforts and one's self as up to the task while doubting that one will have globally significant success. Put that way, it sounds like admirable humility. Maintaining this balance might be difficult but living ethically in such a complex world will always be so.

2.3 Creativity and Improvisation

As mentioned earlier, Marcel (1962, 38) sees hope as a patient and flexible orientation to a future seen as open to one's efforts; our refusal to capitulate has a suppleness and grace. These aesthetic descriptions are suggestive, and I would like to sketch out—even more speculatively than previously—how they might permit a portrait of a person both hopeful and pessimistic. To do so, I draw on work on creativity and improvisation.

R. G. Collingwood (2014, 129) distinguished the creation of art from "technical" making: art objects are typically not made according to a preconceived plan and as a means to a preconceived end, but are yet made deliberately and responsibly by people who know what they are doing, even though they do not know in advance what is going to come of it.[16] The artist, he says, has no idea what the experience is that demands expression until he has expressed it. What he wants to say is not present to him as an end toward which the means have to be devised; it becomes clear to him only as the poem takes shape in his mind, or the clay in his fingers (Collingwood 2014, 29). Artists deliberately work out an idea or emotion, letting the logic and content reveal themselves in and through the creative process.

In his study of jazz, *The Imperfect Art* (1988), Ted Gioia calls for an "aesthetics of imperfection" that can capture the role of improvisation and the apparent lack of formal perfection in that art form. Reminiscent of Collingwood, he distinguishes the "blueprint method" from the "retrospective" method of creating form: the improviser may be unable to look ahead at what he is going to play, but he can look behind at what he has just played; thus each new musical phrase can be shaped in relation to what has gone before. He creates his form *retrospectively* (Gioia 1988, 61). Like Collingwood's artist, the improvising jazz artist does not know and has not planned what is to come—he has no blueprint—but can respond intelligently and sensitively to what he has created before, and to the intrinsic logic and ideas of that ongoing creation. The future unspools, as it were, always connected and responsive to its origin, but going into what is still unknown with formal and substantive intelligence.

"What comes before" is both the "before" of a particular performance and the hours of practice and preparation that any successful musical performance requires. Successful improvisation and creativity require a connection to an internalized past of knowledge, extensive practice, failures, and successes. This past, and the previous moments of creation, inform but do not determine one's actions and decisions now. Some jazz artists therefore speak of a "leap into the unknown," and Andy Hamilton (2000, 181) develops this idea:

> For the improviser, the performance must feel like a "leap into the unknown," and it will be an inspired one when the hours of preparation connect with the requirements of the moment and help to shape a fresh and compelling creation. At the time of performance they must clear their conscious minds of prepared patterns and simply play. Thus it makes sense to talk of preparation for the spontaneous effort. (Hamilton 2000)

In improvisation, errors will inevitably creep in—aimlessness, cliché, and technical mistakes—and Gioia (1988, 66) asks, "Why then are we interested in this haphazard art?" His answer is the central role of the individual in jazz; imperfect improvisation is expressive of the person, and we can always ask, in assessing its merits, "whether it reflects his own unique and incommensurable perspective on his art, whether it makes a statement without which the world would be in some small way, a lesser place" (Gioia 1988, 66). Although in different terms, Collingwood also emphasizes individuality, arguing that creativity is the individual expression of an emotion. Unlike description, which is general and categorizing—"this is a thing of *this* kind"— expression individualizes (Collingwood 2014, 112). This focus on the centrality of the individual response and expression complements my earlier discussion on the need for the pessimist to focus on individuals in her everyday living. This applies to the relationships that contribute to a meaningful life, and here we should remember the intense responsiveness and interactive empathy that musicians need to show to each other when playing together (Hamilton 2000, 183). Even during a solo improvisation a musician must be alert to her fellow musicians; the give-and-take of jazz performances and the intense solidarity and attunement of chamber musicians show that the realization of memorable individual expression often requires others.

For my purposes, the notion of musical improvisation—and by extension all performed improvisation—is perhaps more appropriate than Collingwood's notion of creativity in general, which encompasses more arts than music or performances. In performance, the artist cannot correct a mistake or redo unsatisfactory material, though she may seek to "make amends" for it. A painter or writer can much of the time work over mistakes or change her mind, deleting and amending what she has done in the past. In performance, and particularly in improvised performance where there is no perfected score at hand, one cannot change the past. And so it is in living. We can hope only to respond intelligently and sensitively to our own past and the past of our species; we cannot undo mistakes, though we may take care to understand and not repeat them.

This excursion into aesthetics is suggestive only, of course, and the analogy is limited. In particular, we might think that the "clearing" of consciousness, which Hamilton describes, is less appropriate to the complexities of situations which demand reflection and awareness. However, the excursion does complement much work on ethics that is concerned with individual receptiveness to the particular situation, and to narrative ethics, which explicitly sees a person and her life in aesthetic terms.[17] More to the point here, the openness to the future, the patient suppleness of response to what has gone before, and the emphasis on the individual expressing her own nature in her own "natural rhythm" remind me of Marcel's conception of hope. Despair closes a person into an unbearable and rigid present; in contrast, creativity and improvisation are attitudes of openness to a future one can be integral to creating. The past one has created is significant and one is always receptive to it, but it does not determine a future. Can the pessimist achieve this generous receptivity, this allowance of play and error and imperfection? Can she allow the future to "try itself out," perhaps through her own efforts, and in a way that is faithful to and expressive of who she is?

Doing so would be a way to maintain hopefulness and integrity. Considering her life as a potential personal creation that responds intelligently and sensitively to the past—both her own and her human world's—and "reflects her own unique and incommensurable perspective" could prevent capitulation to the despairing vision that pessimism always risks. The world, says Murdoch (1993, 215), is not given to us on a plate, it is given to us as a creative task.

3. CONCLUSION

I want to conclude by reflecting on what this paper has attempted. As I have stressed, my claims are speculative; we are not "forced" logically to accept them by anything in the substance of either the attitude of hope or of pessimism. However, a part of hope is the ability to construct and maintain images of a sturdy self and an open future; perhaps the possibility of maintaining hope in the ways I have suggested would provide the pessimist with creative resources, the very possibility of which could prove motivating. Whether, as a matter of psychology, pessimism would still slide more easily into misanthropy or cynicism than a realistic love for imperfect creatures, is still open. In any case, in these areas of ethics, so much depends on the particularities and unique complexity of each life—how each one of us will respond to disappointment or despair at the world and our role in it is a matter that cannot be settled in advance. It does help, however, to have images that can disclose possibilities to us, to give us possibilities of how to live with the world we have made for ourselves, to have—in Murdoch's (1993) words again—various "pictures of the human" to guide or inspire us. If we can think of the world as yet valuable in a robust way, and ourselves as valuable despite our harmful record; if we focus on those particular people and relationships that give our lives and selves substance and meaning; and if we can think of ourselves as yet creatively responsible for what we make of the past, perhaps, then, we may remain hopeful despite the pessimism that our own nature also presses upon us.[18]

NOTES

1. My conception of Pessimism is therefore distinguished from the pessimism of, for instance, Schopenhauer or, more recently, Benatar (2006), which is focused on the facts of suffering, however they are caused. Of Schopenhauerian pessimism, Dienstag (2006, 43) writes, "Although there may be, to these pessimists, some particularities of our culture that accentuate our susceptibility to suffering, the sources of that suffering are such that all are subject to them. Human beings inhabit a universe that they would be justified in calling malevolent if it could be shown to have an author."

2. I have explored cynicism in Vice (2011).

3. As Mittleman (2009, 2–3) reminds us. Mittleman is discussing Dante's vision of hell in *The Divine Comedy*.

4. On this standard model, see Day (1969).

5. Ibid. Cf. Brueggemann (1987, 83): "Hope makes it possible not to submit."

6. As Stratton-Lake (1999) notes. Similarly, Bovens (1999, 677) argues that hoping has intrinsic worth, by connecting it to a sense of self-worth; and Blöser and Stahl (2017) also draw out the connection to integrity.

7. At the time I am writing, this is an unpublished manuscript.

8. Seachris helpfully explores the different senses of the notion "sub specie aeternitatis." Again, it is worth asking why the character of the pessimist about meaning is not thought to be as troubling as the character of the pessimist about progress and the good. The seriousness with which this view is taken in the literature on the meaning of life provides some indirect support for taking pessimism seriously as well.

9. This raises the questions of the reason for this visibility. Is it ethical—that evil leaves more trace? Is it psychological—we are attracted to and therefore *see* the bad more than the good?

10. See Nagel (1986 and 1979).

11. See Strawson (1974).

12. We do not, of course, always consciously choose at all, but sometimes simply respond from settled habits or from the clear demands of the situation. But sometimes we must choose, in times of personal conflict or confusion, or when extra sensitivity is called for.

13. For a general account of this tendency, see Blum (2004).

14. See Nussbaum (1993).

15. I am here simply gesturing at the complex debate about the proper roles of partiality and impartiality—between the person and impersonal perspectives—in morality and in the good life more generally. Nagel (1986) influences my views.

16. Strictly speaking, denying that the distinction between planning and execution is necessary for art, Collingwood (2014, 22) says, is not requiring that art always be unplanned.

17. For example, MacIntyre (1984) and Schechtman (1996).

18. My thanks to the editors for their helpful comments on an earlier draft.

REFERENCES

Benatar, David. 2006. *Better Never to Have Been: The Harm of Coming into Existence*. Oxford: Clarendon Press.

Blum, Lawrence. 2004. "Stereotypes and Stereotyping: A Moral Analysis." *Philosophical Papers* 33 (3): 251–89.

Blöser, Claudia, and Titus Stahl. 2017. "Fundamental Hope and Practical Identity." *Philosophical Papers* 46 (3): 345–71.

Bovens, Luc. 1999. "The Value of Hope." *Philosophy and Phenomenological Research* 59 (3): 667–81.

Brueggemann, Walter. 1987. "Living toward a Vision: Grief in the Midst of Technique." In *Hope within History*, 72–91. Atlanta, GA: John Knox Press.

Calhoun, Cheshire. 2019. "Hope Matters." Unpublished manuscript, last accessed March 22, 2019. https://law.vanderbilt.edu/files/archive/CheshireCalhoun_HopeMatters.pdf.

Collingwood, R. G. 2014. *The Principles of Art*. Mansfield Centre, CT: Martino Publishing.

Day, J. P. 1969. Hope. *American Philosophical Quarterly* 6 (92): 89–102.

Dienstag, Joshua Foa. 2006. *Pessimism*. Princeton, NJ: Princeton University Press.

Gioia, Ted.1988. "The Imperfect Art." In *The Imperfect Art*, 50–69. New York and Oxford: Oxford University Press.

Hamilton, Andy. 2000. "The Art of Improvisation and the Aesthetics of Imperfection." *British Journal of Aesthetics* 40 (1): 168–85.

Hampshire, Stuart. 1978. "Morality and Pessimism." In *Public and Private Morality*, 1–22. Cambridge: Cambridge University Press.

Kant, Immanuel. 1960 [1793]. *Religion within the Limits of Reason Alone*. Translated by Theodore M. Greene and Hoyt H. Hudson. New York: Harper and Row.

MacIntyre, A. 1984. *After Virtue: A Study in Moral Theory*. Notre Dame, IN: University of Notre Dame Press.

Marcel, Gabriel. 1962. "Sketch of a Phenomenology and a Metaphysic of Hope." In *Homo Viator: Introduction to a Metaphysic of Hope*, translated by Emma Crauford, 29–67. New York: Harper and Brothers.

Mittleman, Alan. 2009. *Hope in a Democratic Age*. Oxford: Oxford University Press.

Murdoch, Iris. 1993. *Metaphysics as a Guide to Morals*. London: Penguin.

———. 2000. *The Sovereignty of Good*. London: Routledge.

Nagel, Thomas. 1979. "The Absurd." In *Mortal Questions*, 11–23. Cambridge: Cambridge University Press.

———. 1986. *The View from Nowhere*. Oxford: Oxford University Press.

Nussbaum, Martha C. 1993. "Equity and Mercy." *Philosophy and Public Affairs* 22 (2): 83–125.

Pinker, Steven. 2011. *The Better Angels of Our Nature*. London: Penguin.

Prescott, Paul. 2012. "What Pessimism Is." *Journal of Philosophical Research* 37: 337–56.

Seachris, Joshua W. 2013. "The 'Sub Specie Aeternitatis' Perspective and Normative Evaluations of Life's Meaningfulness: A Closer Look." *Ethical Theory and Moral Practice* 16 (3): 605–20.

Schechtman, M. 1996. *The Constitution of Selves*. Ithaca, NY: Cornell University Press.

Stratton-Lake, Philip. 1999. "Marcel, Hope, and Virtue." In *French Existentialism: Consciousness, Ethics and Relations with Others*, edited by James Giles, 139–53. Amsterdam: Rodopi.

Strawson, P. F. 1974. "Freedom and Resentment." In *Freedom and Resentment and Other Essays*, 1–25. London: Methuen.

Sutherland, Stewart R. 1981. "Optimism and Pessimism." *Religious Studies* 17 (4): 537–48.

Vice, Samantha. 2011. "Cynicism and Morality." *Ethical Theory and Moral Practice* 14 (2): 169–84.

Walker, Margaret Urban. 2006. *Moral Repair: Reconstructing Moral Relations after Wrongdoing*. Cambridge: Cambridge University Press.

Chapter Ten

Is Hope a Moral Virtue?

Nancy E. Snow

Elsewhere I have argued that hope can be an intellectual virtue and a demo-cratic civic virtue.[1] In this essay I argue that it can be a moral virtue. In part I, I offer a brief overview of the "belief-desire" model or "bare bones" concep-tion of hope, which is at the heart of many, though not all, philosophical theories of hope currently on offer. In part II, I draw on work by the psychol-ogist Erik Erikson and the philosopher Victoria McGeer to sketch an account of how a general disposition of hope could be developed. In part III, I argue that a particular conception of hope can be a moral virtue, and in part IV, briefly respond to an objection. I conclude with a gesture in the direction of further research on hope.

I. THE "BELIEF-DESIRE" MODEL OF HOPE

The "belief-desire" model or "bare bones" conception of hope can be gleaned from the work of philosophers as diverse as J. P. Day, Thomas Aquinas, Thomas Hobbes, Luc Bovens, Victoria McGeer, Philip Pettit, Margaret Walker, and Ariel Meirav, to name only some of its proponents.[2] The belief-desire model offers insight into the mental state that someone must have in order to be said to hope. According to this account, hope, at its most basic, is the desire for an end or object and the belief that it is possible to attain it. The belief that the end or object is possible carves out a space for hope between certainty and impossibility. If a desired end is certain, it does not make sense to hope for it. If it is impossible, hoping for it is fruitless and can be self-destructive.

Day believes the belief-desire model is necessary and sufficient to explain hope, but most others who hold some version of the model maintain that having the desire for an end or object and the belief that attaining it is possible is necessary, but not sufficient. For example, Martin argues that hope encompasses an incorporation of one's desire into one's agency, that is, the idea of seeing oneself as justified in taking one's desire as a reason for various hopeful activities.[3] Bovens enriches the belief-desire account by adding the element of mental imaging, which is "devotion of mental energy to what it would be like if some projected state of the world were to materialize." Agency theories stress personal agency as a pathway to attaining hoped-for ends, and on hope as enhancing the agency of the individuals who possess it.[4] Agency theorists include philosophers McGeer and Walker, as well as the psychologist C. R. Snyder.[5] Walker stresses that hope is not simply a belief-desire complex, but an emotional attitude consisting of a variety of hope phenomena—such as plans, imaginings, and expectations.[6] All three agency theorists emphasize the motivational force of hope and its connections with agency. Hope, in their view, can motivate us to rise to challenges and undertake tasks that are possible, even though not probable. Clearly, however, some of our hopes outstrip the reach of our agency. For example, we can hope that our team wins, or that we are approved for a new car loan. Other hopes might engage our agency, yet the effects of our hope might be minimal, as when we hope for an end to war, animal abuse, or famine. Addressing this issue, Meirav offers the external factor account of hope, according to which "hope involves a characteristic attitude toward an external factor, on whose operation the hoper takes the prospect's realization to depend causally."[7]

To make the case for hope as a moral virtue, we need to go beyond accounts of the mental states of hopers and explain how we could come to have a disposition to hope. Elsewhere I have argued that

> "Hope" can refer both to an attitude toward particular ends and to a general disposition. To hope for a particular end is to perceive it as a good, desire it, regard its occurrence as uncertain—either probable or possible—and use imagination and agency in efforts to attain it.[8]

Let me state at the outset that, in arguing that hope is a moral virtue, I will remain largely neutral about what other factors must be involved in the mental states of hopers, though I will make points about not hoping for immoral ends and hoping in the right way. The disposition to hope, in my view, is an entrenched character state that gives rise to specific hopes; that is, it is the disposition to form mental states consisting of desires for ends and beliefs that the ends are possible to attain. To be hopes, these mental states, as just mentioned, must contain elements other than mere beliefs and desires, for example, imaginings, such as imagining what one's life would be like should a desired end obtain.

It is a truism that one can hope well or badly. This is true in practical as well as in moral senses. I can be impractical in my hopes and hope for things that are outlandish or that I could never possibly obtain. I can hope for that which is immoral. If one develops a disposition to hope for impractical things, one will frequently be disappointed. If one develops a disposition to hope for immoral ends, one's disposition cannot be a moral virtue. So how one develops the disposition to hope is important to a defense of hope as a moral virtue. To have the disposition to hope as a moral virtue is to be disposed to hope for morally worthy ends. However, given that virtue is often viewed as a "success" term, a measure of practicality must also be admitted. That is, as Aristotle has it, to be truly virtuous one must "hit the target" of virtue in a regular way—*phronēsis* enables the virtuous to do that. Consequently, to give an account of hope as a moral virtue, we must explain how we can develop a disposition to hope for moral ends in a way that is practical—that makes it reasonably possible for us to attain them.

II. DEVELOPING THE DISPOSITION OF HOPE

Erikson discusses how hope is nurtured in children.[9] He believes that persons progress through eight major stages of life cycle development and proposes a schedule of virtues for each stage.[10] He considers hope to be a virtue that starts developing in infancy: "We recognize, for example, an inner affinity between the earliest and deepest mental disturbances and a radical loss of a basic kind of hope."[11] Cultivating hope, or more precisely, its precursors, in infancy is essential for the subsequent psychosocial health of the individual. Maternal care is central to the beginnings of hope, and it is intergenerational: the capacities of mothers to provide care depend on their own experiences as children. For Erikson, the nurturance of hope, too, is intergenerational. Moreover, cultivating hope is not simply a matter of teaching children to have specific hopes for limited objectives. With proper nurturance, children's hopes evolve from limited concrete hopes into a broader and more open-ended attitude of hope.[12] This broader attitude, we can speculate, is the beginnings of the disposition to hope. Though it seems that trust in one's caretaker is essential for the earliest glimmers of hope to emerge,[13] Erikson suggests that mature hope can live where confidence and trust are undermined:

> Hope is both the earliest and the most indispensable virtue inherent in the state of being alive. Others have called this deepest quality *confidence*, and I have referred to *trust* as the earliest positive psychosocial attitude, but if life is to be sustained hope must remain, even where confidence is wounded, trust impaired.[14]

Erikson paints the emergence of hope with broad brushstrokes. McGeer gives more detailed delineation.[15] She draws on the work of psychologist Jerome Bruner to develop a speculative account of the inculcation of hope through the nurturance of children's capacities for agency. She notes that infants and young children have innate capacities for imitation. Parental scaffolding, that is, the support and guidance that parents and other caregivers provide to children early in their lives, capitalizes on capacities to coach children in the successful performance of goal-directed activities. McGeer writes, "Scaffolding here involves a kind of hopeful pretence."[16] The idea is that parents encourage children to perform actions that mimic those performed by adults. Parental scaffolding involves not only urging the child to explore and perform goal-directed actions, but also fostering a sense of exploration and adventure, thereby helping the child to expand the limits of her agential repertoire.

Presumably, children learn how to hope and develop capacities for hope by desiring specific ends and believing that they can attain them. Hope is built by the child's exercising agency in the successful pursuit of these ends. Central to the success of these activities is trust. Children must trust their parents not to lead them into harmful or unduly frustrating activities. McGeer notes the special importance of two factors to this process.[17] The first is that parents must not only cognitively challenge their children, they must also provide them with emotional support when needed. The child who is afraid needs to be encouraged; the child who is hurt needs comforting; and the child who is successful in achieving agential goals needs to be shown approval and given positive feedback. The second important factor is that parents need to model to children how to tolerate frustration when goals are not met.

Teaching the ability to overcome or sidestep frustration and other negative emotions, such as disappointment or dejection, is crucial to developing hope. The child in whom hope takes root is resilient and cognitively savvy. She imitates parents in persevering in the pursuit of attainable goals, as well as in recognizing when goals should be abandoned or adjusted, and is similarly savvy and flexible in her use of means to goal achievement. All of this is consistent with Snyder's agency-pathways theory of hope, according to which high hopers (those who hope well) exhibit cognitive flexibility—the ability to readjust goals and the means to them when confronted with obstacles, as well as the emotional wherewithal to "bounce back"—to continue hoping and not sink into torpor or despair—when hopes are frustrated.

Three central themes emerge from our consideration of Erikson and McGeer. First, early care is essential for cultivating hope. Second, the child should form a secure attachment with her caregiver that provides a supportive base from which early explorations of her environment and the concomitant development of her own capacities can take place. Third, nurturing the child's nascent capacities for goal formation and pursuit, as well as for effective agency, are intimately bound with the development of hope. It would seem, then, that guiding and encouraging in children habits of exploration through action in a context of parental care and support in which children can trust, is a way of cultivating in them a disposition to hope—to form specific hopes that are practical in the sense that, given the child's burgeoning agential capacities, he or she can reasonably expect to attain them, and can expect to grow in her capacities both as an agent and as a good hoper.

III. HOPE AS A MORAL VIRTUE

The previous two sections sketch an explanatory framework that I believe is needed to argue that hope is a moral virtue. In the first section, we garnered insights into the mental states of hopers and stated what we take the disposition to hope to be. In the second section, we drew on other work to offer a developmental account of the formation of this disposition.

In the rest of this section, I will argue that the disposition to hope as articulated in parts I and II is part of a conception of hope as a moral virtue in a broadly Aristotelian sense.[18] Two important caveats should be mentioned. First, hope is not among the virtues listed in Book IV of the *Nicomachean Ethics*. Nonetheless, Gravlee makes the case that hope does appear in Aristotle's work.[19] Whether hope appears in the Aristotelian corpus is not my concern here. Whether hope can plausibly be considered a virtue along broadly Aristotelian lines is.

My second caveat is that, even if hope can be construed as a broadly Aristotelian virtue, it is an imperfect fit, at least as regards the Aristotelian scheme of a virtue as an intermediate state between a single, clearly identified vice of excess and a similarly clear vice of deficiency.[20] Aquinas, for example, believes that hope lies between the extremes of presumption, which is the certainty that good things are to come, and despair, which is the certainty that they won't.[21] For Aquinas, we hope to achieve unification with God at the eschaton. Presumption is the certainty that we will achieve this; despair, the conviction that we won't. Some philosophers question whether hope fits nicely as a mean between extremes in this way. For example, Govier considers four opposites of hope: despair, fear, cynicism, and pessimism.[22] Given the complexities of these issues, I do not insist that hope is an intermediate between only two vices.

My argument that hope can be a broadly Aristotelian moral virtue rests on the following claims: (1) it is possible to give an account of the developmental trajectory of hope that is consistent with the (admittedly few) comments that Aristotle makes about how moral virtue is acquired; (2) in this developmental account, one can chart a progression from having hope as a natural virtue to having hope as a moral virtue, that is, a virtue informed by *phronēsis* or something like it, as well as identify bad forms of hoping to which deficiencies of reason contribute; (3) the motivations and ends characteristic of hope as a moral virtue are consistent with the kinds of motivations and ends of virtues in a broadly Aristotelian sense; and (4) having the disposition of hope is partly constitutive of flourishing lives.

Let us begin with (1) and (2). As is well known, Aristotle gives scant advice about how moral virtues are acquired. In Book II of the *Nicomachean Ethics* he argues that virtuous states of character are acquired through habituation and practice that train us to take pleasure in virtuous actions; this implies roles for parents and families in cultivating virtue in the young. [23] He even states that legislators try to make citizens good through habituation. [24] Though much of his advice is directed toward helping people to achieve the mean and avoid excess and deficiency, a crucial part of his account, for our purposes, is the necessity of moving from mere conformity to genuine understanding. [25] At some point in our developmental trajectory, we must perform virtuous actions as the virtuous person does, with knowledge and understanding of what we are doing and why we are doing it, and not because someone has told us what to do, or because we are merely imitating someone else. As Aristotle puts it, "To be a grammarian, then, we must both produce something grammatical and produce it in the way in which the grammarian produces it, i.e., expressing grammatical knowledge that is in us." [26] This is consistent with remarks in Book VI, in which Aristotle distinguishes natural from full virtue. [27] Natural virtue is not informed by *phronēsis,* or practical wisdom, and can be possessed by children and even animals. Only when one has acquired *phronēsis* can one be said to have virtue in the full sense.

This account meshes well with the more detailed perspective on the development of hope offered by Erikson and McGeer. McGeer's remarks, especially, focus heavily on the development of hope through parentally guided action. Though she does not foreground rationality in her account, the development of children's rational capacities proceeds hand in hand with the development of their traits. As they learn how to be generous, kind, compassionate, and so on, they at first do as they are told by parents or mimic their parents' interactions. Eventually (one hopes), they come to understand the value of virtuous action and act virtuously for its own sake. Reason is key to their acquiring this understanding. The same is true of hope—children develop hope as they develop their agential capacities with the support of parental scaffolding, but eventually, they become effective agents and good hopers in their own right. [28] They are able to do this—to become good hopers as well as develop in other virtues—by increasingly using reason in their judgments and choices of whether and how to act. McGeer's account of how hope develops, I believe, is compatible with multiple roles for reason. To see this, let us examine her remarks more closely.

McGeer not only discusses good hoping but is also sensitive to ways in which the cultivation of hope can go wrong, causing children to become bad hopers. Her remarks on bad hoping shed light on roles for reason in virtuous hoping. She discusses wishful and willful hoping, both of which are bad.[29] She sums up the deficiencies of wishful hoping, also called the "hope of desire" as follows:

> The most glaring defect of wishful hope can be summarized as a failure to take on the full responsibilities of agency in both formulating and working toward the realization of one's hopes. One's capacity for formulating hopes is corrupted through their becoming attached in undisciplined ways to pure desire, and one's capacity for realizing hopes is corrupted by an overreliance on external intervention to secure one's hoped-for ends.[30]

In short, wishful hopers are deficient in two ways: their desires are fanciful and impractical, and their capacity for effective agency in realizing their desires has been impaired by too much dependency on the agency of others.

Willful hoping is the other form of bad hoping. McGeer labels this "the hope of fear," and maintains that it is intimately bound with unreflective dread and ego-anxiety.[31] According to her,

> Willful hopers invest all their energy in the achievement of their ends . . . having little understanding of the self-aggrandizing passions that often drive them to those ends. Willful hopers are therefore quite disciplined in the way they reason from means to ends. . . . But they are also quite unreflective and sometimes unscrupulous, about the impact on self and others of the means they use, always justifying these in terms of the ends pursued. Moreover, they are also quite unreflective, indeed often self-deceived, about their reasons for valuing such ends.[32]

By contrast with wishful hopers, who seem inept in both desire formulation and in their practical abilities to realize their hopes, willful hopers, whose hope is motivated by "self-protective dread or fear" seem neurotically driven to achieve their ends, blind to the passions that animate them, and impervious to the devastation the pursuit of their plans might cause.[33] Unsurprisingly, both wishful and willful hopers can be created by defective parental scaffolding.[34] Since both forms of hoping are defective, neither could count as virtuous hoping.

Why are they defective? A lack of discipline seems to be at the heart of wishful hoping. The wishful hoper is undisciplined in both formulating and realizing her hopes. In formulating her hopes, she allows herself to be guided by "pure" desire, and in realizing her hopes, she relies too much on external factors. Both deficiencies can be attributed to a lack of effective practical reason. In the virtuous, and even in the continent, practical reason guides desire. In the virtuous, of course, practical reason and desire are in harmony;

in the continent, reason masters wayward desire. The wishful hoper seems to be incontinent, allowing whatever rational control she has to be over-whelmed by her desire for a hoped-for end. In formulating her hopes, the wishful hoper is not guided by reason, and in realizing them, her rational agency seems to be in abeyance. The wishful hoper cannot be virtuous be-cause reason has too little influence on how she hopes.

Lack of discipline does not seem to be the problem of the willful hoper, yet deficiencies in reason directly explain why willful hoping goes awry. As McGeer notes in the passage quoted above, willful hopers are unreflective about the reasons for their ends and the impact the pursuit of those ends can have on themselves and on others.[35] Willful hope seems to be blind hope—hope that is neither informed nor restrained by reason.

If both of these bad ways of hoping are caused, in some significant sense, by deficiencies in reason, is there a form of good hoping in which reason plays a central role? McGeer discusses responsive hoping, a form of good hope that she calls "the hope of care."[36] Responsive hoping has both intra-personal and interpersonal dimensions. The intrapersonal features of good hoping include clear-sighted, yet imaginative engagement with reality, resil-ience, flexibility, and the willingness to stretch one's agential capacities. McGeer avers that "peer scaffolding" is paramount for the interpersonal aspects of good hoping.[37] Peer scaffolding is a form of interpersonal support that supplants the structures of parental scaffolding. It is made possible by being part of a community of self-scaffolding hopers—sympathetic, caring others who support one in one's hopes by helping one to formulate and pursue hopes in a positive way. Peer scaffolding helps to keep one on the "straight and narrow" and away from the pitfalls of wishful and willful hoping, as well as to cope with the debilitating emotions that can result when hopes are not realized. Perhaps most importantly, creating a community of responsive hopers fosters clarity—clarity about the limits of our own agency and those of others.[38] All of this points to the importance of care in being a responsive hoper. Care is, in a sense, at the bottom of responsive hoping.[39] We must care for ourselves as well as for others in our guise as agential hopers. This care helps us continually to develop as responsive hopers—to progress in what McGeer calls "the art of good hope."

McGeer's remarks do not directly advocate roles for practical wisdom in good hope. Instead, responsive hoping stresses roles for friends and commu-nity in the development of good hope. This, of course, is consistent with Aristotle's account of the value of friends, especially friends of good charac-ter, and his idea that the flourishing of individuals is not possible outside of the *polis*. Yet we can also argue that reason has key roles to play in respon-sive hoping. Just as parental scaffolding affords guidance to youngsters who have not fully developed reason, so, too, peer scaffolding offers the benefits of collective wisdom to those whose hopes could suffer from rational deficits. Even adults can suffer from deficiencies in hoping—sometimes we desire hoped-for ends too strongly, which causes us to overestimate the probability that we will attain them. Sometimes we are unrealistic in identifying the ends for which we hope. Sometimes we overestimate the effects of our agency on attaining hoped-for ends, or, conversely, underestimate the impact of our own efforts and rely too heavily on external factors. These are cases in which our own powers of reason have become occluded. In such cases, self-correction can be difficult. Our wayward hopes can be adjusted by receiving advice from others, who care about us and are willing to offer us the benefit of their own clear-sighted reason.

To sum up the argument that a hope is a moral virtue thus far, I've argued for (1) and (2) in that I've briefly sketched Aristotle's account of how moral virtue is acquired, and have noted similarities with the more detailed account of the development of hope given by McGeer. A key feature of how virtue is acquired, for Aristotle, is the development of *phronēsis* and its integration into virtue. This transforms natural into full virtue. Similarly, practical reason has roles to play in the development of hope, for it is reasonable to think that hope follows the developmental trajectory of other virtues as children develop their rational capacities along with traits such as generosity, kindness, and compassion. Further consideration of McGeer's remarks reveals how deficiencies in reason contribute, in different ways, to two forms of bad hoping, and how the collective wisdom afforded by peers can guide and correct adult hopers in ways that supplement the functions of parental scaffolding in childhood. McGeer's rich account, I believe, allows for reason to inform good hoping in ways of which Aristotle would approve.

Let us turn now to point (3) in the argument that hope is a moral virtue, namely, that the motivations and ends characteristic of hope as a moral virtue are consistent with the kinds of motivations and ends that Aristotle requires of other moral virtues. The first step in the argument is to note that neither the disposition to hope nor specific hopes need always be virtues or virtuous. For Aristotle as well as for many other virtue ethicists, virtues are orientations toward the good. Thus, the courage of a thief, for example, is a trait, not a virtue, since it is oriented toward the bad end of stealing another's property. This is true of dispositions as well as actions. Consequently, if my disposition to hope is oriented toward a bad end, say, the dominance of neo-Nazism, it does not count as a virtue. The same is true of my particular hopes for bad ends, such as the end that my enemy should suffer, and any actions expressing hope that I might perform in the pursuit of that end, such as poisoning his tea.

On this point I part ways with Kadlac, who, in an interesting paper, argues that hope is a virtue, though not in an Aristotelian sense.[40] Kadlac bases his analysis of the value of hope in large part on Robert Adams's account of structural virtues:

> Structural virtues, such as courage and self-control, are not defined by particular goods or evils one is for or against, but rather by types of strength in rational self-government. A structural virtue is not a matter of having one's heart in the right place, but of being excellently able and willing to govern one's life in accordance with one's own central aims and values, whatever they are. Corresponding to structural virtues are what we may call *structural vices*. They consist not in opposition or indifference to specific goods, but in deficiency in strengths of self-government. Thus, cowardice and incontinence, respectively, are deficiencies of strengths in governing oneself in the face of danger or temptation in general. In this way they are *vices of weakness*.[41]

Kadlac quotes a part of this passage, but not the whole of it, stopping with the phrase "one's central aims and values." I reproduce the entire passage here because I think Kadlac should have paid more attention to Adams's remarks on vice—a point I will pursue in a moment.

Hope, in my view, is what Adams calls a "motivational" virtue: "Motivational virtues are defined in terms of goods one is for, or evils one is against, in having them, as benevolence, for example, is excellence in being for the good of other persons."[42] I take it that this way of thinking about motivational virtues is roughly compatible with an Aristotelian approach, and suggest, to use Adams's framing, that hope is excellence in being oriented toward the attainment of goods. Thus I do not think that hope is a structural virtue in Adams's sense.

Yet Kadlac opts for the view that hope is a structural virtue in this sense. Immediately following the truncated version of the passage quoted above, Kadlac writes,

> In the same way, hope can have myriad objects because we can hope for myriad things. However, as I will argue, the value of hope does not lie in the goodness of its object but rather in its effect on one who hopes—the ways in which it helps one to accurately assess future possibilities, persevere in the pursuit of one's ends, and relate to other human beings in life-enhancing ways.[43]

I agree with this to a great extent but think Kadlac goes awry in denying that the value of hope does not lie in the goodness of its object or end. Commenting on the possibility that a terrorist might display courage in the name of doing God's will, he states that the terrorist could overcome considerable amounts of fear for the sake of doing what he perceives as good, and that we might recognize his courage as a virtue and even grudgingly admire it. We can condemn his behavior as evil even as we find it inspiring. He then extends this analysis to hope, contending that "[i]f such a view of courage is plausible, it seems that a similar assessment would be available to us when individuals hope for things that we do not believe to be good. We can recognize that hope as virtuous without necessarily endorsing its content."[44]

This argument apparently reduces our evaluations of the goodness of hope to assessments of form, or of the manner in which actions are undertaken. This is suggested by other remarks that Kadlac makes about terrorists' commitment, perseverance, and tenacity in the pursuit of their ends.[45] Because we can admire these aspects of their dispositions and actions, Kadlac seems to suggest, we are justified in judging their courage and their hope to be virtuous. I disagree. We might be tempted to admire their courage, commitment, perseverance, and tenacity, though even there I think the value of these qualities as aids to rational self-government is undercut by their being used in the service of an evil end. The main point, however, is that hope is not functioning as a structural virtue in this case. Courage, commitment, tenacity, and perseverance are. Hope is that which gives content to the terrorists' activities. The other virtues give it form and structure. The disposition of hope is functioning as a motivator, but in the case of the terrorists, it cannot be a virtue because it has oriented them toward an end that is not a genuine good. The disposition to hope as a moral virtue enables us to identify proper objects of particular hopes. So, *contra* Kadlac's statement, quoted above, we cannot recognize that hope is morally virtuous unless we can endorse its content.

Moreover, if hope is a structural and not a motivational virtue, on what grounds, apart from the content of hope's ends, would we be justified in deeming the hope of the terrorists to be vicious? We would be forced to make this assessment on purely structural grounds, that is, grounds of form. We could condemn their actions as vicious only if they were noncommittal, lackadaisical, flaccid, and lacking in perseverance and tenacity. Suffice it to say that most virtue ethicists who have written on hope, and certainly virtue ethicists inspired by Aristotle, look to *content* to make judgments of virtue and vice. Strength of commitment and intensity of desire alone do not provide us with a warrant to overlook the actual content of a disposition or an action in evaluating it as virtuous or vicious.

Kadlac comes close to raising what I take to be the decisive objection against the view that hope for bad ends can be virtuous: "One might object to this conclusion on the grounds that the realistic nature of hope is undermined if we grant that genuine hope can coexist with false views about the good."[46] This comes close to the central issue, but does not address it squarely. The problem from a virtue ethical perspective with taking hope for bad ends to be virtuous is not that such hopes, which rely on false views about the good, are unrealistic (though that is problematic), it is that the ends themselves are bad. One might, in fact, regard it as worse when the terrorist hopes with great commitment, perseverance, and tenacity to bring about a bad end than when she hopes noncommittally, lackadaisically, and so on. It is worse because she is more entrenched in evil and error. If her commitment wavers, she could, perhaps, be persuaded to see the error of her ways and be brought to a genuine appreciation of what is truly good.

Thus far I have sought to argue that (3) the motivations and ends characteristic of hope as a moral virtue are consistent with the kinds of motivations and ends of virtues in a broadly Aristotelian sense. The overall gist of the argument has been that having bad motivations and ends disqualifies dispositional hope as well as specific hopes from being considered virtuous. But further refinement is needed. What about what Kadlac calls "idle" hopes? These are hopes that are not very important or valuable. As he puts it, "[I]n order for hope to plausibly be considered virtuous, it must engage us in a particularly strong way. . . . [I]n order to be regarded as virtuous, a hope must not be idle."[47] Clearly some idle hopes are morally neutral, and neither virtuous nor vicious. My hope for good weather for the parade seems to fit into this category. It is not especially virtuous, since it is not of great moment. If it rains, I won't be devastated, though I might be a bit disappointed. For all practical purposes, many hopes that are like this might be indistinguishable from wishes and seem to express nothing of particular importance about our characters. Yet this is not true of all idle hopes; the motivations for some could indeed reveal something about character.[48] Suppose that I hope that it rains on the parade because I am spiteful and want to spoil people's fun. My idle hope links up with other, larger hopes that are morally unworthy and reveals viciousness in my character. The specific hope that it rain on the parade might not engage me deeply, yet is expressive of something unsavory about me—pettiness or mean-spiritedness. Similarly, I might have an idle hope that a colleague encounters obstacles in her career advancement. This hope, too, says something negative about my character—that I am jealous or envious of her. By contrast, suppose that she and I have "locked horns" in the past. As she goes up for promotion, I sincerely hope that she gets it. Perhaps the motivation for my hope is selfish—if she gets the promotion, she will be out of my department and I will no longer have to see her on a daily basis. If she has gratuitously created trouble for me in the past, this hope might not be immoral. It could simply be prudential or common sense. Perhaps, though, my motivation is morally good—I seek to "be big about it," to put the past behind us and wish her well. Or the motivation for my hope could combine a selfish motivation—the desire to be rid of her—with a morally good motivation—the desire to lay the past to rest and move on with a clean slate. So there are circumstances in which even idle hopes, though they do not strongly engage us, can reveal virtue or vice in our characters.

Remarks about (3) naturally lead to a discussion of (4) how having the disposition of hope is partly constitutive of flourishing lives. Conceptions of flourishing differ, and what counts as a flourishing life is a matter of much debate. The Stoics provide an interesting counterexample to the notion that hope is partly constitutive of flourishing lives—they are resigned to their fate in the universe, come what may, and are not hopeful, but flourish nonetheless.[49]

In the spirit of Aristotelianism embraced here, I believe that hope is an important part of a flourishing life that is characterized by self-actualization and wholehearted engagement with one's life circumstances. Having hope is part of a positive, forward-looking outlook that is open to future possibilities and positions the hoper to engage her cognitive, affective, imaginative, and agential capacities in efforts to attain future goods. To see how this orientation is partly constitutive of flourishing, contrast it with someone who lacks hope. Such people can be despairing, apathetic, or lethargic, floating through life in a kind of anomie. Alternatively, they can be cynical about future possibilities. Such lives are devoid of zest, vibrancy, and uplift. The lives of such people might not be blighted but they are not self-actualizing—they live their lives with diminished energy and engagement. They are not wholeheartedly ensconced in the human scene.[50]

CONCLUSION

In this essay, I have argued that hope is a moral virtue in a broadly Aristotelian sense. Elsewhere I have argued that hope can be an intellectual virtue and a democratic civic virtue.[51] In arguing that hope can be a democratic civic virtue as well as an intellectual virtue, my aim was not to adopt a modular approach to virtues such as that endorsed by Adams.[52] Adams makes two causal claims that I do not think provide a promising way of explaining hope.[53] The first is that behavioral dispositions are modular in that they are mutually independent and domain-specific. The second is that such modules can be "added together to form a more inclusive composite disposition."[54] The outline offered here of the development of hope favors a more broad-based approach and is credible as a naturalistic account of how people come to have hope. The capacity to hope is an innate part of our natural endowments, which, through proper care and nurture, can become dispositional and cause its possessors to perceive, think, feel, desire, and act in ways characteristic of hope as a moral virtue. When applied in different domains of life, such as the political domain in a democracy, or the intellectual domain, hope can be a democratic civic virtue or an intellectual virtue.[55] Though these virtues can be further described and theorized in terms of the different domains to which they are applicable, they are, I surmise, not essentially separate from hope in the sense explored here. Fully explaining these relations is a project for another day.[56]

NOTES

1. See Nancy E. Snow, "Hope as an Intellectual Virtue," in *Virtues in Action: New Essays in Applied Virtue Ethics*, ed. Mike Austin (New York: Palgrave Macmillan, 2013), 153–70; and "Hope as a Democratic Civic Virtue," *Metaphilosophy* 49, no. 3 (2018): 407–27.

2. J. P. Day, "Hope," *American Philosophical Quarterly* 6, no. 2 (1969): 89–102; *Hope: A Philosophical Inquiry* (Helsinki: The Philosophical Society of Finland, 1991); and "More about Hope and Fear," *Ethical Theory and Moral Practice* 1 (1998): 121–23; Thomas Aquinas, *Summa Theologica. Secunda Secundæ Partis*, Question 17. http://www.newadvent.org/summa/3017.htm (2008). Accessed March 19, 2017, and July 5, 2018; Thomas Hobbes, *Leviathan*, edited by C. B. MacPherson (Harmondsworth, Middlesex, England: Penguin, 1968); Luc Bovens, "The Value of Hope," *Philosophy and Phenomenological Research* 59, no. 3 (1999): 667–82; Victoria McGeer, "The Art of Good Hope," *Annals of the American Academy of Political and Social Science* 592 (2004): 100–27; Philip Pettit, "Hope and Its Place in Mind," *Annals of the American Academy of Political and Social Science* 592 (2004): 152–65; Margaret Walker, *Moral Repair: Reconstructing Moral Relations after Wrongdoing* (New York: Cambridge University Press, 2006); and Ariel Meirav, "The Nature of Hope" *Ratio* (new series) XXII, no. 2 (2009): 216–33.

3. Adrienne Martin, *How We Hope: A Moral Psychology* (Princeton, NJ: Princeton University Press, 2014).

4. Bovens, "The Value of Hope, 674. Another interesting category of hope theories, here left aside, are those that I call "receptivity" theories. Receptivity theories do not preclude the importance of agency for hope, nor roles for hope in promoting and sustaining effective agency. Instead, they are larger theoretical frameworks within which individual agency and hope's effects on it are theorized and contextualized. According to this type of theory, hope is "received from" or "inspired by" external sources, and then empowers the agency of its possessor. Examples of receptivity theories include those of the French Christian existentialist Gabriel Marcel, *Homo Viator: Introduction to a Metaphysic of Hope*, translated by Peter Smith (Chicago: Gateway Editions, 1978); the East German Marxist Ernst Bloch, *The Principle of Hope*, 3 volumes, translated by Neville Plaice, Stephen Plaice, and Paul Knight (Cambridge, MA: MIT Press, 1986); the Thomist philosopher Josef Pieper, *Faith, Hope, Love* (San Francisco: Ignatius Press, 1997) and *Hope and History: Five Salzburg Lectures*, translated byt Dr. David Kipp (San Francisco: Ignatius Press, 1994); and the conception of hope attributed to the Crow tribe by Jonathan Lear in his book, *Radical Hope: Ethics in the Face of Cultural Devastation* (Cambridge, MA: Harvard University Press, 2006). I leave these theories aside because I believe a more direct focus on accounts incorporating the belief-desire model is the most promising route for arguing that hope is a moral virtue. In articulating the belief-desire model, I draw on Snow, "Hope as a Democratic Civic Virtue."

5. C. R. Snyder, "Hypothesis: There Is Hope," in *Handbook of Hope: Theory, Measures, and Applications*, edited by C. R. Snyder (San Diego, CA: Academic Press, 2000), 3–21.

6. Walker, *Moral Repair*, 47–48.

7. Meirav, "The Nature of Hope," 216. For further discussion, see Meirav, 230–33. His position is that hope that p involves the belief that the external factor(s) relevant for the realization of p is/are good.

8. Snow, "Hope as an Intellectual Virtue," 153–54.

9. Erik H. Erikson, *Insight and Responsibility: Lectures on the Ethical Implications of Psychoanalytic Insight* (New York: Norton, 1964) and *The Life Cycle Completed: Extended Version with New Chapters on the Ninth Stage of Development by Joan M. Erikson* (New York: Norton, 1997).

10. Erikson, *The Life Cycle Completed*, 31–32, 55–56.

11. Erikson, *Insight and Responsibility*, 112.

12. Erikson, *Insight and Responsibility*, 117.

13. See J. W. Santrock, *Life-Span Development* (New York: McGraw-Hill, 2011), 186–87.

14. Erikson, *Insight and Responsibility*, 115; italics his.

15. McGeer, "The Art of Good Hope," 105–8.

16. McGeer, "The Art of Good Hope," 106.

17. McGeer, "The Art of Good Hope," 107–8.

18. For or other accounts of hope as an Aristotelian virtue, see Stan van Hooft, *Hope* (Durham, UK: Acumen Publishing Limited, 2011), and Barbro Fröding, "Hope as a Virtue in an Aristotelian Context," *Philosophy, Psychiatry, and Psychology* 19, no. 3 (2012): 183–86. Unlike my account, van Hooft maintains that hope is an intellectual virtue and is a mean between the extremes of presumption on one hand and despair and recognition on the other (see van Hooft, *Hope*, 2–4, 44–45). Fröding argues that to be virtuous in the Aristotelian sense, one must develop one's capacity for hope, and this is connected with the need for self-care in order to be virtuous (see Fröding, "Hope as a Virtue," 184). For an argument that hope is a virtue, though not in an Aristotelian sense, see Adam Kadlac, "The Virtue of Hope," *Ethical Theory and Moral Practice* 18 (2015): 337–54. For an argument against the view that hope is a moral virtue that is based in the work of Aquinas, see Christopher A. Bobier, "Why Hope Is Not a Moral Virtue: Aquinas's Insight," *Ratio* 32, no. 2 (2018): 214–32.

19. See Scott Gravlee, "Aristotle on Hope," *Journal of the History of Philosophy* 38, no. 4 (2000): 461–77.

20. In this paragraph, I draw on Snow, "Hope as a Democratic Civic Virtue."

21. See Aquinas, *Summa*, Question 17.

22. Trudy Govier, "Hope and Its Opposites," *Journal of Social Philosophy* 42, no. 3 (2011): 239–53. Bovens (personal conversation, December 28, 2014) suggests that fear, as well as despair, is a contrary of hope. For discussions of the complexities of hope, see also Baruch Spinoza, *Spinoza Selections*, edited by John Wild (New York: Charles Scribner's Sons, 1958), 270; David Hume, *A Treatise of Human Nature*, edited by P. H. Nidditch (Clarendon Press: Oxford, England, 1978, 439–48); Day, "Hope," and "More about Hope and Fear"; and Hirokazu Miyazaki, "The Economy of Hope: An Introduction," in *The Economy of Hope*, Hirokazu Miyazaki and Richard Swedberg, editors (Philadelphia: University of Pennsylvania Press, 2017), 3.

23. Aristotle, *Nicomachean Ethics*, translated by Terence Irwin (Indianapolis, IN: Hackett Publishing Company, 1985), 1103a15ff.

24. *Nicomachean Ethics*, 1103b5.

25. *Nicomachean Ethics*, 1105a17–25.

26. *Nicomachean Ethics*, 1105a25.

27. *Nicomachean Ethics*, 1144b3–10.

28. Exactly how this occurs is an interesting question. Two possibilities can be identified: parental scaffolding helps the child to act confidently which then, in a second step, leads the child to develop a sense of hope, or parental scaffolding directly supports the child's development of hopes. I think the two are closely related, and that further thought and perhaps empirical work would be needed to ascertain whether the development of confidence is an intermediate step in the development of hope. I think it not unlikely that confidence comes first, and hope follows. Thanks to Titus Stahl for raising this issue.

29. McGeer, "The Art of Good Hope," 109–24.

30. McGeer, "The Art of Good Hope," 115.

31. McGeer, "The Art of Good Hope," 114.

32. McGeer, "The Art of Good Hope," 115–16.

33. McGeer, "The Art of Good Hope," 116.

34. McGeer, "The Art of Good Hope," 113, 116.

35. McGeer, "The Art of Good Hope," 115–16.

36. McGeer, "The Art of Good Hope," 122.

37. McGeer, "The Art of Good Hope," 118.

38. McGeer, "The Art of Good Hope," 118.

39. McGeer, "The Art of Good Hope," 118.

40. Kadlac, "The Virtue of Hope," 348–49.

41. Robert Merrihew Adams, *A Theory of Virtue: Excellence in Being for the Good* (New York: Oxford University Press, 37; emphasis his), quoted in Kadlac, "The Virtue of Hope," 342.

42. Adams, *A Theory of Virtue*, 37.

43. Kadlac, "The Virtue of Hope," 342.

44. Kadlac, "The Virtue of Hope," 348.
45. Kadlac, "The Virtue of Hope," 348.
46. Kadlac, "The Virtue of Hope," 348.
47. Kadlac, "The Virtue of Hope," 338.
48. Here again, I part ways with Kadlac, who states, "Even if we should acknowledge the existence of idle hopes, it seems implausible to think that their possession is a good reason to praise someone's character," Kadlac, "The Virtue of Hope," 341. By contrast, I think that idle hopes can and sometimes do reveal good and bad aspects of character.
49. Thanks to Claudia Blöser for calling this to my attention.
50. Far more could be said about hope and flourishing. For example, can one hope for bad ends, yet flourish? Can one have false hopes, yet flourish? Unfortunately, space limitations preclude discussion of these issues.
51. See Snow, "Hope as an Intellectual Virtue," and "Hope as a Democratic Civic Virtue."
52. Adams, *A Theory of Virtue*, 125–27.
53. Adams, *A Theory of Virtue*, 125–27.
54. Adams, *A Theory of Virtue*, 126. I do not know what it means to "add" virtues that are operative in one domain to those operative in another to form a "composite" virtue. Though I make no claims about the modularity of virtuous dispositions, I adopt the view that virtues that are at first operative in one domain can be generalized throughout different domains. See Snow, *Virtue as Social Intelligence: An Empirically Grounded Theory* (New York: Routledge Press), "How Habits Make Us Virtuous," in *Developing the Virtues: Integrating Perspectives*, edited by Julia Annas, Darcia Narvaez, and Nancy E. Snow (New York: Oxford University Press), 135–56; and "From Ordinary Virtue to Aristotelian Virtue," in *The Theory and Practice of Virtue Education*, edited by Tom Harrison and David Walker (London: Routledge), 67–81.
55. I am not claiming that all of those who are disposed to have hope in the domains of democratic politics or intellectual life always possess a virtue. There are many ways in which dispositions to hope, in all areas of life, can go awry and fail to be virtuous.
56. I thank Claudia Blöser and Titus Stahl for helpful comments on an earlier version of this essay.

REFERENCES

Adams, Robert Merrihew. 2006. *A Theory of Virtue: Excellence in Being for the Good.* New York: Oxford University Press.
Aquinas, Thomas. 2008. *Summa Theologica. Secunda Secundæ Partis.* Question 17. http://www.newadvent.org/summa/3017.htm.
Aristotle. 1985. *Nicomachean Ethics.* Translated by Terence Irwin. Indianapolis, IN: Hackett Publishing Company.
Bloch, Ernst. 1986. *The Principle of Hope.* 3 vols. Translated by Neville Plaice, Stephen Plaice, and Paul Knight. Cambridge, MA: MIT Press.
Bobier, Christopher A. 2018. "Why Hope Is Not a Moral Virtue: Aquinas's Insight." *Ratio* 32, no. 2 (2018): 214–32.
Bovens, Luc. 1999. "The Value of Hope." *Philosophy and Phenomenological Research* 59, no. 3 (1999): 667–82.
Day, J. P. 1969. "Hope." *American Philosophical Quarterly* 6, no. 2 (1969): 89–102.
———. 1991. *Hope: A Philosophical Inquiry.* Helsinki: The Philosophical Society of Finland.
———. 1998. "More about Hope and Fear." *Ethical Theory and Moral Practice* 1 (1998): 121–23.
Erikson, Erik H. 1964. *Insight and Responsibility: Lectures on the Ethical Implications of Psychoanalytic Insight.* New York: Norton.
———. 1997. *The Life Cycle Completed: Extended Version with New Chapters on the Ninth Stage of Development by Joan M. Erikson.* New York: Norton.
Fröding, Barbro. 2012. "Hope as a Virtue in an Aristotelian Context." *Philosophy, Psychiatry, and Psychology* 19, no. 3 (2012): 183–86.

Govier, Trudy. 2011. "Hope and Its Opposites." *Journal of Social Philosophy* 42, no. 3 (2011): 239–53.

Gravlee, G. Scott. 2000. "Aristotle on Hope." *Journal of the History of Philosophy* 38, no. 4 (2000): 461–77.

Hobbes, Thomas. 1968. *Leviathan*. Edited by C. B. MacPherson. Harmondsworth, Middlesex, UK: Penguin Books.

Hume, David. 1978. *A Treatise of Human Nature*. Edited by P. H. Nidditch. Oxford: Clarendon Press.

Kadlac, Adam. 2015. "The Virtue of Hope." *Ethical Theory and Moral Practice* 18 (2015): 337–54.

Lear, Jonathan. 2006. *Radical Hope: Ethics in the Face of Cultural Devastation*. Cambridge, MA: Harvard University Press.

Marcel, Gabriel. 1978. *Homo Viator: Introduction to a Metaphysic of Hope*. Translated by Peter Smith. Chicago: Gateway Editions.

Martin, Adrienne. 2014. *How We Hope: A Moral Psychology*. Princeton, NJ: Princeton University Press.

Martin, Adrienne M. 2011. "Hopes and Dreams." *Philosophy and Phenomenological Research* LXXXIII, no. 1 (2011): 148–73.

McGeer, Victoria. 2004. "The Art of Good Hope." *Annals of the American Academy of Political and Social Science* 592 (2004): 100–27.

Meirav, Ariel. 2009. "The Nature of Hope." *Ratio* (new series) XXII, no. 2 (2009): 216–33.

Miyazaki, Hirokazu. 2017. "The Economy of Hope: An Introduction." In *The Economy of Hope*, edited by Hirokazu Miyazaki and Richard Swedberg, 1–36. Philadelphia: University of Pennsylvania Press, 2017.

Pettit, Philip. 2004. "Hope and Its Place in Mind." *Annals of the American Academy of Political and Social Science* 592 (2004): 152–65.

Pieper, Josef. 1994. *Hope and History: Five Salzburg Lectures*. Translated by Dr. David Kipp. San Francisco: Ignatius Press.

———. 1997. *Faith, Hope, Love*. San Francisco: Ignatius Press.

Santrock, J. W. 2011. *Life-Span Development*. New York: McGraw-Hill.

Shade, Patrick. 2001. *Habits of Hope: A Pragmatic Theory*. Nashville, TN: Vanderbilt University Press.

Snow, Nancy E. 2010. *Virtue as Social Intelligence: An Empirically Grounded Theory*. New York: Routledge Press.

———. 2013. "Hope as an Intellectual Virtue." In *Virtues in Action: New Essays in Applied Virtue Ethics*, edited by Mike Austin, 153–70. New York: Palgrave Macmillan.

———. 2016. "How Habits Make Us Virtuous." In *Developing the Virtues: Integrating Perspectives*, edited by Julia Annas, Darcia Narvaez, and Nancy E. Snow, 135–56. New York: Oxford University Press.

———. 2018. "From Ordinary Virtue to Aristotelian Virtue." In *The Theory and Practice of Virtue Education*, edited by Tom Harrison and David Walker, 67–81. London: Routledge.

———. 2018. "Hope as a Democratic Civic Virtue." *Metaphilosophy* 49, no. 3 (2018): 407–27.

Snyder, C. R. 2000. "Hypothesis: There Is Hope." In *Handbook of Hope: Theory, Measures, and Applications*, edited by C. R. Snyder, 3–21. San Diego, CA: Academic Press.

Van Hooft, Stan. 2011. *Hope*. Durham, UK: Acumen Publishing Limited.

Walker, Margaret Urban. 2006. *Moral Repair: Reconstructing Moral Relations after Wrongdoing*. New York: Cambridge University Press.

Wild, John, ed., 1958. *Spinoza Selections*. New York: Charles Scribner's Sons.

Chapter Eleven

Hope in Contemporary Psychology

Matthew W. Gallagher, Johann M. D'Souza, and Angela L. Richardson

A HISTORY OF HOPE IN PSYCHOLOGY

Hope has been a topic of interest to philosophers for centuries and has been widely and increasingly examined within psychology in the past century as an important and adaptive trait. In this chapter, we briefly review different models of hope in psychology from the past century before focusing on C. R. Snyder's (2002) model of hope, which is now the most widely studied and empirically supported model of hope within psychology. Then, we will review how hope is typically assessed in psychological research and clinical practice, what we have learned about hope so far, and finally, the trajectory of future hope research.

EARLY MODELS OF HOPE IN PSYCHOLOGY

As the discipline of psychology developed in the early twentieth century, opinions on whether hope was adaptive or harmful were quite mixed. Sigmund Freud took a view consistent with that of Nietzsche: he described hope as a delusion with too much connection to religion (Freud 1928). However, another founder of modern psychology, Carl Jung, described hope as one of the "highest achievements of human effort" (Jung 1933).

Progressively over the course of the twentieth century, psychologists began to develop a more positive perspective on hope as a psychological trait and resource. In 1959, Karl Menninger addressed the American Psychiatric Association on the importance of hope in the science of mental health and how to promote recovery from mental illness. Menninger (1959) highlighted

how the existing literature and practice guidelines had few positive references about the need for mental health professionals to instill hope when
working with patients, because he believed that building and facilitating hope
was a crucial factor in promoting recovery from mental illness. Thus, his
lecture became a call for the psychological community to consider and better
understand how psychologists and psychiatrist can promote hope, and how
hope in turn may help to promote mental health and recovery from mental
illness. He stated that hope is vital in the clinical practice of psychology as it
allows the patient to make more comprehensive and accurate goals for treatment instead of simply passively expecting the best, or conversely, the worst.
Although conceptualizations of hope within psychology have evolved con-
siderably since Menninger's call for action, his statement helped spur hope
research in the subsequent decades.

After Menninger's address, hope was increasingly studied in psychology,
and numerous theories of hope were developed starting in the 1960s and
continuing into the 1970s and 1980s (Callina, Snow, and Murray 2017).
Mowrer emphasized hope's role in learning and behavior in his two-factor
theory of learning. In this theory, hope is conceptualized as an anticipatory
response associated with the expectation of a more favorable outcome
(Mowrer 1960). As the construct of hope continued to be studied, more
researchers began to view hope less as an emotion and more as a component
of one's cognitive processes. For example, Erickson viewed hope as a
thought process, starting at birth that guides individuals toward their goals
(Erickson 1964).

Others have viewed hope as a cognitive process in which the probability
of a goal being actualized is evaluated based on importance, resources, and
goals (Stotland 1969; Gottschalk 1974). One of the first major theoretical
treatises on hope was *The Psychology of Hope* by Stotland (1969). Stotland
conceptualized hope as a cognitive process related to positive expectations of
goal attainment that is accompanied by positive emotions such as motivation.
According to Stotland's theory, hope is dependent upon the predictability
and the importance of the goal. This theory emphasized the role of goals in
the study of motivation. While Stotland's conceptualization of hope reinforced the view of hope as a goal-oriented process or trait, there was still
uncertainty as to how individuals develop hope and how to distinguish hope
from other attitudes of positive expectation such as optimism.

This work was followed by Staats (1989), who conceptualized hope as
both a cognitive and affective trait. Staats's theory posited that the cognitive
side of hope results from an interaction between one's expectations and
wishes, while the affective side of hope encompasses one's expectation of
experiencing negative and positive affect. High hope therefore comes from
high levels of both cognitive and affective components. As hope involves
expectations as well as positive affect, Staats's theory of hope differentiated

hope from optimism, with the latter conceptualized as a more general positive expectation of the future.

A more recent theory from Averill, Catlin, and Chon (1990) conceptualized hope as an emotion, the meaning of which is dependent on the social and cultural environment. According to this theory, hope is best utilized when the individual appreciates the importance of her goal and the goal is acceptable in her society. The motivational component of hope in this theoretical approach is similar to Staats's theory of hope, however Averill and colleagues emphasize the contribution of society and culture on individual motivation.

Other models of hope have demonstrated its utility in the clinical world. Jerome Frank began to emphasize its important role in psychotherapy in his seminal writings on underlying principles across diverse forms of psychotherapy (Frank 1968; Frank and Frank 1993). Frank argued that hope's foundation in positive expectations of goal achievement is vital for effective psychotherapy, positive treatment outcomes, and better therapist-client working alliance. Another theory of hope studied hope in the context of nursing, specifically helping those with chronic illness use hope as a coping skill (Herth 1991). In this model, hope is described as multidimensional, with different attributes (experiential, spiritual, relational, and rational) that enable the hopeful individual to have a subjectively realistic and significant expectation of positive outcomes (Dufault and Martocchio 1985; Herth 2000). Herth subsequently expanded on this model to develop the Hope Process Framework, a set of guidelines for hope interventions aimed at increasing feelings of hope in cancer patients (Herth 2000).

Conceptualizations of hope in psychology therefore shifted over decades from early perspectives in which hope was viewed as a maladaptive trait of the naïve to a more positive view of hope as an adaptive resource that predicted and promoted positive outcomes across many domains. At the same time as psychologists, psychiatrists, and nurses developed models and measures of hope that emphasized the benefits of hope, psychological theories of hope also increasingly conceptualized hope as a cognitive process or trait rather than an emotional process as lay perspectives and definitions of hope often emphasize. The pivotal development that advanced the science and practice of hope within psychology was when Snyder developed a new model of hope, which incorporated some ideas from early models of hope but represented a distinct approach to conceptualizing hope, and this model has now driven hope research in psychology over the past three decades.

SNYDER'S MODEL OF HOPE

Although there have been several theoretical conceptualizations of hope within psychology, many of which continue to be studied empirically, the model proposed by Snyder has the most theoretical and empirical support by far (Rose and Sieben 2017). Snyder's model has been the object of empirical testing for nearly thirty years and has led to a dramatic improvement in our understanding of how hope influences outcomes in many life contexts (Gallagher and Lopez 2017; Snyder 2000; Snyder 2002; Snyder et al. 1991). Snyder began his research on hope building the prevailing understanding of hope as "the perception that one can reach desired goals" (Snyder, Rand, and Sigmon 2017). This interest in goals was sparked while Snyder was studying how one distances themselves from negative emotions associated with mistakes in the form of excuses (Snyder, Higgins, and Stucky 1983). However, Snyder noticed that participants would connect themselves to positive outcomes in addition to distancing themselves from negative outcomes through forming goals (Snyder 2002). Later, as Snyder interviewed people about their goals, he discovered that hopeful people would often discuss both their motivation and the specific strategies by which they would achieve their goals. To incorporate these two components into the definition of hope, Snyder developed a model of hope as a two-fold cognitive trait that represents the ability to identify strategies to achieve one's goals (i.e., pathways thinking) and to have the motivation and determination to successfully implement those pathways (i.e., agency thinking) to achieve the goals (Snyder 2002; Snyder et al. 1991).

The components of Snyder's definition are straightforward; however, it is important to explore how pathways and agency interact to form the higher order construct of hope. First, Snyder's model of hope adopts the widely held and empirically supported perspective that human actions are largely driven by the identification and pursuit of goals (Little, Salmela-Aro, and Phillips 2017; Maslow 1943). Within this understanding of human motivation, attainment of goals must be seen as possible but not guaranteed. Second, Snyder conceptualizes hope primarily as a cognitive trait rather than an emotional process or outcome, in that pathways and agency are described as cognitive resources. Pathways refers to the ability to think of specific ways to achieve goals and is exemplified by thoughts such as "I'll find a way to a solution" (Snyder, Rand, and Sigmon 2017). People with high hope are better able to generate alternative pathways to their goals in the face of obstacles. Agency refers to the ability to implement one's pathways in order to achieve the goal. This includes both initiating and maintaining goal-directed behavior and is exemplified by thoughts like "I can do this" (Snyder 2000). When facing obstacles, people high in hope are better able to choose and implement a particular pathway, and are also flexible and capable of recognizing when it is necessary to disengage from one approach in order to pursue an alternative pathway. The pathways and agency components work in tandem when an individual is pursuing their goals.

Although hope is not conceptualized as an emotion in Snyder's model, the role of emotions is clearly articulated in the model and hope is hypothesized to be a key factor in determining emotional outcomes. Achieving one's goals should be accompanied by positive emotions, whereas failure to achieve goals should result in negative emotions. These emotions would be expected to influence subsequent pathways and agency thoughts through positive and negative reinforcement, which could result in the person modifying the strategy to achieve the goal. Consistent with this theory, many empirical studies have found a significant moderate to high positive correlation between hope and positive emotions and a significant moderate to high negative correlation between hope and negative emotions (Alarcon, Bowling, and Khazon 2013). The interaction between pathways and agency thoughts and positive or negative emotions could influence an individual's behavior from a young age, specifically in how they connect their goals to outcomes (Snyder, Rand, and Sigmon 2017).

MEASURES OF HOPE

As the concept of hope became more refined, psychologists also made great strides in developing valid and reliable measures of hope, which has helped psychologists, in research and practice assess levels of hope and observe associations between hope and other facets of mental health and illness. We first review scales developed from Snyder's hope model, as these are the most widely used assessment tools for measuring hope in psychology, and then we review additional hope measures that have promising empirical support.

Snyder's Measures of Hope

There are three primary hope scales that have been developed to assess hope as conceptualized in Snyder's theoretical framework. The first is the Adult Dispositional Hope Scale, which is often known as the Adult Hope Scale (AHS; Snyder et al. 1991). Snyder's Adult Hope Scale has four pathways items, such as "I can think of many ways to get out of a jam," four agency items, such as "I energetically pursue my goals," and four distraction items, such as "I feel tired most of the time," all rated on an 8-point Likert scale. This scale has demonstrated high validity and reliability (Snyder 2002). A recent meta-analysis using sixteen studies reported the internal consistency at $\alpha = .82$ (Hellman, Pittman, and Munoz 2013). The Adult Hope Scale has demonstrated convergent and discriminant validity as well as structural validity in that it supports Snyder's two-factor structure of hope (Snyder et al. 1991). Scores on the trait hope scale have been found to remain stable across time and across studies (Hellman, Pittman, and Munoz 2013; Snyder et al.

1991). Factor analytic studies have demonstrated that AHS can be used to examine the two components of hope as well as the single overarching hope construct. The AHS has now been translated and used in many languages, with promising evidence that it is valid in different cultures (Abdel-Khalek and Snyder 2007; Carifio and Rhodes 2002; Dubé et al. 2000; Halama 2001; S. M. Y. Ho 2003; McDermott et al. 1997).

Although the AHS remains the most widely used measure for quantifying hope in psychology, it was recognized that assessing hope as a trait may not be ideal in all circumstances, so Snyder and colleagues subsequently developed the State Hope Scale in order to have an additional assessment tool that is more sensitive to variations in levels of hope across time (Snyder et al. 1996). This six-item measure still consists of pathways and agency items, similar to the AHS. Similar to the AHS, the State Hope Scale's reliability and validity have been examined in many studies and there is extensive support for the measurement properties of this scale (Feldman and Snyder 2000). The scale demonstrated Snyder's two-factor structure of hope in a factor analysis. Reliability testing of the State Hope Scale revealed Cronbach alphas of 0.82 and 0.95, which demonstrate high levels of internal consistency within the measure. Based on the scale being strongly and positively correlated with related constructs (i.e., dispositional hope, state self-esteem, and state positive affect) and having a strong, negative association with negative affect, there is strong evidence for convergent validity (Rose and Sieben 2017).

Snyder posited that the experience and benefits of hope was not limited to adults. In line with this idea, he created the Children's Hope Scale (CHS) (Snyder et al. 1997), a developmentally appropriate scale for youth ages eight to nineteen years of age. The CHS is a six-item measure consisting of two scales (pathways and agency), and is also consistent with the two-factor model of hope (Valle, Huebner, and Suldo 2004). As with the AHS and state hope scale, the reliability, validity, and two-factor structure of the children's hope scale is supported by several studies (Moon and Snyder 2000). This scale has a test-retest reliability of $\alpha = 0.73$ and strong convergent validity (Snyder et al. 1997). Using the CHS, higher hope in children was related to higher levels of self-esteem, optimism, and academic success and lower levels of depression (Snyder et al. 1997; Valle, Huebner, and Suldo 2006). Translations of the CHS have also demonstrated structural and convergent validity (Marques, Pais-Ribeiro, and Lopez 2009).

Psychologists also recognized the utility of domain-specific measures of hope in answering questions regarding hope across contexts (Lopez et al. 2000). The Domain-Specific Hope Scale represents one such measure (DSHS; Sympson 1999). The DSHS consists of forty-eight items separated into six domains: social relationships, romantic relationships, leisure, family, work, and academics. The DSHS demonstrated acceptable validity and reliability (Snyder 2000). Since each domain is represented by eight items, researchers have separated the DSHS into scales for specific research questions. One of these is the Academic Hope Scale, which has been used to measure one's disposition to use agency and pathways in one's academic achievement (Gallagher, Marques, and Lopez 2016). Other scales created from the DSHS include the interpersonal hope scale (includes social, family, and romantic hope) and the achievement-oriented hope scale (including academic and work hope; Campbell and Kwon 2001).

Alternative Measures of Hope

One of the first scales developed within psychology to assess hope is the 1975 Hope Scale (Erickson, Post, and Paige 1975). This measure was based on Stotland's theory of hope, specifically the domains of subjective predictability and importance of one's goals. The questionnaire is made up of a list of twenty goals. Individuals rate the degree of importance of each goal on a 7-point Likert scale and assigns the probability of achieving the goal on a scale from 0 to 100. The scores obtained from the 1975 Hope Scale include mean importance and mean probability across all twenty goals. Internal consistencies for each mean sub-score are 0.79 (Importance) and 0.80 (Predictability), demonstrating acceptable reliability.

Based on the theory that hope consists of both a cognitive and affect component, Staats developed two hope scales rather than one in order to assess both factors. The first measure, the eighteen-item Expected Balance scale (EBS; Staats 1989), assesses the affective side of hope by having individuals rate their expectancies of positive and negative affect on a 5-point Likert scale. The EBS was found to have a moderate level of internal consistency. The second and more widely used measure of her two scales is the Hope Index (Staats 1989). The Hope Index contains four subscales: hope in oneself, hope in others, wish, and expect. Staats designed this sixteen-item scale to measure cognitive aspects of hope, specifically the extent to which one wishes for specific goals and expects them to come to fruition. This measure of hope also distinguishes between hope in oneself and hope in others as paralleled by Beck's theory of depression. The Hope Index shows has good evidence demonstrating test-retest reliability and validity (Staats 1989).

The aforementioned measures are all based on subjective self-report, but there are other methods of measuring hope. Gottschalk's Hope Scale can be used to analyze an individual's five-minute speech sample for references to hope (Gottschalk 1974). A weighted scale is used to rate certain categories of the content, and a composite score is calculated from the averaged ratings (Gottschalk 1974). Gottschalk's Hope Scale has been shown to have discriminant validity from constructs such as anxiety and hostility. Another observational measure of hope is the Narrative Hope scale, which assesses the extent to which one has elements of agency and pathways in written stories (Vance 1996). Using the Narrative Hope scale, raters use a given list of thoughts and behaviors designated as consistent with high or low hope. Hope can also be measured in therapy by asking clients questions about their pathways, agency, goals, and obstacles in order to assist the client and clinician with ascertaining the client's levels of hope (Lopez et al. 2000).

DISTINCTION OF HOPE FROM OTHER CONSTRUCTS

Trait hope shows large, statistically significant, associations with similar positive psychology constructs such as optimism and self-efficacy (Snyder, Rand, and Sigmon 2017). All three constructs start from the assumption that human behavior is oriented toward goal pursuit, with motivation increasing as goal attainment appears more likely and as the goal is perceived as more important to the individual. All three are seen as primarily cognitive rather than emotional, and can be measured as stable traits. Finally, they all pertain to positive expectations of the future. Although hope has been shown to have a moderate to high correlation with optimism and self-efficacy, it is conceptually and empirically distinct from these constructs (Snyder, Rand, and Sigmon 2017).

Optimism has been defined as a generalized positive expectancy that good things are more likely to occur than bad things (Carver, Scheier, and Segerstrom 2010). People high in hope and optimism share the view that their goals will be achieved, but, according to Snyder, high hopers as opposed to optimists also believe that their goals will come about through their personal agency. Self-efficacy is the belief that one has the personal ability to do what is necessary to achieve one's goals (Bandura 1997). Hope is similar to self-efficacy in that they both emphasize personal agency or the role of the individual in achieving goals. However, hope takes into account the specific pathways to the goals whereas self-efficacy does not (Luszczynska, Scholz, and Schwarzer 2005). The person high in self-efficacy may not believe his goals will actually be achieved if he is prevented by external forces. The person high in hope, however, believes he will be able to find a way to achieve his goals by adjusting the pathways in light of external conditions or by marshalling the support of others. Hope is distinct from both optimism and self-efficacy in that hope takes into account one's intention to achieve one's goals. People high in optimism simply believe that their goals will be achieved, whereas those high in self-efficacy believe that their goals could be achieved if circumstances are favorable. Empirical studies using confirmatory factor analysis have supported these conceptual differences in finding that hope, optimism, and self-efficacy are better modeled as three distinct latent constructs than one construct (Herbert 2011; Carifio and Rhodes 2002).

HOPE AS A PREDICTOR OF POSITIVE OUTCOMES

Modern psychological theories of hope, such as Snyder's model, suggest that hope is adaptive and promotes positive outcomes across many contexts. Hope is consistently related to better academic performance, physical health, and mental health (Alarcon, Bowling, and Khazon 2013; Snyder 2002). People with higher hope use more adaptive coping strategies such as problem-focused coping and active coping. They are more willing to embrace difficult goals, perceive obstacles as less difficult, and show more resilience in stressful times (Snyder 2002). Furthermore, people with high hope are more likely to achieve their goals, and contrary to the idea that high hopers tend to pursue easy goals, studies have found that high hopers pursue difficult goals and view them as welcome challenges to embrace (Snyder 2002). Although one study found that hope scores were similar across different ethnic groups, the predictors of agency differed between African Americans, Asian Americans, Latinx, and European Americans (Chang and Banks 2007). The examination of the benefits of hope across cultures remains an active area where more research is needed.

Hope and Academic Performance

Hope may promote better academic performance by increasing intention, motivation, effort, and future-oriented perspective (Onwuegbuzie and Snyder 2000; Adelabu 2008). Several studies have found significant positive correlations between scores on the Adult Hope Scale and GPA across age groups (Snyder 2002). One study found that hope uniquely predicted college GPA across four years even after controlling for academic history, self-efficacy, and engagement (Gallagher, Marques, and Lopez 2016). The relationship between hope and academic performance could be due to high hopers being more oriented toward the future (Adelabu 2008). Other studies have found that effort and self-efficacy may contribute to the development of hope in an academic context (Levi et al. 2014; Phan 2013). Hope also protects students from behaviors that negatively impact academic performance, such as substance use (Fite et al. 2014).

Hope and Physical Health

Hope may promote physical health through adaptive illness prevention behaviors such as planning, self-monitoring, and positive social interactions (Berg et al. 2011; Nothwehr, Clark, and Perkins 2013). Not only does hope help in preventing illness and disease, but it also promotes health among individuals with active illness. People with high hope tend to adhere to their medical regimen and use more adaptive ways of coping with stress (Rasmussen et al. 2017). Among individuals with chronic medical conditions, hope predicted positive health behaviors, subjective well-being and even physical functioning after in-patient rehabilitation (Berg et al. 2011; Kortte et al. 2010, 2012). Furthermore, hope may protect people from the effects of pain. Since people with high hope have positive views of their ability to overcome difficulties, they may be less likely to catastrophize while experiencing pain (Hood et al. 2012). In fact, studies have found that people with higher hope are better able to pursue their goals even while experiencing pain (Snyder et al. 2005). Finally, a hope-based intervention even found that after the intervention, individuals had lower levels of pain catastrophizing (Howell, Jacobson, and Larsen 2015). Hope can also help individuals during and after recovery from their illness. Hope predicted posttraumatic growth among cancer survivors, enabling individuals to experience positive personal change after a difficult life event (S. Ho et al. 2011; Yuen, Ho, and Chan 2014).

Hope and Mental Illness

Hope has been proposed to promote mental health, because people with high hope are more likely to use adaptive coping strategies and may therefore be more capable of coping with stress and more resilience to the development of mental illness as a result. Hopelessness is one of the most salient features of depressive disorders. Thus, it comes as no surprise that a recent meta-analysis on hope found significant negative associations with depression ($\rho = -.52$; where ρ is average weighted correlation coefficient corrected for unreliability in both the predictor and criterion variable (Alarcon, Bowling, and Khazon 2013). One reason for this relationship is that people with depression tend to have lower motivation toward goals, create vague goals, and feel they have less control over achieving their goals (Winch, Moberly, and Dickson 2015; Dickson and Moberly 2013). Preliminary research supports the idea that a hope-based intervention can result in lower depression. One study of a hope-based intervention, which was not specifically aimed at lowering depression, found that after eight weeks, participants had a trend toward lower depressive symptoms (Cheavens et al. 2006).

Several studies have found a significant negative correlation between hope and anxiety (Arnau 2017). A study in France that measured anxiety using the Hospital Anxiety and Depression Scale reported a significant correlation of $r = -.25$ between hope and anxiety symptoms (Gana, Daigre, and Ledrich 2013). Similarly, a study using the Arabic version of the Adult Hope Scale found a significant negative correlation of $r = -.29$ (Abdel-Khalek and Snyder 2007). A longitudinal study found that the agency but not pathways component of the AHS significantly predicted less future anxiety even after controlling for baseline anxiety (Arnau 2017).

Hope and Well-Being

Hope not only protects against negative outcomes such as psychopathology, but it also promotes positive functioning such as emotional, eudaimonic, and social well-being (Lee and Gallagher 2017). Emotional or subjective well-being is characterized by high positive affect, low negative affect, and high life satisfaction or subjective happiness (Diener 2009). A meta-analysis found significant positive associations between hope and positive affect ($r =$ .36) and subjective happiness ($r = .45$) (Alarcon, Bowling, and Khazon 2013). Furthermore, recent longitudinal research has demonstrated that hope significantly predicts positive and negative affect after one year ($r = -10$ for negative affect and $r = .24$ for positive affect) (Ciarrochi et al. 2015), and life satisfaction after one year ($r = .41$) (Valle, Huebner, and Suldo 2006). Eudaimonic or psychological well-being is characterized by a sense of meaning or purpose in life. A study using structural equation modeling to control for measurement invariance found that hope significantly predicted eudaimonic well-being even after controlling for levels of optimism (Gallagher and Lopez 2009). Social well-being is characterized by strong relationships and positive social functioning. The previously cited study using structural equation modeling found that hope also significantly predicted social well-being over and above optimism (Gallagher and Lopez 2009). Thus, hope is associated with aspects of complete mental health including well-being, meaning in life, adaptive coping as well as decreased negative outcomes such as anxiety, depression, and PTSD.

HOPE INTERVENTIONS

Research has shown that some people have higher levels of hope than others. Therefore, researchers have developed interventions that focus on increasing levels of hope at the individual level as a way of targeting mental illness. Hope interventions utilize techniques aimed at improving one's use of pathways and agency. Clinicians can increase the use of pathways skills through exercises that generate multiple, realistic routes to a goal, evaluating which route would be most fruitful, and then assessing their own progress on that route at different time points (Cheavens and Guter 2017). Agency can be cultivated through cognitive restructuring, by which individuals increase their flexibility to believe that they have the resources to accomplish their goals. This can be done through monitoring and evaluating the helpfulness of maladaptive thoughts that individuals tell themselves while trying to accomplish their goals (i.e., "My goal is too ambitious"). Furthermore, hope therapy can assist individuals in modifying thoughts to be more encouraging, which could lead to higher expectation of goal achievement (i.e., "I can break up my larger goal into smaller parts") (Cheavens et al. 2006). Hope therapy also helps individuals choose goals that are in line with values, as this will help to promote and maintain motivation toward goals (Cheavens and Ritschel 2014; Koestner et al. 2002).

There is empirical support for the efficacy of hope interventions in increasing levels of hope. In an early test of Snyder's theory, one study placed thirteen older adults (fifty-five years or older) into goal-focused group psychotherapy based on Snyder's hope model (GFGP; Klausner et al. 1998) or a control "reminiscence/life-review" group. Those in the GFGP group showed a small increase in hope and a large increase in agency from pre- to post-treatment. However, there was no statistical difference in overall hope scores between the treatment and control groups (Klausner et al. 1998). A later study led by Cheavens and colleagues introduced a hope therapy manual that included pathways and agency skill-building techniques (Cheavens et al. 2006). Participants learned how to set realistic and meaningful goals, develop strategies to achieve those goals, monitor motivation and progress, and modify goals and strategies as needed along the way. Those in the active treatment condition participated in hope therapy for eight weeks. Participants in this condition exhibited large increases in overall hope and agency scores ($d = 1.04$ and $d = 1.20$, respectively) and moderate increases in pathways scores ($d = 0.68$). Compared to participants in the waitlist condition, participants in the hope therapy group had higher levels of increase in overall hope and agency scores, but not in pathway scores. A more recent study found that after integrating components of Cheavens's hope therapy manual into an intervention for women with cancer, levels of hope and pathways increased, in contrast to previous studies (Thornton et al. 2014).

Along with increases in hope, hope therapy has also demonstrated improvement in state mental health. The complete state model of mental health is often conceptualized as the presence of flourishing (i.e., well-being, hope) simultaneously occurring with absence of mental illness (Keyes 2005). In the hope intervention study conducted by Cheavens, participants in the hope therapy group demonstrated statistically significantly higher levels of self-esteem and meaning in life and lower levels of depression and anxiety compared to those in the waitlist condition group (Cheavens et al. 2006). In another hope intervention trial in which participants met criteria for major depressive disorder, individuals in the goal-oriented (hope) therapy group experienced clinically significant reductions in levels of clinician-rated ($d = 2.5$) and self-reported ($d = 0.91$) depression from baseline to post-treatment (Klausner et al. 1998). A more recent study examining the impact of a brief hope intervention on depressed primary care patients reported a reduction in depression in the hope intervention group that was twice as large as those in a psychoeducational and control group (Heiy and Cheavens 2015). In a group of women diagnosed with cancer participating in group therapy, self-reported levels of anxiety reduced from pre- to post-treatment ($d = 0.6$) (Thornton et al. 2014). Cheavens's study also found a large reduction in anxiety over the course of hope therapy ($d = 0.8$) (Cheavens et al. 2006). This research supports the premise that hope interventions result in substantial reductions in anxiety and depression throughout therapy. Additionally, hope therapy predicts notably larger reductions in psychopathology symptoms and larger increases in aspects of well-being compared to waitlist controls. Finally, even a single ninety-minute hope intervention resulted in higher levels of hope and life purpose as compared to a control group (Feldman and Dreher 2012). Thus, hope therapy may be an intervention that targets hope as well as facets of mental illness and functioning.

Growth in hope scores have also been observed in participants within empirically supported treatments. In several studies, individuals who underwent structured psychological treatment (cognitive-behavioral therapy, dialectical behavior therapy, etc.) demonstrated increases in overall hope, agency, and pathways scores pre- to post-treatment as well as decreases in psychopathology (Harper-Jacques and Foucault 2014; Irving et al. 2004; Ritschel, Cheavens, and Nelson 2012). These results suggest that through participating in structured psychotherapy, one can also increase their hope as well as decrease levels of psychopathology. This observation has led to researchers asking which part comes first in treatment: changes in hope or changes in symptoms.

HOPE AS A MECHANISM OF CHANGE

Early hope intervention trials found that changes in hope were associated with levels of depression and anxiety post-treatment after controlling for pre-treatment hope, anxiety, and depression scores (Cheavens et al. 2006; Ritschel, Cheavens, and Nelson 2012). In a study examining the effectiveness of cognitive processing therapy (CPT) for PTSD, data was collected at multiple time points from pre- to post-treatment, allowing researchers to observe any temporal precedency of one variable over another. In this sample of veterans, hope at pre-treatment predicted post-treatment clinician-rated PTSD symptom severity, and hope at mid-treatment predicted post-treatment self-rated PTSD and depression symptom severity (Gilman, Schumm, and Chard 2012). Interestingly, these relationships were not bidirectional, which demonstrated that hope had temporal precedence as one mechanism through which CPT treats PTSD and depression. More recently, studies have examined hope as a mechanism of change across different CBT protocols and have found that in addition to changes in hope predicting changes in anxiety, changes in hope also preceded reductions in anxiety symptom severity. Therefore, hope is a potential mechanism of change across treatments, suggesting it is a common factor that when intentionally targeted and promoted during empirically supported treatments for anxiety disorders can play an important role in reducing symptoms and improving functioning. Identifying hope as a mechanism of change is important to psychological research as it allows clinicians and researchers to determine efficient and effective ways to treat clinical symptoms. For example, if a client's high severity of PTSD is preventing them from beginning exposure, perhaps using an additional intervention to increase their hope could influence other factors that would then enable the intervention to successfully target symptoms. These findings contribute to the accumulating research examining common elements that explain how psychotherapeutic interventions treat clinical symptoms.

FUTURE DIRECTIONS

Decades of research within psychology have demonstrated that hope predicts many positive outcomes across different domains (mental health, physical health, achievement, etc.). Research within psychology therefore currently views hope as a positive psychological trait that can improve quality of life and should be reinforced and promoted (Snyder 2002). Snyder's hope model has set a strong foundation for the conceptualization of hope, making leaps from how hope was viewed by Freud in the early twentieth century. Moreover, in the past decade, increasingly robust research methods provide stronger evidence to support Snyder's hope theory. Importantly, there is increasing evidence that hope contributes to mental health above and beyond related constructs such as optimism, which indicates that hope impacts one's well-being independent of more generalized positive expectancies (Gallagher and Lopez 2009).

With an abundance of research showing that hope predicts many positive outcomes across domains of an individual's life, it is important to utilize clinical trials to better understand how hope predicts these outcomes. Therefore, future research should utilize more longitudinal rather than cross-sectional studies. Also, future studies could aim to identify whether more agency- or pathways-oriented thinking is necessary for specific outcomes, or if there has to be a sufficient balance of both in order to optimize treatment outcomes.

Most hope research has been conducted on homogenous samples. More studies examining whether hope's effects on mental health are the same for underrepresented samples is warranted. If these effects appear to be different across gender, race/ethnicity, socioeconomic status, or other demographic factors, it is up to psychologists to find out, especially as our society is becoming more diverse (Abdel-Khalek and Snyder 2007). Continuation of studying cultural differences in assessment of hope is essential to ensuring that when comparing levels of hope or effects of hope on psychological outcomes across cultures, the same type of hope is in fact being measured. It has also been suggested that future work should focus on the promotion of hope, the relation between hope and specific positive outcomes such as meaning, coping, and social relationships, and the role of hope within flourishing communities.

REFERENCES

Abdel-Khalek, Ahmed, and C. R. Snyder. 2007. "Correlates and Predictors of an Arabic Translation of the Snyder Hope Scale." *The Journal of Positive Psychology* 2 (4): 228–35. https://doi.org/10.1080/17439760701552337.

Adelabu, D. H. 2008. "Future Time Perspective, Hope, and Ethnic Identity among African American Adolescents." *Urban Education* 43 (3): 347–60.

Alarcon, G. M., N. A. Bowling, and S. Khazon. 2013. "Great Expectations: A Meta-Analytic Examination of Optimism and Hope." *Personality and Individual Differences* 54 (7): 821–27.

Arnau, R. C. 2017. "Hope and Anxiety." In *The Oxford Handbook of Hope*, edited by M. W. Gallagher and S. J. Lopez. Oxford and New York: Oxford University Press.

Averill, J. R., G. Catlin, and K. K. Chon. 1990. *Rules of Hope*. New York: Springer-Verlag.

Bandura, Albert. 1997. *Self-Efficacy: The Exercise of Control*. New York: W. H. Freeman/ Times Books/ Henry Holt & Co.

Berg, Carla J., Lorie A. Ritschel, Deanne W. Swan, Lawrence C. An, and Jasjit S. Ahluwalia. 2011. "The Role of Hope in Engaging in Healthy Behaviors among College Students." *American Journal of Health Behavior* 35 (4): 402–15.

Callina, K. S., N. Snow, and E. D. Murray. 2017. "The History of Philosophical and Psychological Perspectives on Hope: Toward Defining Hope for the Science of Positive Human Development." In *The Oxford Handbook of Hope*, edited by M. W. Gallagher and S. J. Lopez. Oxford and New York: Oxford University Press.

Campbell, Duncan G., and Paul Kwon. 2001. "Domain-Specific Hope and Personal Style: Toward an Integrative Understanding of Dysphoria." *Journal of Social and Clinical Psychology* 20 (4): 498–520.

Carifio, James, and Lauren Rhodes. 2002. "Construct Validities and the Empirical Relationships between Optimism, Hope, Self-Efficacy, and Locus of Control." *Work: Journal of Prevention, Assessment & Rehabilitation* 19 (2): 125–36.

Carver, Charles S., Michael F. Scheier, and Suzanne C. Segerstrom. 2010. "Optimism." *Clinical Psychology Review* 30 (7): 879–89. https://doi.org/10.1016/j.cpr.2010.01.006.

Chang, Edward C., and Kira Hudson Banks. 2007. "The Color and Texture of Hope: Some Preliminary Findings and Implications for Hope Theory and Counseling among Diverse Racial/Ethnic Groups." *Cultural Diversity and Ethnic Minority Psychology* 13 (2): 94–103. https://doi.org/10.1037/1099-9809.13.2.94.

Cheavens, Jennifer S., David B. Feldman, Amber Gum, Scott T. Michael, and C. R. Snyder. 2006. "Hope Therapy in a Community Sample: A Pilot Investigation." *Social Indicators Research* 77 (1): 61–78. https://doi.org/10.1007/s11205-005-5553-0.

Cheavens, Jennifer S., and M. M. Guter. 2017. "Hope Therapy." In *The Oxford Handbook of Hope*, edited by M. W. Gallagher and S. J. Lopez. Oxford and New York: Oxford University Press.

Cheavens, Jennifer S., and Lorie A. Ritschel. 2014. "Hope Theory." In *Handbook of Positive Emotions*, 396–410. New York: Guilford Press.

Ciarrochi, Joseph, Philip Parker, Todd B. Kashdan, Patrick C. L. Heaven, and Emma Barkus. 2015. "Hope and Emotional Well-Being: A Six-Year Study to Distinguish Antecedents, Correlates, and Consequences." *The Journal of Positive Psychology* 10 (6): 520–32. https://doi.org/10.1080/17439760.2015.1015154.

Dickson, Joanne M., and Nicholas J. Moberly. 2013. "Reduced Specificity of Personal Goals and Explanations for Goal Attainment in Major Depression." *PloS One* 8 (5): e64512. https://doi.org/10.1371/journal.pone.0064512.

Diener, Ed, ed. 2009. "Subjective Well-Being." In *The Collected Works of Ed Diener*. Vol. I: *The Science of Well-Being*, 11–58. Dordrecht: Springer.

Dubé, Micheline, Sylvie Lapierre, Léandre Bouffard, and Réal Labelle. 2000. "Le Bien-Être Psychologique Par La Gestion Des Buts Personnels: Une Intervention de Groupe Auprès Des Retraités. [Psychological Well-Being through the Management of Personal Goals: A Group Intervention for Retirees.]" *Revue Québécoise de Psychologie* 21 (2): 255–80.

Dufault, K., and B. C. Martocchio. 1985. "Symposium on Compassionate Care and the Dying Experience. Hope: Its Spheres and Dimensions." *The Nursing Clinics of North America* 20 (2): 379–91.

Erickson, E. H. 1964. *Insight and Responsibility: Lectures on the Ethical Implications of Psychoanalytic Insight*. New York: W. W. Norton.

Erickson, Richard C., Robin D. Post, and Albert B. Paige. 1975. "Hope as a Psychiatric Variable." *Journal of Clinical Psychology* 31 (2): 324–30.

Feldman, D. B., and C. R. Snyder. 2000. "The State Hope Scale." In *A Handbook of Psychological Tests*, edited by J. Maltby, C. A. Lewis, and A. Hill. Lampeter, Wales: Edwin Mellen Press.

Feldman, David B., and Diane E. Dreher. 2012. "Can Hope Be Changed in 90 Minutes? Testing the Efficacy of a Single-Session Goal-Pursuit Intervention for College Students." *Journal of Happiness Studies: An Interdisciplinary Forum on Subjective Well-Being* 13 (4): 745–59. https://doi.org/10.1007/s10902-011-9292-4.

Fite, Paula J., Joy Gabrielli, John L. Cooley, Sarah M. Haas, Andrew Frazer, Sonia L. Rubens, and Michelle Johnson-Motoyama. 2014. "Hope as a Moderator of the Associations between Common Risk Factors and Frequency of Substance Use among Latino Adolescents." *Journal of Psychopathology and Behavioral Assessment* 36 (4): 653–62. https://doi.org/10.1007/s10862-014-9426-1.

Frank, J. 1968. "The Role of Hope in Psychotherapy." *International Journal of Psychiatry* 5 (5): 383–95.

Frank, J. D., and J. B. Frank. 1993. *Persuasion and Healing: A Comparative Study of Psychotherapy*. 3rd ed. Baltimore: Johns Hopkins University Press.

Freud, S. 1928. *The Future of an Illusion*. London: Hogarth.

Gallagher, M. W., and S. J. Lopez, eds. 2017. *The Oxford Handbook of Hope*. Oxford Library of Psychology. Oxford and New York: Oxford University Press.

Gallagher, Matthew W., and Shane J. Lopez. 2009. "Positive Expectancies and Mental Health: Identifying the Unique Contributions of Hope and Optimism." *The Journal of Positive Psychology* 4 (6): 548–56. https://doi.org/10.1080/17439760903157166.

Gallagher, Matthew W., Susana C. Marques, and Shane J. Lopez. 2016. "Hope and the Academic Trajectory of College Students." *Journal of Happiness Studies* 2 (18): 341–52. https://doi.org/10.1007/s10902-016-9727-z.

Gana, Kamel, Stéphanie Daigre, and Julie Ledrich. 2013. "Psychometric Properties of the French Version of the Adult Dispositional Hope Scale." *Assessment* 20 (1): 114–18. https://doi.org/10.1177/1073191112468315.

Gilman, Rich, Jeremiah Schumm, and Kathleen Chard. 2012. "Hope as a Change Mechanism in the Treatment of Posttraumatic Stress Disorder." *Psychological Trauma: Theory, Research, Practice, and Policy* 4 (May): 270–77. https://doi.org/10.1037/a0024252.

Gottschalk, L. 1974. "A Hope Scale Applicable to Verbal Samples." *Archives of General Psychiatry* 30: 779–85.

Halama, Peter. 2001. "The Slovak Version of Snyder's Hope Scale: Translation and Adaptation." *Ceskoslovenská Psychologie* 45 (January): 135–41.

Harper-Jacques, S., and D. Foucault. 2014. "Walk-in Single-Session Therapy: Client Satisfaction and Clinical Outcomes." *Journal of Systemic Therapies* 33: 29–49.

Heiy, J. E., and J. S. Cheavens. 2015. "A Brief Intervention in Primary Care: Increasing Treatment-Seeking and Reducing Symptoms of Depression." Unpublished Manuscript. Ohio State University, Columbus, Ohio.

Hellman, Chan M., Megan K. Pittman, and Ricky T. Munoz. 2013. "The First Twenty Years of the Will and the Ways: An Examination of Score Reliability Distribution on Snyder's Dispositional Hope Scale." *Journal of Happiness Studies: An Interdisciplinary Forum on Subjective Well-Being* 14 (3): 723–29. https://doi.org/10.1007/s10902-012-9351-5.

Herbert, M. 2011. "An Exploration of the Relationships between Psychological Capital (Hope, Optimism, Self-Efficacy, Resilience), Occupational Stress, Burnout and Employee Engagement." Dissertation. Stellenbosh University, South Africa.

Herth, K. 1991. "Development and Refinement of an Instrument to Measure Hope." *Scholarly Inquiry for Nursing Practice* 5 (1): 39–51; discussion 53–56.

———. 2000. "Enhancing Hope in People with a First Recurrence of Cancer." *Journal of Advanced Nursing* 32 (6): 1431–41.

Ho, S. M. Y. 2003. "Hope in Hong Kong." Unpublished Manuscript. University of Hong Kong, China.

Ho, Samuel, Rama Krsna Rajandram, Natalie Chan, Nabil Samman, Colman McGrath, and Roger Arthur Zwahlen. 2011. "The Roles of Hope and Optimism on Posttraumatic Growth in Oral Cavity Cancer Patients." *Oral Oncology* 47 (2): 121–24. https://doi.org/10.1016/j.oraloncology.2010.11.015.

Hood, Anna, Kim Pulvers, Janet Carrillo, Gina Merchant, and Marie Thomas. 2012. "Positive Traits Linked to Less Pain through Lower Pain Catastrophizing." *Personality and Individual Differences* 52 (3): 401–5. https://doi.org/10.1016/j.paid.2011.10.040.

Howell, Andrew J., Ryan M. Jacobson, and Denise J. Larsen. 2015. "Enhanced Psychological Health among Chronic Pain Clients Engaged in Hope-Focused Group Counseling." *The Counseling Psychologist* 43 (4): 586–613. https://doi.org/10.1177/0011000014551421.

Irving, Lori M., C. R. Snyder, Jen Cheavens, Lorraine Gravel, Julie Hanke, Pamela Hilberg, and Nicole Nelson. 2004. "The Relationships between Hope and Outcomes at the Pretreatment, Beginning, and Later Phases of Psychotherapy." *Journal of Psychotherapy Integration* 14 (4): 419–43. https://doi.org/10.1037/1053-0479.14.4.419.

Jung, C. G. 1933. *Modern Man in Search of a Soul*. Oxford: Harcourt, Brace.

Keyes, Corey L. M. 2005. "Mental Illness and/or Mental Health? Investigating Axioms of the Complete State Model of Health." *Journal of Consulting and Clinical Psychology* 73 (3): 539–48. https://doi.org/10.1037/0022-006X.73.3.539.

Klausner, Ellen J., John F. Clarkin, Lisa Spielman, Christopher Pupo, Robert Abrams, and George S. Alexopoulos. 1998. "Late-Life Depression and Functional Disability: The Role of Goal-Focused Group Psychotherapy." *International Journal of Geriatric Psychiatry* 13 (10): 707–16.

Koestner, Richard, Natasha Lekes, Theodore A. Powers, and Emanuel Chicoine. 2002. "Attaining Personal Goals: Self-Concordance plus Implementation Intentions Equals Success." *Journal of Personality and Social Psychology* 83 (1): 231–44. https://doi.org/10.1037/0022-3514.83.1.231.

Kortte, Kathleen B., Mac Gilbert, Peter Gorman, and Stephen T. Wegener. 2010. "Positive Psychological Variables in the Prediction of Life Satisfaction after Spinal Cord Injury." *Rehabilitation Psychology* 55 (1): 40–47. https://doi.org/10.1037/a0018624.

Kortte, Kathleen B., Jennifer E. Stevenson, Megan M. Hosey, Renan Castillo, and Stephen T. Wegener. 2012. "Hope Predicts Positive Functional Role Outcomes in Acute Rehabilitation Populations." *Rehabilitation Psychology* 57 (3): 248–55. https://doi.org/10.1037/a0029004.

Lee, J. Y., and Matthew W. Gallagher. 2017. "Hope and Well-Being." In *The Oxford Handbook of Hope*, edited by M. W. Gallagher and S. J. Lopez. Oxford and New York: Oxford University Press.

Levi, Uzi, Michal Einav, Orit Ziv, Ilana Raskind, and Malka Margalit. 2014. "Academic Expectations and Actual Achievements: The Roles of Hope and Effort." *European Journal of Psychology of Education* 29 (3): 367–86.

Little, Brian R., Katariina Salmela-Aro, and Susan D. Phillips. 2017. *Personal Project Pursuit: Goals, Action, and Human Flourishing*. https://doi.org/10.4324/9781315089928.

Lopez, Shane J., R. Ciarelli, L. Coffman, M. Stone, and L. Wyatt. 2000. "Diagnosing for Strengths: On Measuring Hope Building Blocks." In *Handbook of Hope: Theory, Measures and Applications*, edited by C. R. Snyder. San Diego, CA: Academic Press.

Luszczynska, Aleksandra, Urte Scholz, and Ralf Schwarzer. 2005. "The General Self-Efficacy Scale: Multicultural Validation Studies." *The Journal of Psychology* 139 (5): 439–57. https://doi.org/10.3200/JRLP.139.5.439-457.

Marques, Susana C., J.L. Pais-Ribeiro, and Shane J. Lopez. 2009. "Validation of a Portuguese Version of the Children's Hope Scale." *School Psychology International* 30 (5): 538–51. https://doi.org/10.1177/0143034309107069.

Maslow, A. H. 1943. "A Theory of Human Motivation." *Psychological Review* 50 (4): 370–96. https://doi.org/10.1037/h0054346.

McDermott, Diane, Sarah Hastings, Kelli Gariglietti, Barbara Callahan, Karen Gingerich, and Kandi Diamond. 1997. "A Cross-Cultural Investigation of Hope in Children and Adolescents." Paper presented to the annual meeting of the American Psychological Association, Chicago, Illinois, August 1997.

Menninger, Karl. 1959. "The Academic Lecture: Hope." *The American Journal of Psychiatry* 116: 481–91. https://doi.org/10.1176/ajp.116.6.481.

Moon, C., and C. R. Snyder. 2000. "Children's Hope Scale." In *A Handbook of Psychological Tests*, edited by J. Maltby, C. A. Lewis, and A. Hill. Lampeter, Wales: Edwin Mellen Press.

Mowrer, O. Hobart. 1960. *Learning Theory and Behavior*. Learning Theory and Behavior. Hoboken, NJ: John Wiley & Sons Inc. https://doi.org/10.1037/10802-000.

Nothwehr, Faryle, Daniel O. Clark, and Anthony Perkins. 2013. "Hope and the Use of Behavioral Strategies Related to Diet and Physical Activity." *Journal of Human Nutrition and Dietetics: The Official Journal of the British Dietetic Association* 26 (0 1): 159–63. https://doi.org/10.1111/jhn.12057.

Onwuegbuzie, A. J., and C. R. Snyder. 2000. "Relations between Hope and Graduate Students' Coping Strategies for Studying and Examination-Taking." *Psychological Reports* 86 (3 Pt 1): 803–6. https://doi.org/10.2466/pr0.2000.86.3.803.

Phan, Huy P. 2013. "Examination of Self-Efficacy and Hope: A Developmental Approach Using Latent Growth Modeling." *The Journal of Educational Research* 106 (2): 93–104. https://doi.org/10.1080/00220671.2012.667008.

Rasmussen, H. N., K. K. O'Byrne, M. Vandament, and B. P. Cole. 2017. "Hope and Physical Health." In *The Oxford Handbook of Hope*, edited by M. W. Gallagher and S. J. Lopez. Oxford and New York: Oxford University Press.

Ritschel, Lorie A., Jennifer S. Cheavens, and Juliet Nelson. 2012. "Dialectical Behavior Therapy in an Intensive Outpatient Program with a Mixed-Diagnostic Sample." *Journal of Clinical Psychology* 68 (3): 221–35. https://doi.org/10.1002/jclp.20863.

Rose, S., and N. Sieben. 2017. "Hope Measurement." In *The Oxford Handbook of Hope*, edited by M. W. Gallagher and S. J. Lopez. Oxford and New York: Oxford University Press.

Snyder, C. R., ed. 2000. *Handbook of Hope: Theory, Measures, and Applications*. San Diego, CA: Academic Press.

Snyder, C. R. 2002. "Hope Theory: Rainbows in the Mind." *Psychological Inquiry* 13 (4): 249–75. https://doi.org/10.1207/S15327965PLI1304_01.

Snyder, C. R., Carla Berg, Julia T. Woodward, Amber Gum, Kevin L. Rand, Kristin K. Wrobleski, Jill Brown, and Ashley Hackman. 2005. "Hope against the Cold: Individual Differences in Trait Hope and Acute Pain Tolerance on the Cold Pressor Task." *Journal of Personality* 73 (2): 287–312. https://doi.org/10.1111/j.1467-6494.2005.00318.x.

Snyder, C. R., C. Harris, J. R. Anderson, S. A. Holleran, L. M. Irving, S. T. Sigmon, L. Yoshinobu, J. Gibb, C. Langelle, and P. Harney. 1991. "The Will and the Ways: Development and Validation of an Individual-Differences Measure of Hope." *Journal of Personality and Social Psychology* 60 (4): 570–85.

Snyder, C. R., Raymond L. Higgins, and Rita J. Stucky. 1983. *Excuses: Masquerades in Search of Grace*. Wiley Series on Personality Processes. New York: Wiley.

Snyder, C. R., B. Hoza, W. E. Pelham, M. Rapoff, L. Ware, M. Danovsky, L. Highberger, H. Rubinstein, and K. J. Stahl. 1997. "The Development and Validation of the Children's Hope Scale." *Journal of Pediatric Psychology* 22 (3): 399–421.

Snyder, C. R., Kevin L. Rand, and D. R. Sigmon. 2017. "Hope Theory: A Member of the Positive Psychology Family." In *The Oxford Handbook of Hope*, edited by M. W. Gallagher and S. J. Lopez. Oxford and New York: Oxford University Press.

Snyder, C. R., S. C. Sympson, F. C. Ybasco, T. F. Borders, M. A. Babyak, and R. L. Higgins. 1996. "Development and Validation of the State Hope Scale." *Journal of Personality and Social Psychology* 70 (2): 321–35.

Staats, Sara. 1989. "Hope: A Comparison of Two Self-Report Measures for Adults." *Journal of Personality Assessment* 53 (2): 366–75. https://doi.org/10.1207/s15327752jpa5302_13.

Stotland, Ezra. 1969. *The Psychology of Hope*. San Francisco: Jossey-Bass.

Sympson, S. C. 1999. "Validation of the Domain Specific Hope Scale: Exploring Hope in Life Domains." Unpublished Dissertation. University of Kansas, Lawrence, Kansas.

Thornton, Lisa M., Jennifer S. Cheavens, Carolyn A. Heitzmann, Caroline S. Dorfman, Salene M. Wu, and Barbara L. Andersen. 2014. "Test of Mindfulness and Hope Components in a Psychological Intervention for Women with Cancer Recurrence." *Journal of Consulting and Clinical Psychology* 82 (6): 1087–1100. https://doi.org/10.1037/a0036959.

Valle, Michael F., E. Scott Huebner, and Shannon M. Suldo. 2004. "Further Evaluation of the Children's Hope Scale." *Journal of Psychoeducational Assessment* 22 (4): 320–37. https://doi.org/10.1177/073428290402200403.

———. 2006. "An Analysis of Hope as a Psychological Strength." *Journal of School Psychology* 44 (5): 393–406. https://doi.org/10.1016/j.jsp.2006.03.005.

Vance, M. 1996. "Measuring Hope in Personal Narratives: The Development and Preliminary Validation of the Narrative Hope Scale." Unpublished Dissertation. University of Kansas, Lawrence, Kansas.

Winch, Alison, Nicholas J. Moberly, and Joanne M. Dickson. 2015. "Unique Associations between Anxiety, Depression and Motives for Approach and Avoidance Goal Pursuit." *Cognition & Emotion* 29 (7): 1295–1305. https://doi.org/10.1080/02699931.2014.976544.

Yuen, A. N., S. M. Ho, and C. K. Chan. 2014. "The Mediating Roles of Cancer-Related Rumination in the Relationship between Dispositional Hope and Psychological Outcomes among Childhood Cancer Survivors." *Psycho-Oncology* 23 (4): 412–19. https://doi.org/10.1002/pon.3433.

Chapter Twelve

A Zen Buddhist Conception of Hope in Enlightenment

Rika Dunlap

Hope is an idea that does not seem to fit comfortably into a Buddhist world-view, and hence is rarely discussed by Buddhist philosophers. However, the fact that hope is not discussed explicitly does not mean that it is absent from Buddhist thought. While Buddhist hope is importantly different from how the term is understood in Western philosophy, we can develop a uniquely Buddhist conception of hope by drawing on Buddhist philosophical concepts and doctrines.

Nevertheless, that there is a uniquely Buddhist conception of hope is not a common view among scholars of Buddhism. The idea of hope usually triggers two polarizing reactions among Buddhist scholars and practitioners, though I find neither reaction satisfying.[1] Some accept that hope is important for enlightenment, while others argue that hope is an obstacle to enlightenment.[2] For those who take hope to be an obstacle, hope is understood as an expression of desire or thirst (Pali: *taṇhā*) that causes suffering (Pali: *dukkha*). If one understands hope in this way, hope can only ever be an obstacle.[3]

In another interpretation of Buddhist teachings, one can see hope as an expedient means (Sanskrit: *upāya*). Hope is useful in seeking enlightenment, insofar as the wish to reach enlightenment is a starting point for many Buddhist practitioners. If this wish is seen as hope, namely the hope for enlightenment in one's practice, then some may see hope as an important step toward enlightenment, though hope is nevertheless to be abandoned before enlightenment proper. Hence, while this interpretation can support the idea of hope as a means to an end, it suggests that hope is not central to Buddhist enlightenment, since hope and enlightenment are incompatible at the end. Thich Nhat Hanh claims that hope could be useful in reducing pain, but it does not solve the problem of suffering.[4] So even a favorable view of hope as an *upāya* supports the conclusion that hope is to be abandoned eventually.[5]

With these explanations of the polarizing reactions, the crucial questions emerge as the following: if Buddhist teachings promise to alleviate suffering, does it not have any conception of hope that is uniquely Buddhist in nature? Is hope only a useful means to enlightenment, a stepping-stone at best? Does hope become an obstacle, as Nhat Hanh suggests? Or is there another Buddhist conception of hope that is neither an obstacle nor a stepping-stone?

In this chapter, I answer these questions and claim that we can extract a conception of hope in Zen Buddhism, one that goes beyond the view that hope is a mere means to an end. Here I develop a Buddhist conception of hope by focusing on Dōgen's Zen Buddhist philosophy, a sect of Mahāyāna Buddhism from thirteenth-century Japan. I argue that Dōgen's notion of the nonduality of practice and enlightenment can show that enlightenment involves a paradigm shift in one's perspective and attitude, one that establishes a proper Buddhist conception of hope with three distinct characteristics: (1) hope to live each moment fully through practice; (2) hope to express gratitude for all beings; and (3) hope to express compassion for all beings. Although Dōgen does not use the term "hope" to explain enlightenment, I take the liberty of interpreting a proper attitude of enlightenment as hope for two reasons: first, to clarify a common misunderstanding that the nonduality of practice and enlightenment renders practice unnecessary,[6] and second, to show that practice is an expression of gratitude and compassion that one *hopes* to convey in each moment of one's life with the keen awareness of self as impermanent and dependent on everything else to be. What makes this conception of hope Buddhist is that this hope aims at practice within the present moment without postulating its purpose outside it. With that said, I argue that there are two senses of hope that need to be distinguished: one is an initial hope for enlightenment, in which one sees practice as a mere means and not an end in itself, and the other is a proper hope of enlightenment, namely the hope to live each moment fully through practice to express gratitude and compassion for all beings. My point is that the latter sense of hope is uniquely Zen Buddhist.

This chapter has four parts. The first part summarizes the problems of hope within Mahāyāna Buddhism with some references to the discussion of hope by Thich Nhat Hanh, a contemporary Vietnamese Buddhist monk, scholar, and activist from the Linji school.[7] Nhat Hanh rejects hope as an obstacle to enlightenment, but his reasons for doing so are pertinent to particular ways in which we hope rather than hope *per se*. I argue that if we understand hope as an expression of our fundamental norms and values, then we can establish a Buddhist conception of hope that aligns with Buddhist teachings. The second part introduces the Mahāyāna doctrines of emptiness, the middle way, and *upāya* to establish the theoretical foundation of Zen

Buddhism. The third part explains the process of enlightenment in the *Shōbōgenzō* to distinguish the present-oriented conception of hope from the future-oriented conception of hope. Finally, I will establish a Buddhist conception of hope based on this nonduality of practice and enlightenment.

1. THE PROBLEMS OF HOPE IN BUDDHISM: THE FOUR NOBLE TRUTHS

Before I argue for a Buddhist conception of hope, let me explain why some Buddhists think that hope is an obstacle to enlightenment. Thich Nhat Hanh offers this negative view in *Peace Is Every Step*, arguing that hope is problematic. Although hope is not the main topic of the book, Nhat Hanh provides his own reasons for rejecting hope based on the Mahāyāna understanding of enlightenment: hope does not address the root of the problem; hope is future-oriented; and hope functions only as a means to an end. Nhat Hanh explains:

> Hope is important, because it can make the present moment less difficult to bear. . . . But that is the most that hope can do for us—to make some hardship lighter. When I think deeply about the nature of hope, I see something tragic. Since we cling to our hope in the future, we do not focus our energies and capabilities on the present moment. . . . If you can refrain from hoping, you can bring yourself entirely into the present moment and discover the joy that is already here. . . .Western civilization places so much emphasis on the idea of hope that we sacrifice the present moment. Hope is for the future. It cannot help us discover joy, peace, or enlightenment in the present moment. . . . I do not mean that you should not have hope, but that hope is not enough. Hope can create an obstacle for you, and if you dwell in the energy of hope, you will not bring yourself back entirely into the present moment. [8]

First, Nhat Hanh asserts that hope does not solve the problem of suffering. His reasoning is consistent with the Four Noble Truths, in which the Buddha teaches that one needs to address the root of suffering in order to alleviate pain. In the First Truth, the Buddha identifies the problem: the prevalence of suffering (Pali: *dukkha*). In the Second Truth, the Buddha identifies the root of suffering that is deep within ourselves: thirst or desire (Pali: *taṇhā*). We desire things to be different from what they really are: we wish for things to last when they cannot, clinging to material objects and personal beliefs. The Third Truth is that we need to address the root of suffering in order to alleviate suffering. Finally, the Fourth Truth offers the solution: follow the Buddhist path to address the problem from its root. In asserting that there is something tragic about hope, Nhat Hanh seems to point out that hope is closely related with the root of suffering: *taṇhā*. In hoping for something, we distract ourselves from the reason why we need it in the first place. In the paragraph above, Nhat Hanh makes a strong claim that hope is a

Western conception, arguing that this Buddhist challenge may result in an important realization that hope can actually cause suffering. I believe that he thinks this in light of the Four Noble Truths, the main point of which is to address the cause of suffering, namely *taṇhā*, by taking the Buddhist path. With that said, it is easy to see why hope is considered an obstacle to enlightenment in Buddhism, for hope can be an expression of desire that causes suffering. Without a root cause analysis, Nhat Hanh thinks that we would be trapped in the endless pursuit of relief.[9]

Closely related to this endless pursuit of relief is the second reason for rejecting hope. Insofar as hope is associated with the desire for things to get better eventually, Nhat Hanh thinks that hope diverts our attention from the present, making us look forward to things that are not here and now. In the Four Noble Truths, the Buddha talks about the prevalence of suffering in the First Truth, but Mahāyāna Buddhism, the branch of Buddhism to which Nhat Hanh belongs, instead places an emphasis on the prevalence of enlightenment rather than suffering by developing its own teaching regarding the nonduality between suffering and enlightenment based on the belief that enlightenment is possible here and now through practice.[10] This shift of emphasis toward enlightenment fuels Nhat Hanh's conviction that hope is an obstacle: enlightenment is possible here and now, but hope diverts our attention from the present.

This criticism leads to the last problem with hope: hope functions only as a means to an end. In the quoted passage, Nhat Hanh admits that hope can be useful. However, his main claim is that even if hope as an *upāya* can be useful in reducing pain, one needs to understand how to use this tool properly based on the correct understanding of reality, including what causes suffering. Nhat Hanh does not mention *upāya* in his discussion of hope, but his claim that hope diverts our attention from the present can be interpreted as an argument that the proper understanding of reality is necessary to use an *upāya* so that our use of tools does not contribute to suffering. For this reason, if one sees hope as a means to alleviating suffering but without understanding the necessity to address the cause of suffering, then hope can become detrimental to enlightenment.

I identified these three related reasons for rejecting hope in Nhat Hanh's description of hope, but I argue that these problems are pertinent to particular ways in which we hope rather than hope *per se*. I do not think that hope can be reduced to desire that causes suffering. In fact, I believe that hope has more to do with our fundamental norms and values than suffering-causing desires. If we are to understand hope as an expression of our fundamental norms and values, then we can establish a Buddhist conception of hope, one that is essential to Buddhist teachings. Therefore, to argue for a Buddhist conception of hope in this chapter, I understand hope in the following way: hope is an expression of norms and values, which triggers our conscious

effort or a subconscious working of the mind to affect or influence something, either the state of affairs or our specific perspective that shapes how
this state of affairs appears to us, in accordance with these norms and values.[11] The common usage of the term "hope" has to do with altering the state
of affairs based on what we value ("I hope I get a raise next month," or "I
hope things will improve in the next election"), and there are at least two
problems with this usage of the term according to Buddhism: one is that this
hope is only directed at the state of affairs but not at how we see the state of
affairs, and the other is that the norms and values that determine the content
of hope are misguided.[12] My position is that these problems have to do with
how and *what* we hope but not hope itself, and that we can develop a Buddhist conception of hope as long as we do so with a proper understanding of
reality, truth, and enlightenment according to Buddhism. To show this, I will
now explain the Mahāyāna doctrine of emptiness. According to this doctrine,
enlightenment consists in seeing how things are, namely the emptiness of all.

2. THE MAHĀYĀNA DOCTRINE OF EMPTINESS:
UPĀYA AS *UPĀYA*

In Mahāyāna Buddhism, texts, words, and ideas are considered *upāya*: they
are tools used for reaching enlightenment. The problems of hope are pertinent to particular ways in which we hope but not hope *per se*, just as the
Buddhist idea of *upāya* points out the problematic ways in which we use
words and ideas based on a misguided understanding of them. In this section,
I will stray from the discussion of hope and explain the ideas of emptiness
and *upāya* in order to establish the foundation upon which we can build a
Buddhist conception of hope.

There are two main explanations for the view that words and ideas are a
means to an end in Buddhism: one is a practical reason related to the aim of
teaching a lesson, and the other is a theoretical reason based on a Mahāyāna
understanding of reality and truth. The practical reason comes from the basic
precept within Buddhism, that the Buddha spoke to an audience based on its
level of understanding. Buddhist texts contain contradictory statements, but
this contradiction can be resolved if each is designed specifically for a particular audience to address its needs. The famous analogy of a burning house in
the Parable of the *Lotus Sūtra* can illustrate this point, according to which the
Buddha, knowing that children with a limited understanding would not escape from the burning house when they are so immersed with their toys, tells
white lies and promises new toys to save them. The point of the analogy is to
show that Buddhist texts serve a certain function to make us see how things
are. Buddhists scriptures and words, therefore, are "a finger pointing to the
moon": one needs to see what the finger is pointing to, so studying the finger

closely without looking at what it is pointing to is not going to give one an understanding of the moon. Corresponding to this idea is the two-truth theory, which explains that some texts remain within the realm of conventional truths while some texts may contain the ultimate truth of how things really are. This understanding of truth gave rise to the variety of Buddhist sects with distinct teachings, inasmuch as they disagree upon which texts contain higher truths, each sect adopting a different system of teachings based on the assumption that these texts contain different levels of truths for different audiences.[13]

This practical explanation of *upāya* has room for thinking that there is an ultimate truth about reality, and that some texts will impart this ultimate truth. Nāgārjuna, the founder of the Madhyamaka school of Mahāyāna Buddhism (also known as the middle way school), rejects this point in his philosophy of emptiness (Sanskrit: *śūnyatā*, Japanese: *kū*) by arguing that everything is a conventional truth and an expedient means. In Mahāyāna Buddhism, the Buddhist ideas of impermanence, of the nonexistence of the self, and of dependent origination are clarified with the doctrine of emptiness, which asserts that everything is empty of self-nature (Sanskrit: *svabhāva*, Japanese: *mujishō*). If everything is impermanent and dependent upon everything else to be, then everything is empty of a self-nature. With this understanding of dependent origination, it follows that words and ideas cannot hold on to their objects of reference because there is nothing permanent that these words and ideas can pick out. As soon as one utters a word to point to something, that something has changed already. Nāgārjuna demonstrates that *all* texts and words are conventional truths, inasmuch as the idea of the ultimate truth contains two assumptions: (1) an essentializing view of reality with a certain self-nature and (2) the capacity of words to represent this reality. To challenge these assumptions, Nāgārjuna explains that everything is empty, arguing that emptiness as the lack of self-nature is neither being nor nonbeing. The idea of emptiness is succinctly summarized in the following passage in the *Mūlamadhyamakakārikā*:

1. Whatever is dependently co-arisen
2. That is explained to be emptiness
3. That, being a dependent designation
4. Is itself the middle way.[14]

The first and second lines explain that everything that is of dependent origination is emptiness. In the third and fourth lines, emptiness is considered both a dependent designation (also translated as a provisional name or conventional name) and the middle way: the word, "emptiness" is a provisional name, but emptiness itself is the middle way because it is neither being nor nonbeing. What is more important here, however, is Nāgārjuna's view of truth. He believes that if emptiness is ineffable, then it defies any conceptualization, thus it is impossible to pin down what emptiness is through language.

To this conclusion, however, some may object: even if emptiness is impossible to define, the fact that we can say emptiness is ineffable suggests emptiness can be described after all. Nāgārjuna's view of emptiness, however, is not this. He thinks that even the claim, "Emptiness is ineffable," is a conventional truth. If everything is truly impermanent, interdependent, and thus empty of self-nature, then it is impossible to define emptiness. As soon as we utter a word to grasp or show emptiness, even if it is a claim of its indescribable quality, we give emptiness some form with a name, which means thinking and speaking of emptiness is essentially a self-nature-giving activity. By refuting any ultimate truth about reality, what Nāgārjuna endeavors to accomplish here is the deconstruction of any framework through which we think and speak. Therefore, his arguments do not necessarily describe how things really are to make any claims that correspond to reality, but to challenge the assumptions therein, including an essentializing view of reality and the capacity of words to represent this reality.

Nāgārjuna's philosophy of emptiness and the Madhyamaka school that was established based on his teaching of emptiness as the middle way have left a profound influence on the later Buddhist schools in China, Tibet, Vietnam, Korea, and Japan. For Nāgārjuna, the intellectual exercise to see the limitation of thought is necessary to truly appreciate the Four Noble Truths to address the root of suffering, including an attachment to truth and belief. Emptiness itself is an expedient means, and those who ascribe an ultimate truth to emptiness suffer from the very ailment of a reified view (Sanskrit: *prapañca*) that emptiness is supposed to cure. While the majority of his philosophy is dedicated to deconstruction in order to illustrate this point, the lesson we should take from this is not that it is meaningless and pointless to use language and ideas. Rather, we need to correct our misguided understanding of reality and truth so that we can think and speak properly with an expedient means: we need to learn how to use *upāya* as *upāya*.

The proper use of *upāya* is the key to establishing a Buddhist conception of hope, for we need to learn how and what to hope properly based on the understanding of emptiness. Given that Nāgārjuna is addressing the problem of a reified view, his focus is the deconstruction of perspectives. Later Buddhists schools that emerged in East Asia, on the other hand, focus more on the process of reconstruction based on the Madhyamaka teaching of emptiness and the middle way, and Zen Buddhism (Chinese: Chan) is no exception. Dōgen offers a theory of how we can reconstruct our world in each moment of practice with the keen awareness of emptiness.

In the next section, I will show that Dōgen's Zen Buddhist philosophy is established upon this positive take on emptiness, the main idea of which results in the nonduality of practice and enlightenment that resonates with

Nhat Hanh's understanding of enlightenment in the present moment. Through an analysis of Dōgen's philosophy, I will argue that although Nhat Hanh challenges the idea of hope, the issue is not hope itself but *how* and *what* we hope.

3. ENLIGHTENMENT AND THE PRESENT-ORIENTED CONCEPTION OF HOPE IN THE ZEN BUDDHIST PHILOSOPHY OF DŌGEN

Nāgārjuna's philosophy focuses on the deconstruction of ideas, so some may think Buddhism is nihilistic and far from any conception of hope. However, this deconstruction of truth and reality prepares a ground upon which we can build a Buddhist conception of hope. In this section, I will focus on the Zen Buddhist philosophy of Dōgen, the founder of the Sōtō Zen sect in thirteenth-century Japan. While Nāgārjuna emphasizes the limitation of an expedient means by asserting that emptiness itself is an *upāya*, Dōgen focuses more on the positive side, showing a proper way of using words and ideas. Specifically, Dōgen's understanding of enlightenment in the opening passage of *"Genjōkōan"* in the *Shōbōgenzō* can show that there are two different conceptions of hope that we need to distinguish: one is the future-oriented conception of hope for enlightenment that sees practice as a means to a future end, and the other is the present-oriented conception of hope that sees practice as an end itself. Only the latter conception arises with enlightenment and thus is genuinely Zen Buddhist, whereas the former conception results from the misunderstanding of reality and is only a stepping-stone to enlightenment. To distinguish these two different conceptions, it is necessary first to understand what it means to be enlightened. In this section, I will explain enlightenment in Dōgen's philosophy to show that only the latter conception of hope is compatible with enlightenment.

The opening passage of *"Genjōkōan"* reads like a riddle, as he starts with a dialetheism, in which a contradiction is held simultaneously.[15] What Dōgen aims to demonstrate here is the process of enlightenment in which a practitioner begins with an illusion and achieves enlightenment with the understanding of emptiness. However, Dōgen does not explain the process: he shows it as a dialectical development, in which he affirms, negates, and reaffirms how things appear through the eyes of a practitioner. Let me quote the passage by breaking it down by each sentence:

1. When all beings are Buddha Dharma, there is illusion and enlightenment, practice, birth, death, Buddhas, and sentient beings.
2. When all things are without self, there is no illusion and enlightenment, no birth or death, no Buddhas or sentient beings.
3. The Buddha-Way is originally beyond any fullness and lack,

4. and for that reason, there is birth and death, illusion and enlightenment, sentient beings and Buddhas.[16]

Dōgen's argument can be reformulated as this:

1. When A, then Yi
2. When B, then ~Yi
3. C
4. Therefore, Yii

Lines (1) and (2) here contain a prima facie contradiction, for (1) affirms that there is a distinction between delusion and realization, birth and death, but (2) clearly denies them.[17] Here, (2) indicates the idea of emptiness, that nothing has a self-nature. What is peculiar about this passage, however, is that once Dōgen denies the conventional truth, he reaffirms it in (4). This passage shows the process of becoming enlightened, in which one's understanding of truth and emptiness advances in stages:

1. The assumption of the two-truth theory between conventional and ultimate truths;
2. Reaching the ultimate truth of emptiness;
3. The transcending of this duality by seeing that the ultimate truth of emptiness is also a conventional truth (the middle way as neither being nor nonbeing);
4. And finally, coming back to the conventional truth with a proper understanding of emptiness, what it means to be enlightened, and how to use *upāya* as *upāya*.

In (1), Dōgen affirms the distinction between delusion and realization, birth and death, as well as Buddhas and sentient beings. In the first stage of Buddhist practice, there is an assumption that practice is a means to enlightenment, and the goal is to reach this in the future. In this stage, the practitioner *hopes* for enlightenment, and practice is understood as a means to achieving enlightenment in the future. This initial stage of enlightenment endorses the future-oriented conception of hope.

In (2), Dōgen affirms the doctrine of *svabhārva*, as he explicitly states myriad things are without an abiding self. This is the stage in which the practitioner sees emptiness as the foundation of all myriad things. Upon realizing this, one comes to see that even the idea of emptiness is a conventional truth, an expedient means to seeing how things are. As previously mentioned, this point is an important paradigm shift in the process of enlightenment. Understanding emptiness necessitates some form through which we grasp it, and this activity of giving a form to emptiness is equivalent to giving it a self-nature. In other words, "Emptiness is ineffable" is also an *upāya*: it functions as a finger pointing to the moon. Only through this realization, one can come back to conventional truths with a renewed sense of appreciation, seeing oneself and the world in a new light. In (3), therefore, what Dōgen asserts is the middle way characterized by the nonduality of conventional and ultimate truth (neither being nor nonbeing), that when the distinction between A and B is dissolved, then Yii follows, a new perspective on Yi.

There are two important points here for a Buddhist conception of hope: one is that Dōgen's philosophy has an emphasis on reconstruction (Japanese: *genjō*) rather than deconstruction (Japanese: *datsuraku*), and the other is that enlightenment is a paradigm shift in which one sees the world as *truly* impermanent and interdependent after having understood emptiness as the middle way. First, Dōgen's philosophy goes back to conventional truths in order to clarify what it means to be enlightened: enlightenment is not a state in which one can transcend these conditions of being to eliminate suffering, but enlightenment consists in how we engage in practice and live each moment with an acceptance of these conditions. Given that we are embodied in a certain way, we cannot help but see things with our eyes, hear with our ears, smell with our nose, think with our conceptual frameworks, and speak with our language.[18] Hence, the main point that Dōgen wants to highlight is not just the limitation of these frameworks and the deconstruction of them, but what we do with them in each moment of our lives now that we understand emptiness. *Genjō*, the term included in the title of the fascicle, "*Genjōkōan*," means "letting things manifest themselves" or "manifesting suchness," but I want to translate this as "reconstruction" to distinguish Yi from Yii because letting them manifest is to reconstruct our perspective with a proper understanding of emptiness. Mitsuko Yorizumi explains the opening passage in a similar way, as she asserts the final stage of the dialectical process is the construction of the new world.[19] In the above passage, Dōgen shows that emptiness has two functions: deconstruction that results in (2) and (3), and reconstruction that results in Yii in (4). In short, although the process of deconstruction dissolves the future-oriented conception of hope, it does not mean that we cannot reconstruct a new conception of hope based on this new perspective on the world that we are supposed to cultivate.

But what does this reconstruction entail? What is this new world that we are supposed to see? In other words, what results from enlightenment? These questions lead to the second point that is crucial for a Buddhist conception of hope: enlightenment is a paradigm shift in which one finally sees everything as *truly* impermanent and interdependent. Although we are seeing the same world, we now understand that we are deeply embedded in the network of dependent origination. Once we see this point, we cannot help but engage in practice knowing that what we do emerges in and has an impact on the network of all beings. For this reason, Dōgen emphasizes that enlightenment is not something that we reach through practice, but it is something that we do here and now with the acceptance of dependent origination. In the final section, I will argue that there is a conception of hope that emerges with enlightenment, a Buddhist hope to live each moment fully through practice with the acceptance of self as impermanent and interdependent.

4. A BUDDHIST CONCEPTION OF HOPE IN THE NONDUALITY OF PRACTICE AND ENLIGHTENMENT

In this section, I will establish a Buddhist conception of hope based on the nonduality of practice and enlightenment in the Zen Buddhist philosophy of Dōgen. This nonduality enables us to see practice as an end in itself, rendering it meaningful without having to validate its purpose outside itself. The point is to engage in the act of reconstruction in each moment, for there is nothing beyond this act that one can do. Therefore, a Buddhist conception of hope is not the same as the initial hope for enlightenment, but it instead emerges with enlightenment. I argue that Dōgen's understanding of enlightenment can establish a Buddhist conception of hope with three main characteristics: (1) practice as an end in itself (the present-oriented conception of hope); (2) gratitude for all beings (hope to show gratitude in practice); and (3) compassion for all beings (hope to show compassion in practice). If hope is an expression of norms and values, then a Buddhist hope is an expression of Buddhist norms that promote a certain attitude, which can be best summarized as this: "I engage in practice with the hope to live each moment fully to convey gratitude and compassion for all beings."

Let me clarify the first point that practice is an end in itself. In the previous section, I explained that enlightenment for Dōgen is to reconstruct our perspective of the world through emptiness to see everything as impermanent and interdependent. Since this reconstruction to transform our perspective is only possible in the present moment, enlightenment can only take place here and now. This understanding of enlightenment does not eliminate the possibility of building a Buddhist conception of hope. In fact, I argue that a Buddhist conception of hope is present-oriented, namely the hope to live each moment fully with the acceptance of our own being in the network of dependent origination. Nhat Hanh assumes that hope is future-oriented, but this is not the case: each moment has its own aim, namely, to exercise our capacities to the fullest. In this sense, one can hope to live each moment fully by engaging in practice. This is the proper attitude that a Zen Buddhist should cultivate: an absolute affirmation of life.

But why do we need to live each moment fully? What is the reason for doing so? This question leads to the second element in a Buddhist conception of hope: one hopes to convey gratitude in practice, for enlightenment enables one to see self as dependent on everything else.[20] If we are to understand that we depend on everything else to be, then each moment of our lives should be an expression of gratitude for all beings. Thus, the point of practice is not to hope for something that we do not have, but to express gratitude for what we already have.

This expression of gratitude comes from understanding the Buddhist doctrine of dependent origination, in which one sees the nonduality of self and the world.[21] Dōgen thinks that self and the world are interdependent and arising together because they are both empty without a self-nature.[22] He demonstrates this nonduality of self and the world by challenging our frame of thought and showing how we should reconstruct our conception of self through emptiness. To do this, he plays with language and reverses the subject and object in a sentence: self as the subject seeing the world as the object, and the world as the subject seeing self as the object. Deconstructing how we see things in the relation of subject and object by highlighting the linguistic structure that necessitates the subject and predicate form, Dōgen simultaneously reconstructs a new perspective to see ourselves as arising and deeply embedded in the network of the impermanent and interdependent world. He shows this point with an analogy of fish and birds:

> Fish swim the water and however much they swim, there is no end to the water. Birds fly the skies, and however much they fly, there is no end to the skies. Yet fish never once leave the water, birds never forsake the sky. . . . If a bird leaves the sky, it will soon die. If a fish leaves the water, it at once perishes. *We should grasp that water means life [for the fish], and the sky means life [for the bird]. It must be that the bird means life [for the sky], and the fish means life [for the water]; that life is the bird, life is the fish.* We could continue in this way even further, because practice and realization, and for all that is possessed of life, it is the same.[23]

Here Dōgen aims to do two things: one is to highlight the frameworks through which all beings live, and the other is to see these frameworks as the expressions of the whole world. First, he points out that fish and birds have their own embodied frameworks through which they live their lives. Their activities are connected with the ways of their own beings. This applies to humans as well: we should accept the conditions of our embodied being. Second and more importantly, Dōgen shows that the perspective of emptiness allows us to see self as an expression of the world by reversing the subject and predicate in a sentence (deconstruction). In the above passage, I highlighted the key sentences, in which Dōgen plays with language by switching the subjects, "fish" and "bird," with the predicate "alive" or "life." When we say, "This fish is alive" and "This bird is alive," the subjects are fish and bird. But Dōgen points out that we could also say that life is being this fish, or that life is being this bird by reversing the subject and predicate, in which we can say that life is taking the form of fish or the form of bird.

Through this, Dōgen deconstructs our way of thinking and suggests that the proper reconstruction is to see self as an activity of the whole world. [24]

If we understand practice as an expression of gratitude based on the doctrine of dependent origination, then it makes sense that Dōgen thinks everything we do is a part of practice. In particular, Dōgen thinks, in addition to sitting meditation, cooking is a vital and supreme form of practice, as he regards a *tenzō* (a cook in the Zen monastery) as a master who nourishes people through food. In "Instruction for the Tenzō," Dōgen asserts, "If there is sincerity in your cooking and associated activities, whatever you do will be an act of nourishing the sacred body."[25] Understanding everyday activities as practice, we can say that everything we do in each moment of our lives should aim at showing our gratitude for all beings.

So far, I explained that the proper reconstruction in enlightenment is to see self as an activity of the whole world based on the understanding of dependent origination. This reconstruction encourages one to live each moment fully with the hope to express gratitude for all beings. However, the doctrine of dependent origination indicates that what we do is an effect of everything else, given that our action emerges as an expression of the world. Based on this, some suggest that Buddhism offers a deterministic understanding of reality, thus being at peace with the conditions of our being is a better description of enlightenment.[26] To this, I respond that hope and peace are not mutually exclusive. In fact, being peace is the necessary step for practice, as enlightenment requires our utmost effort to make the most of our lives. Let me explain this point with an analysis of "*Genjōkōan*." If our ways of being are the necessary and important expressions of the world, then this insight sometimes leads to the erroneous attitude that we need not do anything. Indeed, Dōgen's philosophy inherits the doctrine of original enlightenment that was dominant in Tendai Buddhism (Chinese: Tiantai), which asserts that we are already enlightened.[27] Does that mean that there is no need to practice? Dōgen offers his own answer to this question in the concluding paragraph of "*Genjōkōan*" with an analogy of the wind and a fan:

> As Zen master Pao-ch'e of Mount Ma-yü was fanning himself, a monk came up and said, "The nature of the wind is constancy. There is no place it does not reach. Why use a fan?" Pao-ch'e answered, "You only know the nature of the wind is constancy. You haven't yet grasped the meaning of its reaching every place." "What is the meaning of its reaching every place?" asked the monk. The master only fanned himself. The monk bowed deeply.[28]

This conversation is an analogy to explain why practice is necessary at all if our ways of being are the expressions of the world, namely Buddha-nature. To this, Dōgen adds,

> Verification of the Buddha Dharma, the authentic transmission of the vital
> Way, is like this. To say that one should not use a fan because the wind is
> constant, that there will be a wind even when one does not use a fan, fails to
> understand both constancy and the nature of the wind. It is because the nature
> of the wind is constancy that the wind of the house of Buddhism reveals the
> great earth's golden presence and ripens the sweet milk of the long rivers.[29]

To see oneself in the network of dependent origination is to see one's act in
two ways simultaneously: that this act is an effect of everything in the world,
and that this act has an effect on all beings precisely because one is embedded in the world.[30] This acceptance leads to a new appreciation of practice as
enlightenment, in which the present moment is seen as the culmination of all
beings and all moments working together. Therefore, what enables this moment of practice is not just one's own effort, but this effort is being supported
and made possible by everything else. If the whole world is making this
moment of practice possible, then this realization enables us to value practice
as an expression of the whole world, in which we celebrate the working of all
beings in what we do here and now.[31] In emphasizing the constancy of wind,
the student only sees the wind as being everywhere but without understanding why. To understand the constancy of the wind is to practice with the keen
awareness of dependent origination, that one's action is a cause and an effect
of everything else.

Finally, the awareness of self as arising in the network of the world
encourages one to live in such a way to be compassionate for all. Given that
Mahāyāna Buddhism emphasizes the importance of saving all sentient beings
from suffering, enlightenment cultivates the hope of diminishing suffering in
the world.[32] Earlier I argued that the initial hope for enlightenment is to be
overcome, for this hope posits its purpose in the future. Based on this reasoning, some may object that the hope to alleviate suffering is similar to this
initial hope for enlightenment, given that one engages in practice in the
future hope of saving all beings.

I have two responses to this objection. First, the hope to express compassion for all beings is present-oriented, for we can only express our compassion in the present moment of practice. This point leads to my second response: we can hope to alleviate suffering as long as this hope is grounded in
the present practice of compassion. In other words, it is not wrong to act in a
hope for something *as long as* it is done so properly with the understanding
of dependent origination, emptiness, and *upāya*. In the network of dependent
origination, one hopes to make a difference, to make the world a better place,
and to save all beings from suffering by using an *upāya* in the hope of
making others see the moon by pointing to it. Therefore, being nihilistic
about one's own action and its future consequences is not a proper way of
engaging in practice. Indeed, Nhat Hanh's own work on Engaged Buddhism

would not make sense if his work were not done with the hope of alleviating suffering.[33] Only that this hope needs to be grounded with the present practice to convey gratitude and compassion for all beings. Keeping that in mind, we can see why peace work is important for Nhat Hanh, as he concludes his remark on hope by stressing that peace work is not a means to an end but an end in itself:

> A. J. Muste, the mid-twentieth-century leader of the peace movement in America who inspired millions of people, said, "There is no way to peace, peace is the way." This means that we can realize peace right in the present moment with our look, our smile, our words, and our actions. Peace work is not a means. Each step we make should be peace. . . . We don't need the future. We can smile and relax. Everything we want is right here in the present moment.[34]

Through this example, Nhat Hanh illustrates his view that corresponds to the nonduality of practice and enlightenment in Dōgen's philosophy: whatever we do here and now is enlightenment, thus hoping for enlightenment in the future is mistaken. However, it does not mean that there is no conception of hope in Buddhism.

5. CONCLUSION

Nhat Hanh asserts that hope is an obstacle if we think that enlightenment is possible only in the future. As I showed in this chapter, Nhat Hanh offers a specific *upāya* to combat our tendency to see practice as a mere means to an end. This mistake is characterized as the first stage of enlightenment in the opening passage of "*Genjōkōan*." As Dōgen shows in the fascicle, one should realize that practice is not a means to a future end of enlightenment, but practice *is* enlightenment. This nonduality of practice and enlightenment means that practice and enlightenment are the cause and effect of each other simultaneously: one is to see practice as the result of enlightenment, and the other is to see enlightenment as the result of practice. The first point is strongly connected with the nonduality of self and the world, in which one celebrates each moment as the presencing of the whole world.[35] Given that everything is an expression of the world, one need not hope for more, yet one should hope to live in such a way to cherish each moment as the "present" of all beings. Obviously, the "present" is a pun, but not a haphazard one: this moment is a manifestation of all beings in the past and future, and practice is an act of gratitude for this present. Simultaneously, we need to see that whatever we do here and now affects everything else precisely because we are entrenched in the network of dependent origination. Thus, Mahāyāna Buddhism highlights the importance of compassion, and saving all beings from suffering is an important reason for practice.

In this chapter, I focused on Dōgen's Zen Buddhism to establish a Buddhist conception of hope. Needless to say, Dōgen's philosophy is not representative of all Buddhist teachings, and some may challenge my interpretation of Dōgen's philosophy with an idea of hope here, especially when Dōgen does not speak of hope in his writings. To establish my point, I made references to Nhat Hanh's elucidation of hope, but I did my utmost to give a charitable reading of his explanation in light of Buddhist teachings. Therefore, it was not my aim to dismiss Nhat Hanh's claim entirely, but rather to clarify what he means from a Zen perspective and build upon his discussion of hope. I believe that there is a conception of hope in Buddhism, inasmuch as the main concern of Mahāyāna Buddhism in particular is to save all from suffering. The aim of my philosophical inquiry was to bring out these implications of Buddhist teachings to extract what we may rightly call a Buddhist conception of hope even in the silence of Buddhist texts.[36]

NOTES

1. I have talked to some Buddhist practitioners and scholars about hope, and I received these polarizing reactions. In this chapter, I will focus on Thich Nhat Hanh's discussion of hope.

2. Thich Nhat Hanh argues that hope becomes an obstacle because it distracts us from the present. I will discuss this point later.

3. Amy Donahue, a specialist in Indian philosophy and Theravāda Buddhism at Kennesaw State University, thinks that hope is closely related to the Theravāda understanding of suffering, *dukkha*. Although I will not focus on Theravāda Buddhism in this chapter, I would like to thank her for her feedback on my work on hope.

4. Thich Nhat Hanh, *Peace Is Every Step: The Path of Mindfulness* (New York: Bantam Books, 1991), 41–42.

5. Nhat Hanh admits that hope can be useful, but that it is more detrimental to achieving enlightenment after all. For this reason, Nhat Hanh does not have a favorable view of hope. My point is not that Nhat Hanh has a favorable view of hope as an *upāya*, but rather that if some Buddhists think hope is important and useful for enlightenment, then it is most likely because they think it functions as an *upāya* or a stepping stone to enlightenment.

6. Dōgen's Zen Buddhism endorses the doctrine of original enlightenment that was dominant in Tendai Buddhism, according to which everything is already enlightened. As a result, some misunderstand that there is no need to practice to be enlightened.

7. Chan is Chinese, and it refers to Zen Buddhism in Japan. Within Chan, there are multiple schools, one of which is Linji, to which Nhat Hanh belongs, and Sōtō is another school, whose teachings Dōgen transmitted from the Caodong school of China. The common features of these Zen schools include an emphasis on meditation as practice, the uses of riddles to showcase the limitation of language, and the nonduality of practice and enlightenment.

8. Nhat Hanh, *Peace*, 41–42.

9. A root cause analysis is used in the medical field to identify and address the cause of a disease rather than the symptoms. In Buddhism, the Buddha is compared to a physician, and what the Buddha engages in the Four Noble Truths is a root cause analysis to address the source of suffering rather than treating the symptoms.

10. In the *Heart of the Buddha's Teaching*, Nhat Hanh explains that the Three Dharma Seals are impermanence, no self, and nirvana. See *The Heart of the Buddha's Teaching* (New York: Harmony Books, 1998), 131. He points out that in Theravāda Buddhism (the Southern Transmission), the last Dharma Seal is suffering (*dukkha*), but he emphasizes the nonduality of

suffering and enlightenment based on the *Samyukta Agama*. Theravāda focuses on the Pali canon with its emphasis on the prevalence of suffering and the importance of monastic life for enlightenment. Mahāyāna, on the other hand, focuses on the prevalence of enlightenment and its emphasis on everyday activities as practice.

11. I say subconsciousness here because sometimes our values are not as transparent as we might assume. In other words, we can learn our values from what we actually hope. In developing a Buddhist conception of hope, I want to emphasize that hope does not have to be directed at the state of affairs but how we see the state of affairs.

12. Zen Buddhists would point out that seeing the state of affairs requires a perspective. Therefore, we need to realize that any discussion of the state of affairs has a perspective (or a framework through which we see the state of affairs) already built into it. For this reason, any discussion of the state of affairs is relative to the framework of this perspective.

13. The *panjao* system was the classification of Buddhist texts in China.

14. Nāgārjuna, "Examination of the Four Noble Truths," in *The Fundamental Wisdom of the Middle Way: Nāgārjuna's Mūlamadhyamakakārikā*, translated by Jay Garfield (New York: Oxford University Press, 1995), chapter 24, 18.

15. Yasuo Deguchi, Jay Garfield, and Graham Priest, "A Mountain by Any Other Name," *Philosophy East and West* 63, no. 3 (2013): 338.

16. Dōgen, "*Genjōkōan*," in *The Heart of Dōgen's Shōbōgenzō*, translated by Masao Abe and Normal Waddell (Albany: State University of New York, 2002), 40.

17. The antecedents in (1) and (2) are identical in meaning, for Buddha Dharma is that all things/beings are without self. So these conditional sentences present a contradiction.

18. Steven Heine also emphasizes this point and the boundary of horizon in "What Is on the Other Side? Delusion and Realization in '*Genjōkōan*,'" in *Dōgen: Textual and Historical Studies*, edited by Steven Hein (New York: Oxford University Press, 2012), 42.

19. Mitsuko Yorizumi, *Shōbōgenzō Nyūmon* (Tokyo: Kadokawa Bunko, 2014), 44. She uses "*kōchiku*," which means construction.

20. This nonduality of self and the world leads to the importance of the earth for Dōgen. Some of the scholarships on the environment include *Visions of Awakening Space and Time* by Taigen Dan Leighton and *Mountains, Rivers, and the Great Earth* by Jason Wirth.

21. Dōgen explains that everything in this world *is* Buddha-nature instead of the common reading of the *Nirvāṇa Sūtra* that all sentient beings without exception have Buddha-nature. See the fascicle of "*Busshō* (Buddha-nature)" in the *Shōbōgenzō*.

22. Emptiness is a way of explaining the true nature of reality as impermanent and interdependent. If we focus on the temporal aspect, we can say that everything is impermanent. If we focus on the spatial aspect, we can say that everything is interdependent.

23. Dōgen, "*Genjōkōan*," in *The Heart*, 43–44.

24. Technically, there are two perspectives that one needs to hold simultaneously: to see oneself as oneself ("I am me") and to see oneself as the world ("I am the world" or "The world is me"). If we reduce self to one or the other, then it is not quite right, for one can say that whatever I do is the result of the world, so I am not at all responsible for what I do. This view is obviously mistaken. I am responsible for what I do, yet there are conditions that influence what I do here and now.

25. Dōgen, "Instruction for the Tenzō," in *Moon in a Dewdrop: Writings of Zen Master Dōgen*, ed. Kazuaki Tanahashi (New York: North Point Press, 1995), 58.

26. Multiple people brought up this point when I talked about hope and Buddhism in the past. Nhat Hanh also has a similar idea that enlightenment brings peace, thus there is no room for hope.

27. According to original enlightenment, we practice in order to realize that we are already enlightened. To illustrate this point, Dōgen claims that we do not have Buddha-nature, but we *are* Buddha-nature. Traditionally, Buddha-nature is considered a potentiality for enlightenment, but Dōgen changes the meaning of Buddha-nature to say that we are already enlightened. Read "*Busshō* (Buddha-nature)" in the *Shōbōgenzō*.

28. Dōgen, "*Genjōkōan*," in *The Heart*, 45.

29. Dōgen, "*Genjōkōan*," in *The Heart*, 45.

30. Because of this interdependence of all beings, some believe that Zen Buddhist philosophy has important implications for environmental philosophy.

31. The fascicle, *"Zenki* ("The Whole Activity" or "Undivided Activity")," focuses on this point in the *Shōbōgenzō*.

32. Mahāyāna means the great vehicle, and this name emerged with the criticism of Theravāda Buddhism, which early Mahāyāna Buddhists called Hīnayāna, the small vehicle, because of its emphasis on monastic life, an elitist approach to enlightenment.

33. Nhat Hanh is a central figure in Engaged Buddhism, the social and political movement that endeavors to resolve social and political issues based on the teachings of Buddhism.

34. Nhat Hanh, *Peace*, 42.

35. I use "presencing" to emphasize that each moment manifests itself as a process of presencing suchness. This expression is often used in Buddhist philosophy to refer to this process.

36. I would like to thank my friends and colleagues, Jason Wirth and Michael Hemmingsen, and the editors of this book, Claudia Blöser and Titus Stahl, for their helpful comments on earlier drafts of this chapter.

REFERENCES

Deguchi, Yasuo, Jay Garfield, and Graham Priest. 2013. "A Mountain by Any Other Name." *Philosophy East and West* 63, no. 3: 335–343.

Dōgen. 1995. *Moon in a Dewdrop: Writings of Zen Master Dōgen.* Edited by Kazuaki Tanahashi. New York: North Point Press.

Dōgen. 2002. *The Heart of Dōgen's Shōbōgenzō.* Translated by Masao Abe and Norman Waddell. Albany: State University of New York.

Heine, Steven. 2012. "What Is on the Other Side? Delusion and Realization in *'Genjōkōan.'*" In *Dōgen: Textual and Historical Studies*, edited by Steven Heine, 42–74. New York: Oxford University Press.

Leighton, Taigen Dan. 2007. *Vision of Awakening Space and Time: Dōgen and the Lotus Sutra.* Oxford: Oxford University Press.

Nāgārjuna. 1995. *The Fundamental Wisdom of the Middle Way: Nāgārjuna's Mūlamadhyamakakārikā.* Translated by Jay Garfield. New York: Oxford University Press.

Nhat Hanh, Thich. 1991. *Peace Is Every Step: The Path of Mindfulness.* New York: Bantam Books.

———. 1998. *The Heart of the Buddha's Teaching.* New York: Harmony Books.

Wirth, Jason. 2017. *Mountains, Rivers, and the Great Earth: Reading Gary Snyder and Dōgen in an Age of Ecological Crisis.* Albany: State University of New York Press.

Yorizumi, Mitsuko. 2014. *Shōbōgenzō Nyūmon.* Tokyo: Kadokawa Bunko.

III

Social Contexts of Hope

Chapter Thirteen

Interpersonal Hope

Adrienne M. Martin

The subject of this chapter is what I call *interpersonal hope*, or hope invested by one person in another. Although the philosophical literature on hope is fairly sizable, specifically interpersonal hope does not bulk large. I aim to demonstrate that it is a fruitful subject matter, yielding insights about both agency and interpersonal relations. Interpersonal hope is also a prevalent and significant element of ordinary human life, deserving philosophical investigation in its own right. To point the reader's intuitions in the right direction, here is an example of interpersonal hope: a father hopes his daughter will have a more comfortable and fulfilling life than he has. This hope is the basis for a number of expectations the father presses on himself, centered around the ideas of providing opportunities for his child and raising her to take advantage of those opportunities. As she nears adulthood, the hope also becomes the basis for a number of expectations the father holds *her* to, centered around the ideas of taking advantage of opportunities. At the point where he forms these expectations of his daughter, the father's hope for his daughter becomes an interpersonal hope. He invests his hope *in* his daughter; he hopes *in her* for her better life.

I will argue that this hope, and hopes like it, should be conceptualized in terms of *socially extended agency*—when we invest hope *in each other*, in a distinctive way I will identify, what we hope for is to extend our agency through each other. The father's hope is a hope to achieve the end of a better life for his daughter, in part through her agency as an extension of his. (Lest this sound creepily controlling, let me anticipate a point I will develop later: the extension of agency does not imply retaining control over that agency, and can take many forms, even a complete hand-off of material resources.) I will argue that conceptualizing interpersonal hope in these terms sheds light on the nature of hope in general (that is, not only hope invested *in people*, but hope wherever and however we inhabit it), and also provides a framework for understanding several emotional attitudes—let-down, pride in another, pride in oneself, trust, betrayal, and gratitude—that bear an intuitive but elusive connection to more frequently theorized Strawsonian "reactive attitudes" like resentment and indignation. I conclude by describing three kinds of constraint on good interpersonal hope, which is not, I argue, an intrinsically moral or virtuous phenomenon.

1. SOCIALLY EXTENDED AGENCY AND FEELING LET DOWN BY A PERSON

My most direct argument for conceptualizing interpersonal hope in terms of socially extended agency takes this form: I begin by identifying a key mark of interpersonal hope. This mark is that, when we invest hope in a person, we can be described as "counting on" the investee, and this means being positioned to feel *let down by* the investee, if they do fail. I then demonstrate that this positioning makes sense if investing hope in a person is hoping to extend one's agency through theirs.

First, the mark of interpersonal hope: in our exemplar, the father comes to hold his daughter to certain expectations about taking advantage of the opportunities he has worked to make available to her. These expectations amount to "counting on" his daughter to take her opportunities, such that, if she fritters them away, he is disposed to feel *let down by* her. This form of "let-down" is distinct from another. First, there is the "disappointment" or "let-down" of desire for an outcome or situation that you have only predictive expectations for—the disappointment of rain on your wedding day. It is also possible to feel this form of disappointment regarding a person's actions or attitudes. Thus you might want a new friend to develop an interest in some activity you enjoy and feel "let down" when they dislike it but not feel they have let *you* down. Then there is different sense of feeling "let down by" a person that is my focus—here, you hold someone to an expectation in a personal way, such that the failure to live up to it is felt to demonstrate a lack of appreciation *for you* or that it was *your* expectation they were supposed to live up to. In our exemplar, the father could have either of these expectations and be disposed to feel both forms of "disappointment" or "let down." It is, however, only the second sense that marks the investment of what I'm calling interpersonal hope.

Second, my proposed conception of interpersonal hope, which I will argue provides a compelling explanation of this feeling of let-down, is this: when we invest hope in people, we hope to create a certain intertwining of agencies. Put suggestively, the feeling that a person has let you down marks a hit on your agency. Moving toward a more concrete account of this conception of interpersonal hope, what I have in mind is *socially extended agency*, modeled on standard treatments of *socially extended cognition*. In Clark's and Chalmers's account, a person's cognition is extended "outside of skull and skin" when the person's thought processes are reliably coupled with some external entity, such that the thought processes and the external entity both play active causal roles and jointly govern the person's behavior. A person's cognition is *socially* extended when that external entity is another person's mind. Socially extended *agency* arises from a reliable coupling of one's agency with that of another person. Collective action is a clear case of socially extended agency. However, collective action involves shared and joint intentions, and mutual awareness of these intentions among the members of the collective. Socially extended agency does not necessarily involve these elements. All that is required for extended agency is the reliable causal coupling of a person's agency with some external entity, and all that is required for socially extended agency is that the external entity is another person's agency.

The metaphor of *investment* is a good one for socially extended agency. First, there is the familiar sense of "investment," where an investor is someone who puts money, time, or effort into a fund or project, with some anticipation of return. In this sense, when a person puts their agency or agency-relevant resources in another person's project, with some anticipation of return in the form of the success of the project, they may thereby produce a reliable coupling of theirs and the investee's agency. Second, there is the sense of "investment," where an investor is someone who imbues another with a right or a power. There are many ways a person many be invested with power, and a large number of them make the invested person into the agent of the investor—for example, when a person is invested with the power to perform civil marriages, they thereby become the agent of the state, so that the *state* performs the marriage through them. This is a circumstance of socially extended agency, where the state's agency is reliably coupled with that of the officiant.

Next, I want to set this concept of socially extended agency inside a characterization of hope, very broadly construed. This will deepen the explanation of the connection between interpersonal hope and the feeling of being let down by a person. There are multiple methods for generating a "characterization" of an attitude, a state of being, or an experience. So, if one reads widely enough about hope, one will encounter many approaches to describing it. Not all of these approaches involve breaking hope into its component parts, but this is a useful way to investigate hope's interaction with other attitudes, states of being, and experiences. Among philosophers and psychologists who take such an "analytic" approach to describing hope, I believe it is fair to say a rough consensus has recently emerged, that hope has three primary component parts: first, a belief that the hoped-for outcome is possible but not guaranteed; second, a desire or preference for that outcome; and some third thing that amounts to a positively-toned "what-if" attitude toward a future containing that outcome.[1]

According to what has come to be called the "standard" or "orthodox" view of hope, it consists in a desire for a possible but uncertain outcome. Several philosophers have observed, however, that this view doesn't easily distinguish hope from other attitudes, such as despair. Hence some third element seems needed, and philosophers have proposed several, including mental imaging of the hoped-for outcome (Bovens 1999); viewing some external factor on which the hoped-for outcome depends as good (Meirav 2009); taking an agential interest in the future containing the outcome (McGeer 2008); setting the probability of the outcome "offline" and acting as if it is likely to obtain (Pettit 2004); seeing the possible-but-uncertain desired outcome as encouraging (Milona and Stockdale 2018); seeing the probability of the outcome as sufficient to license hopeful thoughts, feelings, and plans (Martin 2014); and a phenomenological idea of the future containing the hoped-for outcome (Calhoun 2018). The commonality across these proposals is that a person who hopes, allows the possibility of the hoped-for outcome to positively color their engagement with the future. The question "*What if* the future contains what I desire?" positively affects their thoughts, feelings, plans, or simply ways of being in the present.

We can now put my proposal about interpersonal hope in the following terms. When hope is interpersonally invested it has these three components: irst, a belief that it is possible but not guaranteed that one's agency will be extended through another person's and thereby contribute to the realization of the hoped-for outcome; second, a desire or preference for that extension; and some third thing that amounts to a positively-toned "what-if" attitude toward a future containing that outcome produced through a process that includes this extension of agency. In our exemplar, the father hopes in his child for her better future, insofar as he believes it is possible but not guaranteed that his agency will be extended through hers in the creation of this better future, and both desires and entertains a positively-toned "what-if" attitude toward this outcome.

The postulate that hoping in a person is hoping to extend one's agency through the investee's agency explains why failed or thwarted interpersonal hopes are marked by the attitude that one has been *let down* by that person. For, on this account, the investment is essentially a desiderative and affective orientation toward the possibility of *reliance*. When we build into our efforts particular events or objects, such that our efforts rely on those things, and those things do not eventuate, the bottom drops out of our agency or our agency rests on a base of reduced stability. The realization that a hoped-for base of stability is unavailable is marked by the sinking feeling of disappointment. When we hope to extend our agency through another person's, we rely on their responsible agency, and so the feeling of disappointment acquires a reactive aspect—that aspect that distinguishes the feeling of having personally been let down by someone, which I will discuss more in short order—and becomes the attitude that they have let us down.

In both cases, we might say the disappointment marks the dissolution of the what-if attitude. The disappointed person has lost the possibility of living under the positive guidance of the question "*What if* the future contains what I desire?" and they've lost this possibility not because they've let go of the desire but because their circumstances no longer adequately support the question. In the case of interpersonal hope, the person who is let down perceives that the person in whom they had invested hope will not extend their agency.

Thus, there is a direct connection between interpersonal hope, if it is conceptualized in terms of socially extended agency, and the feeling of being let down. In the next phase of my argument, I aim to demonstrate that the socially extended agency conception of interpersonal hope also fits well with a set of observations about the similarities and differences between feeling let down by a person and reacting to them with moral anger. For a first point of comparison, the attitude that one has been let down and moral anger have this in common: they both presuppose the responsible agency of their targets; that is, it appears they are both modes of "participant" relation, to use Peter Strawson's term. Participant relations contrast with *objective* relations, where a person is treated as an object of, for example, study, policy, or manipulation. Strawson's focus was on the idea that relating to people as "participants" implies they are *free and responsible agents*. The reactive attitudes, Strawson argued, imply the responsible agency of their targets; we suspend them when we believe the person we are interacting with is excused or exempt from responsibility. It is also helpful on this point to include certain speech acts we may use in efforts to get people to live up to our expectations. Most philosophers writing on the subject tend to associate reactive attitudes with *demands*. That is, it is very common to characterize the reactive attitudes and the participant stance as *demanding*. However, we should attend to the fact that *demands* are only a particularly imperatival instantiation of the broader category of *directive* speech acts or speech acts that try to make their hearer do something. In addition to other imperatival speech acts like commands, there are also are directives that tend to be performed in a more precative mood, such as entreating, pleading, and urging. *Urging* is of particular interest for present purposes, because it is a common tool we deploy when we fear someone may let us down: "Don't let me down!" we may urge. Coming back to my original point, then, both the feeling of *let-down*, and now *urging,* are participant modes of relation—like moral anger and the demand for basic recognition respect, they imply the responsible agency of their targets.

Like certain other reactive attitudes, feeling let down by a person is *positional*—it implies something about your position relative to the target of the feeling. Uninformatively, it implies that they let you down. This observation can become more informative, however, again through comparison with moral anger. First, compare feeling let down with feeling morally indignant toward them, conceived as Strawson does. Indignation implies that its target wronged somebody other than you—hence, Strawson calls it a "vicarious" reactive attitude. Indignation thus seems to imply both its target's moral agency—they are someone it is apt to represent as a "wrongdoer"—and the moral subjectivity on the person on behalf of whom you feel indignant. Next consider resentment, once again conceived as Strawson does. Resentment implies *you* are the person wronged. If that's right, then resentment implies not only the moral agency of its target and your moral subjectivity; it also implies your position relative to its target, and vice versa. Let-down, like resentment, implies your position relative to that person. We can connect this point about the positionality of both resentment and let-down with the earlier distinction between ways of holding a person to an expectation. Both resenting and feeling let down by a person indicate that you held them to an expectation in a "personal" way, such that the failure to live up to the expectation is felt to demonstrate a lack of appreciation *for you.* Hence Strawson called resentment a "personal" reactive attitude.

This brings us to the key difference between let-down and resentment. The *grounding* of the two attitudes is different—for what it takes to be positioned to be let down is different from what it takes to be wronged. It is standard to think the positionality presupposed by resentment is co-membership in moral community. That is, any member of the moral community is capable of being wronged by any other member. In one sense, this is a trivial claim: to be capable of being wronged, one must be a member of the "community" of beings capable of being wronged. But given certain common assumptions about the scope of that "community"—that it is all of humanity, or all creatures with certain capacities—this becomes a substantive claim, and implies that one does not have to be in a more particular relation*ship* to be positioned either, on the one side, to wrong another person or, on the other side, to aptly resent another person who has wronged you. On this view, resentment is the appropriate response to moral wronging because wronging is a violation of moral *status*, the status a person has simply in virtue of membership in the moral community. Moral status sets up boundaries; resentment marks the violation of something meant to be inviolable.

Letting a person down, by contrast, is not failing to respect their moral status. Rather it is failing to appreciate a prior *personal relationship*—a relationship describable only through reference to the particular people involved and their history together. A useful comparison is with *hurt feelings*, which appears on Strawson's suggestive list of reactive attitudes. Overtures of friendship and offers of help provide one context for hurt feelings—that is, when our *offers* of relationship are refused, we can be hurt. It's not especially appropriate to feel *let down* by such refusals, however, for feeling let down presupposes the context of an *existing* relationship. Hurt feelings can be a response to a failure to appreciate an existing relationship, too—when a family member forgets your birthday or your adult child never calls, for example. And feeling let down is not typically an apt response to such forms of neglect. So, we want to specify the nature of the relationship that "let down" fails to appreciate.

My proposal here is that the difference between let-down and hurt feelings, too, can be captured by the idea of socially extended agency. Why is the father let down by his daughter's failure to appreciate the opportunities he's worked to make available to her? Why doesn't he instead suffer from hurt feelings? The answer is that his agency is bound up in the creation of the opportunities, in a way it is not bound up in things like wanting his daughter to remember his birthday and stay in touch.

Personal relationships are not exhausted by social extensions of agency. And what it takes to properly appreciate our personal relationships is also not exhausted by appreciating how people's agency is extended through us, or how others seek to extend their agency through us. However, personal relationships are the contexts where we are most likely to seek to extend our agency through other people. Thus, it makes sense that interpersonal hope, conceived in terms of socially extended agency, is bound up in particular personal relationships in at least three ways: First, we often invest such hope in the context of preexisting relationships. Friendship, romantic love, project collaboration, activist coalitions—these are all relationships within which people develop shared ends, adopt each other's ends, hope to receive help with their ends, and to help others with their ends. Second, when a person invests hope in another, it tends to create a new relationship or change preexisting relationships. Love and friendship, for example, often come into being, and deepen or change, in part as a result of invested hope. Such evolutions of personal relationships constitute changes in opportunities for extended agency, and thereby shifting patterns of personal expectations and potential sources of let-down. Finally, interpersonally invested hope itself *is* a hope for relationship: a relationship where hopeful person's agency is extended through the investee.

To socially extend our agency, we provide *agential resources* for use by the investee. Agential resources take many forms. In our exemplar, the father provides material resources to create opportunities for his child. He also provides educational labor and support in an effort to both make her capable of making good use of her opportunities and shape her values and goals so that she will see the point in pursuing these opportunities. And he provides emotional resources and support in at least two ways: first, he provides the emotional labor involved in raising and educating her; second, he invests his emotions—which are tied to agency at least insofar as they are involved in motivation—in her and her efforts. Although it is tricky to do this well, and many of us do not do it well, parents can lend agential support to their children's efforts simply by being present and appreciative onlookers. So interpersonal hope can manifest in many ways, ranging from the provision of material resources to the investee's projects or well-being, to simple emotional investment in the same.

This brings me to another demonstration of the explanatory power of the socially extended agency conception of interpersonal hope. Previously, I observed that complete strangers cannot let each other down. However, this observation is not entirely accurate. As a matter of fact, people do sometimes appear to invest hope in people they don't know and to feel let down by them. It is common enough for people to become extremely invested in athletes and sports teams and develop a range of hopeful expectations of good sportsmanship, dedication, and excellence. This is true even for many fans who live far away from "their" team or athlete, who rarely or never have the opportunity to see them in live competition. It is also common for people to invest hope in politicians and candidates for political office, and develop a range of hopeful expectations of commitment, integrity, and deliverance on professed values. This is true even for many people who do not join or contribute to political campaigns. Moreover, it is often seen as reasonable—or at least not plumb loco—for the fans of athletic or political celebrities to "feel let down by" poor performance or failures to uphold values the fans felt they had in common.

Considered from a distance, this is a strange phenomenon. How is the athlete who cheats or competes poorly letting down someone in another city, whom they have never met, sitting on the couch in their living room? How is the candidate for an office in another state, for whom I do not even have the opportunity to vote, and for whom I have not provided any material support, letting *me* down when it's revealed they are a serial harrasser? The socially extended agency account of interpersonal hope provides two avenues of explanation, one deflationary and one not. Both avenues involve first attending to the roles occupied by public figures. These roles invite people to have a sense of "relationship" with those occupying them, and the "relationship" is usually construed as one of "support."

The rituals of being a sports fan are largely centered on a kind of magical thinking—by wearing the shirt and cheering and thereby "participating" in the win. There are more direct avenues available for supporting a political candidate, but it is also possible to "support" a political candidate only in your mind and heart. Thus, on the deflationary explanation, let-down in such cases is a technically an error, but one the hopeful person has been invited, even seduced, into making. Your agency is not extended through the public figures you "invest" in, but those roles and the rituals that have grown up around them make it seem reasonable to hope it could be.

On the non-deflationary explanation, those roles and rituals gain enough substance for it to be reasonable to talk of genuine, if only symbolically, extended agency. On either explanation, it makes sense that poor play by the athlete or political candidate would feel like the frustration of an agential effort and produce the feeling that a person for whom you had some expectations has let *you*, personally, down.

2. INTERLUDE

I have been demonstrating the explanatory power of my socially extended agency conception of interpersonal hope, in relation to the feeling of let-down, why it has the phenomenology it does, why it appears in the context of personal relationships, and also why it appears to make sense in some fringe scenarios where the person feeling let down has no relationship with the target of the feeling. I next turn to demonstrating the fruitfulness of this conception for understanding the relations between, first, interpersonal hope and other forms of hope and, second, interpersonal hope and two more robust participant relationships, trust and benefaction. Before I turn to this, though, I want to briefly compare the socially extended agency conception of interpersonal hope to my previous work on "normative hope."

I previously attempted to understand the connection between interpersonal hope and let-down (or "disappointment") in my discussion of *normative hope*, where the hopeful person specifically hopes another person will "conform to a norm." In relation to the rough consensus characterization of hope, a normative hope is one where the hopeful person desires that another person conform to a norm, believes conformity is an "achievable challenge" for that person, and adopts a positively toned "what-if" attitude toward a future where they conform to the norm. Central examples include hoping one's teenage children will be honest, when their developmental stage makes this difficult; hoping a stranger will be considerate, when the surrounding culture encourages selfishness; hoping a powerful set of people will act justly, when their corrupt character impedes their moral vision (Martin 2014).

Unfortunately, normative hope, so conceived, does not *explain* the propriety of feeling let down when the teenager lies, or the stranger is a jerk, or the powerful act unjustly. The cases I started with, such as "lying teenager," led me to think about this attitude primarily in the context of obstacles to achievement (such as the teenage brain, or social practices of selfishness). Hence, it seemed central to let-down that it marks failures to meet expectations levied differently from the way *requirements* are levied. If requirements are levied as things the target *must* accomplish, the natural contrast seemed expectations levied as more optional, though nevertheless urgent or pressing or highly desirable—hence the idea of an "achievable challenge." But it's possible to let a person down by failing to do something not at all challenging. Moreover, it's possible to represent conformity to a certain norm as an achievable challenge for a person without thereby positioning yourself to feel let down. I can hope scientists make steps toward figuring out how humans can colonize Mars—representing such progress as an achievable challenge—but an attitude that the scientists let me down with a lackluster performance remains unfitting or inapt in the absence of any real "investment" on my part. In short, representing conformity to a norm as an achievable challenge leaves open whether one is invested in that conformity.

Additionally, I should note that, as far as normative hope is concerned, I now believe we should broaden the language describing the hoped-for outcome, and not limit it to "norm-conformity." An interpersonal hope need not invoke "conformity to a norm" in any substantive way. Granted, we can describe, for example, the daughter's efforts as "conforming to a norm of taking advantage of the opportunities provided by loved ones." However, even if such a description is always in principle available, it need not substantially feature in the interpersonal hope's components. Hence, interpersonal hope is for the investee to make some specific kind or degree of effort in pursuit of an outcome, where that effort may or may not be a matter of norm-compliance. As before, it was the cases I used to begin investigating normative hope—namely, cases where the hoped-for outcome has *moral* significance for the hopeful person—that mislead me somewhat. Taking expectations that people meet moral requirements as the model inclined me to think in terms of norms, while altering the description of how those norms are pressed on the target of expectation. Adding to the starting data cases where the hoped-for outcome is not of moral significance (such as investing hope in a team for a championship, or hope in one's child for a better future for that child—which could be but is not necessarily morally significant) makes the concept of *investment* far more salient than that of *challenge*.

3. A TAXONOMY OF HOPE

If we think of feeling let down as marking the dissolution of the hopeful what-if attitude, it is natural to also ask about the *positive* resolution of the latter—what happens when the hopeful person realizes they are now physically occupying the future they once occupied only through fantasy, imagination, or as a "phenomenological idea"? In the case of impersonal hope, the answer is some kind of happiness or joy. In the case of interpersonal hope, the positive resolution means the hoped-for extension of agency has been successful, that the hopeful person has, via the investee, brought about the hoped-for outcome. *Pride* is thus the natural response, but since the hopeful person's success is largely due to another person, it is pride *in another,* rather than the form of pride that has received more attention in philosophy: pride in oneself. (Previously I proposed that the satisfaction of normative hope produces gratitude, but as I will discuss below, I now think gratitude occupies a different place in the taxonomy framed by interpersonal hope.)

However, now that pride is on the scene, we should realize an important fact about "impersonal" hope: a good deal of impersonal hope is actually *intra*personal hope, or the hope to achieve something through one's own efforts or agency. Hence, there are cases we might have been inclined to categorize as "impersonal hope," because they contrast with *inter*personal hope, where failure causes the hopeful person to feel disappointed *in themselves*; while success makes them proud *of themselves*. So, we can draw a diagram (see Figure 13.1).

In fact, hope is most paradigmatically mix of impersonal, intrapersonal, and interpersonal—when the hopeful person perceives that the outcome they desire is best realized through a mix of their own efforts, the efforts of others, and fortunate events. Hope usually positions people to adopt a range of both

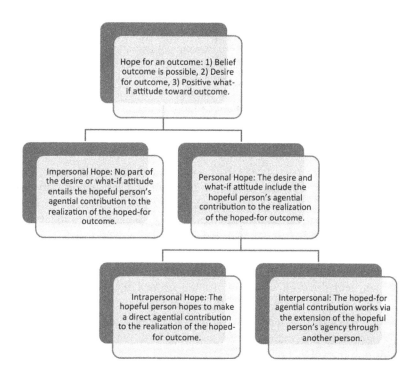

Figure 13.1. Taxonomy of Hope

"objective" and "participant" attitudes, including objective disappointment, the feeling of having been let down by oneself or another, objective happiness, and pride in oneself or another. Which attitudes are most prominent depends on the circumstances contributing to the dissolution or positive resolution of the hopeful what-if attitude. There are also hopes that bind together the intra- and interpersonal: *hoping in* us *for our growth together in mutual presence.*

Not only is hope paradigmatically multi-faceted in this way, but *hoping well* paradigmatically requires all these facets. Hope shades into wishful thinking, for example, when there are avenues open to the hopeful person—avenues whose difficulty suits the strength of the hopeful person's desire that they either are unwilling to take or are culpably unable to see. That is, hoping well paradigmatically requires not hoping in a purely impersonal way, but also investing int*ra*personal hope in oneself. A purely impersonal hope where intrapersonal hope is available is an *idle* hope. And sometimes an idle hope is fine, but other times it is not. Similarly, as previously stated, hoping well paradigmatically requires not hoping in a purely personal way because investing no hope in the fortunate or congenial turn of events is failing to recognize the limits of human agency. This is what I would take from Victoria McGeer, when she writes,

> [N]o matter what the circumstance, hoping is a matter, not only of recognizing but also of actively engaging with our own current limitations in affecting the future we want to inhabit. . . . Thus, hope . . . is . . . about taking an agential interest in the future and in the opportunities it may afford. It is about saying the following: although there may be nothing we can do now to bring about what we desire, our energy is still oriented toward the future, limitations notwithstanding. (McGeer 2004, 104)

I think McGeer overstates the connection between the hopeful person's hope and their agency—it is not true that hoping for an outcome always means being disposed to act in pursuit of it, should the opportunity arise. There are genuine idle hopes, and hopes directed at the past, or at present events dependent entirely on fortune. However, a normative or ethical proposition is true: sometimes (often) we should not be satisfied with idle hopes but should rather invest some of our hope in our own agency. And, as McGeer also makes clear in her insightful discussion of the connection between hope and the recognition of limited agency, usually we should not invest *all* our hope in agents—either ourselves or others.

For the rest of this chapter, I focus on int*er*personal hope, arguing that it is the broader genus that includes trust and generous benefaction as species. I then return to the subject of constraints on ethical interpersonal hope. A good deal of what I will say about interpersonal hope has analogous iterations in the categories of impersonal and intrapersonal hope, that I will leave to the reader to consider.

4. INTERPERSONAL HOPE: THE GENUS

The relationship interpersonal hope constitutes can be a relatively "thin" one. By this, I mean it can obtain between people who are, otherwise, relatively distant or unconnected. Nevertheless, we can see that an advantage of analyzing interpersonal hope in terms of socially extended agency already offers a more systematic account than we had previously for two nondemanding reactive attitudes: *pride* and *appreciation*. Pride, as I have already detailed, marks the positive resolution of a hopeful what-if attitude, when the question that attitude poses is *What if their agency extends mine, and brings about what I desire?* I have also already indicated, somewhat less directly, the place of appreciation; let-down, I have suggested, marks a person's failure to act in a way that is adequately *appreciative of* the relationship of extended agency. In connection with the possibility of *acting appreciatively* (or failing to), there is an *attitude* of appreciation that can play an important role in familial relationships, friendships, and collaborations. It is important to these relationships that the participants appreciate each other—and that includes appreciating the various ways the participants extend their agency through each other.

The presence of appreciation points us toward *gratitude*, which I will come to shortly. First, though, let's consider *trust* as a mode of relation that involves a specific kind of appreciation characteristic of interpersonal hope. Trusting is a mode of relation that clearly belongs to Strawson's participant stance but, like interpersonal hope and the attitudes I have connected with it, trust is not easy to directly connect with the *moral* modes of relation and attitudes. My proposal is that trust is a thickening of interpersonal hope.

Begin with Karen Jones's definition of trust: "Trust is an attitude of optimism that the goodwill and competence of another will extend to cover the domain of our interaction with her, together with the expectation that the one trusted will be directly and favorably moved by the thought that we are counting on her" (Jones 1996, 4). The first element of trust, on this definition, an "attitude of optimism that the goodwill and competence of another will extend to cover the domain of our interaction with her," is essentially the same as a positively toned "what-if" attitude about the trusted person's goodwill and competence in that domain. The latter is a somewhat better characterization of the positivity of both hope and trust, because "optimism" can easily be read as precluding a low subjective probability estimate, and both hope and trust are consistent with believing the desired outcome is extremely unlikely. In trust, the prime example is willed trust, such as Richard Holton discusses (Holton 1994). In some circumstances, we are able to decide to trust a person despite being fairly pessimistic about their trustworthiness; we succeed in our trusting effort when we are able to, despite our pessimism, approach our relationship with the trusted person through this positive question: "What if they manage to be trustworthy?"

The second element of Jones's definition, the "expectation that the one trusted will be directly and favorably moved by the thought that we are counting on her," is what we might call a "participant" rather than "predictive" expectation. That is, it is not essential to trust that the trusting person predicts the trusted will be directly and favorably moved by the thought that the trusting person is counting on her, in either the way we predict the weather or other natural events, or the way we predict people's behavior when we run the odds. The expectation involved in trust is, rather, the sort of expectation we express when we say, "I *expected better* of you," to someone who has let us down. Jones writes that the sense of "expectation" she intends generates "disappointment, frustration, let down, or—in cases where what we are counting on is the agency of another and our relationship is one of trust—with feelings of betrayal" (Jones 2017, 3). Key here is that trust involves counting on the *agency of another*—this is indicated in Jones's definition by the way that the "optimism" is about the trusted person's "goodwill and competence" and that the expectation is about how the trusted person will be "moved." Is there reason to think the trusting person not only counts on the trusted person's agency but specifically counts on the extension of their own agency through the trusted person's? Some reflections from Annette Baier support this interpretation. Baier observes that we find occasion to trust others when our own ability to secure, protect, or nourish the things we value reaches its limits. We trust others, she says, because "we need their help in creating, and then in not merely guarding but looking after the things we most value" (Baier 1986, 236). Thus, trust, at least insofar as it is modeled on *en*trusting, is "letting other persons . . . take care of something the truster cares about, where such 'caring for' involves some exercise of discretionary powers" (241). Like hope, trust is in part "a matter, not only of recognizing but also of actively engaging with our own current limitations in affecting the future we want to inhabit" (McGeer 2004, 104)—where that future is, specifically, the creation, protection, nourishment, and so on, of something we care about. It is clear, then, that trusting a person means hoping they will use their agential resources to tend to something toward which in other circumstances we would direct our own agency. In addition, Jones's "expectation that the one trusted will be directly and favorably moved by the thought that we are counting on her" describes a hope for the kind of causal coupling I've proposed in connection with extended agency: the coupling of the trusting person's concerns and expectations and the trusted person's motivation.

Thus, Jones reveals what we need to add to interpersonal hope to get trust. First, we need to add some specifics about the desired outcome—namely that it has to do with the "domain of [the investor's] interaction with [the investee]." By contrast, one person can invest mere *interpersonal hope* in another for an outcome outside of that domain—such as the child's life or character after the parent is dead, or the improved law or policy that affects people other than oneself, and so forth. Second, we need to add some specifics about how the investee will be motivated in their efforts to bring about the desired outcome—namely that they will be moved by "goodwill" and the "thought that [the investee] is counting on [them]." And again, by contrast, one person can invest mere interpersonal hope in another without expecting (or hoping for) this *specific* mechanism of causal coupling. Finally, and, implied by these specifications, the attitude of let down that arises at the dissolution of hope's what-if attitude is perhaps the more extreme sense of *betrayal* when that hope takes the form of trust.

A different thickening of interpersonal hope gives us *benefaction*. Or, to be more careful, it gives us one important form of benefaction: the benefaction linked with *gratitude*, which could be characterized as *generous* benefaction (Chappell 2019). Benefaction motivated by generosity implies the belief that one's contribution to the beneficiary is a potential benefit, something they can use to better their condition or achieve something good. Generosity also implies an *unconditional* desire to provide such a contribution to the beneficiary—the benefactor isn't aiming to get something in return. It is consistent with the benefactor's generosity that they see the beneficiary's good as part of their own good, but their motivation does not depend on this.

Generous benefaction seeks to create an ongoing connection between benefactor and beneficiary. A good way to see this is to consider things from the beneficiary's perspective. The beneficiary of generosity usually feels, to some degree, *on the hook* to the benefactor. They feel they should "make good" on the benefactor's investment. There's often flexibility along more than one dimension, in what counts as "making good." For example, if a generous contribution was given (perhaps because solicited) for a particular purpose with a specific deadline, and the beneficiary does not achieve that purpose by that deadline, they may seek to make good on the investment in another way or at a later date. The idea of "paying it forward" is another example. The important point, for present purposes, is that the sense of being on the hook corresponds to a sense, on the part of the beneficiary, that the benefactor *continues to care* about their well-being. Generosity thus threads a tricky needle: As said, it is unconditional in a certain way, so it does not carry a strong or strict *expectation* that the beneficiary will use the contribution in a particular way. Nevertheless, it does convey an on-going care or concern for the beneficiary—this is evident in the fact that it would be normal for a beneficiary to, themselves, feel a bit disappointed or let down if they found out that their benefactor wasn't at all concerned about their failure to make good.

Putting the point slightly differently, while a good and truly generous *benefactor* does not carry strong expectations of the beneficiary, a good *beneficiary* feels a sense of obligation to their benefactor. In fact, an excellent beneficiary finds a way to convey appreciation for their benefactor without doing anything that might imply that the benefactor has any expectations of the beneficiary—this is why "making good" and "paying it forward" are often the best ways of demonstrating appreciation for a person's generosity toward you. A beneficiary who treats the benefaction as if it were a loan or similar transaction insults the benefactor, discounting their generosity.

The connection generous benefaction seeks could be shared agency, or perhaps shared valuing, but these connections are more robust and reflexively intentional than generosity necessarily implies. The question is whether generosity seeks a connection *more* robust than, say, simply caring about the beneficiary. I think that it does, that generosity typically seeks a causal coupling of the benefactor's and beneficiary's agency, or extended agency. We can see this by considering what it means to the benefactor when the beneficiary does not use the resources provided by the benefactor. Generosity does not achieve its purpose unless the beneficiary uses the provided resources to advance toward some end sufficiently related to the original purpose of the benefaction. This is true even if the beneficiary who does not actually use the provided resources nevertheless demonstrates appreciation for the benefaction; and it is true even if the beneficiary achieves the original purpose of the benefaction through some other means. If the connection sought by generosity were only the demonstration of care or concern for the beneficiary, it should be able to count as a success as long as the beneficiary achieves the purpose of the benefaction, regardless the means. Therefore I say generous benefaction seeks to extend the benefactor's agency through the beneficiary.

Thus, what we need to add to interpersonal hope to get generous benefaction are as follows: First, some specifics about the desired outcome—namely that it involves the extension of one's (the benefactor's) agency through the beneficiary's, in contribution to the beneficiary's improved condition or achievement of a purpose or goal desired by the beneficiary (keeping in mind that generosity usually implies significant flexibility about what counts as an "improved condition" and/or "achieved purpose"). By comparison, mere interpersonal hope does not require that the desired outcome center on the investee's well-being or a purpose the investee also cares about—witness the case of hoping in one's child for a better future for *oneself.* In addition, in the case of generous benefaction, this desire is unconditional; whereas mere interpersonal hope is consistent with, for example, an expectation of return—that is, it is possible for interpersonal hope to be transactional or otherwise conditional. Finally, these additions imply a certain weakening of the hopeful disposition to feel disappointment at the dissolution of the what-if attitude. Along one dimension, the generosity of motive that shapes how the desired outcome is conceptualized means that the what-if attitude should be relatively durable; because relatively open-ended, it is not easy to disappoint a truly generous benefactor. Along another, although generosity does imply the presence of a positively-toned what-if attitude, the benefactor has before them, to some degree, something like *"What if* my contribution means my beneficiary will succeed?" It also implies weak or minimal "expectations" of the beneficiary; so if the what-if attitude does dissolve, it should generate only mild or minimal disappointment.

5. CONSTRAINTS ON INTERPERSONAL HOPE

As a final matter, I want to sketch, in a programmatic way, an evaluative framework for interpersonal hope, trust, and generous benefaction. My thought is that the right systematic treatment of the constraints on these participant modes of relation may resolve a significant amount of the resistance readers might feel toward my account—in particular, many seeming counterexamples may prove to be unproblematic, if we can accurately relate them to the limits on interpersonal hope. I will present these limits in relation to the reactive attitudes that feature in interpersonal hope, trust, and generous benefaction.

The reactive attitudes constituting hopeful relationships—let-down or betrayal, pride in oneself or another, appreciation or gratitude—are subject to at least three kinds of constraints. First, there are internal, conceptual constraints: these attitudes imply certain propositions, and if those propositions are false, the attitudes are unfitting, or misleading. Feeling let down by a person who did not let you down, or in whom you had not invested; feeling proud of a person in whom you had not invested; feeling betrayed by someone whom you did not trust; feeling grateful to someone who has not shown you generosity (and expecting gratitude from someone to whom you have not shown generosity)—each of these is *unfitting* or, on analogy with the infelicitous speech acts that might express them, a kind of *misfire*.

Second, there are external, ethical constraints imposed by the particular personal relationships on the scene. As discussed previously, we frequently invest hope in people in the context of preexisting relationships. The roles people occupy in different kinds of relationships are defined in part by ethical norms that say what it is and is not good to do. For example, good parents do not invest purely selfish hope in their children and are sensitive to how hope creates pressure on the child. A good friend may sometimes invest purely selfish hope in their friend, but perhaps only by mutual understanding.

So, feeling let down can be conceptually in order but still indicate one is not doing a good job filling one's role in the relationship. Good employers do not trust their employees not to seek to improve their station. So, feeling betrayed when they move up can be conceptually in order but indicate one is not a good employer. Good citizens do not hope for their fellow citizens to "uphold the social contract" on their own. To borrow and perhaps modify a point from Martin Luther King Jr.'s "Letter from Birmingham Jail," the white moderate who sees themselves as wanting the same political changes as civil rights activists but hopes those activists will act entirely within the scope of existing unjust laws is not a good fellow democratic citizen. The sense of disappointment King himself expresses in this document measures the hope he had been willing to place in those who then let Black Americans down by condemning nonviolent protest.

Third, given certain standard assumptions about the scope of morality, and some perhaps more contentious assumptions about ethical personal relationships, it's possible for hope to conform to the ethics of particular personal relationships yet be immoral. It may be useful to sub-divide violations of moral constraints into those that wrong people outside of the hopeful relationship and those that wrong specifically the investee. In the first subcategory, a hopeful investment conforms to the ethics of a preexisting relationship while wronging third parties—mob loyalty might be an example; a parental investment that contributes to maintaining an unjust distribution of societal resources might be another. On a certain kind of picture of morality and personal relationships, that is, it's possible to be a good mobster or a good parent, while acting immorally. In such cases, when the mobster feels betrayed, or the parent feels let down, these reactive attitudes mark the investee's failure to live up to a genuine trust or hope that, morally speaking, they should never have been expected to uphold.

In the second subcategory, a hopeful investment conforms to the ethics of a preexisting relationships while nevertheless wronging the investee. *Unwelcome* investments seem likely examples, since they might run afoul of a general moral requirement of respect for autonomy. Cases where this is easy to see are those where there isn't much of a preexisting relationship, and the investee for one reason or another did not want to receive a particular investment or an investment from a particular person. In such cases, the hopeful person's sense that they have been let down could conceivably be in order, both conceptually and ethically speaking, while still marking a hope that has been immorally foisted on the investee. Scenarios where there are preexisting relationships are more complicated to analyze because it can be difficult to separate the general moral requirement forbidding (at least most) unwelcome investments from the ethics of particular personal relationships. Good parents don't foist unwelcome hopes on their children, both because, morally speaking, respect for autonomy limits the hopes any person can invest in another and because, speaking in terms of the ethics of parenting, parents shouldn't invest selfish hopes in their children.

6. CONCLUSION

My argument in this chapter has been, overall, in the mode of reflective equilibrium. There are a number of interesting and, from the perspective of daily life, important phenomena that feel and operate as if they must have much in common: personal relationships, dependence, vulnerability, support, and reliance; as well non-juridical modes of relation and attitudes like hope, trust, generosity, pride, gratitude, disappointment, let-down, betrayal. Some of these, philosophers have grappled with and found some trouble fitting them into standard moral and ethical frameworks; others have been largely unattended to. I've suggested here that they may all coalesce around interpersonal hope or the hope for socially extended agency.[2]

NOTES

1. Milona argues that the third component is unnecessary, given his preferred conception of desire and what he calls "the basing relation."
2. I would like to thank Matthew Benton, Agnes Callard, Paul Hurley, Anne Jeffrey, Berislav Marušić, Alex Rajczi, and the participants in the Claremont Colleges Philosophy Works-in-Progress Group for their help with this essay.

REFERENCES

Baier, Annette. 1986. "Trust and Antitrust." *Ethics* 96 (2): 231–60.
Bovens, Luc. 1999. "The Value of Hope." *Philosophy and Phenomenological Research* 59 (3): 667–81.
Calhoun, Cheshire. 2018. "Motivating Hope." In *Doing Valuable Time*, 68–89. Oxford University Press.
Chappell, Sophie-Grace. 2019. "Gratitude as a Virtue." In *The Moral Psychology of Gratitude*, 245–67. Rowman & Littlefield International.
Holton, Richard. 1994. "Deciding to Trust, Coming to Believe." *Australasian Journal of Philosophy* 72 (1): 63–76. https://doi.org/10.1080/00048409412345881.
Jones, Karen. 1996. "Trust as an Affective Attitude." *Ethics* 107 (1): 4–25.
———. 2017. "But I Was Counting on You!" In *The Philosophy of Trust*, edited by Paul Faulkner and Thomas Simpson. Oxford University Press. https://doi.org/10.1093/acprof:oso/9780198732549.001.0001.
Martin, Adrienne. 2014. *How We Hope: A Moral Psychology*. Princeton University Press.
Marušić, Berislav. 2017. "Trust, Reliance and the Participant Stance." *Philosophers' Imprint* 17 (17): 1–10.
McGeer, Victoria. 2004. "The Art of Good Hope." *Annals of the American Academy of Political and Social Science* 1: 100–27.
———. 2008. "Trust, Hope and Empowerment." *Australasian Journal of Philosophy* 86 (2): 237–54.
Meirav, Ariel. 2009. "The Nature of Hope." *Ratio* 22 (2): 216–33. https://doi.org/10.1111/j.1467-9329.2009.00427.x.

Milona, Michael, and Katie Stockdale. 2018. "A Perceptual Theory of Hope." *Ergo, an Open Access Journal of Philosophy* 5 (20181115). https://doi.org/10.3998/ergo.124 05314.0005.008.

Pettit, Phillip. 2004. "Hope and Its Place in Mind." *Annals of the American Academy of Political and Social Science* 1: 152–65.

Chapter Fourteen

Hope for Material Progress in the Age of the Anthropocene

Darrel Moellendorf

Growth in our capacity to produce has resulted in prosperity unimaginable to earlier generations.[1] But such prosperity is hardly generalized. Poverty still afflicts billions of people. And although that suggests that dismantling serious injustice requires egalitarian political movements, the pursuit of generalized prosperity could not be achieved merely by redistributing the fruits of production. The current global gross domestic product (GDP) per capita is approximately $11,000 (World Bank 2019). So, even if equalizing at current levels of production would create gains for many people worldwide, it certainly would not result in prosperity for everyone. Justice may be best served by much more equality, but massive productive growth is still needed if prosperity is to be generalized across the globe. So, we have good reason to promote growth in productive capacity in order to overcome the scourge of poverty and to provide the material basis for generalized prosperity or so it seems. Such growth could fundamentally transform our lives for the better. As productive capacity grows, human labor power could be transformed from a means for the production of the goods that sustain our lives, often now realized by various means of compulsion, into a capacity for free expression. Accounts of such progress are the foundation of materialist accounts of history in many Marxist writings, and hope for future abundance under communism is a central theme in Ernst Bloch's writings (Bloch 1986). I am not, however, going to assume the traditional Marxist path of exit out of capitalism into socialism and from there into communism. I don't think we know enough to be confident about how such generalized prosperity might come about, and in particular whether socialism would be needed to achieve it, as Marx thought. My concern here is with a source of anxiety about the path toward abundance. Growth in productive capacity in the era of capitalism has been the source of very significant environmental destruction, ushering into existence a new epoch in the history of the planet, the *Anthropocene.* Environmental damage now threatens to cross planetary boundaries and to disrupt the stability of planetary systems that made human civilization possible during the *Holocene*. Hope for human prosperity may be crowded out by anxiety about environmental destruction.

In this paper I shall argue that it remains rational to hope for generalized human prosperity. The features of our makeup, our intelligence and rationality, guided us in the pursuit of unrivaled prosperity, and for some, it might also help to find a way to avoid the worst aspects of environmental destruction and to secure the abundance. I begin with hope.

1. HOPE

I am not going to discuss what kind of psychological state hope is. I intend my discussion to be neutral between two kinds of accounts. The first, dominant in most contemporary discussions, are those that could be called "compound accounts." These accounts see hope as consisting in a belief about the possibility of the object of hope and a pro-attitude about the attainment of that object (Moellendorf 2006, 415). Since despair or anxiety might also consist in a nonconfident belief about X and a desire for X, compound accounts need to also identify a third element that differentiates hope from despair. The difference between these accounts concerns the character of that third, additional feature, of hope that would serve to distinguish hope from despair (Meirav 2009). The other accounts might be called "simple accounts" (Moellendorf 2006, 417). These accounts take hope to be a simple state or concept, neither a belief nor a desire (Segal and Textor 2015; Blöser 2019), but perhaps some sort of *besire*, both cognitive and motivational (Atham 1986, 284–85; Blackburn 1988, 97–100). Although most current accounts of hope opt for the former understanding, I don't see a knockdown argument in favor of it. Elsewhere I have appealed to psychological parsimony in its favor. The idea is that if hope can be explained by a desire and a belief plus something else, there is no reason to add another state, hope, to our psychology (Moellendorf 2006, 415–16). But that's not an especially weighty reason in favor of a compound account. Any defense of an explanation on grounds that it has fewer parts in the *explanans* has no answer to the charge that reality simply might not be as elegant as the theory. A more parsimonious explanation might also distort reality by shoehorning it into a narrow fitting theoretical space, rather than capturing its complicated fullness. Moreover, the case for parsimony can also, in a different way, be appealed to in defense of the simple state view insofar as it does with one attitude what the compound accounts do with two or three. In short, I no longer see a reason to favor compound accounts on grounds of parsimony.

Hopes seem to exist within the space of reasons. They are attitudes that we endorse or criticize in ourselves and others based on reasons. Regarding reasons *for* attitudes, there are at least two kinds. Some reasons serve as permissions, others as requirements. Take belief. Given sufficient evidence, argument, or explanation and lack of compelling counterevidence, argument, and explanation we might be *permitted* to believe a claim. And given even more of the evidence, argument, and explanation, we might be *required* to believe the claim. In the case of intentions to act, there may be some that are *permitted* but not required given the circumstances, such as to make great personal sacrifices to help another in need, and others that are *required*, all else being equal, such as to honor a promise. With respect to hoping, it seems clear that reasons sometimes *permit* justified hoping. Insofar as that is the case, reasons could also then rule out unjustified hoping. Whether hoping is ever *required* by reasons is less clear to me. But that is not my concern in this paper. Instead, I focus on what might provide permission for hoping for a specific kind of material progress.

Hope has both an epistemic and an evaluative character. First a word about the epistemic character. Hope includes a belief or a belief-like aspect about the possibility of the object of hope. One way in which particular hopes might be criticized has to do with the extreme unlikelihood of the object coming to pass. In the shared space of reasons for assessing the possibility of an outcome or event, the evidence for the belief counts, rather than facts beyond evidential warrant, since only evidence is available to us. We have access to the evidence that points to the fact or the possible fact that we can assess, share, and dispute. The space of reasons in which hope comes under scrutiny, then, is evidence-relative (Parfit 2011, 150–51). One question is, whether in relation to the evidence, hope is rational? That question suggests an evidence-relative threshold of improbability for the object of hope, at the limit the object's impossibility, beyond which hope is unjustified. Hope, however, does not tightly parallel belief. Justified hope is far more tolerant of doubt than is belief (Moellendorf 2006, 417). Hope naturally arises when an event or outcome is uncertain, because either it has not yet occurred or if it has occurred its occurrence is not known. Doubt is a typical part of such an experience. As the credence in the occurrence increases, hope seems to get squeezed out by confident belief.

Regarding its evaluative character, hope includes either desire or a desire-like aspect for the event or outcome. In the space of reasons, we may endorse or criticize our hopes in this regard as well. Hope, whether our own or another's, for that which is wrong or bad, is itself wrong or objectionable. Such a standard applied to hope seems simply to rely on a justified axiological or normative understanding. If it is wrong to act in some way, or if an outcome would be bad, then hoping for the success of the act or the existence of the outcome also seems wrong. This second basis for evaluating hope seems to tightly parallel the assessment of actions and outcomes.

The space of reasons is shared. To the extent that there are reasons for evaluating the permissibility of hoping, these must be, in principle, intelligible to others. If hoping is constrained by both a threshold of evidence of probability and an axiological or normative evaluation of the object, then a person has some basic responsibility to modify her hopes in light of the reasons that can be marshalled for or against them. In the shared space of reasons, we appeal to the evidence accessible to each of us for the facts and to accounts that seem to explain the evidence, as well as to the values and norms that evaluate outcomes and actions. Evidence and their explanations serve as reasons that permit beliefs. Such evidence and explanation might be called "belief-makers," and with respect to hope, we might call them "hope-makers." Given sufficient hope-makers, hope is permissible. This idea features in the following discussion of hope for prosperity in the *Anthropocene*.

Attitudes that are sensitive to reasons seem to involve a complicated dispositional structure. That structure is central in evaluating the permissibility of attitude. T. M. Scanlon's description of the dispositional structure of beliefs and intentions is instructive:

> [A] person who believes that P will tend to have feelings of conviction about P when the question arises, will normally be prepared to affirm P and to use it as a premise in further reasoning, will tend to think of P as a piece of counterevidence when claims incompatible with it are advanced, and so on. Similarly, a person who intends to do A will not only feel favorably disposed, on balance, to that course of action, but will also tend to look out for ways of carrying on out this intention . . . and will think of this intention as a prima facie objection when incompatible courses are proposed. (Scanlon 1998, 21)

The dispositional structure that Scanlon identifies for both beliefs and actions includes the following: (1) pro-feelings, (2) readiness to act, and (3) preparedness to object in the face possible attitudes that are incompatible. These dispositions are justified, if they are, considering evidence and explanation of putative facts, in light of attitude-makers.

Now suppose that hope-makers are sufficiently present to make hope for H permissible. Scanlon's account of the dispositional structure of attitudes applied to this case would have it that the following is the case. A person would be permitted (1) to enjoy the anticipation of H; (2) to act positively in some way, either by contributing to H or in positive planning for the occurrence of H; and (3) to reject attitudes, such as anxiety about H or demoralization in regards to H, that are incompatible with hoping that H. Notice then that hoping for H involves some personal commitment to H. If one hopes for the success of a political campaign, it would be irrational to fear its success, to knowingly act to undermine it, and to be demoralized by the prospects of its success. Some feelings, actions, and attitudes are ruled out by hoping for an outcome or action. If there were no dispositional implications to hoping, if hoping were completely idle, this would not be the case and there would be little reason to assess its permissibility. But insofar as hoping for H involves the possession of certain dispositions, it rules out the possession of certain other ones, and therefore also other attitudes to the contrary, among them other hopes to the contrary.

The active or psychic commitments of attitudes entail personal opportunity costs. Some feelings, actions, and attitudes are ruled out. This is the case with hoping, and it may distinguish hoping from idle wishing. Because my hoping for the success of a campaign normally involves some active or psychic commitment to its success, I cannot simultaneously hope for the success of a rival campaign. That hope has personal opportunity costs is relevant to assessing the strength of possible hope-makers. For the acquisition of these opportunity costs requires justification in the shared space of reasons, and the justification is made by appeal to hope-makers. When one appeals to evidence and explanations in the shared space of reasons to justify the permissibility of one's hope, one is also by implication justifying the permissibility of others hoping similarly in similar circumstances. The license provided by reasons is not issued only to one person. It is held by all who are similarly situated. Still, even if hope-makers are constituted by evidence and explanation, reasonable persons may disagree about how much credence to give these because one's epistemic access to hope-makers may differ. Consider how Rawls talks about the burdens of judgment, the source of reasonable disagreement about beliefs. He cites six categories of sources of reasonable disagreement, including the complexity of determining the relevance of the evidence for claims, disagreement about how to weigh the relevant evidence, conceptual vagueness, differing perspectives produced by a multitude of life experiences, competing normative considerations, and finally the inability to realize all moral and political values in any institutional framework (Rawls 1993, 55). Taken together these factors might produce different assessments among reasonable people examining the same set of evidence for the existence of reasons to believe and to affirm political values. If this is broadly correct, then the claim that hopes require justification in the shared space of reasons does not entail that agreement will yield a verdict more demanding than a permission to hope. The burdens of judgment seem particularly to cast doubt on a requirement to hope.

Some threshold of evidence and explanation is required to make sense of the permission to hope. Immanuel Kant is well known for adopting the lowest possible threshold. In his "Theory and Practice" essay he asserts this minimal position as follows: "History may well give rise to endless doubts about my hopes, and if these doubts could be proved, they might persuade me to desist from my apparently futile task" (Kant 1970, 89). For Kant, it seems, hope for historical progress is justified as long as it is not demonstrably impossible. This, I think, is too permissive a standard for justified hope. Because there are opportunity costs to hoping, it is implausible that one is justified in hoping despite the costs. The threshold must be higher than the lack of demonstrable impossibility. When we hope for H, we foreclose the possibility of cultivating feelings, pursuing actions, and adopting attitudes that may be incompatible with H. The costs associated with hoping for H justify the demand that there be more reason for hoping for H than merely that it is not demonstrably impossible. Consider the analogous case of intentions to act. Working in one political campaign, we rule out actively supporting another campaign. The decision of which campaign to pursue will be based partially on the weight of the values, but not only. The longer the odds are for one campaign, the more rational it would be to support another that is more likely, but less valuable. As the likelihood drops to merely not impossible, so the case diminishes for pursuing it at the expenses of other valuable campaigns. What's true of intentions, I believe, is true also of hopes, and for roughly the same reasons. If there were no opportunity costs for hoping, Kantian minimalism about hope-makers might be reasonable. The greater the costs assumed, however, in hoping for H, the greater credence we would need to make hoping for H rational. The credence will always be substantially below justified belief, but it will surely be above the absence of impossibility.

The two points about the existence of reasonable disagreement in hoping and the need for more than mere minimalism about hope-makers work together to support the idea that hope for the achievement of valuable social and political commitments is bolstered to the extent that the credence in the realization the ends of the cause is bolstered.

2. THE ABUNDANT SPRINGS OF COOPERATIVE WEALTH

The above discussion of hope generally informs my discussion of hope for generalized prosperity. The idea of this kind of prosperity features prominently in the works of Karl Marx and other Marxists. It's role often seems to be to offer a hopeful vision of human liberation in which our productive capacity is not dictated by any form of social compulsion. Marx and Engels imagine that "in communist society . . . nobody has one exclusive sphere of activity but each can become accomplished in any branch he wishes" (Marx and Engels 1947, 22). Generalizing freedom of that sort, Marx and Engels thought, would be possible only if prosperity had also become generalized. And that would be accomplished by means of a massive increase in productive capacity. Liberation, according to this view, requires dramatic material progress.

From his early writings through to some of his final polemics, Marx maintained that the development of productive capacity was necessary for human liberation. A passage in *The German Ideology*, which was a favorite of Leon Trotsky's (Trotsky 1987, 56), Marx and Engels hold that the "development of productive forces . . . is absolutely necessary as a practical premise: firstly, for the reason that without it only *want* is made general, and with want the struggle for necessities and all the old filthy business would necessarily be reproduced" (Marx and Engels 1947, 56). Despite appreciating capitalism's unprecedented productive power, Marx and Engels famously claim in *The Communist Manifesto* that under capitalist property relations there occurs "an epidemic that, in all earlier epochs, would have seemed an absurdity—the epidemic of overproduction" (Marx and Engels 1972, 478). Marx, of course, cannot be confused for an advocate of de-growth. The "absurdity" of overproduction is not that more is produced than is necessary to meet needs, but rather that more is produced than can be profitably sold. The productive capacity unleashed cannot be fully utilized because of capitalist property relations. In order "to increase the total of productive forces as rapidly as possible" to make possible generalized prosperity, of which capitalism provides only a glimpse, *The Manifesto* asserts that working-class control over finance and heavy industry would be necessary (Marx and Engels 1972, 490). Later in the *Critique of the Gotha Programme* Marx imagines that in "a higher phase of communist society," there will occur "the all-round development of the individual," which is made possible because "the springs of co-operative wealth flow more abundantly" (Marx 1938, 10).

The Marxian vision is one in which humanity generally, and not merely a minority ruling class, is not constrained by the roles that producers must play in the reproduction of the necessities of life. The "all-round development of the individual" for everyone is possible only if productive capacity is so great that little time has to be spent producing goods necessary for survival. The realization of the vision requires the springs of cooperative wealth flowing more abundantly. So, the Marxian account of generalized prosperity rests on the hope that productive forces can be developed sufficiently to permit a generalized and massive reduction in the amount of time and effort required to reproduce the necessities of life. Support for that hope is provided by a Marxian account of the historical development of productive forces, which may be the most important aspect of the account of historical materialism, even if it is often neglected. G. A. Cohen offers an especially sophisticated interpretation of that aspect of historical materialism, and it is to his interpretation that I turn in the next section.

3. THE DEVELOPMENT OF PRODUCTIVE CAPACITY AS A HOPE-MAKER

In *Karl Marx's Theory of History*, Cohen reconstructs and defends the central claim of Marx regarding the historical development of productive forces. This Cohen calls the Development Thesis. The thesis is stated as follows: "The productive forces tend to develop throughout history" (Cohen 2000, 135). Cohen takes productive forces to consist in labor power and the means of production, the latter includes the instruments of production, raw materials, and the space in which production can occur (ibid., 55). Productive force or capacity can be thought of as the amount of labor required to produce a given amount of product. Growth in productive forces is measurable and identifiable as either an increase is the size of the product of the labor for a given amount of labor or the maintenance of the size of the product but produced with less labor (ibid., 56). These could also be combined; somewhat more could be produced with somewhat less labor. Growth in productive capacity understood in this way would seem to count as progress toward the Marxian vision of liberation. Perhaps, it's more accurate to say that it is necessary for progress since growth in productive capacity is merely the material precondition. It does not ensure that people in fact spend less time working; they might instead spend the same amount of time producing more. Still, for those who are broadly sympathetic to the Marxian vision of liberation, material progress is valuable as a necessary means.

Cohen does not take the Development Thesis to be an empirical generalization. On the contrary, he claims that it identifies the existence of a *tendency* for productive forces to develop. As such, it is consistent with productive forces not developing or developing due to some other causes in some particular epoch. To be clear, the existence of a tendency to X does not always explain the existence of X, when it exists, since something else could also cause it to exist. The existence of a cancer that tends to produce death rapidly does not necessarily explain the death of a patient. Moreover, the existence of a tendency is only weakly predictive of X; for unless it is an undefeatable tendency, other causal factors could intervene. The tendency of the tree outside my window to bloom in early April can be defeated by prolonged drought.

If historically productive forces have in fact developed, an account of a tendency toward such development is a general explanation of the events, not in every case as explained in the previous paragraph, but as a default explanation. If the tendency is to be accounted for adequately, the cause that produces the growth in product force must be identified. But, as Jon Elster points out, appealing to a cause does not necessarily involve appealing to a law like relation. Causal laws generally apply when the necessary and sufficient conditions are made explicit. In such cases, we expect the effect to follow without exception given the cause. Appealing to causal mechanisms is far less robust than appealing to a causal law. Because no conditions are set out, the invoking of a causal mechanism does not entail that the effect follows with strict necessity (Elster 1986, 10). When a mechanism is invoked to explain in general the tendency of productive forces to grow, an explanation is offered, but appealing to the mechanism is only weakly predictive for two reasons. One is that the tendency can be defeated, and the other is that conditions for the operation of the mechanism are vague.

Cohen accounts for the tendency of productive forces to grow by appealing to three alleged facts about human nature and our historical circumstances:

1. The historical situation of humanity is one of scarcity. I call this "the fact of scarcity."
2. Humans possess sufficient intelligence to enable them to make improvements on their situations. I call this "the fact of intelligence."
3. Humans are sufficiently rational to seize the means to make improvements. I call this "the fact of rationality."

Taken together these three claims comprise a mechanism of the kind that Elster discusses. These alleged facts would explain a historical tendency toward replacing less productive forces by more productive ones roughly as follows: insofar as it is the case that existing productive forces are insufficient to satisfy their needs (the fact of scarcity), humans will set about discovering and testing the means to improve upon existing productive forces (that fact of intelligence), and once appropriate means of improvement are found, humans arrange things and themselves to employ the means (the fact of rationality). As the previous sentence suggests, I take the fact of rationality to include collective rationality. The tendency so understood entails that serious collective action problems are, with sufficient time, resolved. A shorthand statement of this mechanism is the following: the facts of human intelligence and rationality tend to produce changes in productive forces when doing so responds to human needs.

So stated, however, the mechanism is clearly implausible. Human prehistory during the *Pleistocene* suggests this. If the three facts to which Cohen appealed sufficed to explain growth of productive forces, we should expect periods of stagnation or decline to be the exception. Appealing to a tendency toward growth allows setbacks, but it would be remarkable if the mechanism were mostly defeated. In fact that seems to be the case. So far as we understand the evidence, *Homo Sapiens* and archaic humans used stone tools, with little development for over two million years. And during roughly the first 190,000 years of their existence, anatomically modern humans were unable to produce any sustained growth in productive forces. The mechanism comprising Cohen's three claims is inconsistent with this record.

There is a debate among those studying the available evidence about whether what is referred to as "behavioral modernity" arose suddenly. Some scholars defend a so-called "human revolution," perhaps accompanied by a genetic change that occurred about fifty thousand years ago, a revolution characterized by the development of tools, greater dissemination of art, and the development of complex languages (Klein 1995 and Tattersall 2009). Other scholars claim that these changes were the result of tens of thousands of years of very slow development (McBrearty and Books 2000). In either case, for more than one hundred thousand years there was hardly any growth in productive forces. And as developments occurred, they were slow for tens of thousands of years thereafter. An additional reason to think that there was little progress in the development of productive forces during the *Pleistocene* is that the available evidence suggests no significant population growth (Hawks 2000).

The reason for this stagnation seems to be that the environment of the *Pleistocene*, in which humans hunted and gathered, made survival exceedingly difficult and time consuming. It was not particularly hospitable for preserving the gains of knowledge and passing them on from one generation to the next. The *Pleistocene* was beset with repeated glaciation and warming in roughly one-hundred-thousand-year cycles. But around eleven thousand years ago, as *Holocene* began, the global mean temperature increased and climatic variations became comparatively mild. The *Holocene* climate was conducive to human flourishing. Circumstances for passing on improvements in productive forces improved. In several locations groups of people transitioned from hunting and gathering to settled agricultural communities. Over time civilizations emerged in several places—Mesopotamia, Egypt, the Indus River basin, China, and Mesoamerica. The fortuitous coincidence of a stable and relatively mild climate and human intelligence and rationality permitted material progress.

Consideration of the account above suggests that the mechanism that explains the tendency of productive forces to grow must include a fourth element (Moellendorf 2017):

> 4) Environmental circumstances are sufficiently favorable that when humans labor, improvements can be passed on to at least some successor generations. I call this "the fact of climatic favorability."

Cohen's three claims and my amendment comprise a more plausible mechanism of the growth of productive forces. The mechanism is the application of human intelligence and rationality to a natural environment that is inhospitable enough to require work but not so inhospitable that the fruits of labor cannot persist. Development occurs when the application of human powers to the natural environment yields gains and both the gains and the increased powers are passed down.

The most recent period of the *Holocene* had produced rapid growth in productive capacity under capitalist property relations. The Industrial Revolution constituted a major advance in material progress. The economist Thomas Piketty reports that global economic growth per capita from 1700 to 2012 was on average 0.8 percent annually, which amounts to more than a 1,000-percent increase over the entire period. According to Piketty, "Average global per capita income is currently around 760 euros per month; in 1700 it was less than 70" (Piketty 2014, 86). This growth has brought many benefits. Increased longevity is one. In the United Kingdom at the dawn of the Industrial Revolution, life expectancy at birth was about forty years. It is now about eighty years. Longevity has increased even in many poorer parts of the world. For example, at the turn of the twentieth century, life expectancy in India was about twenty-four years, and it's now about sixty-five years (Roser 2013a). Better education is another benefit. At the time of the Industrial Revolution, over 80 percent of the global population was illiterate; now it is less than 15 percent (Roser and Ortiz-Ospina 2016). And increased leisure time is a third benefit. Retirement has only recently been possible on a wide scale. In 1850, the majority of the male population sixty-five and older living in the United States was still working. Today, less than a quarter of that population is working (Roser 2013b). Freedom from toil has long been a Utopian dream of those who must spend at good portion of their day engaged in work that is not valuable for its own sake. As technological developments improved productivity, working-class movements were able to struggle for a shortened working day and for old-age pension schemes.

Even the revised mechanism comprising the four claims stated above can offer no insurance against exogenous shocks. War, pestilence, and famine remained threats throughout the *Holocene*. But insofar as the general explanation for growth employs a plausible mechanism, there is reason to hope for continued growth in productive capacity. The sufficient conditions may be lacking, or exogenous shocks may still occur. So, no confident prediction of developmental growth is possible.

The mechanism, in its revised version, is a hope-maker. It establishes reason to hope that productive capacity will continue to grow as long as humans are compelled to ingenuity as a result of scarcity. Why is it not instead sufficient reason to believe in such growth? Why is it not in other words a belief-maker? The ever-present possibility of exogenous shocks raises doubts about the future continuance of growth. Pandemics and gigantic meteor strikes cannot be ruled out. But for the present discussion a more important source of grave doubt is due the problems that growth causes. The industrial, chemical, and technological means by which prosperity is produced have created unintended consequences that could undermine the environmental basis of prosperity by eroding the fact of climatic favorability.

4. ANTHROPOCENIC THREATS

The environmental costs of much of the recent remarkable growth in productive capacity have been high. So high in fact, that many natural scientists argue that the Earth has been fundamentally altered by human activity and that it has entered a new geologic epoch, the *Anthropocene* (Crutzen and Stoermer 2000; Waters et al. 2016). Recent industrial, agricultural, commercial, and military activities have so profoundly affected basic planetary systems that scientists have begun to warn that we risk crossing planetary boundaries that could place the planetary stability of the *Holocene* in doubt (Rockström et al. 2009). This suggests that the mechanism for continued growth and prosperity appealed to in the previous section could be undermined. The *Anthropocene*, brought into existence by tremendous technological advances causing rapid growth in productive capacity, could undermine the very environmental basis of that capacity. Rather than ushering into existence generalized prosperity, continued productive growth by could be courting disaster.

In the previous section I discussed the mechanism that, according to Cohen, produces growth in productive capacity. That mechanism is the application of human intelligence and rationality to a natural environment that is inhospitable enough to require work but not so inhospitable that the fruits of labor cannot persist. I suggested the mechanism could be thought of as a hope-maker. The threats of the *Anthropocene* suggest that the mechanism may invite anxiety instead. One plausible way to think about this is that the mechanism is in an important sense self-defeating. The growth that the mechanism explains has produced conditions that may undermine continued material progress by degrading an aspect of the mechanism itself, the fact of climatic favorability. Put that way, it is far from obvious that the mechanism is a hope-maker. It instead issues an invitation to anxiety.

If, however, the facts of intelligence and rationality are taken seriously, permission to hope may still be warranted. The anxiety is that production and consumption is undermining the environmental conditions for the pursuit of material progress. But the mechanism is constituted by, among other things, the facts of intelligence and rationality applied to productive problems The hope, then, is that these can be marshalled to solve the problem of environmental destruction, which is itself becoming a productive problem. Even if we are not confident that catastrophic environmental destruction can be avoided, and indeed it seems very hard to have such confidence, taking the facts of intelligence and rationality seriously, which one must do to rely on the mechanism in historical explanation, provides the basis for hope. Insofar as the tools for defeating the threats posed by the unintended consequences of productive growth are our own motivated intelligence and rationality, which have been so successful in solving productive problems in the past, hope seems permissible.

It doesn't follow from the analysis above that the problem of pursuing generalized prosperity while avoiding environmental destruction is merely a matter of hoping. Hope is not the solution, even if hope may play an important role in getting us there. If hope in progress is necessary for solving the problems that confront us, it surely isn't sufficient. Motivated rationality and intelligence may confront serious social obstacles. Consider an additional argument adapted from Cohen about the problems of capitalist growth (Cohen 2000, 302–7):

1. Under capitalist property relations economic competition between firms requires continual productivity gains.
2. Improvements in productivity can be used either to reduce labor while maintaining outputs or output may be increased while labor stays the same (or some combination of both).
3. Capitalist production tends to promote output production since the other threatens profits garnered from sales, and therefore loss of competitive strength.
4. Output production depletes resources and creates pollution and is a fundamental contributor to stress placed on planetary systems.
5. Therefore, capitalism tends to deplete resources, creates pollution, and contributes in a fundamental way to stress of planetary systems.

This is an argument for the existence of another tendency. This tendency consists not in features of human nature under specific environmental conditions but in capitalism's tendency to use productivity gains to promote output production. Insofar as massive increases in production tend both to deplete natural resource and pollute the environment, stresses to planetary systems are the expected results.

Insofar as productivity gains could also be used to reduce toil and approximate generalized prosperity, capitalism rather than human nature might be thought to be the source of the problem of the stress placed on planetary boundaries in the *Anthropocene*. But since growth in productive capacity is still needed, merely changing property relations to achieve more egalitarian entitlements, even if incentives to produce were not diminished, would not result in generalized prosperity. Output growth is still needed, and historically we have witnessed no better way to achieve that than by means of market competition.

Market competition has produced huge growth in human productive capacity. It has also had the unintended consequence of creating environmental destruction that threatens the very basis of that growth. It threatens to undermine that fact of climatic favorability and other fundamental planetary processes. There is the need for continued growth of the kind that market competition has been capable of producing, but there is also need for a reduction of the risks disrupting the environmental stability that makes abundance possible (Moellendorf 2019). Our reasons for hoping that the course of sustainable growth can be found rest in the facts of intelligence and rationality, our capacities to intelligently devise and to rationally pursue solutions to the problems of human production.

The Development Thesis is standardly understood, even by Cohen himself, as a claim about the engine that drives growth in productive forces. Still, if there is in fact a tendency in capitalism toward environmental destruction, perhaps the facts of intelligence and rationality can be called upon to mitigate that tendency. Whether that requires reforming capitalism and redirecting its productive capacity or replacing it but preserving the capacity for production under broader public control is unclear. In either case, the solution is beyond the standard interpretation of the Development Thesis since it involves matters of political and social policy and contestation.

5. CONCLUSION

I have argued that hope is rationally permitted given the existence of sufficient hope-makers, evidence, and explanatory theories that provide reasons to hope. The mechanism offered by Cohen that explains the tendency of productive forces to grow, amended with the addition of the fact of climatic favorability, is a hope-maker for the achievement of eventual generalized prosperity. But that mechanism risks being self-defeating as growth in consumption and production erode the fact of climatic favorability. Moreover, the very social processes that seem best suited to producing such prosperity, namely market competition, also threaten to undermine the fact of climatic favorability by depleting resources and creating pollution that threatens planetary boundaries. Hope for the creation of generalized prosperity, without disrupting the planetary stability, is directed then not only to technological advancement, but also to the solving of a serious social problem. The aim must be either to harness capitalist growth while preventing further environmental destruction or to transition to a different form of property relations with more egalitarian entitlements, a form of property relations that is capable of maintaining growth incentives but that is better able to prevent environmental destruction.

NOTE

1. An earlier version of this paper was presented at the conference *"Karl Marx's Theory of History: A Defence*, 40 Years On," at Goethe University, Frankfurt, Oct. 25–26, 2018. I'm thankful to the participants for the feedback and to the editors of this volume for their helpful comments.

REFERENCES

Atham, J. E. J. 1986. "The Legacy of Emotivism." In *Fact, Science and Morality: Essays on A. J. Ayer's Language, Truth, and Logic*, edited by Graham McDonald and Crispin Wright, 275–88. Oxford: Blackwell.

Blackburn, Simon. 1988. *Ruling Passions.* Oxford: Claredon Press.

Bloch, Ernst. 1986. *The Principle of Hope.* Cambridge, MA: MIT Press.

Blöser, Claudia. 2019. "Hope as an Irreducible Concept." *Ratio* Online First. https://doi.org/10.1111/rati.12236.

Cohen, G. A. 2000, *Karl Marx's Theory of History: A Defence.* Expanded edition. Princeton: Princeton University Press.

Crutzen, Paul J., and Eugene F. Stoermer. 2000. "The Anthropocene." *Global Change Newsletter* 41, no. 41 (May):17–18.

Elster, Jon. 1986. *Nuts and Bolts for the Social Sciences.* Cambridge: Cambridge University Press.

Hawks, John. 2000. "Population Bottlenecks and Pleistocene Human Evolution." *Molecular Biology and Human Evolution* 17, no. 1 (January): 2–22.

Kant, Immanuel. 1970. "On the Common Saying: 'This May Be True in Theory, but It Does Not Apply in Practice.'" In *Kant's Political Writings*, edited by Hans Reiss. Cambridge: Cambridge University Press.

Klein, Richard. 1995. "Anatomy, Behavior, and Modern Human Origins." *Journal of World Prehistory* 9, no. 2 (June): 167–98.

Marx, Karl. 1938. *Critique of the Gotha Programme.* New York: International Publishers.

Marx, Karl, and Friedrich Engels. 1947. *The German Ideology.* New York: International Publishers.

Marx, Karl, and Friedrich Engels. 1972. "The Manifesto of the Communist Party." In *The Marx Engels Reader*, edited by Robert C. Tucker. New York: W. W. Norton Co.

McBrearty, Sally, and Allison Brooks. 2000. "The Revolution That Wasn't: A New Interpretation of the Origin of Modern Human Behavior." *Journal of Human Evolution* 39, no. 5 (November): 453–63.

Meirav, Ariel. 2009. "The Nature of Hope." *Ratio* 22, no. 2 (June): 216–33.

Moellendorf, Darrel. 2006. "Hope as a Political Virtue." *Philosophical Papers* 35, no. 1 (November): 413–33.

Moellendorf, Darrel. 2017. "Progress, Destruction, and the Anthropocene." *Social Philosophy and Policy* 34, no. 4 (Winter): 66–88.

Moellendorf, Darrel. 2019. "Three Interpretations of the Anthropocene: Hope and Anxiety at the End of Nature." *Ethics, Politics & Society*, forthcoming.

Parfit, Derek. 2011. *On What Matters,* Vol. 1. Oxford: Oxford University Press.

Piketty, Thomas. 2014. *Capital in the Twenty-First Century.* Cambridge, MA: Harvard University Press.

Rawls, John. 1993. *Political Liberalism.* New York: Columbia University Press.

Rockström, Johann, et al. 2009. "A Safe Operating Space for Humanity." *Nature* 461 (September 23): 472–75.

Roser, Max. 2013a. "Life Expectancy." *Our World in Data*, May. https://ourworldindata.org/life-expectancy.

Roser, Max. 2013b. "Economic Growth." *Our World in Data*, November. https://ourworldindata.org/economic-growth.

Roser, Max, and Esteban Ortiz-Ospina. 2016. "Global Rise of Education." *Our World in Data*, https://ourworldindata.org/global-rise-of-education.

Segal, Gabriel Segal, and Mark Textor. 2015. "Hope as a Primitive Mental State." *Ratio* 28, no. 2 (June): 207–22.

Scanlon, T. M. 1998. *What We Owe to Each Other.* Cambridge, MA: Harvard University Press.

Tattersall, Ian. 2009. "Human Origins: Out of Africa." *PNAS* 106, no. 38 (September 22): 16018–21.

Trotsky, Leon. 1987. *The Revolution Betrayed.* New York: Pathfinder Press.

Waters, Colin N., et al. 2016. "The Anthropocene Is Functionally and Stratigraphically Distinct from the Holocene." *Science* 351, no. 6292 (January 8): 137–47.

World Bank. 2019. "GDP per Capita (Current US$)." World Bank Open Data. 2019. https://data.worldbank.org/indicator/NY.GDP.PCAP.CD.

Chapter Fifteen

Political Hope
and Cooperative Community

Titus Stahl

The philosophical literature on hope often focuses on how people hope for outcomes that affect them personally. This is clearly not the only important kind of hope that we find in social reality, however. Many people have strong hopes for social change (or the absence of such change), and these hopes often deeply influence their relationship to society at-large. This is not surprising; social outcomes are typically only achievable by collective action and are therefore constitutively beyond the control of the individual. Because the cooperation of others in achieving or avoiding social change is something of which we can never be completely confident, hope—traditionally analyzed as a compound state that involves a belief in the possibility, but not the certainty, of an outcome and a desire for that outcome—is a typical and appropriate relationship to such outcomes (as far as we desire them).

The importance of hope for political agents is reflected in the regular appearance of the language of hope in political rhetoric. The religiously inspired references to hope in the U.S. Civil Rights movement (see, for example, Lloyd 2018) provide perhaps the most famous example of this, reflecting a situation in which activists sought radical social change but were aware of the need for the cooperation of a majority population that was highly uncertain. The rhetoric of hope also seems to be especially powerful in situations where public trust in the expertise of purely technocratic policy-makers is in decline and where there is a feeling that citizens themselves must effect the change they are seeking. The iconic use of the language of hope in Barack Obama's 2008 U.S. presidential campaign and in the subsequent post-crisis European election campaigns is a testament to this tendency (Ferrara 2013; Príncipe 2015).

This raises the question of what systematic importance political philosophers should assign to hope. In particular, we might ask whether citizens ought to have hopes of certain kinds for specifically political reasons, and whether the fact that people have certain hopes enters into political justification. The first question is about whether it is a characteristic of a just society that citizens not only affirm certain moral beliefs (e.g., mutual respect), but also entertain certain hopes. The second question concerns the structure of political justification. Typically, the question of whether certain political arrangements are legitimate depends on whether all citizens can rationally agree to them. Whether they can do so will depend partly on the beliefs that they can adopt based on evidence, and partly on their needs and desires. But it may also depend on whether they are rationally entitled to hope for certain outcomes.

While the classics of political philosophy have typically not paid much attention to the attitude of hope, there is a fragmented tradition which has centered on hope, the most famous representative of which is Ernst Bloch, whose 1959 *Principle of Hope* is a breath-taking attempt to integrate into the then-dominant discourse of "scientific Marxism" the idea that it is actually hope, rather than knowledge, that is at the center of radical politics. Perhaps more widely read today is Richard Rorty's engagement with the idea that hope can be the basis of a non-foundationalist liberal theory. Next to these well-known attempts to think about hope, we are witnessing the beginnings of less idiosyncratic, more systematic reflections on the role of hope in liberal political theory.

This chapter will pursue three aims: First, I will propose three different roles that hope can play in political philosophy—one instrumental, one constitutive, and the other justificatory (section 1). I will then examine three major approaches to political hope, exemplified by Bloch, Rorty, and contemporary liberal authors (section 2) in order to distinguish three approaches to the justificatory question. I will argue that they make opposite mistakes with regard to the importance of hope. Whereas Bloch solves the problem of justification by introducing a metaphysics to support hope, thereby adopting an overambitious concept of hope, Rorty and contemporary liberals assign it too small a role. Based on this discussion, I then argue for my own proposal (section 3): the view that, while ethical pluralism rules out any expectation that we can achieve more ambitious forms of community than political liberalism seems to allow, the requirements of justice may still require us to hope for the emergence of such forms of community.

1. THE ROLE OF HOPE IN POLITICAL PHILOSOPHY

This section will systematically examine the different functions that hope can have within political theory. This task is made slightly difficult by the fact that most political theorists in the Western tradition do not devote much thought to hope. Of course, one reason for this may be that hope is considered uninteresting from the perspective of political theory, which tends to view it as an attitude which either only has significance for the private emotional life of citizens or, even worse, impedes the participation of citizens in politics.

The latter claim is often endorsed by philosophers who assimilate hope with optimism, that is, the belief that uncertain outcomes are likely to obtain. Optimism can therefore mislead people into thinking that an outcome will be easier to achieve than it actually is, thereby undercutting the rationality of their actions. This can either undermine political institutions (when people act irrationally so as to risk the success of collective endeavors) or strengthen unjust institutions (when skilled political leaders know how to manipulate the hopes of the population to their own ends).

Both arguments are advanced by Spinoza in his *Theological-Political Treatise*. There, Spinoza argues from the premise that hope is a problematic attitude since it reflects epistemic uncertainty that does not grasp the actual necessity of all events. Because of this insufficient cognitive grasp of reality, hope leads to superstition (Mason 1997, 145). This argument makes an appearance as early as the first paragraph of the *Treatise*, where Spinoza writes,

> If men were able to exercise complete control over all their circumstances, or if continuous good fortune were always their lot, they would never be prey to superstition. But since they are often reduced to such straits as to be without any resource, and their immoderate greed for fortune's fickle favours often makes them the wretched victims of alternating hopes and fears, the result is that, for the most part, their credulity knows no bounds. In critical times they are swayed this way or that by the slightest impulse, especially so when they are wavering between the emotions of hope and fear; yet at other times they are overconfident, boastful and arrogant. (Spinoza [1670] 2002, 388)

He draws from this the political conclusion

> that superstition, like all other instances of hallucination and frenzy, is bound to assume very varied and unstable forms, and that, finally, it is sustained only by hope, hatred, anger and deceit. . . . [M]en's readiness to fall victim to any kind of superstition makes it correspondingly difficult to persuade them to adhere to one and the same kind. . . . This inconstancy has been the cause of many terrible uprisings and wars. . . . So it is readily induced, under the guise of religion, now to worship its rulers as gods, and then again to curse and condemn them as mankind's common bane. (Spinoza [1670] 2002, 389)

This argument already assumes that hope is irrational in two ways: First, it assumes that hope is never justified in the sense that our hoping correctly reflects reasons and evidence, an assumption that depends on Spinoza's metaphysical views about the necessity of all events. Second, it assumes that hope is never practically rational, that it never informs our actions in justifiable ways. These assumptions are clearly problematic and much recent thinking about hope holds that hopes can be theoretically and practically rational insofar as they are compound states that involve a belief in the possibility (but also the uncertainty) of a given outcome, a desire for that outcome, and other elements, such as the incorporation of the possibility and the desire into our practical agency (see Martin 2013; Blöser and Stahl 2017). The belief component can be rational insofar as it is true that an outcome is possible, but uncertain, and the desire and incorporation components can be practically rational as far as the outcome is genuinely good (for the agent) and the incorporation of the possibility and the desire into the agent's agency, licensing certain actions, indeed contributes to that agent's pursuit of his or her good.

If we thus reject the premise that hoping as such is irrational, a question arises concerning the ways in which political institutions, movements, and actions might be informed by or even need to rely on the rational hopes of citizens. I would like to distinguish between three types of overall positive functions of hope in relation to the political, all of which can be extracted from the literature.

The first function is an *instrumental* one. Instrumentalist accounts argue that hope is politically important because certain valuable institutional arrangements are promoted by, or even instrumentally depend on, people hoping in certain ways. The weaker version of that argument, that hoping is conducive to but not necessary for desirable political institutions, often takes a psychological form. One might argue, for example, that political progress toward more just forms of government often faces collective action problems, such that "first movers" face costs that can be rationally accepted only under the assumption that other people will cooperate. As there is bound to be uncertainty at best about such cooperation, a form of hope that takes the possibility of such cooperation and one's desire for it as reasons to move first may be a decisive factor in the likelihood of progress. Similarly, when Katie Stockdale analyzes the political dimension of hope in terms of the way in which oppression can damage such hope, the importance of taking such damages into account relies on her argument that "hope thus seems to be practically rational for members of oppressed groups to cultivate in resisting oppression" (Stockdale 2019, 37).

A stronger version of the instrumental argument is provided by Kant, who argues that we have a moral duty to strive toward political progress, and that this duty persists as long as we have reason to believe that such progress is possible. Based on this belief in the possibility of progress, we are licensed to hope for such progress, as this is a necessary condition of our being able to fulfill our moral duties (for general discussions of Kant on hope, see O'Neill 1996, 284; Chignell 2013; and the chapter by Claudia Blöser in this volume; for the specifically political dimension, see Huber 2019, 5–6).

Jakob Huber summarizes Kant's argument as follows:

> Kant seems to assume that, for psychological reasons, we can only act and sustain our commitment to action over time if we regard it as at least possible for us to make a difference, i.e. to causally contribute to the realisation of our goals. . . . Hence, in cases where the odds of making a difference are dim, we need hope in order to sustain our commitment to action. . . . In scenarios such as these, where the odds of actually making a difference seem vanishingly low, it becomes extraordinarily hard to fend off despair and ultimately even to retain our resolve to act at all. Only hope, Kant argues, can then protect us from demoralisation and keep us going by sustaining the idea of a future hospitable to our agency. (Huber 2019, 9)

Notice that here the function of hope is still instrumental: Hope is important because it is a condition of something (political agency) that is valuable because of its contribution to some other valuable outcome (political progress). If it were possible to fulfill our moral duties without hoping—for example, if we were purely rational beings that were motivated by moral reasons alone—then hope would cease to have any value in politics.

A second function is *constitutive* in nature. This means that hope is valuable not because it makes the achievement of valued political outcomes more likely but because it is a precondition for the emergence of a political sphere in the first place. It is in Hobbes and, surprisingly, again in Spinoza that we find at least hints of this argument. In Hobbes, hope figures in the explanation of both the features of the state of nature and the possibility of overcoming it. In the state of nature, Hobbes famously argues, people are equal in the sense that no one can ever rationally expect to control all others. More precisely, he argues that there is an "equality of hope" (Hobbes [1651] 1996, 83) that explains why the risk of war never disappears: Even the weaker party can always reasonably hope to overpower the stronger one in the future. The hope in question is thus a hope for achieving individual outcomes by one's own capacities. At the same time, Hobbes holds it to be a *law of nature* that we must strive toward civic peace—and thus toward the emergence of a political state—as long as we have any hope of its possibility (Hobbes [1651] 1996, 87). The hope in question, however, is not the hope that one will be able to bring about such a state in virtue of one's own capacities, but rather the hope that others will cooperate (which Hobbes judges to be reasonable). One can therefore say that the very possibility of political action (that is, entering into a covenant) depends on the balance between *intersubjective hope in others* and *individual hope in oneself*. Here, hope's role is not merely instrumental; the presence of citizens' hope in one another is a condition for the very intelligibility of political action.

In the passages where he discusses hope more positively, Spinoza argues that political communities can be held together either by fear (as in the case of submission to a powerful ruler) or by hope. What Spinoza primarily seems to have in mind is that citizens cooperate with political structures because they hope that they will thereby secure future rewards (Spinoza [1670] 2002, 439). Hope is preferable to fear initially because when people are motivated by hope they cooperate willingly (Spinoza [1677] 2002, 750), and therefore freely. While this seems to be an instrumental argument about incentives on the individual level, the contrast to fear shows that Spinoza also has a constitutive argument in mind. Because fear weakens the agential power of the individual, a community held together by fear is therefore also collectively less powerful and less free than a community held together by hope (Spinoza [1670] 2002, 700; Tucker 2018). Collective political agency is thus increased if individual hope is the mechanism of solidarity. As Justin Steinberg argues, the specific form of *civic hope* that interests Spinoza also implies *devotion to others*, because it induces citizens to see each other as the source of benefits (Steinberg 2018, 90–91). Again, it turns out that a specific form of intersubjective hope is a foundation for political freedom.

A third function relates to the *justificatory* role of hope. According to this argument, the question to which hope provides a solution is one about how we can show that certain political arrangements are acceptable to all citizens. There are two variations of this argument. I will only briefly mention them here as they will be discussed more extensively in the later sections of this chapter. On the one hand, one can argue for specific institutional structures by pointing out that they promote a spirit of hopefulness or even specific hopes, thereby providing a good to citizens, insofar as hopefulness supports their efficacy and autonomy. Here, the promotion of hope is a reason-giving feature of the outcome that is argued for. On the other hand, one can also ask about the shared premises on which citizens may rely when engaging in public, political argument. True beliefs and normatively relevant desires and interests are typically taken to be a basis for arguments that one can legitimately introduce into public debate. But it might also be true that people can rely on shared hopes as a source of political argument when they deliberate with other citizens. In this case, hope is a reason-giving feature of the present on which one can build an argument for political change.

These three functions of hope in relation to the political are not to be thought of as providing an exhaustive list. In particular, I have focused on the role that one can see particular hopes for particular outcomes play in the political sphere. The categorization does not capture, for example, the idea of "radical hope" famously developed by Jonathan Lear (Lear 2006; Eagleton

2015, ch. 4). Radical hope, according to Lear, is a form of hope that individuals and groups can exhibit in situations in which a previously existing framework of meaning that could have informed particular hopes has been lost. In such situations, radical hope can inform politics by enabling agents to remain directed in their agency toward an essentially undetermined future. While the importance of this idea for the analysis of hope in the case of severely oppressed groups must not be underestimated, it is equally clear that such radical hope is neither a form of hope in the literal sense—since it lacks an object—nor the basis for a positive political project.

2. THREE MODELS OF POLITICAL HOPE

Having distinguished the different functions that hope can play in political theory, this analytical framework can now be employed to examine the insights of two political philosophers who have assigned hope a central place in their work, namely Ernst Bloch and Richard Rorty, as well as recent attempts in liberal theory to come to terms with hope systematically. I focus on these three approaches not because they happen to contain the most explicit discussions of hope but because they represent three fundamental strategies for using hope for justificatory purposes that have significance beyond the idiosyncrasies of the individual authors' positions.

In particular, Bloch must be read responding to the form of political justification endorsed by orthodox Marxism, which is grounded in beliefs about scientific social truth and as an attempt to provide a politically less disempowering alternative to it. Rorty, by contrast, rejects the idea of grounding political justification entirely and presents reliance as hope precisely as a replacement for such grounding. Finally, in contemporary liberal work—for which the discussion of hope by Darrel Moellendorf will serve as my main example—hope is assigned an auxiliary function under nonideal circumstances where other forms of grounding are not yet accessible. I will argue that all three responses contain valuable insights but that they miss the mark to some extent by either under- or overestimating the justificatory potential of hope.

2.1 Bloch

Any summary of Bloch's three-volume *Principle of Hope* is bound to do injustice to his work. While most of the work is concerned with analyses of literary or cultural phenomena, and while Bloch does not explicitly address the issue of political justification, one can still read the philosophical parts of the book as a critique of the orthodox Marxist interpretation of the political implications of materialism that has consequences for this issue.

According to Marx, materialism is the insight that the forms of thinking in any given society, including the forms of its political arguments, are a reflection of the dominant forms of material interaction in that society (Marx and Engels [1846] 1976, 36–37). This premise leads Marx to reject the standard understanding of political justification that departs from moral principles. If political ideals, moral principles and so forth are a mere reflection of the material basis of society, then political criticism cannot take these elements as a premise, as they are intrinsically tied to the society being criticized. Marx has instead been widely understood to base his own political criticism on the diagnosis of tensions within the "material basis of society." In any class society, Marx argues, the ruling class must represent its own interests as the interests of society as a whole (Marx and Engels [1846] 1976, 60)—as indeed they are, as long as the rule of the dominant class is functional for the development of the productive forces (Marx and Engels [1846] 1976, 52; Cohen 2000). As soon as their rule becomes dysfunctional with regard to the further development, however, there emerges an opposition between that class and subordinated classes whose interests are no longer effectively promoted.

This tension is expressed, on the level of ideas as a contradiction between the ruling class's pretense that it pursues general interests and the social reality in which it pursues merely its own partial interest. Materialist political criticism, Marx argues, departs from such contradictions without needing any "external" moral standpoint. On this model, the entire task of political justification falls to a social analysis that uncovers irreparable tensions within a given social order between a certain mode of class rule and the requirements of the development of the productive forces. In other words, what political critics rely on are beliefs that are derived from a social-scientific analysis of the existing society.

This materialist picture is the implicit object of Bloch's critique in *The Principle of Hope*. Here, Bloch takes up the widespread criticism that the orthodox Marxist model cannot account for genuinely politically motivated action. The present state of society is either such that no open contradictions have yet emerged, in which case there is no oppressed class on which a political movement could draw (rendering political criticism premature and pointless), or there are indeed such contradictions and therefore a class that is already motivated, through its objective social position, to overthrow the social order in which case political criticism that goes beyond merely educating that class about its position is unnecessary.

Bloch tries to solve this dilemma by developing an alternative form of materialism that conceives of itself not as a scientific analysis of what has already realized in the given society but as an analysis of the not-yet realized potential of that society. Grounding this materialism in both a metaphysics of the not-yet realized (Bloch [1959] 1986, chs. 17 and 18) and a psychological theory of how hope allows us to cognitively relate to these not-yet realized potentials (Bloch [1959] 1986, ch. 14), he aims to supplement the "cold stream" in Marxism—that is, its scientific analysis of existing society—with a "warm stream," an affective mode of capturing how society could be (Bloch [1959] 1986, 205).

The aim of Bloch's theory is to hold on to a certain version of immanent political critique: the idea that political critique and political action can relate to norms that are not external to a given social order (in the way that subjectively endorsed moral principles or the agents' brute desires are) but rather grounded in the material conditions of those societies (Stahl 2013). At the same time, such criticism must be more than a retrospective affirmation of what happens anyway. He thereby grasps a central problem for a theory of the justificatory function of political hope. If we understand hope as a compound attitude composed of beliefs and desires, it seems that only the belief component is capable of truth and that the desire component either does not admit of justification or merely admits of intrasubjective justification opposed to genuinely intersubjective political justification. If we add to this view the plausible idea that belief in the mere possibility of some future outcome is not sufficient to justify actions toward that outcome, this means either that hope does not play a role in political justification at all or that it introduces into the political process desires that remain external to it. In other words, a political critique based on hope cannot be an immanent critique.

Bloch wants to solve this problem by assimilating desire (or rather, the anticipatory components of hope) to the cognitive grasp of a form of material reality that is described with a metaphysical terminology that is invented more or less merely for this purpose. By redefining hope in its entirety such that it becomes a form of political knowledge, he attempts to formulate a theory of political justification that is both immanent (in contrast to other understandings of political hope) and practically relevant (in contrast to orthodox Marxism).

That this solution is insufficient, however, can be shown by considering the way in which hope in Bloch remains external to the process of political justification. While through hoping people can grasp the not-yet-realized potential of reality, such insights are viewed not as something contestable within the political process but as exercising normative constraint on that process from the outside. Bloch thus ultimately ends up with a form of moral realism that undermines his aim to provide a materialist, immanent critique. He thereby also remains bound to an interpretation of Marx's materialism that assumes that a materialist critique of society can only be based on insights about material reality that are to some extent capable of truth. Thus he fails to solve the genuine problem of how hope can play a role in intersubjective justification and does not ask the more interesting question of whether one can imagine a Marxist materialist view that allows for the political justification of people's desires.

2.2 Richard Rorty

While it is certainly more well known than Bloch's, Richard Rorty's theory of political justification remains marginal in the contemporary debate in political theory. In some sense, it reverses the strategy chosen by Bloch (Smith 2010, 18) but with the interesting result that hope, again, becomes central to his idea.

Rorty famously argues not only that a certain kind of grounding of intersubjective political justification in a "final vocabulary"—be it normative, religious, or metaphysical—is unachievable, but that the attempt to discover such a grounding is typically also dangerous. Instead, Rorty advocates "liberal irony" (Rorty 1989, ch. 4), that is, public commitment to a certain liberal vocabulary combined with private awareness that this commitment and its accompanying vocabulary are always in doubt and lack metaphysical certainty.

This rejection of a liberalism backed by moral truth puts Rorty in a position toward orthodox liberal thought that is similar to Bloch's attitude toward orthodox Marxist thought. In contrast to Bloch, however, Rorty turns to hope not as an attitude that gives us access to other metaphysical grounds but rather as a replacement for any cognitive access to such grounds whatsoever. Rorty in particular introduces hope in his response to the worry that, once liberals admit that there are no true moral claims in a final vocabulary that can provide intersubjective justification, liberalism as a system of ideas will lose its ability to account for the social integration of societies (Rorty 1989, 85).

In response to this worry, Rorty argues that a liberalism based not on philosophical knowledge but rather on hope for a better future society is less susceptible to being undermined by reflexive critique:

> The reason liberalism has been strengthened by this switch is that whereas belief in an immortal soul kept being buffeted by scientific discoveries and by philosophers' attempts to keep pace with natural science, it is not clear that any shift in scientific or philosophical opinion could hurt the sort of social hope which characterizes modern liberal societies—the hope that life will eventually be freer, less cruel, more leisured, richer in goods and experiences, not just for our descendants, but for everybody's descendants. If you tell someone whose life is given meaning by this hope that philosophers are waxing ironic over real essence, the objectivity of truth and the existence of an ahistorical human nature, you are unlikely to arouse much interest, much less do any damage. The idea that liberal societies are bound together by philosophical beliefs seems to me ludicrous. What binds societies together are common vocabularies and common hopes. The vocabularies are, typically, parasitic on

the hopes—in the sense that the principal function of the vocabularies is to tell stories about future outcomes which compensate for present sacrifices. (Rorty 1989, 86)

In other words, Rorty assumes that the shared anticipation of a collective future is what accounts for the binding force of hope. Hopes, importantly, do not provide any additional justification beyond the fact that we have them and are attached to them. On this account, they instead supply the motivation for which justificatory arguments are necessary, according traditional philosophical theories.

Rorty therefore not only makes an argument that in some sense reverses the view adopted by Bloch by drawing exclusively on the anticipation or desire component of hope rather than its belief argument but also faces the opposite problem: If the hope that liberals have to draw on is strictly speaking "unjustifiable" (Rorty 1982, 208; Rorty 2002, 58; Smith 2005, 91), then it is hard to see how this hope is more than the description of actually existing consensus and how it might help to solve any conflicts concerning the meaning of "freer" or "less cruel," or their relative importance, when such conflicts emerge in a given society. When Rorty compares the metaphysical foundations of liberalism to religious beliefs and argues that, like the latter, the former are unnecessary for motivating people to make sacrifices, he states that "willingness to endure suffering for the sake of future reward [is] transferable from individual rewards to social ones, from one's hopes for paradise to one's hopes for one's grandchildren" (Rorty 1989, 85). While it may be true that people are willing to endure sacrifices for their grandchildren without needing metaphysical reassurance, many political choices require that groups sacrifice their present welfare or privileges for the sake of ensuring that unrelated others are treated justly. It is unclear whether the motivation to make such sacrifices can be generated without a reasonable basis for which the desires that people already share might be insufficient. In other words, the justificatory role of hope in Rorty is likely too weak to fulfill its assigned function.

2.3 Contemporary Liberal Thought

In contemporary political theory, there have been a number of attempts to capture the significance of hope (Aronson 2017; Eagleton 2015; Stockdale 2019; Snow 2018). The most systematic defense of the importance of hope in this literature is to be found in an article by Darrel Moellendorf (Moellendorf 2006). His argument is centered not on the question of grounding liberal principles, as in Rorty, but on the question of whether hope is an attitude that is required from political agents along with the related question of whether we have reason to demand that political institutions should promote and enable certain kinds of hopes, namely hopes for the realization of social justice.

In particular, Moellendorf argues that

> securing the institutional bases of hope is a virtue of state institutions, particularly in states in transition from severe injustice. And . . . when the bases are secure, a person who fails to hope for the political future is in that regard *prima facie* blameworthy. (Moellendorf 2006, 414)

This claim is justified by reference to two ways in which hope is politically valuable from a liberal perspective: First, hope for social justice is *instrumentally* valuable as it motivates agents to take steps toward realizing it. Second, hope is also *intrinsically* valuable because it contributes to agents' confidence and thereby to their self-respect:

> Hope contributes to the development and maintenance of the confidence of agents by sustaining them in the face of uncertainty. . . . Such confidence is a characteristic of persons who take themselves to be entitled to just political institutions. Therefore, . . . hope contributes to a person's attitude that she is entitled to just political institutions. (Moellendorf 2006, 424)

While these arguments suggest an external relationship between political institutions and hope—hope is seen either as a precondition for individuals' political actions or as a desirable outcome of political arrangements—Moellendorf also assumes that there is a more internal connection. Sometimes we have reason to endorse social arrangements that are partially unjust because they provide the best basis for overcoming social injustice in the future. In such cases, we can take as a reason to endorse these arrangements the fact that they provide "institutional bases for hope," that is, that they make it reasonable for citizens to hope (and perhaps to be optimistic to a minimal degree) that injustice will be overcome. While Moellendorf acknowledges that hope as a psychological state cannot be the object of policy (Moellendorf 2006, 429), the institutional bases can be, and they can be best understood as those features of an institutional order that license hope.

It is evident that this connects to some degree with Bloch's idea that hope is a way to capture the potentialities of a given social order. In contrast to Bloch, Moellendorf spells this out without introducing any contested metaphysical claims. This is possible because, in contrast to Bloch, he does not assume that social progress depends on contradictions within a mode of production and instead argues from the premise that, given the right institutional arrangements, social progress will be pursued by citizens. In comparison to Rorty, Moellendorf does not intend hope to replace other philosophical commitments to specific principles of justice but rather treats the institutional bases of hope as a feature of a society that allows us to rationally choose partially unjust social arrangements if they are better suited to ultimately arriving at arrangements that are as just as possible. The normative weight is still carried by this ultimate goal, which is defined independently of its capacities to engender hope. For this reason, Moellendorf limits his discussion of the political value of hope to transitional societies (Moellendorf 2006, 426).

While I find Moellendorf's arguments for the political value of the institutional bases of hope convincing, it is clearly the most limited of the three discussed thus far. That a given institutional transitory arrangement licenses hope for the realization of another ultimate arrangement plays a justificatory role. However, it does so only because the ultimate arrangement is not currently attainable. Furthermore, the hope is valuable only in virtue of the desirable features of the ultimate arrangement. In other words, what we ought to hope for is a situation in which hope no longer plays a political role. That the role of hope is limited in this way is of course no argument against this account. It suggests, however, that people can reasonably regret that all that is available to them is hope, and it is unclear whether this is the most robust role we can assign to hope.

3. HOPE FOR A COOPERATIVE COMMUNITY

The discussion of the three models of political hope in the last section seems to lead the theory of political hope into a dilemma: We need to avoid the mistake of claiming interpersonal validity for hope-based arguments by introducing metaphysical premises (as Bloch attempts), but we must equally avoid the opposite mistake of conceptualizing political hope so weakly that hope-based justifications cannot help us to decide on any substantial political questions (as Rorty does). But then references to hope in political discourse must seemingly achieve the impossible: They must serve as arguments in a debate between citizens with radically different comprehensive doctrines and conceptions of the good in a way that mere belief cannot.

Yet if the belief component does not carry the entire weight of hope-based arguments (in which case we would not need to refer to hope in the first place), the desire or anticipation component must play a substantive role. Without any metaphysical support of the type envisaged by Bloch, however, according to which our anticipations are capable of truth, there seems to be little reason to believe that there could be an "overlapping consensus" (Rawls [1993] 2005, 144–53) regarding hope in a pluralistic society.

In this section, I will argue that there is indeed an argument for the claim that, even in an ideally just society of the Rawlsian type, citizens reasonably can and perhaps ought to share certain hopes that can motivate their political actions (for a shorter version of this argument, see Stahl 2018). My argument will rest on a critique of liberal societies that we find in the writings of the early Marx. Unlike Marx, however, I will use this critique for the present purposes not to reject liberalism but to point to shortcomings of even ideally just liberal societies—shortcomings that we cannot *expect* to overcome even if we assume that all citizens are rational and affirm liberal principles of justice. In the absence of warrant to *expect* more, I argue that we should still allow for and perhaps even require citizens who are committed to justice to *hope* that the preconditions under which these shortcomings can be overcome will emerge.

As is well known, Rawls's *Theory of Justice* endorses the idea that there will be a pluralism of reasonable conceptions of the good in modern societies (Murray 2014). This is rephrased in *Political Liberalism* as the idea of a pluralism of what Rawls calls "comprehensive doctrines" that include conceptions of the good (Rawls [1993] 2005, 13). Because of the "burdens of judgment" (Rawls [1993] 2005, 55), this pluralism is, Rawls argues, an "inevitable outcome of free human reason" (Rawls [1993] 2005, 37). The central argument of *Political Liberalism* is that this need not undermine our hope for overlapping consensus with regard to purely *political* doctrines, but Rawls takes it to render irrational any expectation for an overlapping consensus beyond such political doctrines. In particular, the latter feature makes it impossible for a well-ordered liberal society to have the features of a *community* (Rawls [1993] 2005, 42–43). While Rawls quite narrowly defines community as "a society governed by a shared comprehensive religious, philosophical, or moral doctrine" (Rawls [1993] 2005, 42), he clearly also takes his argument to rule out the idea that a well-ordered society could require that citizens be attached to each other in other ways or to share ideals beyond political ones. Such attachments can be part of private, voluntary associations, but they can never be part of the political culture.

This is where Marx's critique of liberalism connects to the Rawlsian project. In his early writings from around 1843 and 1844, Marx develops both a critique of liberalism and a positive argument for what he first terms "human emancipation" and then later calls the "true community of men," a community that Dan Brudney calls the "true communist society" (Brudney 2010, 151). The critique is most clearly spelled out in *On the Jewish Question*. There, Marx argues that the liberal view of the political splits the person in two, with the political citizen on the one hand and the private human being on the other. Neither role allows us to achieve genuine emancipation: Whereas in the private, economic life of citizens people are isolated from their community by virtue of relating to others only via competitive market relations, in political life, as citizens, they see themselves as part of a mutually supportive community, but this role is disconnected from their day-to-day activities and ultimately exists only in their imagination (Marx [1844b] 2010, 154).

The positive counterpart to this picture is supplied in Marx's *Comments on James Mill* where he considers a form of true community in which producers are connected to each other by genuine concern for each other's conception of the good and organize their production accordingly (Marx [1844a] 2010, 227–28; Brudney 2014, 455). Only in such a community, Marx argues, can people relate to each other in a way that adequately expresses moral concern for each other (Brudney 2001, 378).

That this critique of liberalism applies to the Rawlsian model can be seen relatively easily once one considers that Rawls views "the social bases of self-respect" as "perhaps the most important primary good" (Rawls 1999, 386) available to all citizens in a well-ordered society. The development of self-respect is only possible, however, if others affirm the worth of our particular life plans. This leads Rawls to the following conclusion:

> Putting these remarks together, the conditions for persons respecting themselves and one another would seem to require that their common plans be both rational and complementary: they call upon their educated endowments and arouse in each a sense of mastery, and they fit together into one scheme of activity that all can appreciate and enjoy. (Rawls 1999, 387)

This seems to entail Marx's argument that this is only possible in a community in which people affirm each other's pursuit of the good life as valuable. Rawls therefore worries "that only in a limited association of . . . individuals united in the pursuit of common . . . social ends is anything of this sort possible" (Rawls 1999, 387). He responds to this worry, however, by arguing that it is sufficient if for each individual there exists one particular community of shared interests where he or she can encounter this attitude, a condition which is met if "in public life citizens respect one another's ends and adjudicate their political claims in ways that also support their self-esteem" (Rawls 1999, 388), that is, if they affirm the principles of justice. In other words, whenever there is a political culture in which liberal principles are affirmed, then the conditions necessary for the emergence of more particular communities that can support people's self-respect are met.

The reason for Rawls's delegation of the task of securing interpersonal attitudes necessary for people's self-respect to more particular communities rather than requiring that the political community as a whole be characterized by them is that we cannot expect the emergence, on that level, of evaluative consensus that could sustain those attitudes.

Clearly, however, this will not be sufficient for anyone impressed by Marx's critique of liberalism. First, a liberal political culture is a necessary, but not a sufficient, condition for the achievement of self-respect since the

particular kind of community of interest that would affirm a given conception of the good may fail to develop. Second, and more importantly, smaller
communities as a whole might consider a lack of affirmation by the political
community as a whole as a form of disrespect, which then undermines their
members' self-respect.

There is thus a tension between the need to secure the social bases of self-
respect in Rawls and his idea of the inevitable pluralism of forms of life. He
sometimes seems to argue that this tension is inevitable in the sense that in
any liberal society, the free exercise of reason will necessary lead to a form
of pluralism that rules out the emergence of any more ambitious form of
community at the political level. There is, however, no reason to assume this.
The free exercise of reason is perfectly compatible with the idea that everyone adopts a conception of the good that involves pursuing a more particular
good *within a cooperative community in which all such projects are mutually
valued* (see also Honneth 2014). It is merely unreasonable to *expect* that this
outcome will emerge.

We can thus reformulate Rawls's argument as an epistemic one: our
conception of a just society must be constrained by what it is reasonable to
expect in terms of possible consensus. The fact that it would be unreasonable
to believe that citizens will converge on a range of conceptions of the good
that include a cooperative attitude toward those with other conceptions within that range therefore motivates Rawls's choice of the weaker strategy of
merely requiring affirmation of the political principles under which, he
hopes, more limited cooperative communities will emerge (Brudney 2014,
460). Rawls is correct, I assume, to rule out confidence in anything more than
that. But one could argue that this does not rule out the hope that, unlikely as
it might be, a liberal society will one day converge on a more demanding
ideal of community. If Marx is right that such a community would more
robustly support people's self-respect than Rawls's thinner liberal vision,
then it seems to follow that, in its absence, already citizens' knowledge that
others also hope for such a community itself contributes to their self-respect.
If such hope is not irrational (given that the belief in the possibility of such a
community is true and that it is practically rational for a liberal community to
endorse a collective desire for such a community), then we might include the
fact that such hope is shared among the citizens as part of what it means to
affirm the idea of justice. Given the right institutions, it seems feasible to
cultivate such hopes, and therefore, as a feasible and desirable ideal of a
social order that supplies more of one of the central primary goods than other
such orders, we might even say that a perfectly just society is required to take
institutional steps toward such cultivation.

This argument is clearly stronger than the liberal argument discussed in
the last section: It does not recommend the cultivation of hope merely in
circumstances in which genuine justice is not yet achievable, but rather en-

visages it as part of a perfectly just society (the justice of which is not undercut by the fact that it does not necessarily form an ambitious community). It is also clearly stronger than Rorty's argument as it takes seriously the idea that we lack any metaphysical guarantee that a more ambitious form of liberal community will emerge. This does not mean, however, that hope is a replacement for normative foundations; rather, it means that hope is an appropriate way to relate to that which can be shown to be desirable from the perspective of a whole range of cooperative conceptions of the good life. Finally, while the argument as described is based on the premises of contemporary liberal theory, it can easily be extended to take up some of the Marxist intuitions that also drive Bloch's discussion. Once we assume that more ambitious forms of community that go beyond an individualist market society are already developing within that social structure (or, as Marx ([1859] 2010) would say, that "the material conditions of their existence have matured within the framework of the old society"), such hope can be analyzed as grasping the potential of social reality without adding any contestable metaphysical claims.

4. CONCLUSION

Hope can play different roles in the narratives of political theory. In particular, I have distinguished between instrumental, constitutive, and justificatory functions of hope; and I have discussed three main strategies for spelling out the justificatory function in the existing literature, briefly considering the ways in which these strategies remain unsatisfactory. In the last section, I argued that there is another option for liberals when it comes to thinking about hope, which relates to the tension between the necessity of ambitious form of community for the supply of the central primary social good of self-respect and the epistemic argument that it would be unreasonable to think of such forms of community as being sufficiently likely to be included in our concept of a well-ordered society.

In order to complete the argument, it must be examined in what sense the argument that a just liberal society is one in which hopes for more ambitious forms of community are cultivated assigns a justificatory role to hope. It is easy to see that it does so in the first sense: The existence of such hope is described as a desirable form of a just society as far as it is assumed that the very fact that citizens share in such hoping will already support the development of self-respect. However, the argument also assigns hope a justificatory role of the kind discussed in section 2 insofar as it supports the idea that normative and descriptive beliefs are not the only relevant arguments in public debate. The shared hope for a more ambitious form of community—if it is indeed shared—can support arguments for institutional changes that bring such a community within reach of society as it is presently. While this does not resolve the tension between pluralism and large-scale community, it allows us to see that it is not illegitimate to hope that this tension will be gradually resolved and to work toward this goal.

REFERENCES

Aronson, Ronald. 2017. *We: Reviving Social Hope*. Chicago: The University of Chicago Press. https://www.press.uchicago.edu/ucp/books/book/chicago/W/bo22501588.html.

Bloch, Ernst. (1959) 1986. *The Principle of Hope*. Oxford: Basil Blackwell.

Blöser, Claudia, and Titus Stahl. 2017. "Fundamental Hope and Practical Identity." *Philosophical Papers* 46 (3): 345–71. https://doi.org/10.1080/05568641.2017.1400918.

Brudney, Daniel. 2001. "Justifying a Conception of the Good Life: The Problem of the 1844 Marx." *Political Theory* 29 (3): 364–94. https://doi.org/10.1177/0090591701029003003.

———. 2010. "Producing for Others." In *The Philosophy of Recognition: Historical and Contemporary Perspectives*, edited by Hans-Christoph Schmidt am Busch and Christopher F. Zurn, 151–88. London: Rowman & Littlefield.

———. 2014. "The Young Marx and the Middle-Aged Rawls." In *A Companion to Rawls*, edited by Jon Mandle and David A. Reidy, 450–71. Hoboken, NJ: John Wiley & Sons, Ltd. https://doi.org/10.1002/9781118328460.ch26.

Chignell, Andrew. 2013. "Rational Hope, Moral Order, and the Revolution of the Will." In *Divine Order, Human Order, and the Order of Nature*, edited by Eric Watkins, 197–218. Oxford: Oxford University Press.

Cohen, G. A. 2000. *Karl Marx's Theory of History: A Defence*. Princeton: Princeton University Press.

Eagleton, Terry. 2015. *Hope without Optimism*. New Haven: Yale University Press.

Ferrara, Mark S. 2013. *Barack Obama and the Rhetoric of Hope*. Jefferson, North Carolina: McFarland & Company, Inc., Publishers.

Hobbes, Thomas. (1651) 1996. *Leviathan*. Edited by Richard Tuck. Cambridge: Cambridge University Press.

Honneth, Axel. 2014. *Freedom's Right. The Social Foundations of Democratic Life*. Translated by Joseph Ganahl. Cambridge: Polity Press.

Huber, Jakob. 2019. "Defying Democratic Despair: A Kantian Account of Hope in Politics." *European Journal of Political Theory*. Online first preprint (May). https://doi.org/10.1177/1474885119847308.

Lear, Jonathan. 2006. *Radical Hope: Ethics in the Face of Cultural Devastation*. Cambridge: Harvard University Press.

Lloyd, Vincent. 2018. "'A Moral Astigmatism': King on Hope and Illusion." *Telos* 2018 (182): 121–38. https://doi.org/10.3817/0318182121.

Martin, Adrienne. 2013. *How We Hope: A Moral Psychology*. Princeton: Princeton University Press.

Marx, Karl. (1844a) 2010. "Comments on James Mill, Elémens d'économie Politique." In *tripleC: Communication, Capitalism & Critique* 3: 211–28. Collected Works. London: Lawrence & Wishart Ltd.

———. (1844b) 2010. "On the Jewish Question." In *Collected Works March 1843–August 1844*, 3: 146–74. Collected Works. London: Lawrence & Wishart Ltd.

———. (1859) 2010. "Preface to 'A Contribution to the Critique of Political Economy.'" In *Collected Works: 185–16*, 29: 261–66. Collected Works. London: Lawrence & Wishart Ltd.

Marx, Karl, and Friedrich Engels. (1846) 1976. "The German Ideology." In *Collected Works: 1845–47*, 5: 19–539. Collected Works. New York: International Publishers.

Mason, Richard. 1997. *The God of Spinoz: A Philosophical Study*. Cambridge: Cambridge University Press.

Moellendorf, Darrel. 2006. "Hope as a Political Virtue." *Philosophical Papers* 35 (3): 413–33. http://www.tandfonline.com/doi/abs/10.1080/05568640609485189.

Murray, Pete. 2014. "Conception of the Good." Edited by Jon Mandle and David A. Reidy. *The Cambridge Rawls Lexicon*. Cambridge: Cambridge University Press. https://doi.org/10.1017/CBO9781139026741.042.

O'Neill, Onora. 1996. *Kant on Reason and Religion*. Tanner Lectures on Human Values. http://tannerlectures.utah.edu/_documents/a-to-z/o/oneill97.pdf.

Príncipe, Catarina. 2015. "Hope Is on the Way." *Jacobin*, January 2015. https://jacobinmag.com/2015/01/syriza-election-european-left/.

Rawls, John. 1999. *A Theory of Justice*. Revised edition. Cambridge, MA: Belknap Press of Harvard University Press.

———. (1993) 2005. *Political Liberalism*. New York: University Press Group Ltd.

Rorty, Richard. 1982. *Consequences of Pragmatism*. Minneapolis: University of Minnesota Press.

———. 1989. *Contingency, Irony and Solidarity*. Cambridge: Cambridge University Press.

Rorty, Richard M. 2002. *Against Bosses, Against Oligarchies: A Conversation with Richard Rorty*. Edited by Kent Puckett. Chicago: Prickly Paradigm Press.

Smith, Nicholas H. 2010. "From the Concept of Hope to the Principle of Hope." In *Hope Against Hope: Philosophies, Cultures and Politics of Possibility and Doubt*, edited by Janet Horrigan and Ed Wiltse, 3–22. Amsterdam: Rodopi.

Smith, Nicholas H. 2005. "Rorty on Religion and Hope." *Inquiry* 48 (1): 76–98. https://doi.org/10.1080/00201740510015365.

Snow, Nancy E. 2018. "Hope as a Democratic Civic Virtue." *Metaphilosophy* 49 (3): 407–27. https://doi.org/10.1111/meta.12299.

Spinoza, Benedictus de. (1677) 2002. "Political Treatise." In *Complete Works*, edited by Michael L. Morgan, translated by Samuel Shirley, 676–754. Indianapolis: Hackett Publishing.

———. (1670) 2002. "Theological-Political Treatise." In *Complete Works*, edited by Michael L. Morgan, translated by Samuel Shirley, 383–583. Indianapolis: Hackett Publishing.

Stahl, Titus. 2013. "What Is Immanent Critique?" *SSRN Electronic Journal*, November. https://doi.org/10.2139/ssrn.2357957.

———. 2018. "Why Politics Needs Hope (but No Longer Inspires It)." *Aeon Magazine*, July. https://aeon.co/ideas/why-politics-needs-hope-but-no-longer-inspires-it.

Steinberg, Justin. 2018. *Spinoza's Political Psychology: The Taming of Fortune and Fear*. Cambridge: Cambridge University Press.

Stockdale, Katie. 2019. "Social and Political Dimensions of Hope." *Journal of Social Philosophy* 50 (1): 28–44. https://doi.org/10.1111/josp.12270.

Tucker, Ericka. 2018. "Hope, Hate and Indignation: Spinoza on Political Emotion in the Trump Era." In *Trump and Political Philosophy*, edited by M. B. Sable and A. J. Torres, 131–58. New York: Palgrave Macmillan.

Index

About the Contributors

Matthew A. Benton is Assistant Professor of Philosophy at Seattle Pacific University. Prior to that he held postdoctoral research fellowships at the University of Notre Dame and the University of Oxford; he earned a PhD in philosophy from Rutgers University. He writes mainly in epistemology, philosophy of language, and philosophy of religion, and has published articles in *The Philosophical Quarterly, Analysis, Noûs, Philosophy & Phenomenological Research, Synthese, Philosophical Studies, Philosophical Perspectives, Res Philosophica*, and *Oxford Studies in Philosophy of Religion*, among other journals. He is coeditor of *Knowledge, Belief, and God: New Insights in Religious Epistemology* (2018), and of *Religious Disagreement and Pluralism* (forthcoming).

Claudia Blöser is Assistant Professor of Philosophy at the Goethe University Frankfurt. Her main areas of research are practical philosophy, especially Kant's practical philosophy and moral psychology. Her publications include *Zurechnung bei Kant* (2014), articles in *Ethical Theory and Moral Practice, Kantian Review*, and *Philosophia, Ratio*. Together with Titus Stahl, she has coauthored the Stanford Encyclopedia article on hope (2017) and "Fundamental Hope and Practical Identity" (*Philosophical Papers*, 2017).

Douglas Cairns (FRSE, FBA, MAE) is Professor of Classics in the University of Edinburgh. His most recent books are *Sophocles: Antigone* (2016), *Emotions in the Classical World: Methods, Approaches, and Directions* (with Damien Nelis, 2017), *Greek Laughter and Tears: Antiquity and After* (with Margaret Alexiou, 2017), *Seneca's Tragic Passions* (with Damien Nelis, 2017), *Distributed Cognition in Classical Antiquity* (with Miranda Anderson and Mark Sprevak, 2018), and *A Cultural History of the Emotions in Antiquity* (2019).

Johann M. D'Souza, MA, received his master's degree in psychology from Boston University and is pursuing a PhD in clinical psychology at University of Houston under a presidential fellowship. His research interests focus on the intersection between positive psychology and psychopathology. Clinically, he is interested in forms of Cognitive Behavior Therapy (CBT) that utilize mindfulness, acceptance, and values-based action, such as Acceptance and Commitment Therapy (ACT). In addition, he is a research affiliate of the Human Flourishing Program at Harvard University.

Rika Dunlap is Assistant Professor of Philosophy at the University of Guam. Her areas of research are Asian philosophy, ethics, and applied ethics. Her recent publications include: "Hope without the Future: Zen Buddhist Hope in Dōgen's *Shōbōgenzō*" in the *Journal of Japanese Philosophy* and "From Freedom to Equality: Rancière and the Aesthetic Experience of Equality," in *Continental Philosophy Review*.

Roe Fremstedal is Associate Professor of Philosophy at Norwegian University of Science and Technology (NTNU Trondheim) and Full Professor of Practical Philosophy at University of Tromsø – The Arctic University of Norway. His publications include *Kierkegaard and Kant on Radical Evil and the Highest Good* (2014) and articles in *Inquiry, Journal of Value Inquiry, Kantian Review, Kierkegaard Studies Yearbook, Journal of Religious Ethics,* and *Religious Studies.*

Matthew W. Gallagher, PhD, is Associate Professor in the Department of Psychology and Texas Institute for Measurement, Evaluation, and Statistics at the University of Houston. Dr. Gallagher received his PhD in clinical and quantitative psychology in 2011 from the University of Kansas. He completed a postdoctoral fellowship at the Center for Anxiety and Related Disorders at Boston University. Dr. Gallagher was previously a staff psychologist in the Behavioral Science Division of the National Center for PTSD and Assistant Professor of Psychiatry at Boston University School of Medicine. His research interests include evaluating the efficacy of transdiagnostic treatments for PTSD and anxiety disorders, identifying mechanisms of change of empirically supported treatments, and understanding how positive thinking (e.g., hope, optimism, self-efficacy) promotes well-being and provides resilience to PTSD and other anxiety disorders. His research has been funded by the National Institute of Mental Health (NIMH), the Society for Multivariate Experimental Psychology (SMEP), and the Department of Defense (DoD). He is the author of over one hundred articles, chapters, and books, including the *Oxford Handbook of Hope* with Shane Lopez, and is a licensed clinical psychologist.

Anne Jeffrey is Assistant Professor of Philosophy at Baylor University. She earned her PhD at Georgetown University and was a postdoctoral researcher at Notre Dame on the Hope and Optimism project. Her main areas of research are metaethics and normative ethics in the virtue tradition. She is the author of *God and Morality* (2019) as well as articles appearing in *Episteme, Ethical Theory and Moral Practice, International Journal for Philosophy of Religion*, and *Religious Studies*.

Adrienne M. Martin is the Akshata Murty 2002 and Rishi Sunak Associate Professor of Philosophy, Politics, and Economics, and George R. Roberts Fellow at Claremont McKenna College. She is the author of *How We Hope: A Moral Psychology* (2013) and the editor of *The Routledge Handbook of Love in Philosophy* (2019).

Darrel Moellendorf is Professor of International Political Theory and Professor of Philosophy at Johann Wolfgang Universität Frankfurt am Main. He is the author of *Cosmopolitan Justice* (2002), *Global Inequality Matters* (2009), and *The Moral Challenge of Dangerous Climate Change: Values, Poverty, and Policy* (2014). He coedited (with Christopher J. Roederer) *Jurisprudence* (2004); (with Gillian Brock) *Current Debates in Global Justice* (2005); (with Thomas Pogge) *Global Justice: Seminal Essays* (2008); and (with Heather Widdows) *The Routledge Handbook of Global Ethics* (2014). He has published articles in journals such as *Climatic Change, Ethics, Ethics and International Affairs, Journal of Political Philosophy, Social Philosophy and Policy, Social Theory and Practice, The Monist*, and various other journals.

Angela L. Richardson, MA, received her master's degree in psychology from Boston University and is currently pursuing a PhD in clinical psychology at the University of Houston with Dr. Gallagher as her faculty advisor. She is in her second year of doctoral study, working as a research assistant under a National Institutes of Health grant fellowship. Her line of research focuses on identifying factors of resilience in trauma and anxiety-related disorders, with an interest in military and women populations. These factors of interest include hope, gratitude, and psychological well-being.

Nancy E. Snow is Professor of Philosophy and director of the Institute for the Study of Human Flourishing at the University of Oklahoma. She is the author of *Virtue as Social Intelligence: An Empirically Grounded Theory* (2010) and over forty-five papers on virtue and ethics more broadly. She has also edited or coedited seven volumes: *In the Company of Others: Perspectives on Community, Family, and Culture* (1996), *Legal Philosophy: Multiple Perspectives* with Larry May and Angela Bolte (1999), *Stem Cell Research: New Frontiers in Science and Ethics* (2004), *Cultivating Virtue: Perspectives from Philosophy, Theology, and Psychology* (2014), *The Philosophy and Psychology of Character and Happiness* with Franco V. Trivigno (2014), *Developing the Virtues: Integrating Perspectives* with Julia Annas and Darcia Narvaez (2016), and *The Oxford Handbook of Virtue* (2018). She is currently revising a monograph on hope, writing one on virtue ethics and virtue epistemology, and coauthoring a book on virtue measurement. She is the series editor of "The Virtues," a fifteen-book series published by Oxford University Press featuring interdisciplinary volumes on virtues or clusters of virtues. The first volume in this series, *Justice*, edited by Mark LeBar, was published in 2018.

Sarah M. Stitzlein is Professor of Education and Affiliate Professor of Philosophy at the University of Cincinnati. She primarily employs pragmatist and political philosophy to study education and democracy. She is president of the John Dewey Society and coeditor of *Democracy & Education*.

Titus Stahl is Assistant Professor of Philosophy at the University of Groningen. He works on social and political philosophy, critical social theory, privacy theory, and the history of political thought. He has published in *Constellations*, *Critical Horizons*, *Social Theory and Practice*, and *Ethics and Information Technology*. His book *Immanent Critique* will be published in 2020. Together with Claudia Blöser, he has authored the Stanford Encylopedia article on hope (2017) and "Fundamental Hope and Practical Identity" (*Philosophical Papers*, 2017).

Katie Stockdale is Assistant Professor of Philosophy at the University of Victoria. She works primarily on the nature and value of emotions in moral, social, and political life. She has published articles in *Journal of Social Philosophy*, *Ergo*, *Hypatia*, *International Journal of Feminist Approaches to Bioethics*, and *Social Theory and Practice*. She is currently writing a book manuscript on hope and oppression.

Samantha Vice is Professor of Philosophy at the University of the Witwatersrand. She works in ethics, aesthetics, and social philosophy, and has published papers on beauty, goodness, impartiality and partiality, privilege and race, and moral psychology. She is coeditor of *Ethics at the Cinema*, *The Moral Life*, and a special issue of *Philosophical Papers* on aging, and she is currently working on a manuscript on the ethics of animal beauty.

Printed in the USA
CPSIA information can be obtained
at www.ICGtesting.com
LVHW010505201023
761597LV00008B/118